ADVANCED LEVEL
BIOLOGY - PRACTICAL

Jane Hawkes
Head of Biology Dept, Mander Portman Woodward
and
Fiona Eldridge
Head of Science Faculty, Mander Portman Woodward

To all at MPW Birmingham

Fiona Eldridge.

DP PUBLICATIONS LTD.
Aldine Place, 142-144 Uxbridge Road,
Shepherds Bush Green, London W12 8AA

1989

ACKNOWLEDGEMENTS

We should like to thank students and colleagues at Mander Portman Woodward for their help and encouragement in the prepration of this book, Dr Gillian W Watson of the CAB International Institute of Entomology for her careful proof reading and advice, and Gavin Purves and Ann Jefferies-Kelly of the HPM Group for their assistance with page layout and design work.

We are also grateful for permission to reproduce past examination questions to the Oxford and Cambridge Schools Examination Board, the University of Cambridge Local Examinations Syndicate, the University of London School Examinations Board and the University of Oxford Delegacy of Local Examinations.

A CIP catalogue record for this book is available from the British Library.

ISBN 1 870941 357

First published in Great Britain 1989

Copyright DP Publications Ltd. 1989©

Designed & Typeset by
HPM Group
PO Box 44
Godalming
Surrey GU7 2SH

Printed by
The Bath Press
Lower Bristol Road
Bath BA2 3BL

PREFACE

Practical skills form a major part of the assessment of an A level candidate's ability. The practical paper contributes between 20 and 33.33% towards the final grade. In addition, many parts of the theory papers contain questions referring to, and requiring knowledge of, the practical aspects of the subject.

The aims of this book are to help students to:

★ work effectively during practical classes

★ make accurate drawings and reports of their practical work

★ increase their confidence in tackling practical examination questions.

The text includes:

★ hand drawn diagrams to show the level of detail required

★ annotations for drawings of specimens to give diagnostic classification features

★ plant and animal tissue drawings

★ tables relating structure of tissues to their functions

★ the necessary procedures, precautions and controls for physiological experiments

★ background theory information for physiological experiments

★ hints boxes to emphasise the key practical requirements in each section

Throughout the text there are example questions drawn from several of the major examination Boards and suggestions for answer techniques. Following each question is a code for the examination Boards:

C – Cambridge
L – London
O – Oxford
O&C – Oxford and Cambridge

The book evolved in response to students' requests for a single text concentrating on aspects of practical Biology specifically required for the examination. It is based on the combined fifteen year teaching experience of the authors.

CONTENTS

INTRODUCTION

This book has been written for students of 'A' level Biology and concentrates on the practical aspects of the examination. It can be used during class practicals and also when preparing for assessments and the final practical examination. We concentrate on the practical skills required by the 'A' level examinations and this text aims to help students to achieve a high standard. Guidelines for practicals are often lacking in the standard 'A' level text books.

This book gives details of the techniques needed for the successful completion of practical assessments and examinations. The drawings in the text have been hand drawn to show the detail and size that students are expected to produce themselves in their examination. The chapter on physiological experiments gives explanations of procedures, background theoretical information and presentation of method and discussions.

We have used past examination questions from the major examination boards to illustrate the main *types* of question set by the boards; students should realise that they can then apply their acquired skills to *any* examination question.

The division of the book into six chapters is based on self-contained sections of the syllabus, with the exception of Chapter 6 on statistical and graphical techniques, which has been included to help students interpret the data that they produce from their experiments and investigations. The order of the chapters in the book is not intended to suggest a particular order of study.

Chapter 1: The Study of Whole Organisms

This covers the study of whole organisms. The classification details that we have used are based on an analysis of the requirements of the major examination boards. Although it is not a comprehensive survey of the five Kingdoms, it provides students with all they should need for their examination. The illustrations that we have used demonstrate the major classification features of each class. Students may need to relate these features to different specimens belonging to the same class. For example, the characteristics exhibited by a rat, illustrated in this chapter, will also be shown by another specimen from the same class, such as the mouse, which students might be given in their examination.

Chaper 2: Simple Physiological Experiments

This chaper, on simple physiological experiments, covers the experimental questions set by the examination boards. These questions demand greater interpretive skills from students, and require more background theoretical knowledge than other types of practical quesions. We have provided the essential background information and key definitions which should also be useful for theory revision.

Chapter 3: Plant Tissue Drawings

This chapter describes and illustrates the major plant tissues. The specimens that we have chosen to illustrate the types of plant tissues *may not be* the same as students will be given in their examination. However, the types of tissues *will be common* to alternative specimens and students, having learned for example to recognise parenchyma on one slide should then be able to recognise it in a section of *any* plant organ.

Chapter 4: Animal Tissues and Organs

This chapter describes and illustrates animal tissues and organs and is constructed in a similar way to Chapter 3 on plant tissues. We have tabulated the key features of the tissues and organs for quick reference.

Chapter 5: Dissection

The instructions given in this chapter describe the dissection of three systems of a mouse. We chose a mouse for these dissections because it is commonly used in the examination, is widely available and is used by many schools for their practical work.

They also have less subcutaneous fat than rats and can be conveniently displayed under water. The instructions given in this chapter can be used by students during their assessment work, as a practical handbook guide, since they no longer have to be able to dissect and display from memory.

Chapter 6: Representing and Interpreting Data

This chapter describes the mathematical skills that students need for interpreting data that they have gathered from their experiments, long term investigations and field work. Whilst some of the techniques are likely to have been taught as part of a GCSE mathematical syllabus, others are only in 'A' level mathematics syllabuses which students may, or may not, have studied. We have discovered from our class experience that many students struggle to adapt mathematical techniques to biological work. We hope that our use of biological examples will help such students to understand the underlying mathematical techniques.

Jane Hawkes
Fiona Eldridge
London 1989

ADVANCED LEVEL
BIOLOGY - PRACTICAL

1

THE STUDY OF WHOLE ORGANISMS

All exam boards require a study of a range of plants and animals so that students gain an appreciation of the variety of life and different levels of organisation. The majority of the exam boards set practical questions on this section of the syllabus. These can ask for specific classification features, construction of simple dichotomous keys, comparative morphology based on whole or parts of organisms or the relationship between external features and mode of life. Questions can also ask for explanations of any ecological relationships between the specimens. The information in this section will also be useful for theory examinations where named examples of organisms are required.

The chapter is divided into three sections:

■ Classification

■ Construction of keys

■ Comparative morphology

The easiest way to familiarise yourself with the organisms is to produce a set of drawings as this involves careful observation of their external features. You would not be expected to reproduce these drawings from memory but you would need to know the main classification features.

CLASSIFICATION

DICHOTOMOUS KEYS

COMPARATIVE MORPHOLOGY

HINTS BOX ✔

DRAWING TIPS

- Position the organism so that the majority of the features are clearly visible.
- Make sure that the specimen is not damaged.
- Use a hand lens or microscope if necessary.
- Make simple line drawings using a sharp H or HB pencil.
- Do not shade or use colour.
- Leave sufficient space for labels and annotations.
- Include classification features and adaptations to mode of life in your annotations.
- Head each drawing with the major group (*phylum*) and sub-group (*class* and *genus*) names.
- Add notes on *habitat* and *mode of nutrition*.

These hints should help you to produce a set of drawings for your revision.
Under exam conditions you are expected to draw whole or parts of organisms in comparative morphology questions only. *You should aim to complete a drawing in 10 - 15 minutes*.

We shall begin with details of the major classification groups, and then go on to examples of the main types of practical exam question set on this section of the syllabus.

CLASSIFICATION

The function of any classification scheme is to group together objects (in this case organisms) which share similar characteristics. With this in mind, modern Taxonomists base their classification of the organisms on five Kingdoms. In this guide we follow this system; you may find that it is different to that you have used previously but you should check your syllabus for the precise scheme required.

In common with other systems the major groupings are:

KINGDOM
PHYLUM (called *DIVISION* in Botany)
CLASS
ORDER
FAMILY
GENUS
SPECIES

These groupings represent different levels of organisation with Kingdom being the largest and species the smallest. The diagram below illustrates the relationships between the different levels of a typical group; the Arthropods. Family has been omitted because it is not necessarily needed in exam questions.

```
                         KINGDOM
                         ANIMALIA
              ┌─────────────────┴─────────┐
         other phyla              PHYLUM
                                  ARTHROPODA
     ┌────────────────────────────┼─────────────────────────────┐
   CLASS                        CLASS                          CLASS
   CRUSTACEA                    INSECTA                        ARACHNIDA
     ┌──────────────┬─────────────┴────┐                        │
   ORDER        other orders         ORDER                     ORDER
   LEPIDOPTERA                       HYMENOPTERA                ORTHOPTERA
                              ┌──────────┴──────┐
                         other genera        GENUS
                                             APIS
                                      ┌────────┴────────┐
                                   other            SPECIES
                                   species          MELLIFERA
```

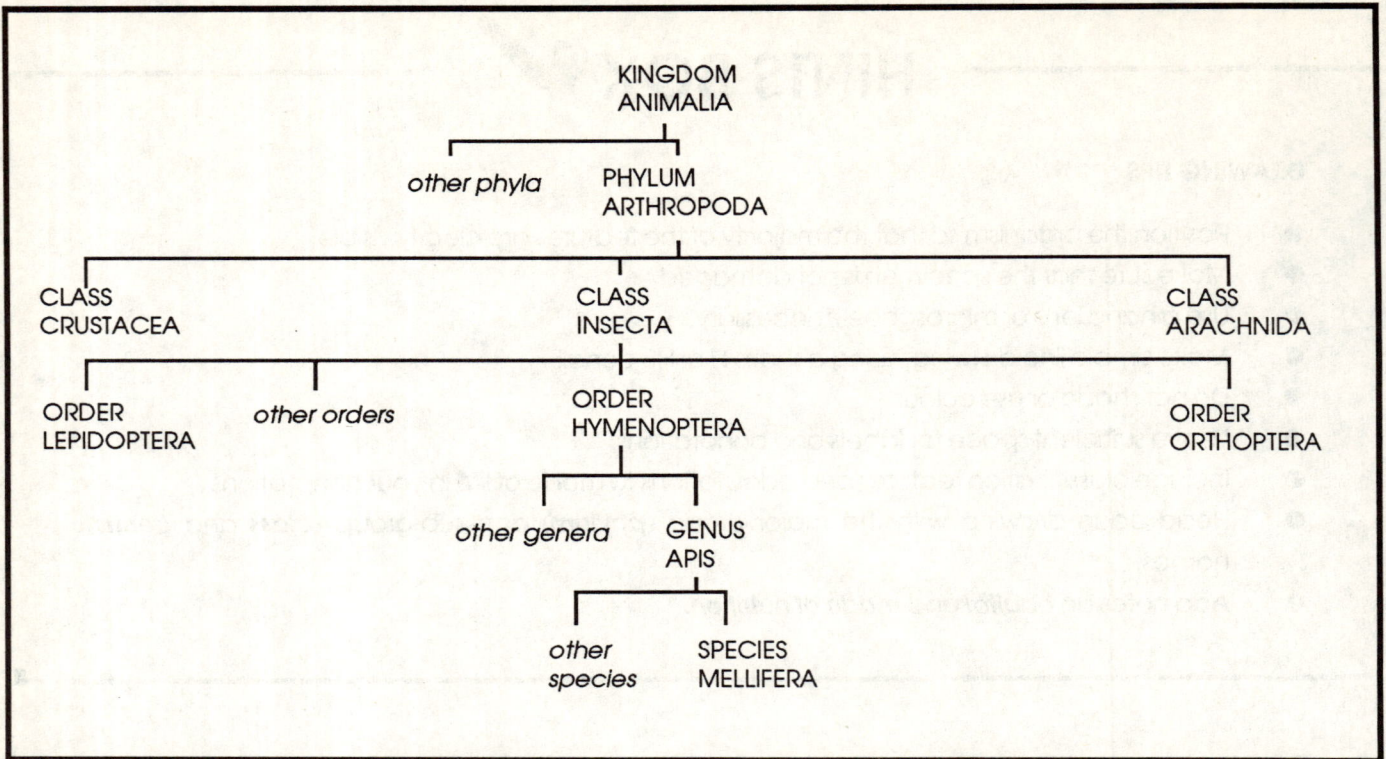

The five kingdoms are:

○ *MONERA*
○ *PROTISTA*
○ *FUNGI*
○ *PLANTAE*
○ *ANIMALIA*

On the following pages a description of the major groupings will be given together with examples of organisms which exhibit the characteristics of those groupings. This only constitutes a very brief summary, but it should provide you with sufficient information for the practical exam. For each organism, you are generally expected to know only the features of the phylum (or division) and one sub-group, usually the class.

If any of the terms are unfamiliar to you, make sure that you either ask your teacher for clarification or refer to a textbook.

KINGDOM *MONERA*

This Kingdom includes Bacteria, Viruses and Blue-green algae (Cyanobacter). These organisms are without a true nucleus *ie.* Prokaryotes. They also lack membrane bound organelles such as mitochondria or chloroplasts. Most of the organisms in this Kingdom are heterotrophic but the Blue-green algae are an exception as they are photosynthetic and hence autotrophic.

The members of this Kingdom are ubiquitous in distribution (*ie.* found in all habitats). Both free-living and parasitic forms can be found. Bacteria are especially important as decomposers in ecosystems.

Illustrations of examples of members of Kingdom monera are not included here because you would not be given them in your practical exam.

KINGDOM *PROTISTA*

This Kingdom includes the Protozoans. They are all unicellular organisms with a true (membrane bound) nucleus *ie*. Eukaryotes. They have many complex, membrane bound organelles *eg*. mitochondria and endoplasmic reticulum. The Protista are generally heterotrophic but some "intermediate organisms" such as *Euglena* are also autotrophic. None of the members of this Kingdom have a cellulose cell wall.
They are mainly found in aquatic habitats although some are found in damp terrestrial habitats. Some members have become highly specialised parasites and live in the body fluids of other, higher organisms.

Illustrations have been included for three classes of the Phylum Protozoa: Sarcodina, Ciliata and Flagellata. See *pages 6 - 9*.

KINGDOM *FUNGI*

This Kingdom includes moulds, mushrooms, toadstools, smuts and rusts.
They are all Eukaryotic organisms and most are multicellular although some such as yeast are unicellular. They are all heterotrophic, containing no photosynthetic pigments. They all have cell walls consisting of fungal cellulose and some may also contain chitin.
Fungi are found widely distributed in terrestrial habitats and a few are aquatic. They may be either saprotrophic or parasitic. Many fungi are important decomposers in ecosystems.

Illustrations have been included for two classes of the Division Eumycophyta: Phycomycetes and Basidiomycetes. See *pages 10 - 12*.

KINGDOM *PLANTAE*

This Kingdom includes algae, mosses, clubmosses, ferns, conifers and flowering plants. They are all Eukaryotic organisms and most are multicellular with the exception of some of the algae *eg*. *Chlamydomonas*. They are virtually all autotrophic, containing chlorophylls and other photosynthetic pigments, with the exception of a small number of parasitic plants. All members have cellulose cell walls.
Plants are ubiquitous in distribution; they are the producers in virtually every ecosystem.

Illustrations have been included for:
two Divisions of algae; Chlorophyta and Phaeophyta, and for
Divisions Bryophyta, Pteridophyta and Spermatophyta. See *pages 13-24*.

KINGDOM *ANIMALIA*

This Kingdom includes coelenterates, flatworms, segmented worms, arthropods, molluscs, echinoderms and vertebrates. They are all Eukaryotic, multicellular organisms. They are all heterotrophic and lack any form of photosynthetic pigment. Animal cells do not have cell walls.
Animals are found in all habitats; they are the consumers.

Illustrations have been included for the following Phyla: Coelenterata, Platyhelminthes, Annelida, Arthropoda, Mollusca, Echinodermata and Chordata. See *pages 25-55*.

We shall describe the major characteristics of each of the main Phyla required by the examining Boards. Following each Phylum we shall give the characteristics of some of its sub-groups, again concentrating on those required for the practical exam. Each sub-group is also represented by a diagram which should help you to learn the important diagnostic features and to identify the specimens. Most of the characteristics given are externally visible structures which can be seen with the naked eye or with the aid of a hand lens or microscope.

KINGDOM *PROTISTA*

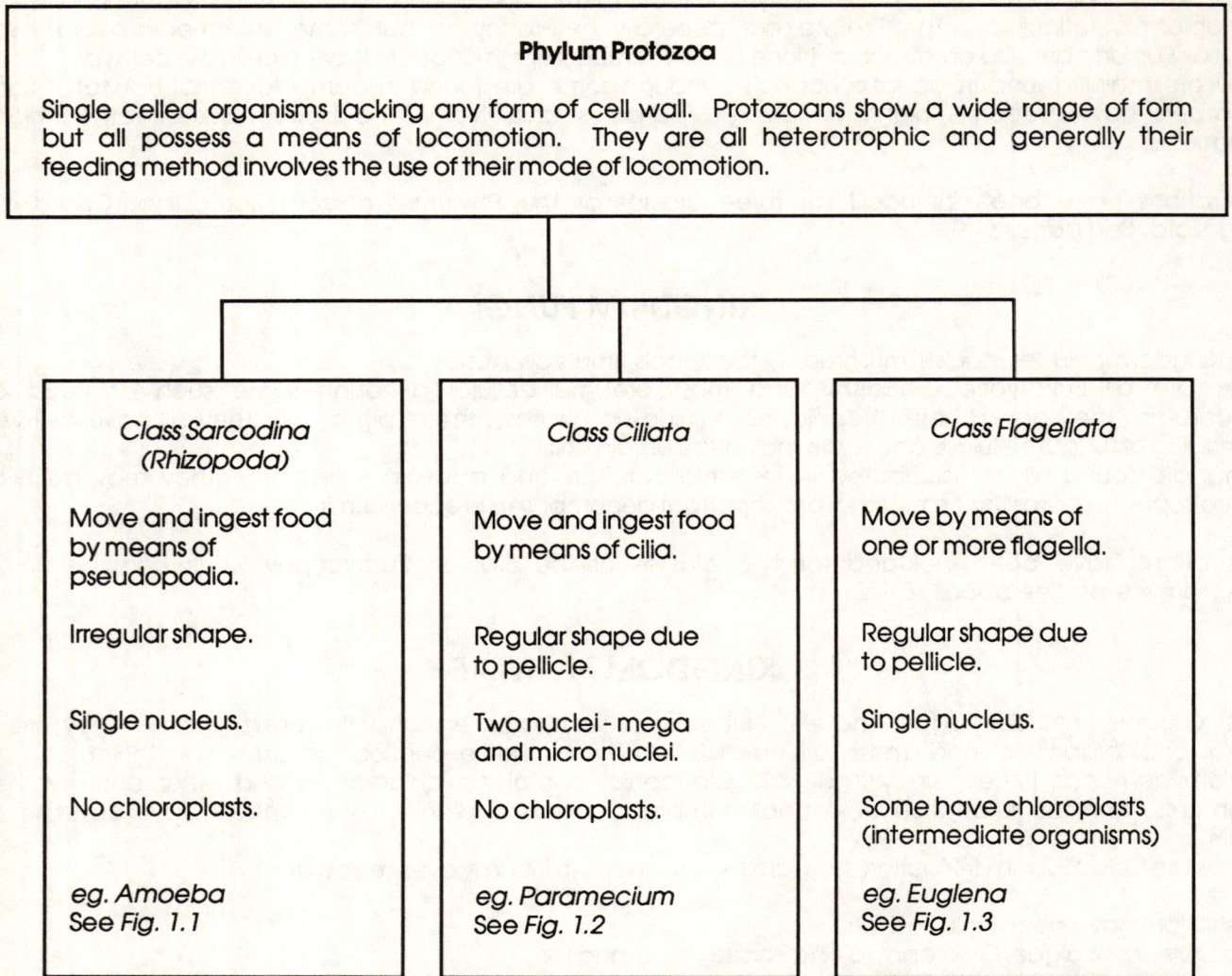

Phylum Protozoa

Single celled organisms lacking any form of cell wall. Protozoans show a wide range of form but all possess a means of locomotion. They are all heterotrophic and generally their feeding method involves the use of their mode of locomotion.

Class Sarcodina (Rhizopoda)

Move and ingest food by means of pseudopodia.

Irregular shape.

Single nucleus.

No chloroplasts.

eg. *Amoeba*
See *Fig. 1.1*

Class Ciliata

Move and ingest food by means of cilia.

Regular shape due to pellicle.

Two nuclei - mega and micro nuclei.

No chloroplasts.

eg. *Paramecium*
See *Fig. 1.2*

Class Flagellata

Move by means of one or more flagella.

Regular shape due to pellicle.

Single nucleus.

Some have chloroplasts (intermediate organisms)

eg. *Euglena*
See *Fig. 1.3*

KINGDOM *PROTISTA*

PHYLUM *PROTOZOA*

CLASS *SARCODINA*

GENUS *AMOEBA* X 400

Fig. 1.1

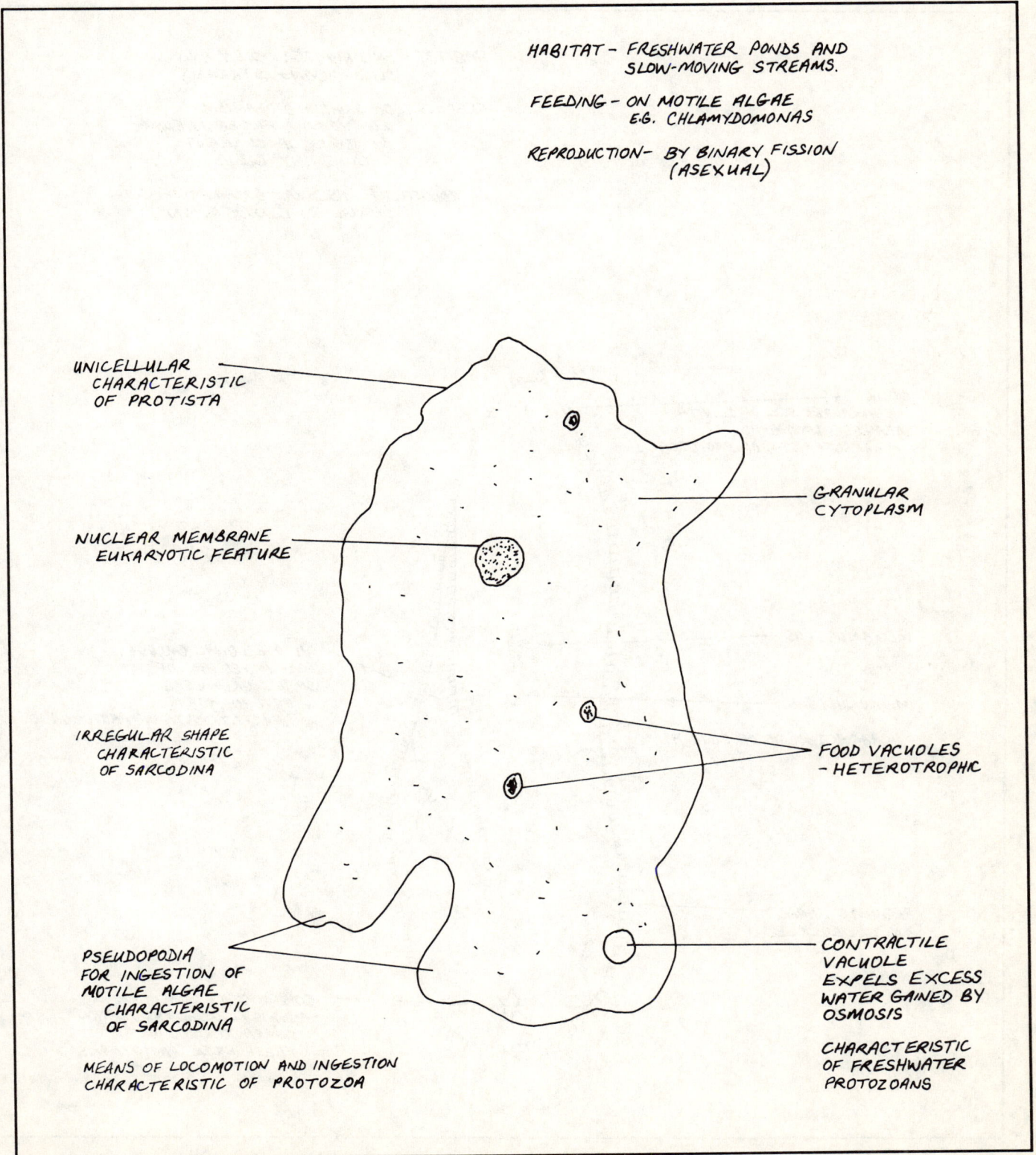

HABITAT – FRESHWATER PONDS AND
SLOW-MOVING STREAMS.

FEEDING – ON MOTILE ALGAE
E.G. CHLAMYDOMONAS

REPRODUCTION – BY BINARY FISSION
(ASEXUAL)

UNICELLULAR
CHARACTERISTIC
OF PROTISTA

GRANULAR
CYTOPLASM

NUCLEAR MEMBRANE
EUKARYOTIC FEATURE

IRREGULAR SHAPE
CHARACTERISTIC
OF SARCODINA

FOOD VACUOLES
– HETEROTROPHIC

PSEUDOPODIA
FOR INGESTION OF
MOTILE ALGAE
CHARACTERISTIC
OF SARCODINA

CONTRACTILE
VACUOLE
EXPELS EXCESS
WATER GAINED BY
OSMOSIS

CHARACTERISTIC
OF FRESHWATER
PROTOZOANS

MEANS OF LOCOMOTION AND INGESTION
CHARACTERISTIC OF PROTOZOA

KINGDOM *PROTISTA*

PHYLUM *PROTOZOA*

CLASS *CILIATA*

GENUS *PARAMECIUM*   X 400

Fig. 1.2

HABITAT- FRESHWATER PONDS AND
SLOW-MOVING STREAMS

FEEDING - ON SMALL ORGANISMS
EG. YEAST, FILTER FEEDING
BY MEANS OF CURRENTS
CREATED BY CILIA

REPRODUCTION- ASEXUAL BY BINARY FISSION,
SEXUAL BY CONJUGATION

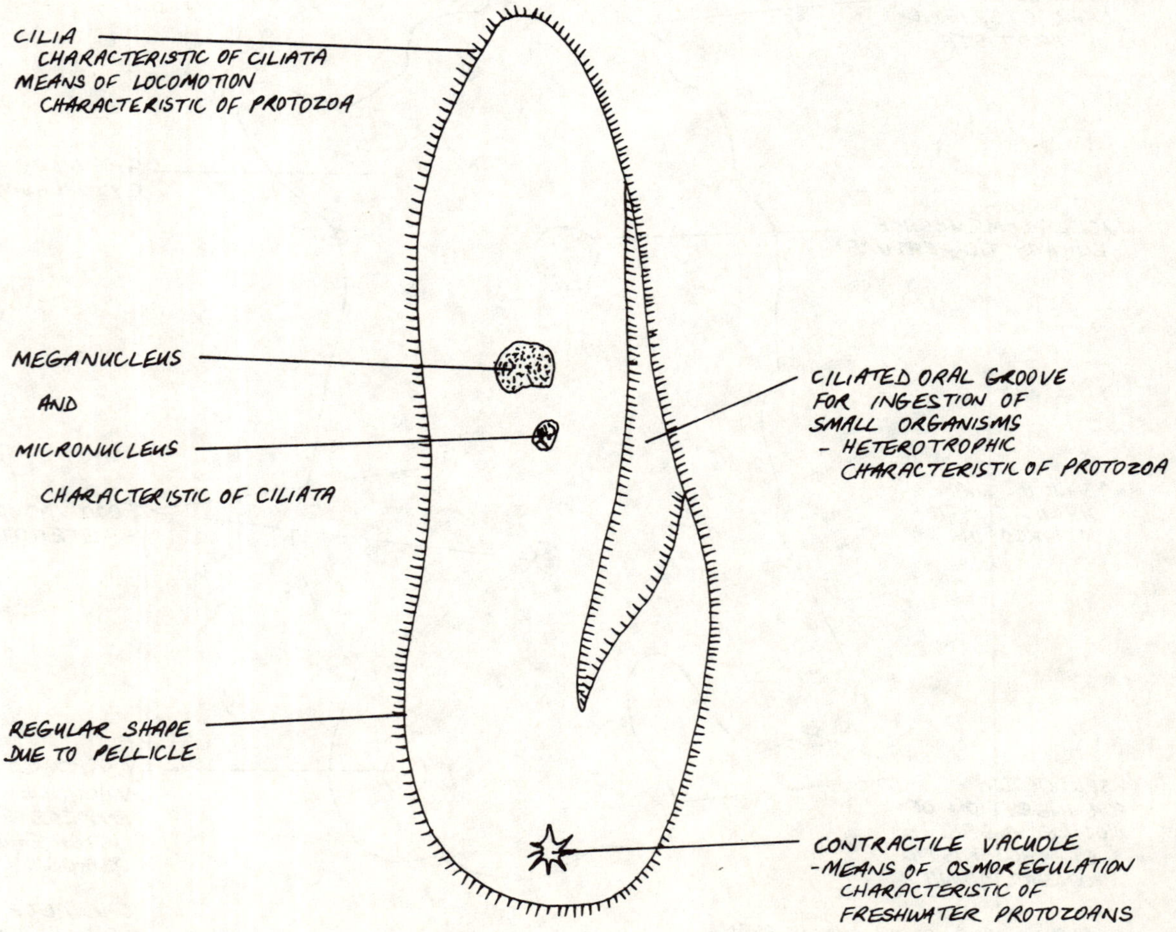

CILIA
CHARACTERISTIC OF CILIATA
MEANS OF LOCOMOTION
CHARACTERISTIC OF PROTOZOA

MEGANUCLEUS

AND

MICRONUCLEUS

CHARACTERISTIC OF CILIATA

CILIATED ORAL GROOVE
FOR INGESTION OF
SMALL ORGANISMS
- HETEROTROPHIC
CHARACTERISTIC OF PROTOZOA

REGULAR SHAPE
DUE TO PELLICLE

CONTRACTILE VACUOLE
-MEANS OF OSMOREGULATION
CHARACTERISTIC OF
FRESHWATER PROTOZOANS

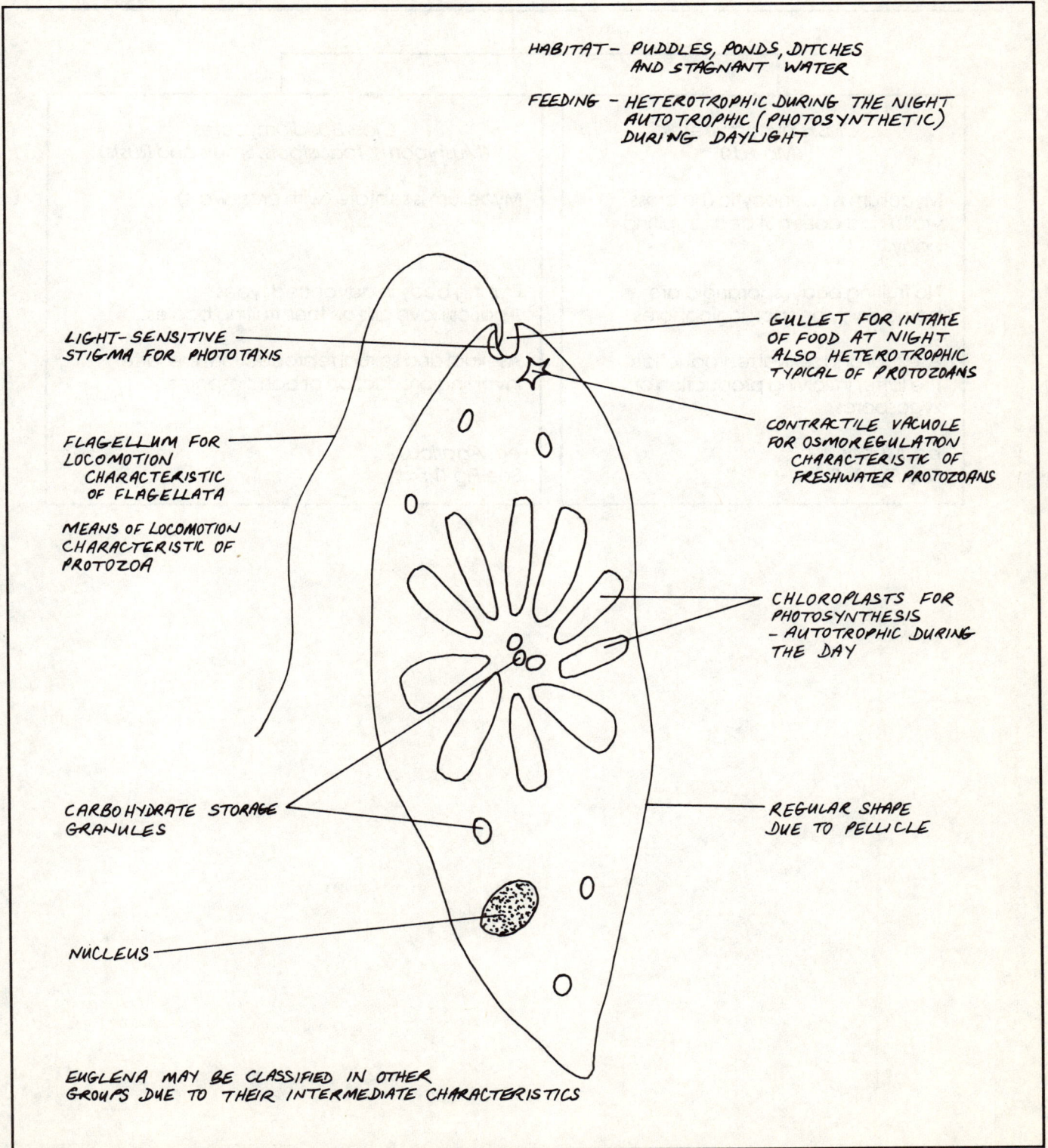

KINGDOM *PROTISTA*

PHYLUM *PROTOZOA*

CLASS *FLAGELLATA*

GENUS *EUGLENA*   X 600

Fig. 1.3

HABITAT – PUDDLES, PONDS, DITCHES
AND STAGNANT WATER

FEEDING – HETEROTROPHIC DURING THE NIGHT
AUTOTROPHIC (PHOTOSYNTHETIC)
DURING DAYLIGHT

LIGHT-SENSITIVE
STIGMA FOR PHOTOTAXIS

GULLET FOR INTAKE
OF FOOD AT NIGHT
ALSO HETEROTROPHIC
TYPICAL OF PROTOZOANS

CONTRACTILE VACUOLE
FOR OSMOREGULATION
CHARACTERISTIC OF
FRESHWATER PROTOZOANS

FLAGELLUM FOR
LOCOMOTION
CHARACTERISTIC
OF FLAGELLATA

MEANS OF LOCOMOTION
CHARACTERISTIC OF
PROTOZOA

CHLOROPLASTS FOR
PHOTOSYNTHESIS
– AUTOTROPHIC DURING
THE DAY

CARBOHYDRATE STORAGE
GRANULES

REGULAR SHAPE
DUE TO PELLICLE

NUCLEUS

EUGLENA MAY BE CLASSIFIED IN OTHER
GROUPS DUE TO THEIR INTERMEDIATE CHARACTERISTICS

KINGDOM *FUNGI*

Division Eumycophyta (True Fungi)

Most Eumycophytes have a mycelium of thread-like hyphae. The body may be unicellular or filamentous. The majority are terrestrial - growing in soil or on remains of animals or plants; a few are aquatic. Some, called mycorrhizae, form symbiotic relationships with higher plants such as oak trees. This group also forms the fungal component of lichens.

Class Phycomycetes
(Moulds)

Mycelium is coenocytic (no cross walls) and does not bear a fruiting body.

No fruiting body: sporangia are borne singly on sporangiophores.

Asexual and sexual reproduction, the latter involving production of zygospores.

eg. Mucor
See *Fig. 1.4*

Class Basidiomycetes
(Mushrooms, Toadstools, Smuts and Rusts)

Mycelium is septate (with cross walls).

Fruiting body in advanced types
Agarics have gills on their fruiting bodies.

Asexual and sexual reproduction, the latter involving production of basidiospores.

eg. Agaricus
See *Fig. 1.5*

DIVISION *EUMYCOPHYTA*

CLASS *PHYCOMYCETES*

GENUS *MUCOR*   X 400

Fig. 1.4

HABITAT - DUNG OF HORSES AND CATTLE ON FOODS E.G. BREAD

FEEDING - AS A SAPROTROPH (SAPROPHYTE) ON DEAD ORGANIC MATTER

ASEXUAL REPRODUCTION

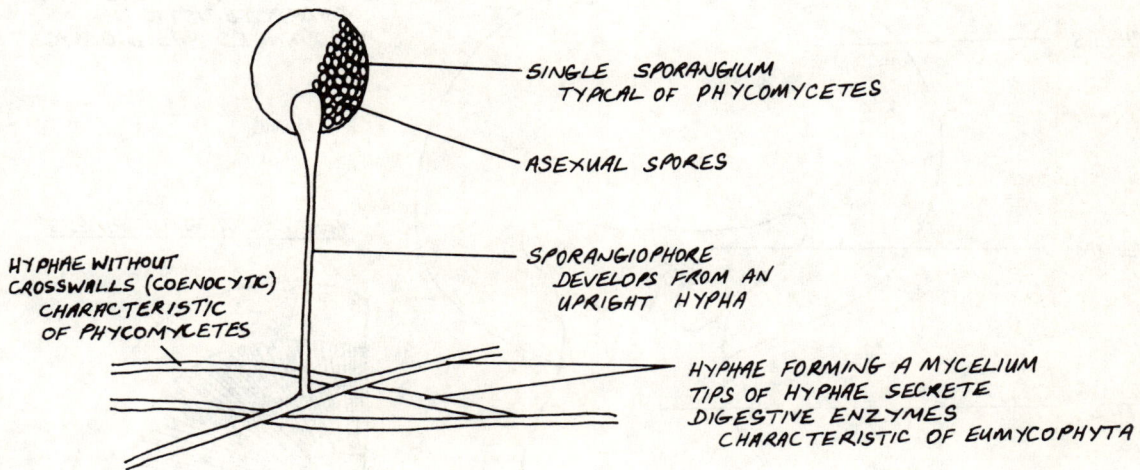

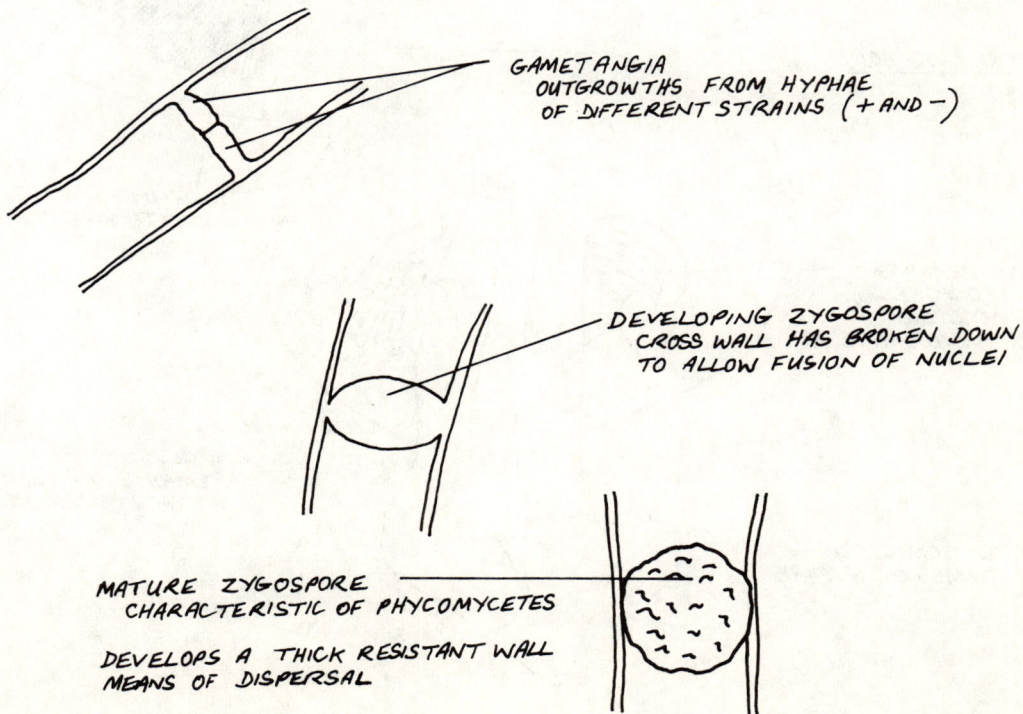

SINGLE SPORANGIUM TYPICAL OF PHYCOMYCETES

ASEXUAL SPORES

SPORANGIOPHORE DEVELOPS FROM AN UPRIGHT HYPHA

HYPHAE WITHOUT CROSSWALLS (COENOCYTIC) CHARACTERISTIC OF PHYCOMYCETES

HYPHAE FORMING A MYCELIUM TIPS OF HYPHAE SECRETE DIGESTIVE ENZYMES CHARACTERISTIC OF EUMYCOPHYTA

SEXUAL REPRODUCTION

GAMETANGIA OUTGROWTHS FROM HYPHAE OF DIFFERENT STRAINS (+ AND -)

DEVELOPING ZYGOSPORE CROSS WALL HAS BROKEN DOWN TO ALLOW FUSION OF NUCLEI

MATURE ZYGOSPORE CHARACTERISTIC OF PHYCOMYCETES

DEVELOPS A THICK RESISTANT WALL MEANS OF DISPERSAL

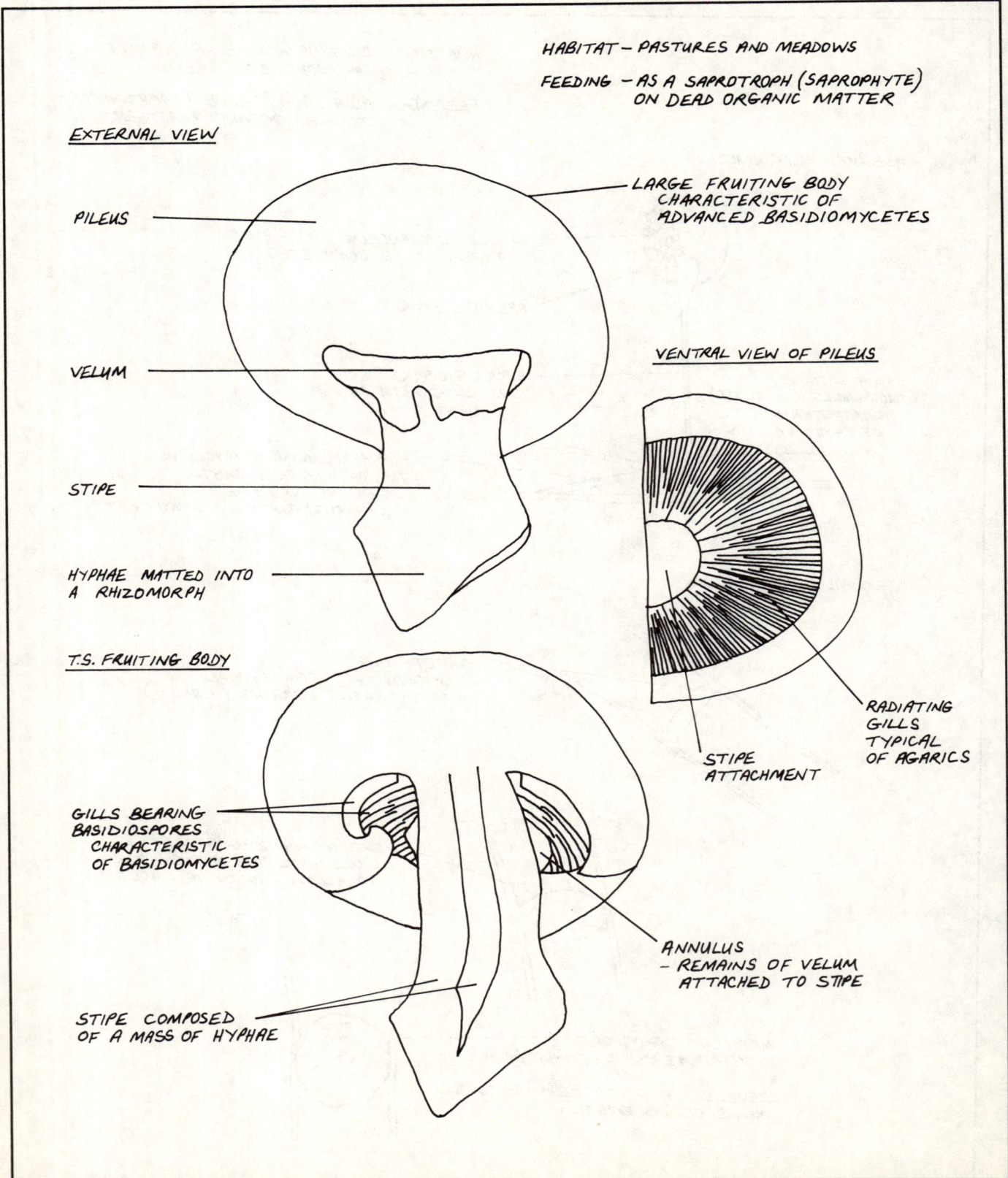

DIVISION *EUMYCOPHYTA*

CLASS *BASIDIOMYCETES*

GENUS *AGARICUS*

Fig. 1.5

HABITAT — PASTURES AND MEADOWS

FEEDING — AS A SAPROTROPH (SAPROPHYTE) ON DEAD ORGANIC MATTER

EXTERNAL VIEW

PILEUS

VELUM

STIPE

HYPHAE MATTED INTO A RHIZOMORPH

LARGE FRUITING BODY CHARACTERISTIC OF ADVANCED BASIDIOMYCETES

VENTRAL VIEW OF PILEUS

RADIATING GILLS TYPICAL OF AGARICS

STIPE ATTACHMENT

T.S. FRUITING BODY

GILLS BEARING BASIDIOSPORES CHARACTERISTIC OF BASIDIOMYCETES

STIPE COMPOSED OF A MASS OF HYPHAE

ANNULUS — REMAINS OF VELUM ATTACHED TO STIPE

KINGDOM *PLANTAE*

The Algae are so diverse that they have been divided into separate Divisions based mainly on their photosynthetic pigments. Each Division has only one Class, therefore Class and Division have the same characteristics. For sub-group features you will need to learn those of the various Orders.

Division Chlorophyta (Green algae)
Class Chlorophyceae

Unicellular, filamentous and thalloid forms. Contain chlorophylls a and b, carotenes and xanthophylls. Chloroplasts have pyrenoids which store starch. 90% are found in freshwater; terrestrial forms occur on rocks, soil and damp wood. Some form symbiotic associations *eg.* zoochlorellae in Hydra and others are the algal partners in lichens.

Order Conjugales

Unicellular or filamentous.
Cylindrical cells joined end to end to form unbranched filaments.

Cell walls have an inner cellulose layer and an outer pectic layer.

Nucleus suspended in the centre of large vacuoles by cytoplasmic strands.

Chloroplasts are elaborate *eg.* spiral.

eg. Spirogyra
See *Fig. 1.6*

Order Volvocales

Unicellular or colonial.
Cells are biflagellate.

Cellulose cell walls often have external, gelatinous sheath.

Single central nucleus.

Chloroplasts are usually cup-shaped.

eg. Chlamydomonas
See *Fig. 1.7*

Division Phaeophyta (Brown algae)
Class Phaeophyceae

Filamentous or thalloid forms. Contain chlorophylls a and c, carotene and xanthophylls including fucoxanthin. No pyrenoids. Storage products are laminarin and mannitol, not starch. All marine except 3 freshwater species; many are characteristic flora of the intertidal zone.

Order Fucales

Thalloid. Growth by dichotomous branching of apex

Body divided into lamina, stipe and holdfast

No asexual reproduction. Sexual reproduction involves development of specialised organs on the thallus tip (receptacle) within cavities called conceptacles

eg. Fucus vesiculosus - Bladder wrack
See *Fig. 1.8*

DIVISION *CHLOROPHYTA*

CLASS *CHLOROPHYCEAE*

GENUS *SPIROGYRA*   X 400

Fig. 1.6

HABITAT — FRESHWATER PONDS AND STREAMS

REPRODUCTION — ASEXUAL BY FRAGMENTATION,
SEXUAL BY CONJUGATION.

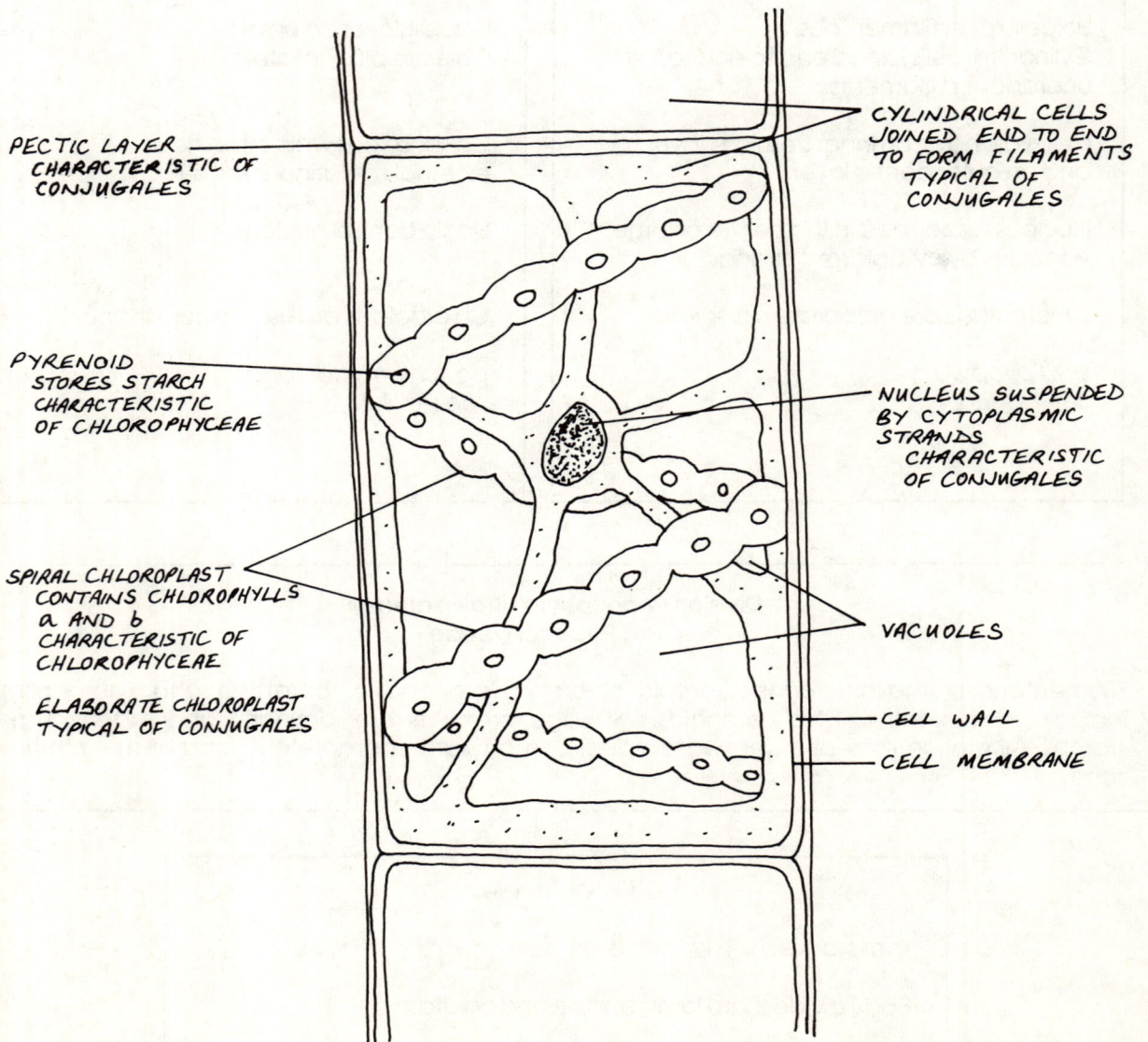

PECTIC LAYER
CHARACTERISTIC OF
CONJUGALES

CYLINDRICAL CELLS
JOINED END TO END
TO FORM FILAMENTS
TYPICAL OF
CONJUGALES

PYRENOID
STORES STARCH
CHARACTERISTIC
OF CHLOROPHYCEAE

NUCLEUS SUSPENDED
BY CYTOPLASMIC
STRANDS
CHARACTERISTIC
OF CONJUGALES

SPIRAL CHLOROPLAST
CONTAINS CHLOROPHYLLS
a AND b
CHARACTERISTIC OF
CHLOROPHYCEAE

VACUOLES

ELABORATE CHLOROPLAST
TYPICAL OF CONJUGALES

CELL WALL

CELL MEMBRANE

DIVISION *CHLOROPHYTA*

CLASS *CHLOROPHYCEAE*

ORDER *VOLVOCALES*

GENUS *CHLAMYDOMONAS*   X 600

Fig. 1.7

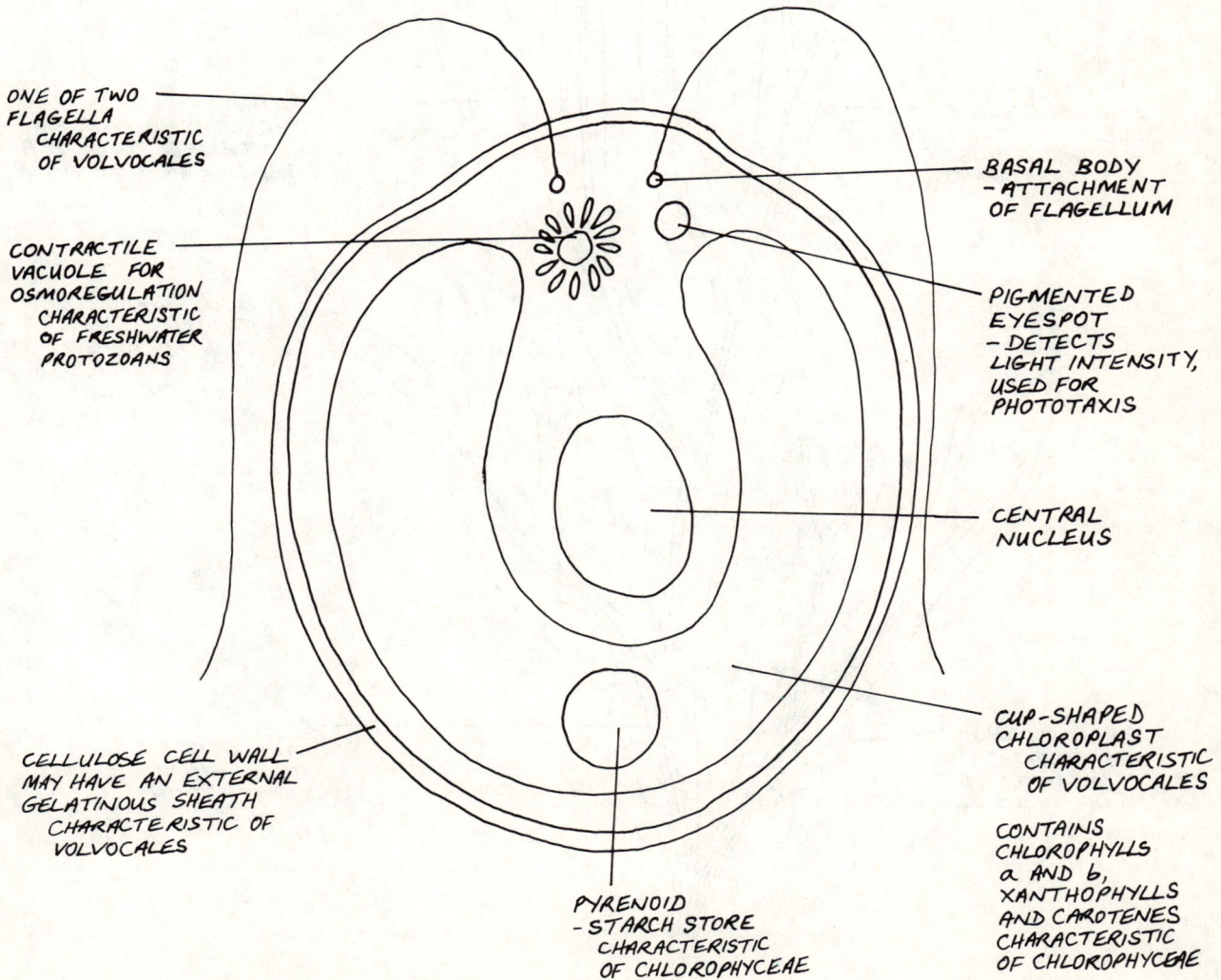

HABITAT - FRESHWATER PONDS
AND DITCHES

LOCOMOTION - BY FLAGELLA

REPRODUCTION - ASEXUAL BY FISSION
SEXUAL BY FUSION

ONE OF TWO
FLAGELLA
CHARACTERISTIC
OF VOLVOCALES

CONTRACTILE
VACUOLE FOR
OSMOREGULATION
CHARACTERISTIC
OF FRESHWATER
PROTOZOANS

BASAL BODY
- ATTACHMENT
OF FLAGELLUM

PIGMENTED
EYESPOT
- DETECTS
LIGHT INTENSITY,
USED FOR
PHOTOTAXIS

CENTRAL
NUCLEUS

CELLULOSE CELL WALL
MAY HAVE AN EXTERNAL
GELATINOUS SHEATH
CHARACTERISTIC OF
VOLVOCALES

CUP-SHAPED
CHLOROPLAST
CHARACTERISTIC
OF VOLVOCALES

CONTAINS
CHLOROPHYLLS
a AND b,
XANTHOPHYLLS
AND CAROTENES
CHARACTERISTIC
OF CHLOROPHYCEAE

PYRENOID
- STARCH STORE
CHARACTERISTIC
OF CHLOROPHYCEAE

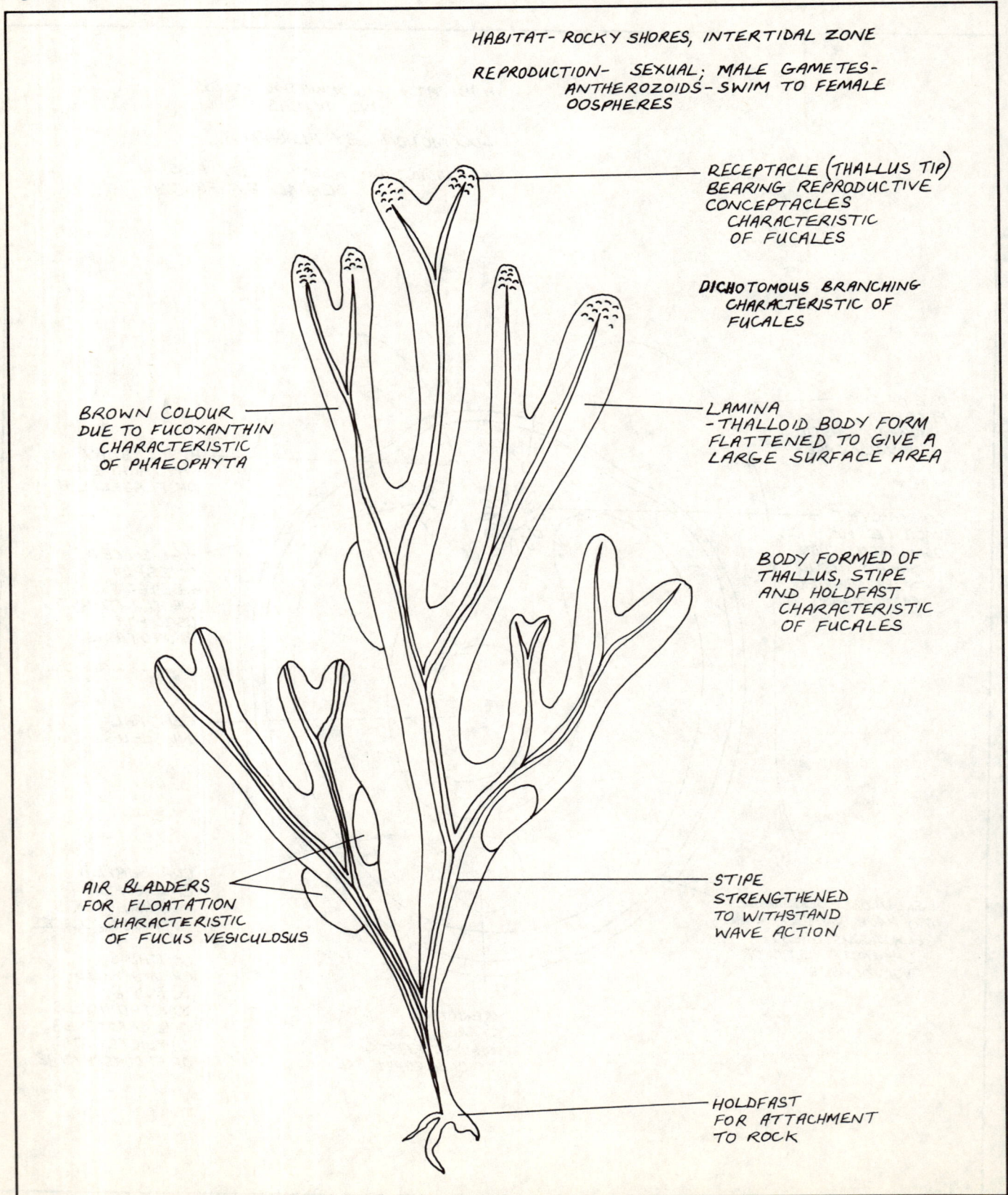

DIVISION *PHAEOPHYTA*

CLASS *PHAEOPHYCEAE*

ORDER *FUCALES*

GENUS *FUCUS*   X 1

Fig. 1.8

HABITAT- ROCKY SHORES, INTERTIDAL ZONE

REPRODUCTION- SEXUAL; MALE GAMETES-
ANTHEROZOIDS - SWIM TO FEMALE
OOSPHERES

RECEPTACLE (THALLUS TIP)
BEARING REPRODUCTIVE
CONCEPTACLES
CHARACTERISTIC
OF FUCALES

DICHOTOMOUS BRANCHING
CHARACTERISTIC OF
FUCALES

BROWN COLOUR
DUE TO FUCOXANTHIN
CHARACTERISTIC
OF PHAEOPHYTA

LAMINA
-THALLOID BODY FORM
FLATTENED TO GIVE A
LARGE SURFACE AREA

BODY FORMED OF
THALLUS, STIPE
AND HOLDFAST
CHARACTERISTIC
OF FUCALES

AIR BLADDERS
FOR FLOATATION
CHARACTERISTIC
OF FUCUS VESICULOSUS

STIPE
STRENGTHENED
TO WITHSTAND
WAVE ACTION

HOLDFAST
FOR ATTACHMENT
TO ROCK

Division Bryophyta

A thalloid plant body which represents the persistant gametophyte generation. No true roots, stems or leaves *ie.* do not contain vascular tissue. Rhizoids for attachments to substratum and absorption. Bear archegonia and antheridia; male gametes are biflagellate and motile.
Found mainly in damp terrestrial habitats.

Class Musci (Mosses)

Colonial, may be upright or prostrate.
Plant body is stem-like and bears leaf-like appendages.

'Leaves' are arranged spirally and contain chlorophylls a and b, carotene and xanthophyll.

Apical sex organs - female leaf clusters containing archegonia and male rosettes containing antheridia.

Spores germinate into a protonema.

eg. Polytrichum
See *Fig. 1.9*

Division Pteridophyta

Body differentiated into true stems, roots and leaves which form the persistant sporophyte generation. Contains vascular tissue - xylem consists of tracheids. Sporophyte bears sporangia on specialised sporophylls.

Class Lycopsida (Club mosses)

Small leaves arranged spirally around stem.

Sporangia grouped into strobili or cones. Sporangia borne on the upper surface or in the axils of the sporophylls.

eg. Lycopodium
See *Fig. 1.10*

Class Pteropsida (Ferns)

Large leaves (fronds) which are deeply divided (pinnate) arranged spirally around stem.

Sporangia borne in groups called sori on the underside or margins of the sporophylls.

eg. Dryopteris
See *Fig. 1.11*

DIVISION *BRYOPHYTA*

CLASS *MUSCI*

GENUS *POLYTRICHUM*　　　X4

Fig. 1.9

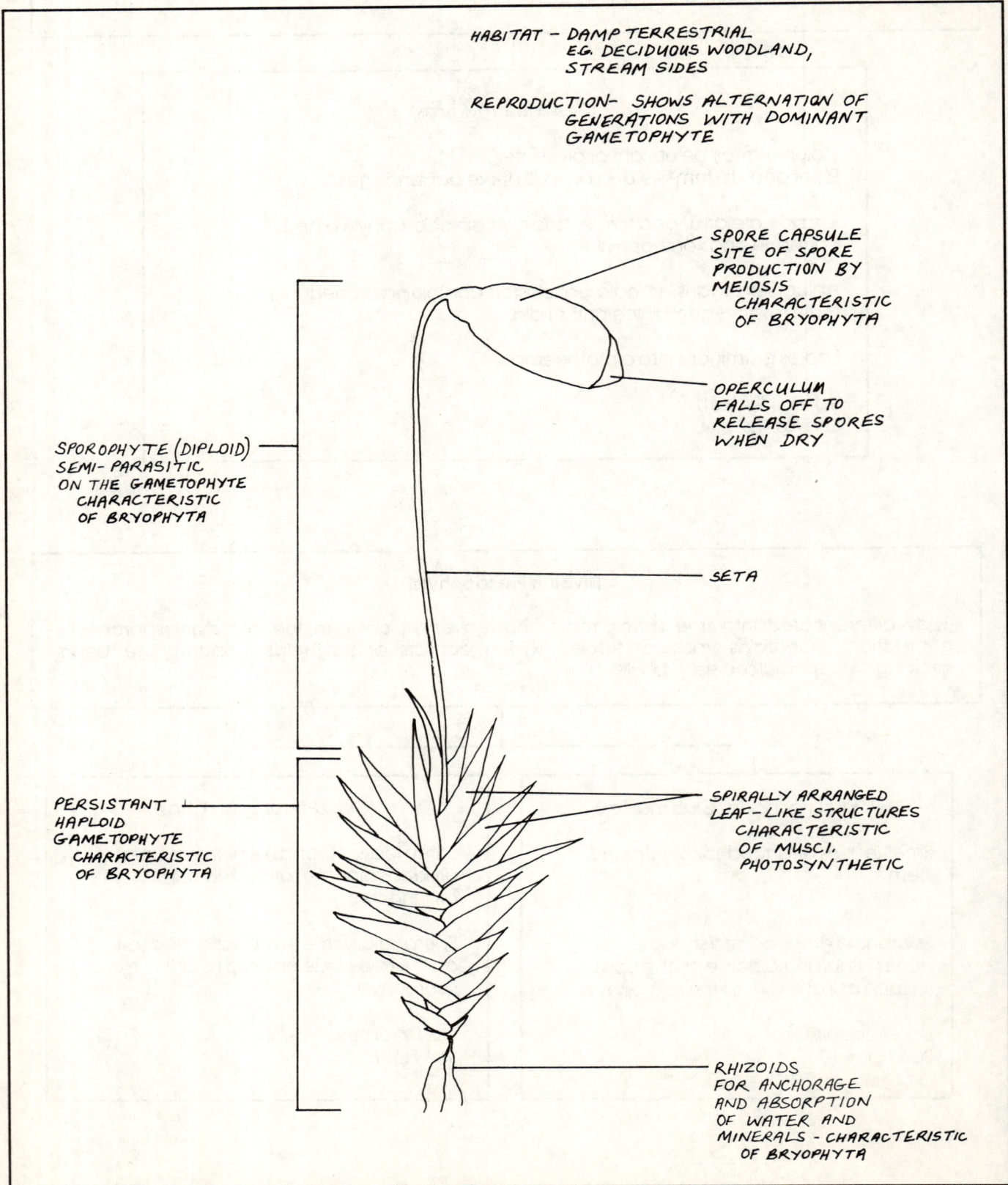

HABITAT – DAMP TERRESTRIAL
E.G. DECIDUOUS WOODLAND,
STREAM SIDES

REPRODUCTION– SHOWS ALTERNATION OF
GENERATIONS WITH DOMINANT
GAMETOPHYTE

SPORE CAPSULE
SITE OF SPORE
PRODUCTION BY
MEIOSIS
CHARACTERISTIC
OF BRYOPHYTA

OPERCULUM
FALLS OFF TO
RELEASE SPORES
WHEN DRY

SPOROPHYTE (DIPLOID)
SEMI-PARASITIC
ON THE GAMETOPHYTE
CHARACTERISTIC
OF BRYOPHYTA

SETA

PERSISTANT
HAPLOID
GAMETOPHYTE
CHARACTERISTIC
OF BRYOPHYTA

SPIRALLY ARRANGED
LEAF-LIKE STRUCTURES
CHARACTERISTIC
OF MUSCI.
PHOTOSYNTHETIC

RHIZOIDS
FOR ANCHORAGE
AND ABSORPTION
OF WATER AND
MINERALS - CHARACTERISTIC
OF BRYOPHYTA

DIVISION *PTERIDOPHYTA*

CLASS *LYCOPSIDA*

GENUS *LYCOPODIUM*   X 2

Fig. 1.10

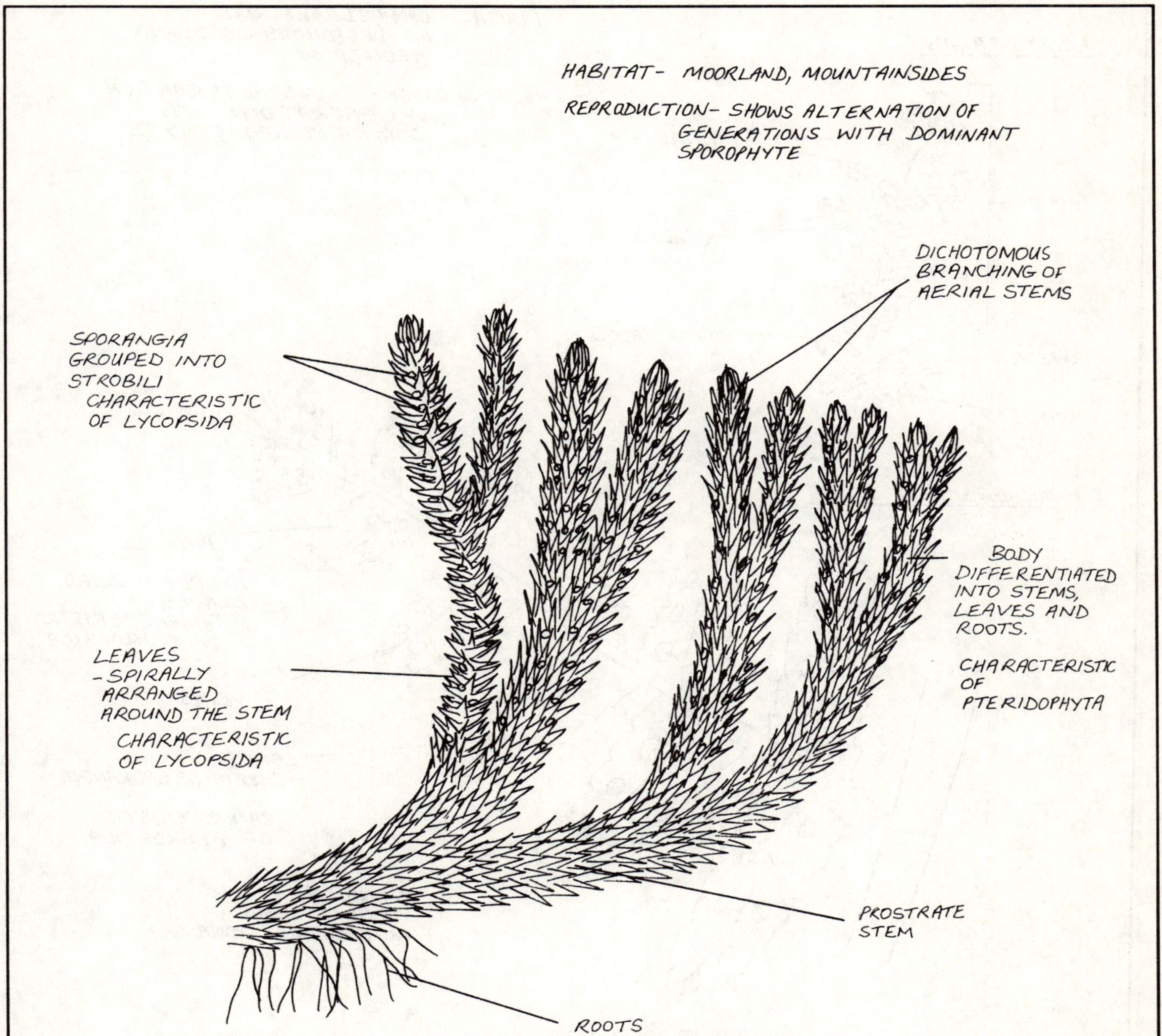

HABITAT- MOORLAND, MOUNTAINSIDES

REPRODUCTION- SHOWS ALTERNATION OF GENERATIONS WITH DOMINANT SPOROPHYTE

DICHOTOMOUS BRANCHING OF AERIAL STEMS

SPORANGIA GROUPED INTO STROBILI CHARACTERISTIC OF LYCOPSIDA

BODY DIFFERENTIATED INTO STEMS, LEAVES AND ROOTS.

CHARACTERISTIC OF PTERIDOPHYTA

LEAVES -SPIRALLY ARRANGED AROUND THE STEM CHARACTERISTIC OF LYCOPSIDA

PROSTRATE STEM

ROOTS FOR ANCHORAGE AND ABSORPTION

DIVISION *PTERIDOPHYTA*

CLASS *PTEROPSIDA*

GENUS *DRYOPTERIS*

Fig. 1.11

HABIT DRAWING

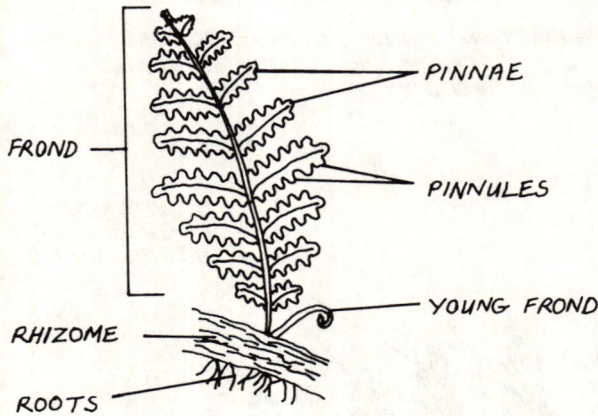

PINNAE

FROND

PINNULES

YOUNG FROND

RHIZOME

ROOTS

HABITAT - DAMP TERRESTRIAL
E.G. DECIDUOUS WOODLAND
HEDGEROW

REPRODUCTION - SHOWS ALTERNATION
OF GENERATIONS WITH
DOMINANT SPOROPHYTE

UNDERSIDE OF PINNA

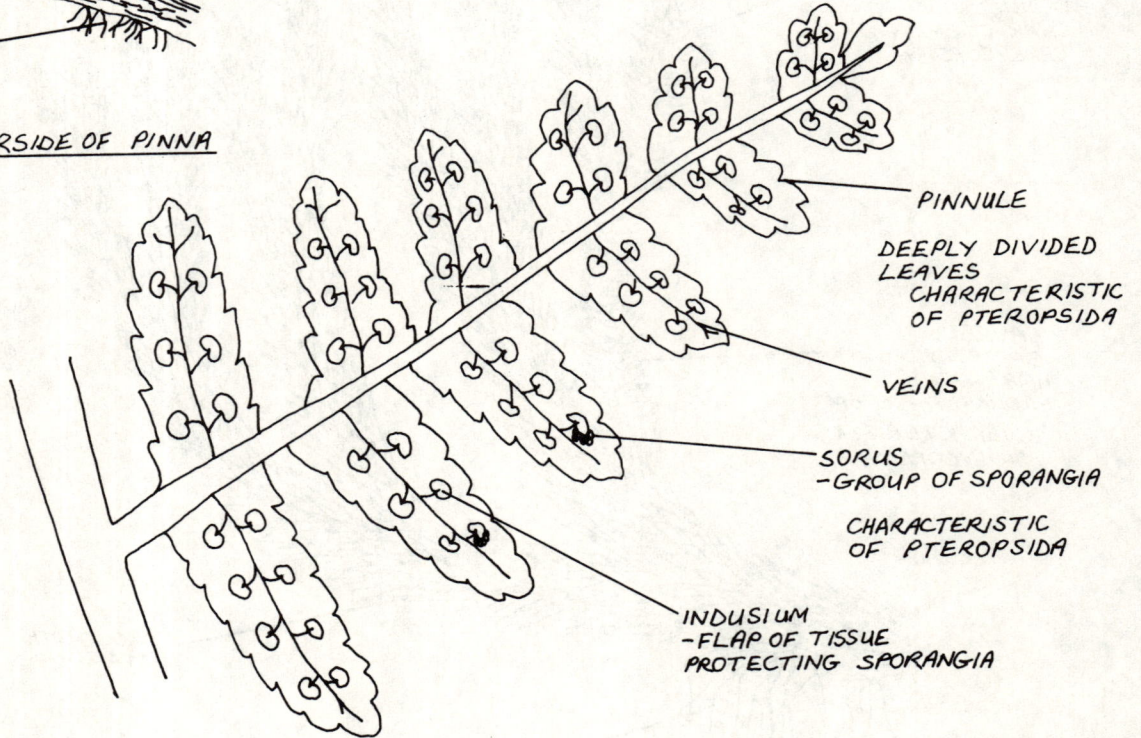

PINNULE

DEEPLY DIVIDED
LEAVES
CHARACTERISTIC
OF PTEROPSIDA

VEINS

SORUS
- GROUP OF SPORANGIA

CHARACTERISTIC
OF PTEROPSIDA

INDUSIUM
- FLAP OF TISSUE
PROTECTING SPORANGIA

T.S. THROUGH SORUS

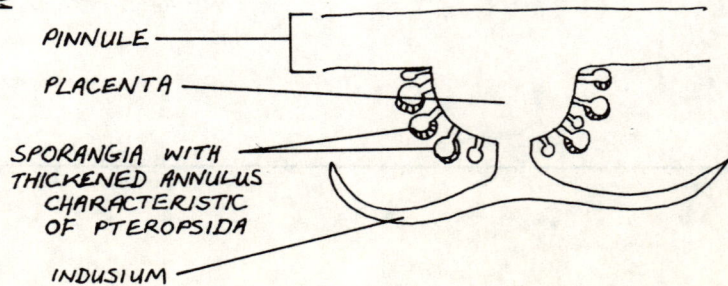

PINNULE

PLACENTA

SPORANGIA WITH
THICKENED ANNULUS
CHARACTERISTIC
OF PTEROPSIDA

INDUSIUM

Division Spermatophyta

The sporophyte consists of true root, stem and leaves; the gametophyte is never independent. There is a wide range of form from herbaceous plants to trees. They are found in nearly all types of habitat. Internal tissues show a high degree of differentiation and in the more advanced types, vessels are present as well as tracheids in the xylem. Secondary thickening is common. The sporophyte bears specialised reproductive structures; either cones or flowers. Both male and female gametophytes are very reduced; the male is found within the pollen grain and the female within the megaspore. Seeds are either naked or enclosed in a fruit.

Class Gymnospermae

Sporophyte always a woody shrub or a tree. Usually evergreen and often have reduced leaves.

Reproductive structures borne on unisexual cones. Following fertilisation the seeds develop on the surface of the megasporophyll, they are not enclosed.

eg. *Pinus* - Pine
See *Fig. 1.12*

Class Angiospermae

Sporophytes vary in size, shape and type; may be herbaceous or woody.

Reproductive structures are flowers; these may occur singly or in groups (inflorescences). Seeds develop within specialised fruits.

Sub-class Monocotyledones

Mainly herbaceous perennial plants with underground storage organs such as corms, bulbs and rhizomes.

Leaves narrow with parallel venation.

Floral parts arranged in threes or multiples of three.

eg. *Tulipa* - Tulip
See *Fig. 1.13*

Sub-class Dicotyledones

Annual, biennial and perennial herbs, shrubs and trees.

Leaves broad with net venation.

Floral parts arranged in fours or fives (or multiples).

eg. *Primula* - Primrose
See *Fig. 1.14*

DIVISION *SPERMATOPHYTA*

CLASS *GYMNOSPERMAE*

GENUS *PINUS*

Fig. 1.12

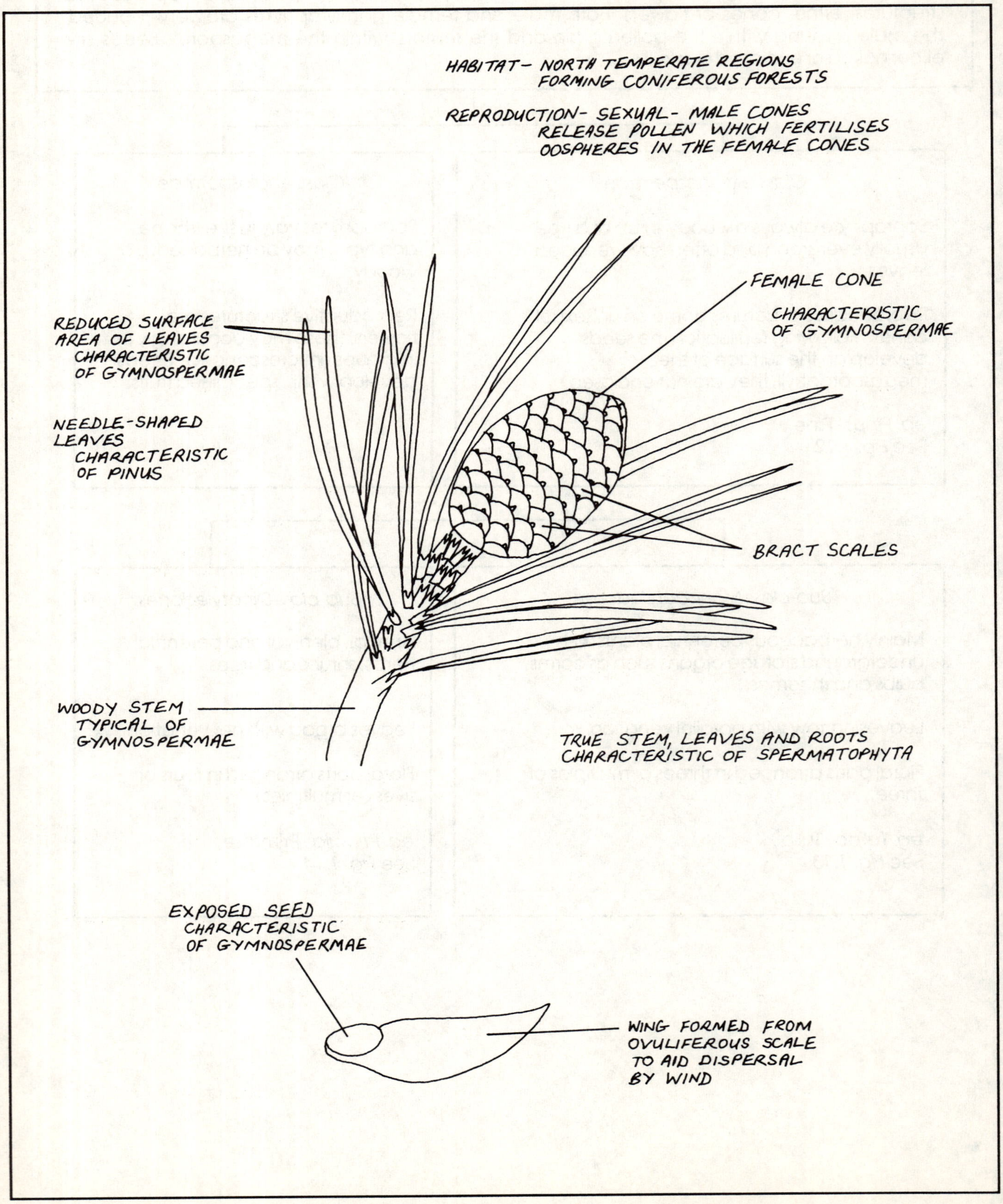

HABITAT – NORTH TEMPERATE REGIONS
FORMING CONIFEROUS FORESTS

REPRODUCTION – SEXUAL – MALE CONES
RELEASE POLLEN WHICH FERTILISES
OOSPHERES IN THE FEMALE CONES

FEMALE CONE
CHARACTERISTIC
OF GYMNOSPERMAE

REDUCED SURFACE
AREA OF LEAVES
CHARACTERISTIC
OF GYMNOSPERMAE

NEEDLE-SHAPED
LEAVES
CHARACTERISTIC
OF PINUS

BRACT SCALES

WOODY STEM
TYPICAL OF
GYMNOSPERMAE

TRUE STEM, LEAVES AND ROOTS
CHARACTERISTIC OF SPERMATOPHYTA

EXPOSED SEED
CHARACTERISTIC
OF GYMNOSPERMAE

WING FORMED FROM
OVULIFEROUS SCALE
TO AID DISPERSAL
BY WIND

DIVISION *SPERMATOPHYTA*

CLASS *ANGIOSPERMAE*

SUB-CLASS *MONOCOTYLEDONES*

GENUS *TULIPA*

Fig. 1.13

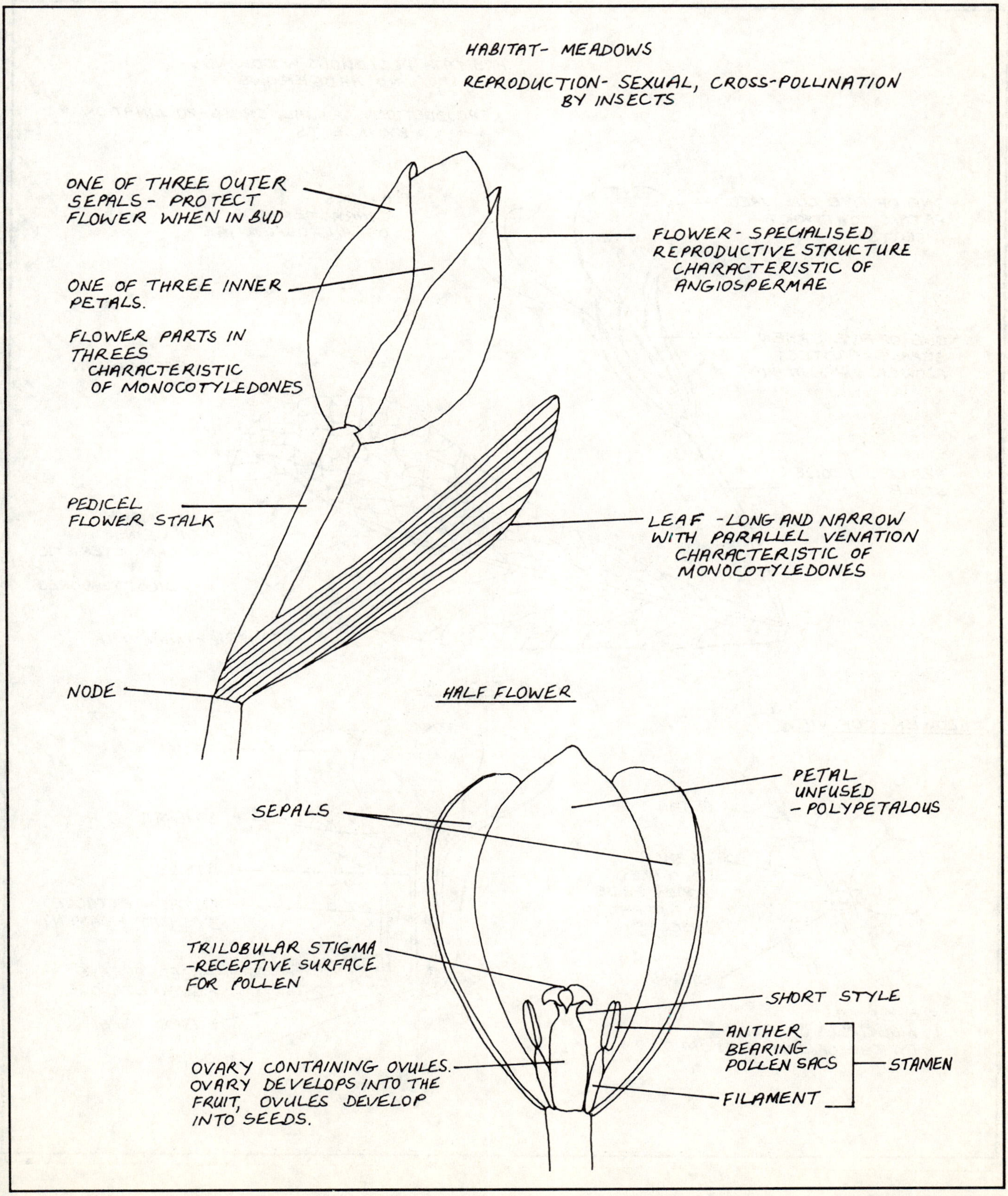

HABITAT- MEADOWS

REPRODUCTION- SEXUAL, CROSS-POLLINATION BY INSECTS

ONE OF THREE OUTER SEPALS - PROTECT FLOWER WHEN IN BUD

ONE OF THREE INNER PETALS.

FLOWER PARTS IN THREES CHARACTERISTIC OF MONOCOTYLEDONES

PEDICEL FLOWER STALK

NODE

FLOWER - SPECIALISED REPRODUCTIVE STRUCTURE CHARACTERISTIC OF ANGIOSPERMAE

LEAF -LONG AND NARROW WITH PARALLEL VENATION CHARACTERISTIC OF MONOCOTYLEDONES

HALF FLOWER

SEPALS

PETAL UNFUSED - POLYPETALOUS

TRILOBULAR STIGMA -RECEPTIVE SURFACE FOR POLLEN

SHORT STYLE

ANTHER BEARING POLLEN SACS

STAMEN

OVARY CONTAINING OVULES. OVARY DEVELOPS INTO THE FRUIT, OVULES DEVELOP INTO SEEDS.

FILAMENT

DIVISION *SPERMATOPHYTA*

CLASS *ANGIOSPERMAE*

SUB-CLASS *DICOTYLEDONES*

GENUS *PRIMULA*

Fig. 1.14

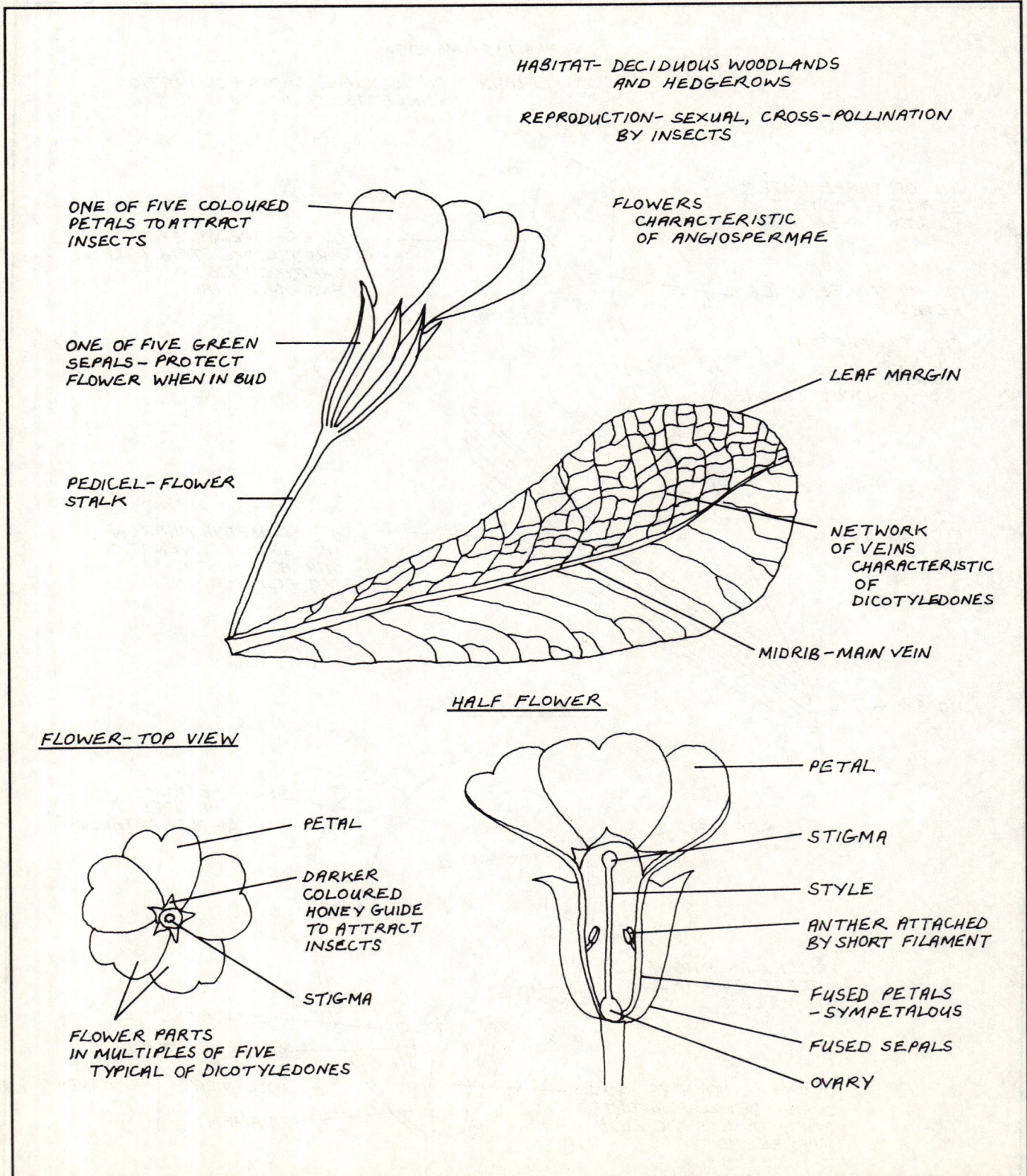

HABITAT- DECIDUOUS WOODLANDS AND HEDGEROWS

REPRODUCTION- SEXUAL, CROSS-POLLINATION BY INSECTS

ONE OF FIVE COLOURED PETALS TO ATTRACT INSECTS

FLOWERS CHARACTERISTIC OF ANGIOSPERMAE

ONE OF FIVE GREEN SEPALS - PROTECT FLOWER WHEN IN BUD

LEAF MARGIN

PEDICEL- FLOWER STALK

NETWORK OF VEINS CHARACTERISTIC OF DICOTYLEDONES

MIDRIB-MAIN VEIN

HALF FLOWER

FLOWER- TOP VIEW

PETAL

DARKER COLOURED HONEY GUIDE TO ATTRACT INSECTS

STIGMA

FLOWER PARTS IN MULTIPLES OF FIVE TYPICAL OF DICOTYLEDONES

PETAL

STIGMA

STYLE

ANTHER ATTACHED BY SHORT FILAMENT

FUSED PETALS - SYMPETALOUS

FUSED SEPALS

OVARY

KINGDOM *ANIMALIA*

Phylum Coelenterata

Radially symmetrical, diploblastic (two body layers) organisms. The body cavity, the enteron, has a single opening. The mouth is surrounded by a row of mobile tentacles armed with stinging nematocysts. Symbiotic algae present in the endoderm. They are often polymorphic with medusoid (jellyfish-like) and hydroid (sedentary polyp) forms. Found widely distributed in aquatic habitats although most are marine.

Class Hydrozoa

Usually colonial.

Both hydroid and medusoid forms.

May secrete a chitinous skeleton; the perisarc.

eg. Hydra and *Obelia*
See *Figs. 1.15* and *1.16*

Class Anthozoa

Solitary and colonial forms.

No medusoid forms.

Only colonial forms secrete a calcareous skeleton.

eg. Actinia - Sea Anemone
See *Fig. 1.17*

PHYLUM *COELENTERATA*

CLASS *HYDROZOA*

GENUS *HYDRA*　　X 50

Fig. 1.15

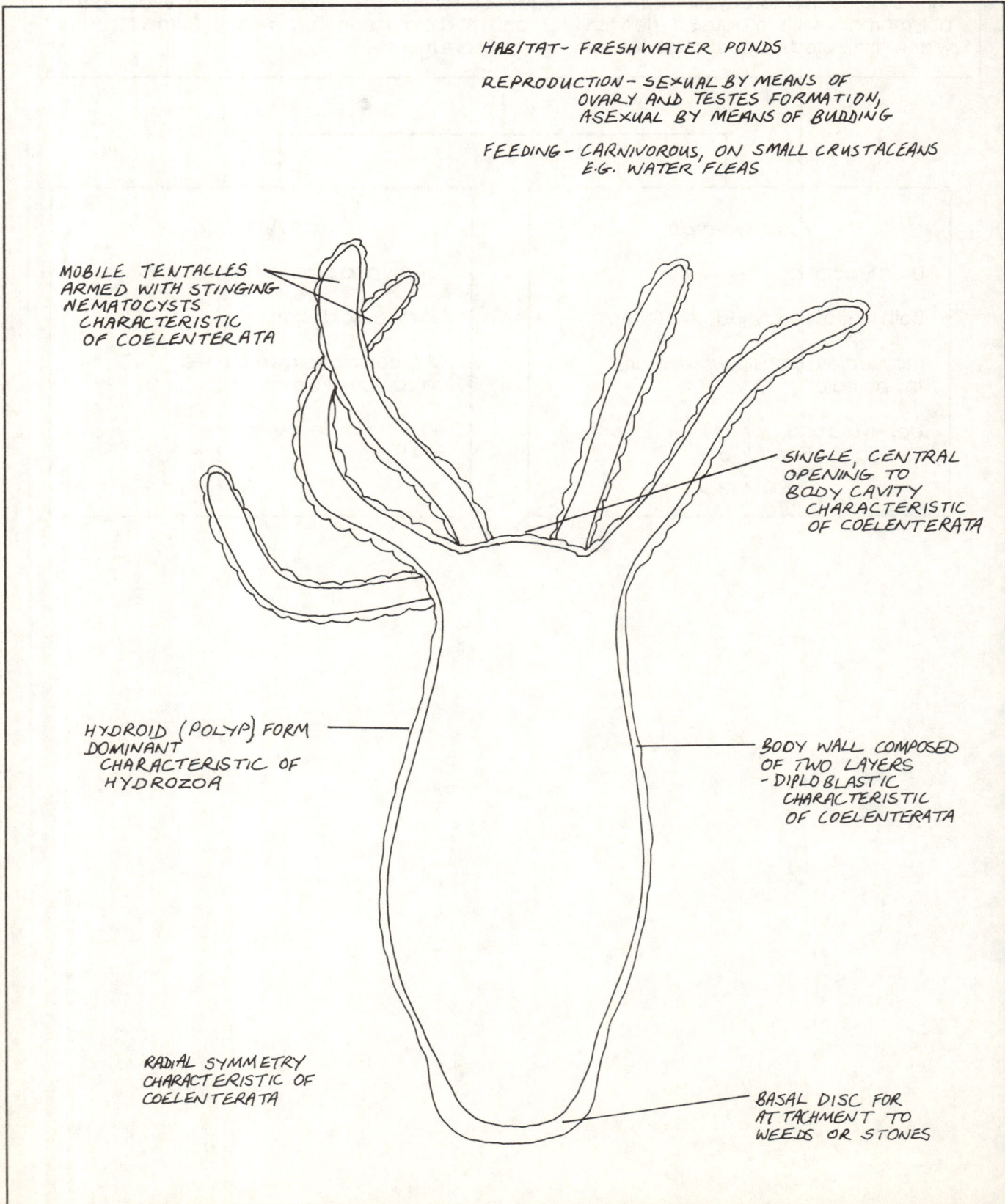

HABITAT - FRESHWATER PONDS

REPRODUCTION - SEXUAL BY MEANS OF OVARY AND TESTES FORMATION, ASEXUAL BY MEANS OF BUDDING

FEEDING - CARNIVOROUS, ON SMALL CRUSTACEANS E.G. WATER FLEAS

MOBILE TENTACLES ARMED WITH STINGING NEMATOCYSTS CHARACTERISTIC OF COELENTERATA

SINGLE, CENTRAL OPENING TO BODY CAVITY CHARACTERISTIC OF COELENTERATA

HYDROID (POLYP) FORM DOMINANT CHARACTERISTIC OF HYDROZOA

BODY WALL COMPOSED OF TWO LAYERS - DIPLOBLASTIC CHARACTERISTIC OF COELENTERATA

RADIAL SYMMETRY CHARACTERISTIC OF COELENTERATA

BASAL DISC FOR ATTACHMENT TO WEEDS OR STONES

PHYLUM *COELENTERATA*

CLASS *HYDROZOA*

GENUS *OBELIA*   X 100

Fig. 1.16

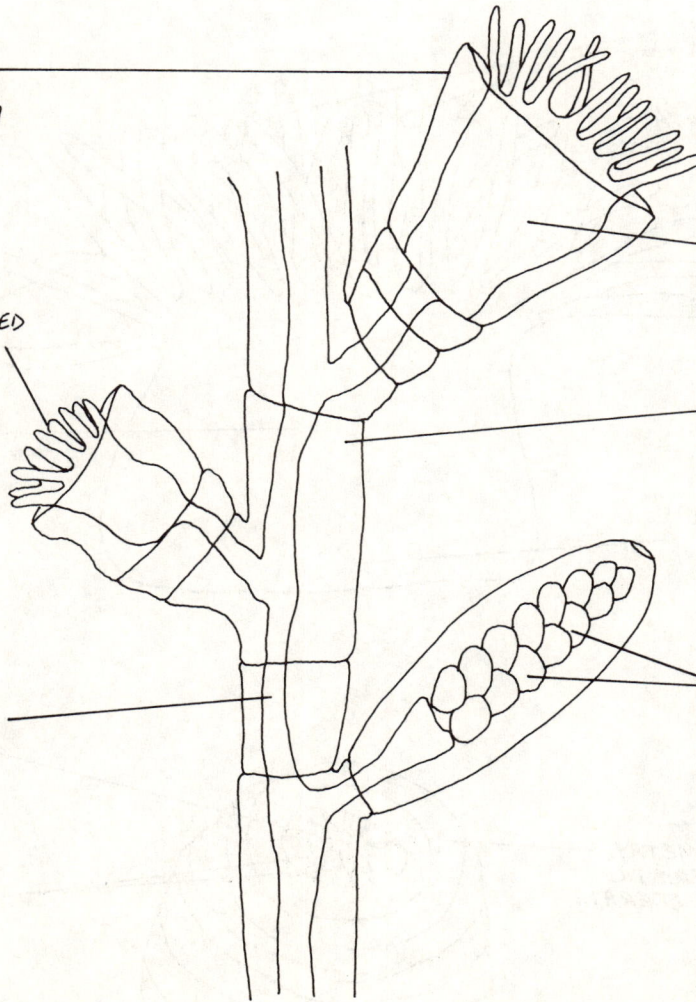

HABITAT – MARINE, ATTACHED TO SEAWEEDS AT LOW TIDE LEVEL

FEEDING – CARNIVOROUS, ON LARVAE AND PLANKTON

REPRODUCTION– ASEXUAL BY BUDDING FROM HYDROID POLYPS; SEXUAL BY RELEASE OF GAMETES FROM MOTILE MEDUSAE

RADIAL SYMMETRY CHARACTERISTIC OF COELENTERATA

MOUTH SURROUNDED BY TENTACLES ARMED WITH STINGING NEMATOCYSTS CHARACTERISTIC OF COELENTERATA

HOLLOW COENOSARC CONNECTING THE COLONY

HYDRANTH –HYDROID POLYP

PERISARC –CHITINOUS SKELETON TYPICAL OF HYDROZOA

DEVELOPING MEDUSAE –SEXUAL STAGE AND MOTILE DISPERSAL STAGE

PHYLUM *COELENTERATA*

CLASS *ANTHOZOA*

GENUS *ACTINIA*   X 1.5

Fig. 1.17

HABITAT— ROCKY SHORE, IN SHALLOW WATER

FEEDING— CARNIVOROUS, CATCHING CRUSTACEANS AND SMALL FISH

REPRODUCTION— SEXUAL—GAMETES FUSE TO FORM A ZYGOTE WHICH DEVELOPS INTO A CILIATED PLANULA LARVA. THE LARVA SETTLES AND DEVELOPS INTO A NEW ANEMONE.

EXPANDED

MOBILE TENTACLES ARMED WITH STINGING NEMATOCYSTS CHARACTERISTIC OF COELENTERATA

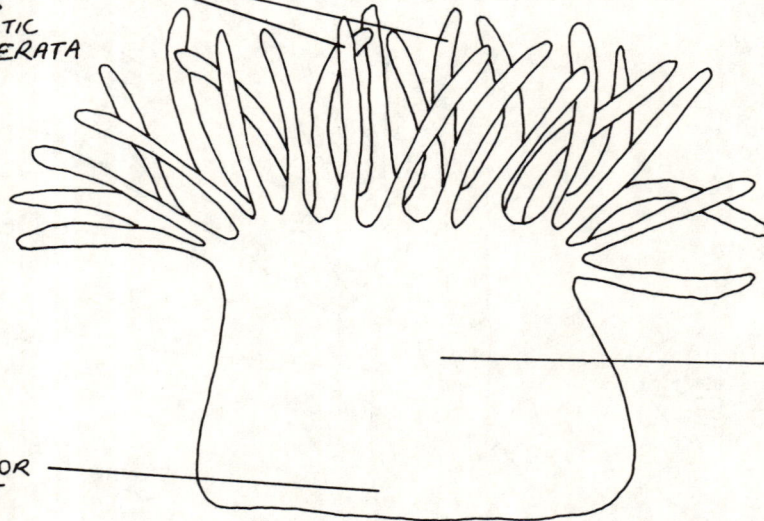

HYDROID FORM ONLY CHARACTERISTIC OF ANTHOZOA

BASAL DISC FOR ATTACHMENT TO ROCKS

CONTRACTED

SINGLE OPENING TO BODY CAVITY CHARACTERISTIC OF COELENTERATA

RADIAL SYMMETRY CHARACTERISTIC OF COELENTERATA

TENTACLES

Phylum Platyhelminthes

Dorso-ventrally flattened organisms. They are triploblastic (three body layers) showing bilateral symmetry. The gut (if present) is very branched with only one opening. They are hermaphrodites with both male and female reproductive systems. Found in aquatic habitats where they may be either free-living or parasitic.

Class Turbellaria

Leaf-like body with slight differentiation of head.

Ciliated epidermis glides over the surface of mud in ponds.

Branched gut with eversible pharynx.

No suckers.

eg. Planaria - Flatworm
See *Fig. 1.18*

Class Trematoda

Leaf-like body without differentiation of head.

Thick cuticle without cilia.

Branched gut with sucking pharynx.

One oral and one ventral sucker.

eg. Fasciola - Liverfluke
See *Fig. 1.19*

Class Cestoda

Long tape-like body with slight head (scolex).

Thick cuticle without cilia.

No gut.

Several suckers and hooks on scolex.

eg. Taenia - Tapeworm
See *Fig. 1.20*

PHYLUM *PLATYHELMINTHES*

CLASS *TURBELLARIA*

GENUS *PLANARIA*

Fig. 1.18

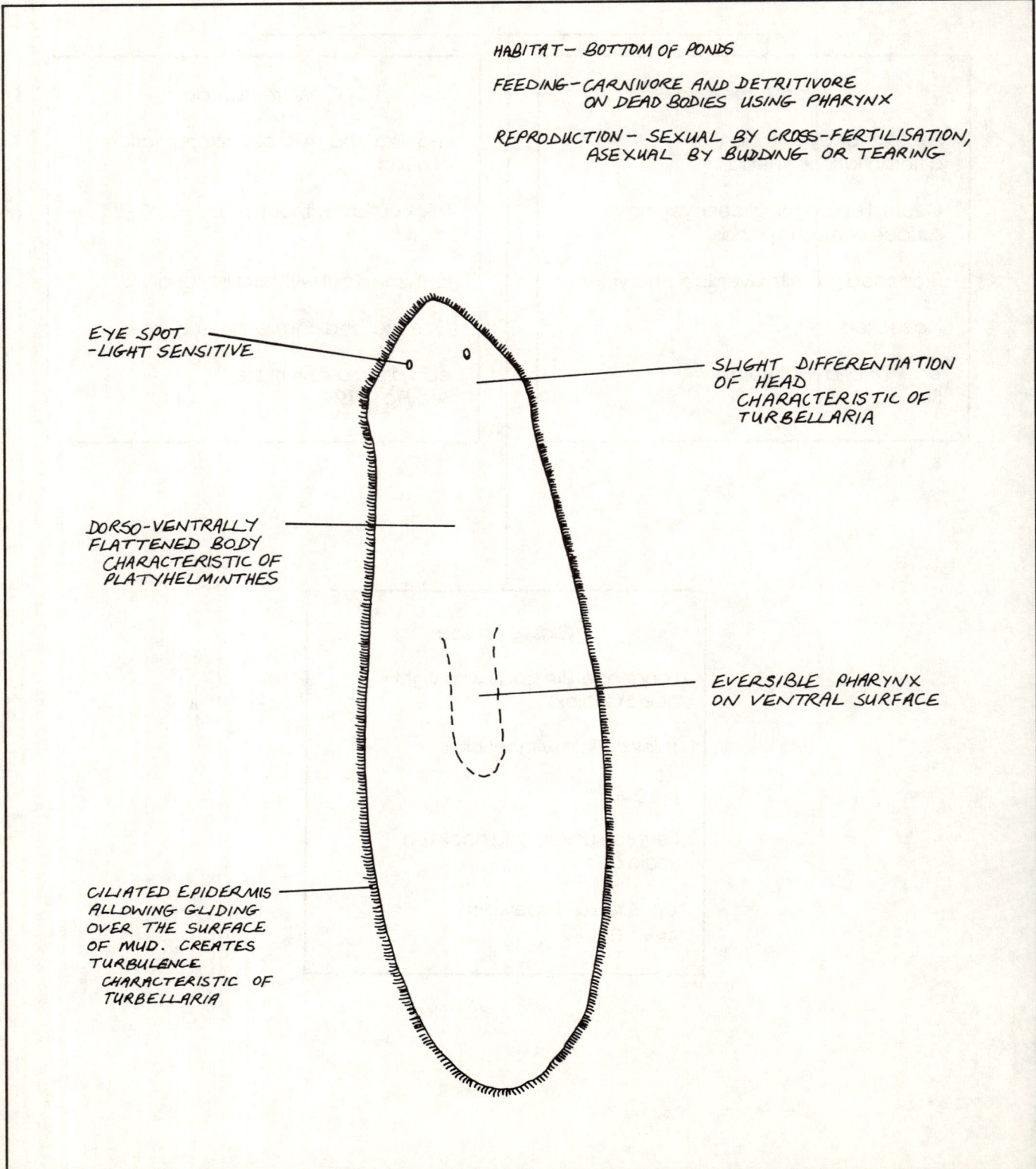

HABITAT – BOTTOM OF PONDS

FEEDING – CARNIVORE AND DETRITIVORE
ON DEAD BODIES USING PHARYNX

REPRODUCTION – SEXUAL BY CROSS-FERTILISATION,
ASEXUAL BY BUDDING OR TEARING

EYE SPOT
– LIGHT SENSITIVE

SLIGHT DIFFERENTIATION
OF HEAD
CHARACTERISTIC OF
TURBELLARIA

DORSO-VENTRALLY
FLATTENED BODY
CHARACTERISTIC OF
PLATYHELMINTHES

EVERSIBLE PHARYNX
ON VENTRAL SURFACE

CILIATED EPIDERMIS
ALLOWING GLIDING
OVER THE SURFACE
OF MUD. CREATES
TURBULENCE
CHARACTERISTIC OF
TURBELLARIA

PHYLUM *PLATYHELMINTHES*

CLASS *TREMATODA*

GENUS *FASCIOLA*   X 4

Fig. 1.19

HABITAT - ADULT IN THE BILE DUCT
OF VERTEBRATES E.G. SHEEP

FEEDING - PARASITIC, ON BLOOD AND
EPITHELIAL CELLS VIA PHARYNX

REPRODUCTION - SEXUAL, SELF-FERTILISATION
(HERMAPHRODITE)

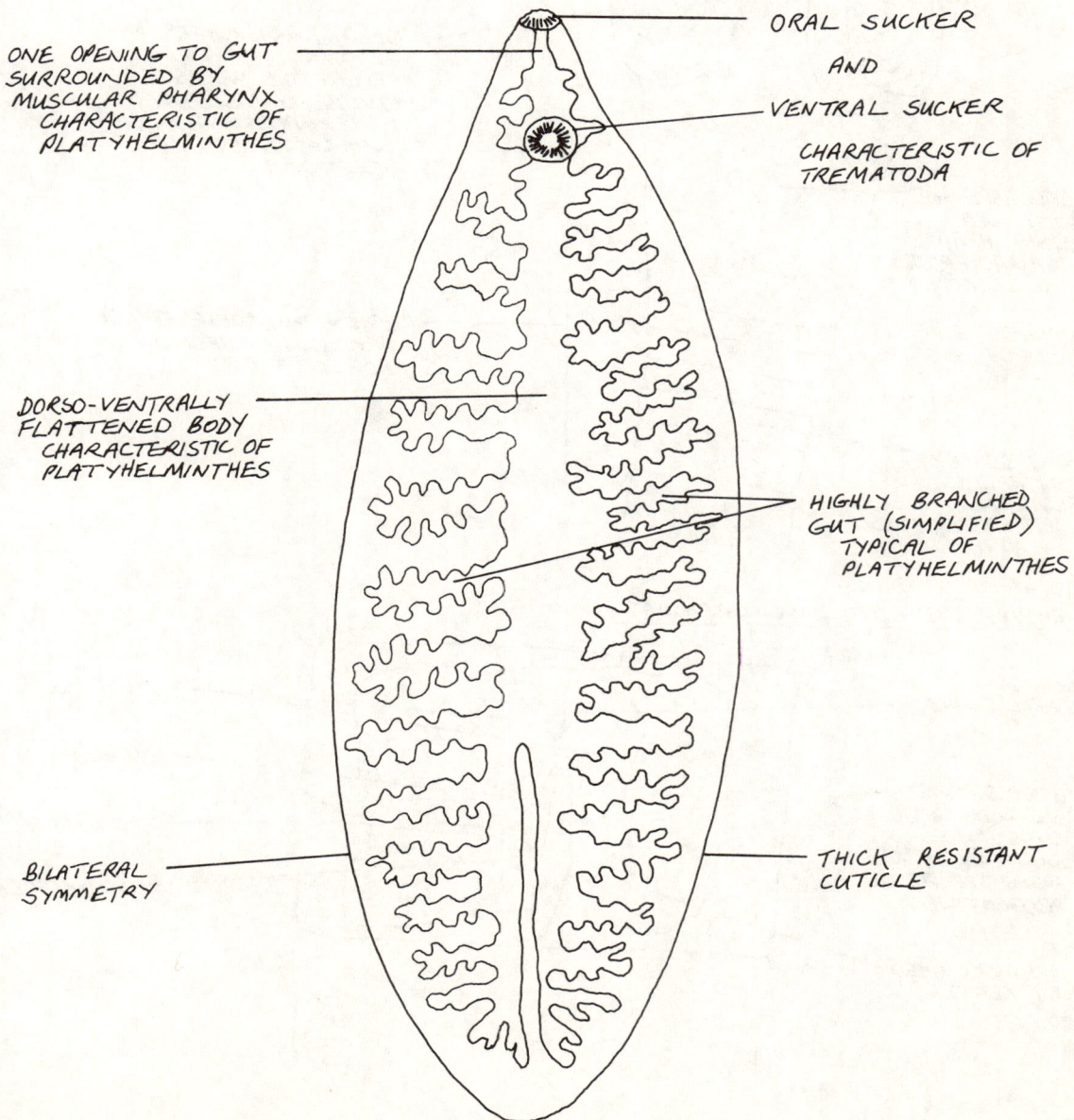

ONE OPENING TO GUT
SURROUNDED BY
MUSCULAR PHARYNX
CHARACTERISTIC OF
PLATYHELMINTHES

ORAL SUCKER

AND

VENTRAL SUCKER

CHARACTERISTIC OF
TREMATODA

DORSO-VENTRALLY
FLATTENED BODY
CHARACTERISTIC OF
PLATYHELMINTHES

HIGHLY BRANCHED
GUT (SIMPLIFIED)
TYPICAL OF
PLATYHELMINTHES

BILATERAL
SYMMETRY

THICK RESISTANT
CUTICLE

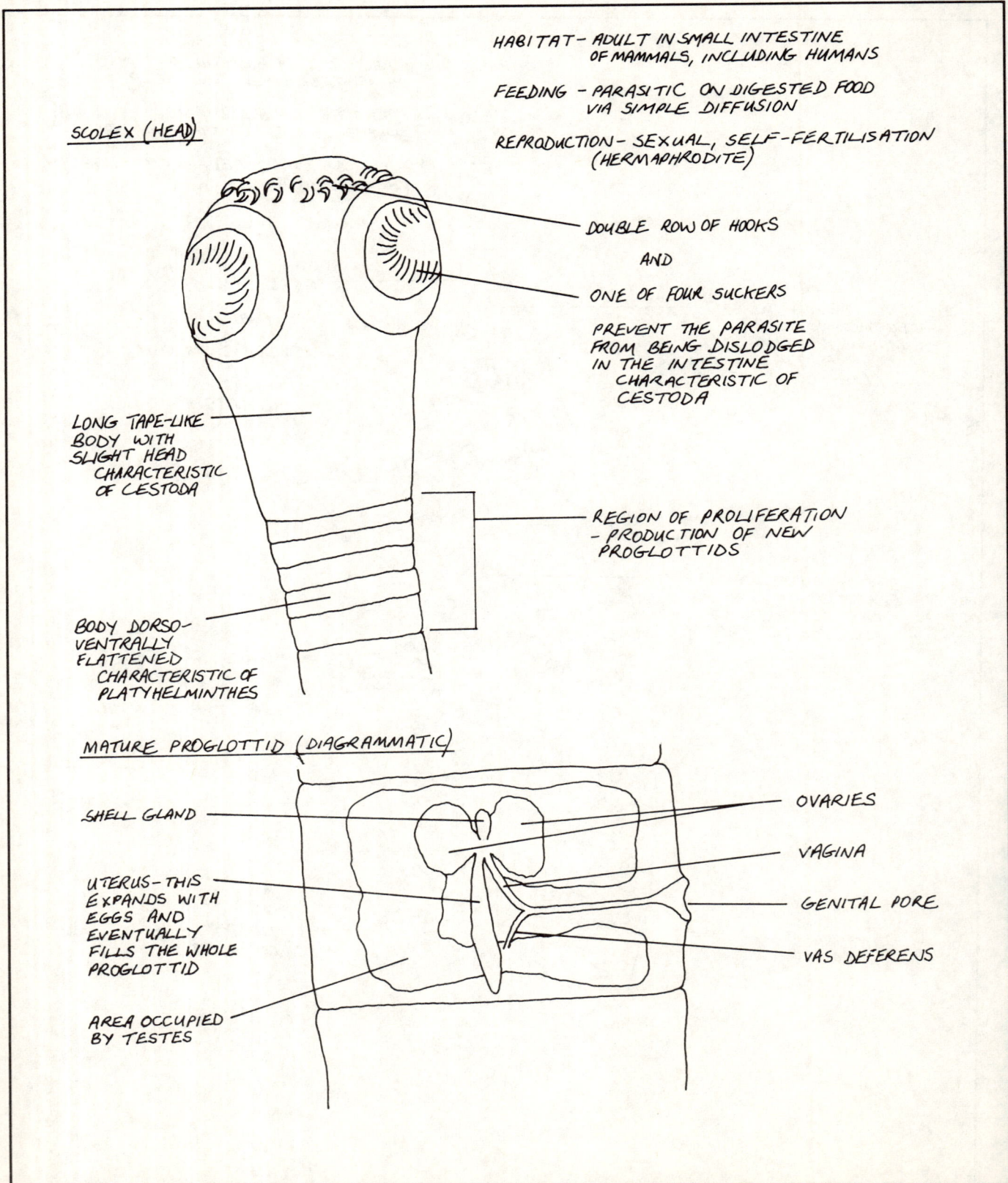

PHYLUM *PLATYHELMINTHES*

CLASS *CESTODA*

GENUS *TAENIA*   X 100

Fig. 1.20

HABITAT - ADULT IN SMALL INTESTINE
OF MAMMALS, INCLUDING HUMANS

FEEDING - PARASITIC ON DIGESTED FOOD
VIA SIMPLE DIFFUSION

REPRODUCTION - SEXUAL, SELF-FERTILISATION
(HERMAPHRODITE)

SCOLEX (HEAD)

DOUBLE ROW OF HOOKS

AND

ONE OF FOUR SUCKERS

PREVENT THE PARASITE
FROM BEING DISLODGED
IN THE INTESTINE
CHARACTERISTIC OF
CESTODA

LONG TAPE-LIKE
BODY WITH
SLIGHT HEAD
CHARACTERISTIC
OF CESTODA

REGION OF PROLIFERATION
- PRODUCTION OF NEW
PROGLOTTIDS

BODY DORSO-
VENTRALLY
FLATTENED
CHARACTERISTIC OF
PLATYHELMINTHES

MATURE PROGLOTTID (DIAGRAMMATIC)

SHELL GLAND

OVARIES

VAGINA

GENITAL PORE

UTERUS - THIS
EXPANDS WITH
EGGS AND
EVENTUALLY
FILLS THE WHOLE
PROGLOTTID

VAS DEFERENS

AREA OCCUPIED
BY TESTES

Phylum *Annelida*
Metamerically segmented, coelomate (with a fluid-filled cavity) worms. The body is covered by thin collagen cuticle which is used for gaseous exchange. Tentacles, parapodia or external gills may be used to increase the surface area for gaseous exchange. Chitinous chaetae typically present as are simple eyes. They are found mainly in aquatic habitats.

Class Polychaeta

Distinct head with appendages and eyes.

Parapodia present with many chaetae.

Lack a clitellum.

eg. Nereis - Ragworm
See *Fig. 1.21*

Class Oligochaeta

Indistinct head with no appendages or eyes.

No parapodia and only a few small chaetae.

Clitellum (saddle) present - used for cocoon production.

eg. Lumbricus - Earthworm
See *Fig. 1.22*

PHYLUM *ANNELIDA*

CLASS *POLYCHAETA*

GENUS *NEREIS*   X 2

Fig. 1.21

HABITAT – BURROWING IN MUD OR SAND
IN THE INTERTIDAL REGION

FEEDING – MAINLY CARNIVOROUS, BUT
ALSO A DETRITIVORE

REPRODUCTION – SEXUAL, CROSS-FERTILISATION

CLERLY DEFINED HEAD
EVERTIBLE PHARYNX
BEARS JAWS

TACTILE PALP

TACTILE TENTACLES

METAMERIC
SEGMENTATION
– BODY DIVIDED INTO
COMPARTMENTS
CHARACTERISTIC OF
ANNELIDA

PARAPODIA
– LATERAL APPENDAGES
FOR LOCOMOTION
CONTAIN BLOOD
CAPILLARIES FOR
GASEOUS EXCHANGE
CHARACTERISTIC
OF POLYCHAETA

CHITINOUS CHAETAE
TYPICAL OF ANNELIDA

MANY CHAETAE
BORNE ON
PARAPODIA FOR
ANCHORAGE
CHARACTERISTIC
OF POLYCHAETA

DORSAL BLOOD
VESSEL

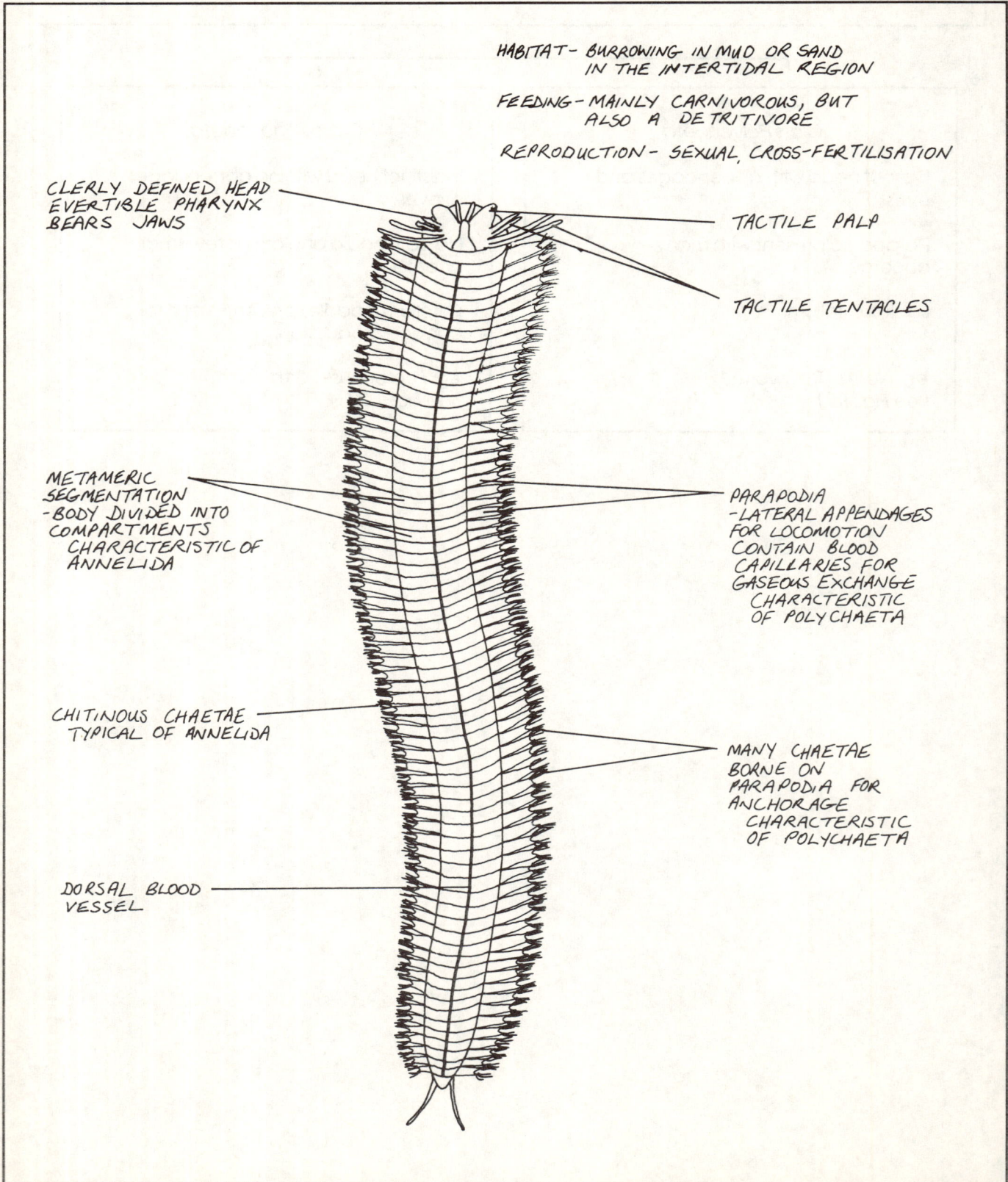

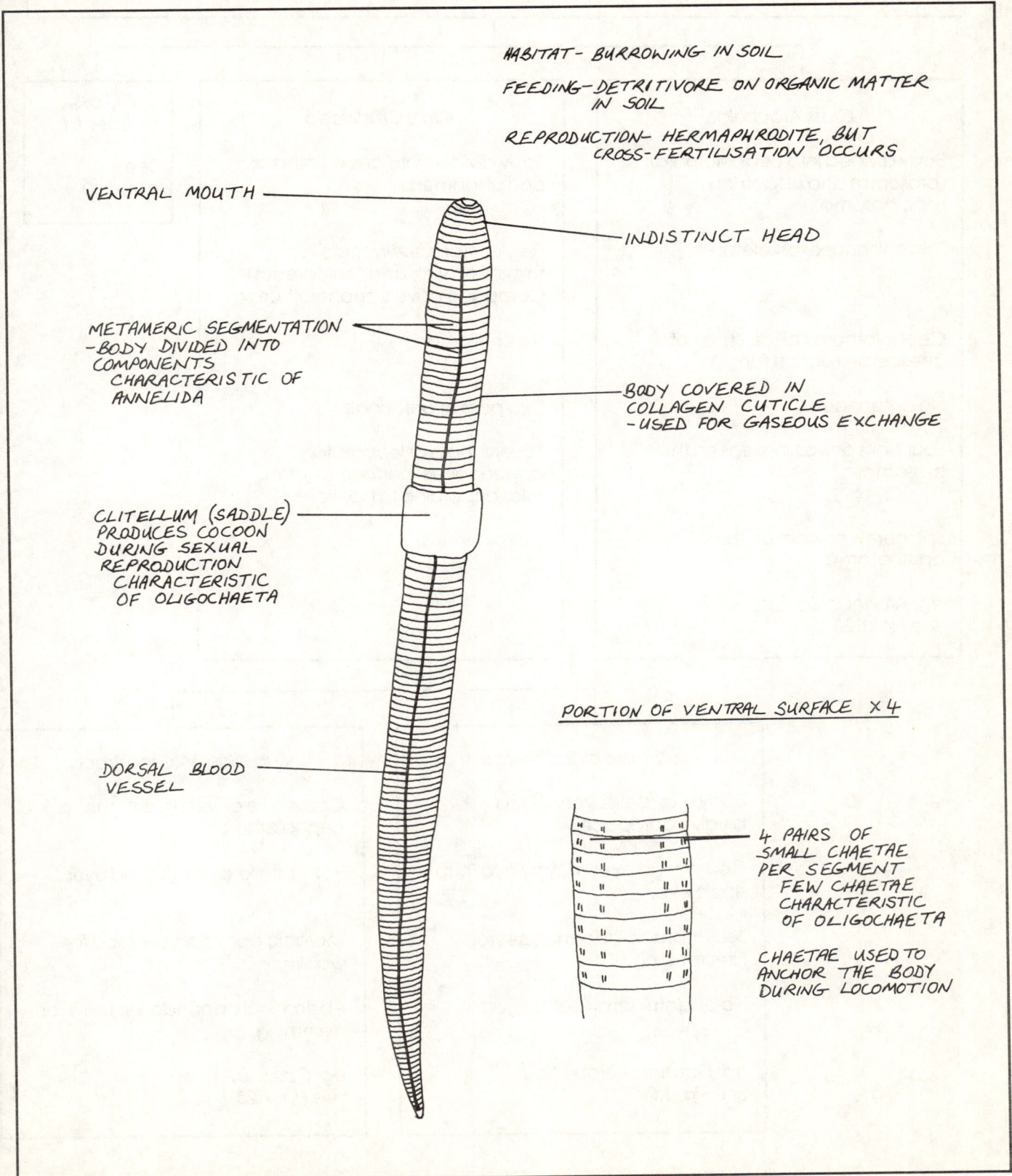

PHYLUM *ANNELIDA*

CLASS *OLIGOCHAETA*

GENUS *LUMBRICUS*   X2

Fig. 1.22

HABITAT- BURROWING IN SOIL

FEEDING- DETRITIVORE ON ORGANIC MATTER IN SOIL

REPRODUCTION- HERMAPHRODITE, BUT CROSS-FERTILISATION OCCURS

VENTRAL MOUTH

INDISTINCT HEAD

METAMERIC SEGMENTATION -BODY DIVIDED INTO COMPONENTS CHARACTERISTIC OF ANNELIDA

BODY COVERED IN COLLAGEN CUTICLE -USED FOR GASEOUS EXCHANGE

CLITELLUM (SADDLE) PRODUCES COCOON DURING SEXUAL REPRODUCTION CHARACTERISTIC OF OLIGOCHAETA

DORSAL BLOOD VESSEL

PORTION OF VENTRAL SURFACE X4

4 PAIRS OF SMALL CHAETAE PER SEGMENT FEW CHAETAE CHARACTERISTIC OF OLIGOCHAETA

CHAETAE USED TO ANCHOR THE BODY DURING LOCOMOTION

Phylum Arthropoda
The body is covered by a chitinous exoskeleton. They have pairs of jointed appendages; some may be modified to form mouthparts. Compound eyes may be present. There is a well-developed head, with the rest of the body divided into the thorax and abdomen. The anus is terminal. Found widely distributed, forms may be free-living or parasitic.

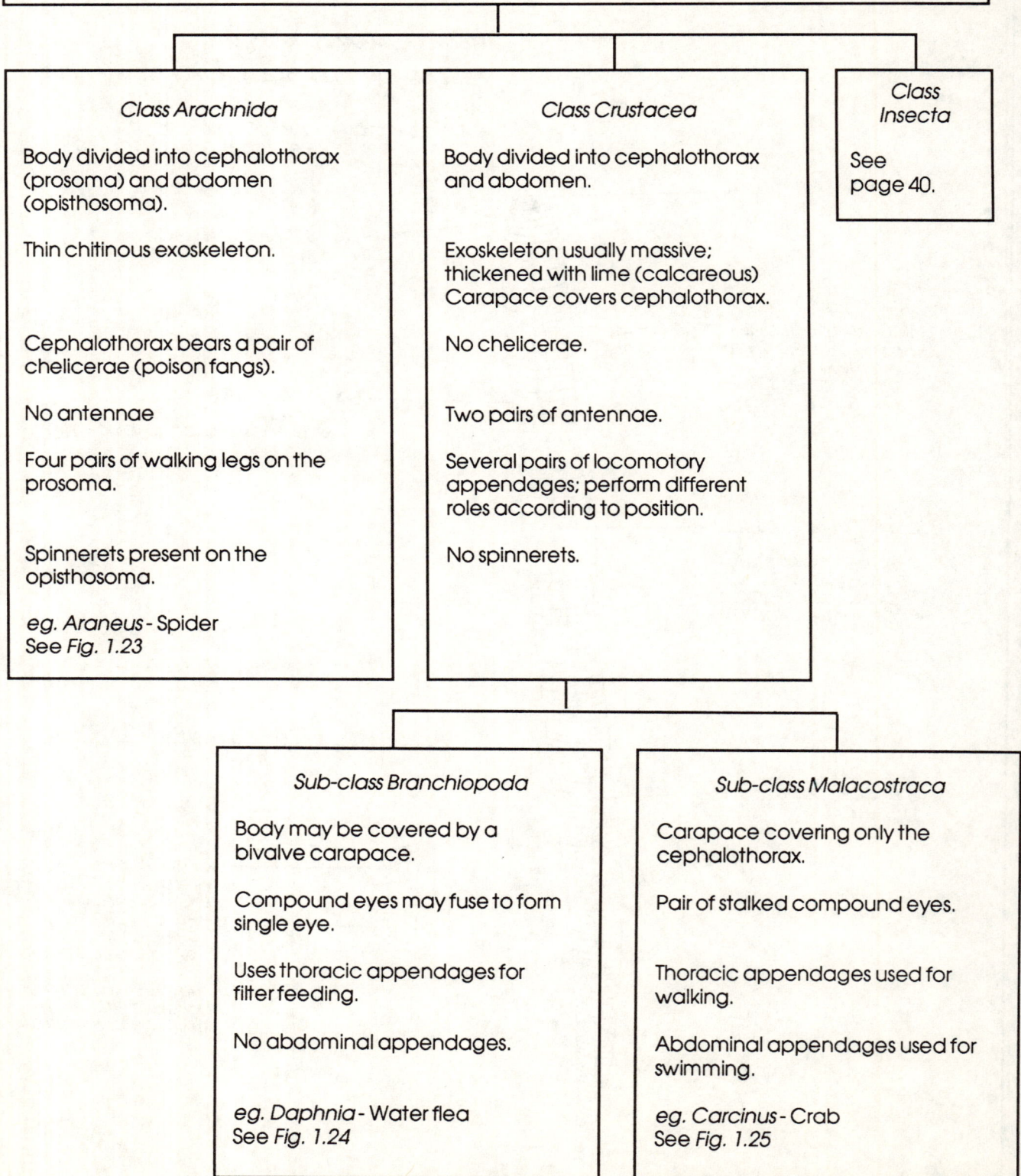

Class Arachnida

Body divided into cephalothorax (prosoma) and abdomen (opisthosoma).

Thin chitinous exoskeleton.

Cephalothorax bears a pair of chelicerae (poison fangs).

No antennae

Four pairs of walking legs on the prosoma.

Spinnerets present on the opisthosoma.

eg. Araneus - Spider
See *Fig. 1.23*

Class Crustacea

Body divided into cephalothorax and abdomen.

Exoskeleton usually massive; thickened with lime (calcareous) Carapace covers cephalothorax.

No chelicerae.

Two pairs of antennae.

Several pairs of locomotory appendages; perform different roles according to position.

No spinnerets.

Class Insecta

See
page 40.

Sub-class Branchiopoda

Body may be covered by a bivalve carapace.

Compound eyes may fuse to form single eye.

Uses thoracic appendages for filter feeding.

No abdominal appendages.

eg. Daphnia - Water flea
See *Fig. 1.24*

Sub-class Malacostraca

Carapace covering only the cephalothorax.

Pair of stalked compound eyes.

Thoracic appendages used for walking.

Abdominal appendages used for swimming.

eg. Carcinus - Crab
See *Fig. 1.25*

PHYLUM *ARTHROPODA*

CLASS *ARACHNIDA*

GENUS *ARANEUS*   X6

Fig. 1.23

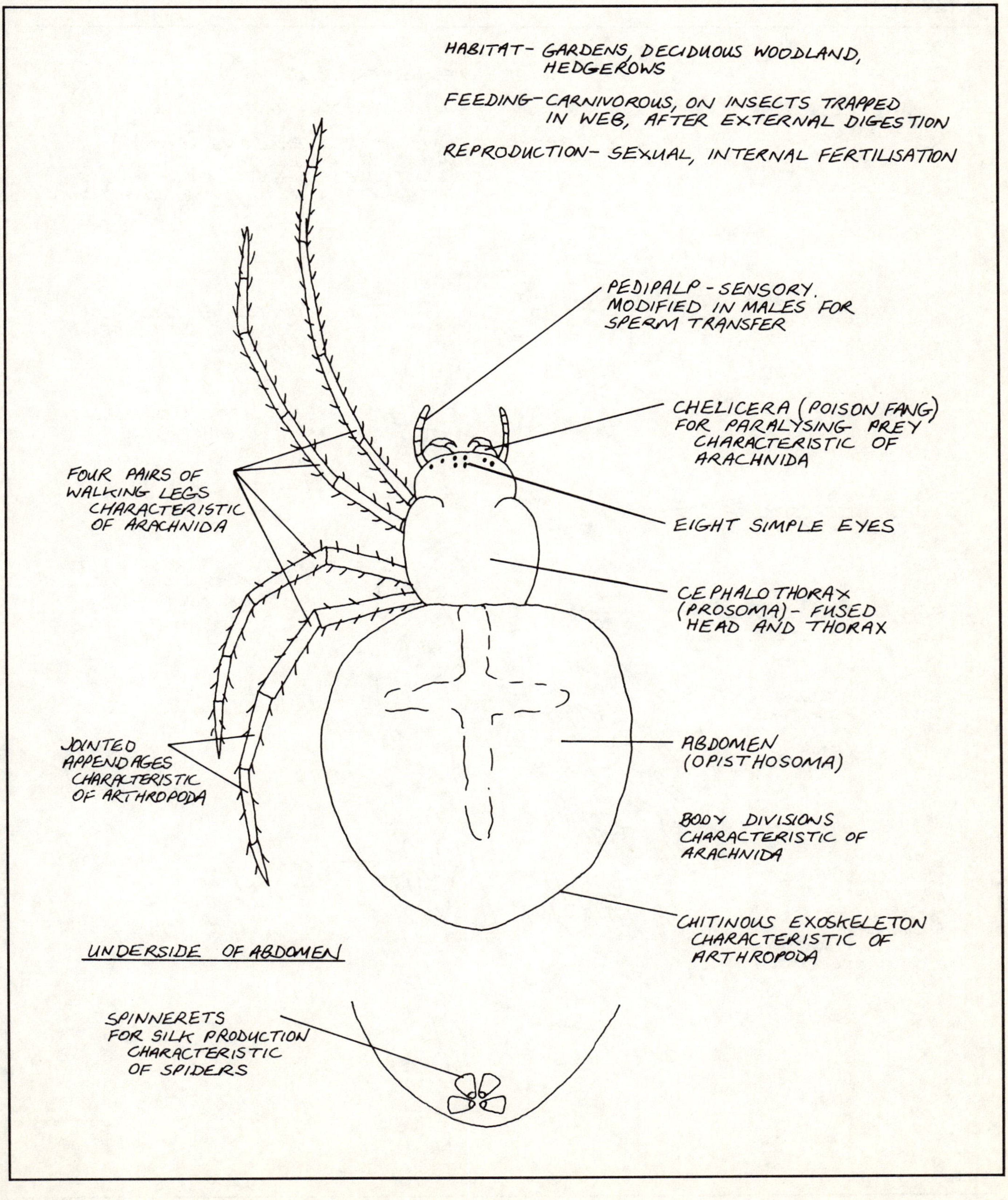

HABITAT- GARDENS, DECIDUOUS WOODLAND, HEDGEROWS

FEEDING- CARNIVOROUS, ON INSECTS TRAPPED IN WEB, AFTER EXTERNAL DIGESTION

REPRODUCTION- SEXUAL, INTERNAL FERTILISATION

PEDIPALP - SENSORY. MODIFIED IN MALES FOR SPERM TRANSFER

CHELICERA (POISON FANG) FOR PARALYSING PREY CHARACTERISTIC OF ARACHNIDA

FOUR PAIRS OF WALKING LEGS CHARACTERISTIC OF ARACHNIDA

EIGHT SIMPLE EYES

CEPHALOTHORAX (PROSOMA) - FUSED HEAD AND THORAX

JOINTED APPENDAGES CHARACTERISTIC OF ARTHROPODA

ABDOMEN (OPISTHOSOMA)

BODY DIVISIONS CHARACTERISTIC OF ARACHNIDA

CHITINOUS EXOSKELETON CHARACTERISTIC OF ARTHROPODA

UNDERSIDE OF ABDOMEN

SPINNERETS FOR SILK PRODUCTION CHARACTERISTIC OF SPIDERS

37

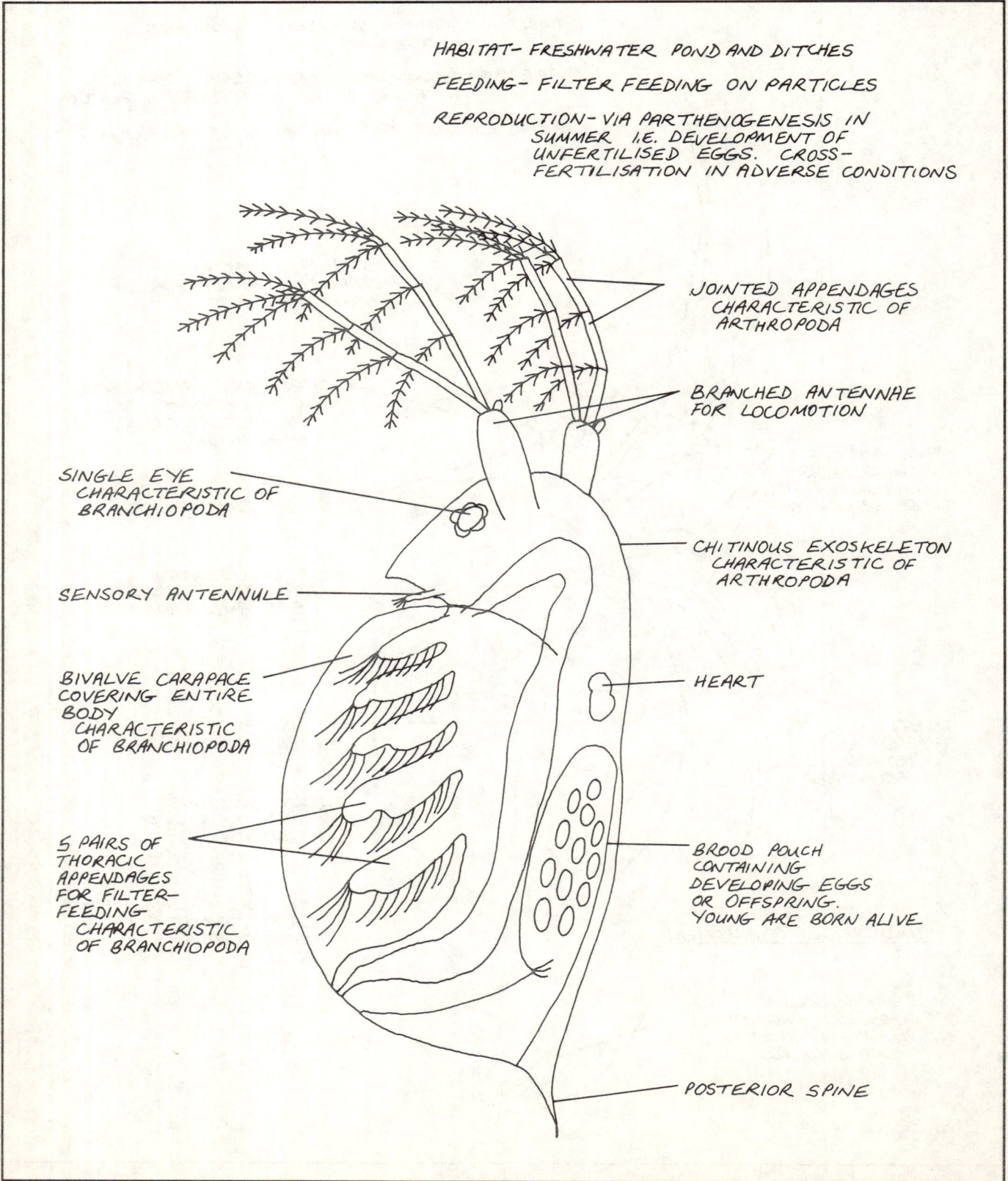

PHYLUM *ARTHROPODA*

CLASS *CRUSTACEA*

SUB-CLASS *BRANCHIOPODA*

GENUS *DAPHNIA*   X 100

Fig. 1.24

HABITAT- FRESHWATER POND AND DITCHES

FEEDING- FILTER FEEDING ON PARTICLES

REPRODUCTION- VIA PARTHENOGENESIS IN
SUMMER I.E. DEVELOPMENT OF
UNFERTILISED EGGS. CROSS-
FERTILISATION IN ADVERSE CONDITIONS

JOINTED APPENDAGES
CHARACTERISTIC OF
ARTHROPODA

BRANCHED ANTENNAE
FOR LOCOMOTION

SINGLE EYE
CHARACTERISTIC OF
BRANCHIOPODA

CHITINOUS EXOSKELETON
CHARACTERISTIC OF
ARTHROPODA

SENSORY ANTENNULE

BIVALVE CARAPACE
COVERING ENTIRE
BODY
CHARACTERISTIC
OF BRANCHIOPODA

HEART

5 PAIRS OF
THORACIC
APPENDAGES
FOR FILTER-
FEEDING
CHARACTERISTIC
OF BRANCHIOPODA

BROOD POUCH
CONTAINING
DEVELOPING EGGS
OR OFFSPRING.
YOUNG ARE BORN ALIVE

POSTERIOR SPINE

PHYLUM *ARTHROPODA*

CLASS *CRUSTACEA*

SUB-CLASS *MALACOSTRACA*

GENUS *CARCINUS*   X2

Fig. 1.25

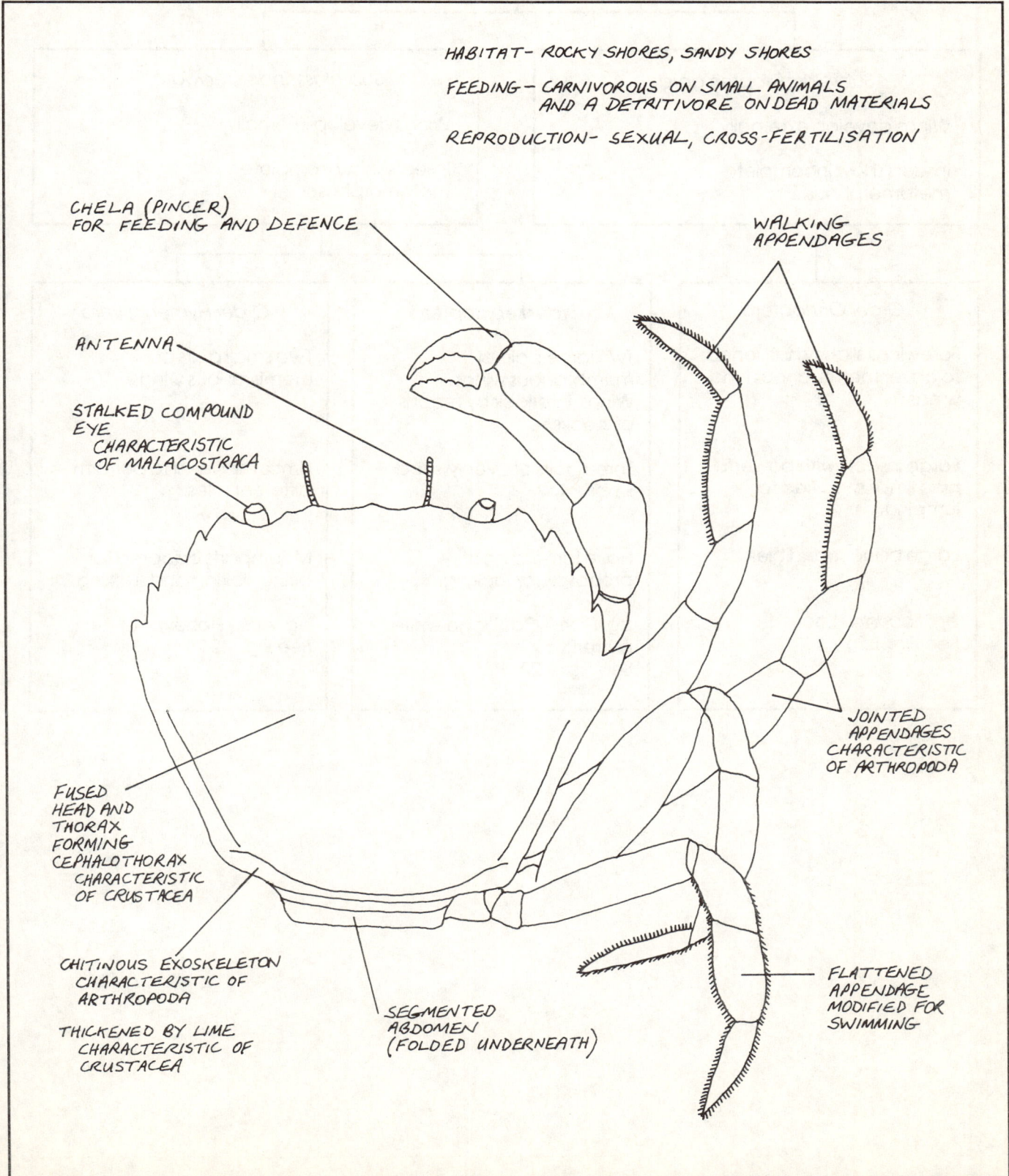

HABITAT- ROCKY SHORES, SANDY SHORES

FEEDING- CARNIVOROUS ON SMALL ANIMALS AND A DETRITIVORE ON DEAD MATERIALS

REPRODUCTION- SEXUAL, CROSS-FERTILISATION

CHELA (PINCER) FOR FEEDING AND DEFENCE

WALKING APPENDAGES

ANTENNA

STALKED COMPOUND EYE CHARACTERISTIC OF MALACOSTRACA

JOINTED APPENDAGES CHARACTERISTIC OF ARTHROPODA

FUSED HEAD AND THORAX FORMING CEPHALOTHORAX CHARACTERISTIC OF CRUSTACEA

CHITINOUS EXOSKELETON CHARACTERISTIC OF ARTHROPODA

THICKENED BY LIME CHARACTERISTIC OF CRUSTACEA

SEGMENTED ABDOMEN (FOLDED UNDERNEATH)

FLATTENED APPENDAGE MODIFIED FOR SWIMMING

Phylum Arthropoda

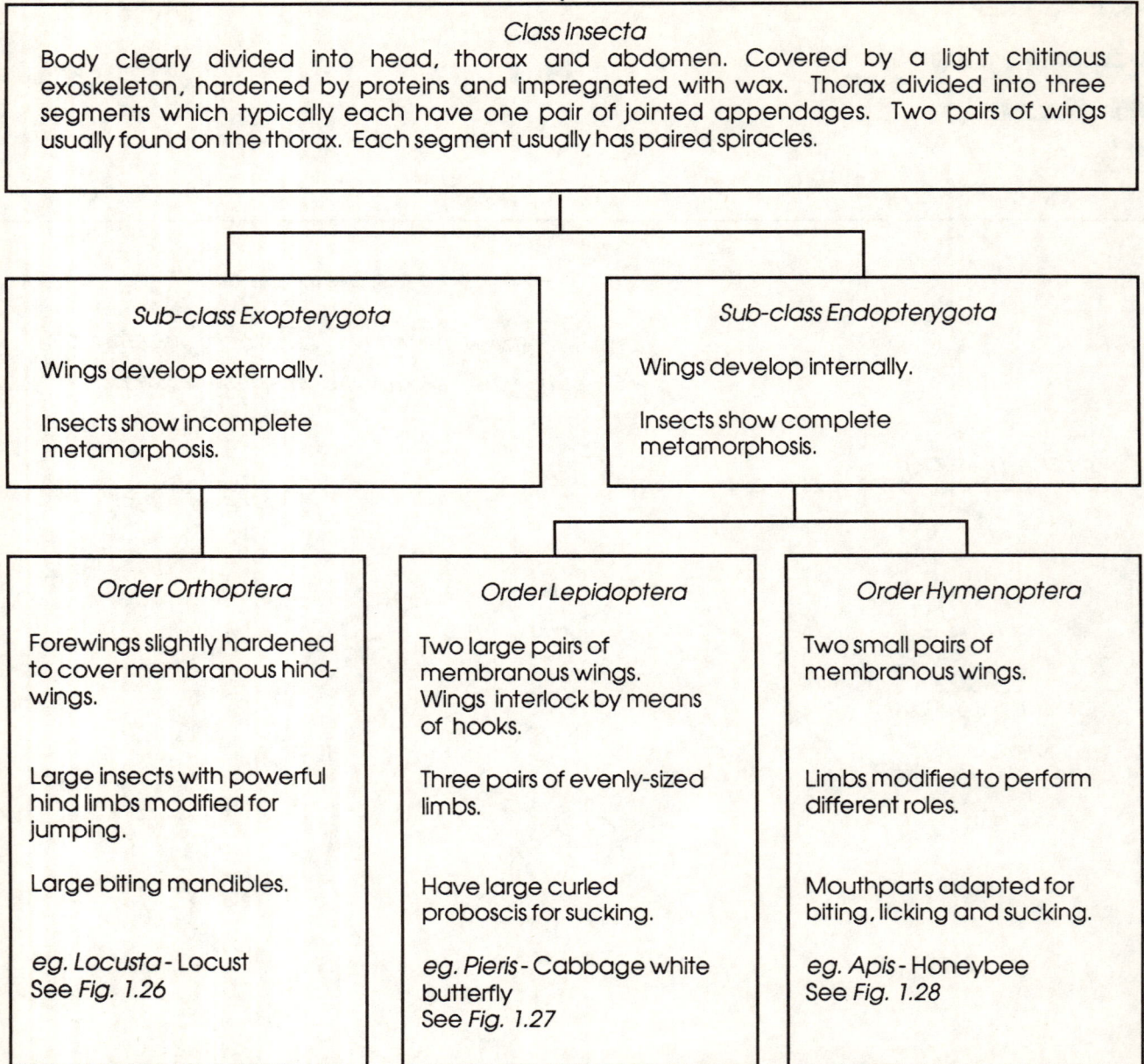

Class Insecta

Body clearly divided into head, thorax and abdomen. Covered by a light chitinous exoskeleton, hardened by proteins and impregnated with wax. Thorax divided into three segments which typically each have one pair of jointed appendages. Two pairs of wings usually found on the thorax. Each segment usually has paired spiracles.

Sub-class Exopterygota

Wings develop externally.

Insects show incomplete metamorphosis.

Sub-class Endopterygota

Wings develop internally.

Insects show complete metamorphosis.

Order Orthoptera

Forewings slightly hardened to cover membranous hind-wings.

Large insects with powerful hind limbs modified for jumping.

Large biting mandibles.

eg. Locusta - Locust
See Fig. 1.26

Order Lepidoptera

Two large pairs of membranous wings. Wings interlock by means of hooks.

Three pairs of evenly-sized limbs.

Have large curled proboscis for sucking.

eg. Pieris - Cabbage white butterfly
See Fig. 1.27

Order Hymenoptera

Two small pairs of membranous wings.

Limbs modified to perform different roles.

Mouthparts adapted for biting, licking and sucking.

eg. Apis - Honeybee
See Fig. 1.28

PHYLUM *ARTHROPODA*

CLASS *INSECTA*

SUB-CLASS *EXOPTERYGOTA*

ORDER *ORTHOPTERA*

GENUS *LOCUSTA*   X 2

Fig. 1.26

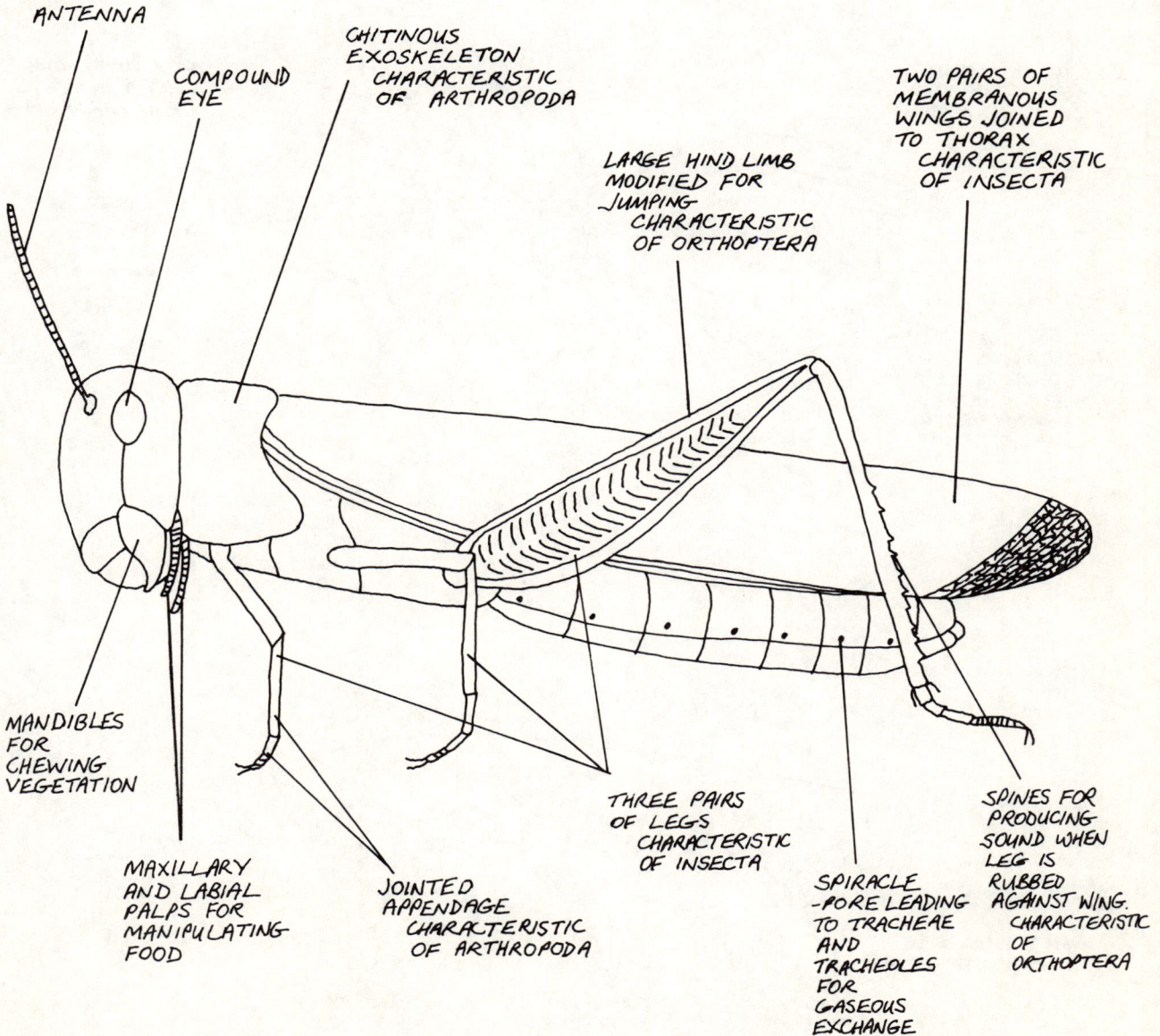

HABITAT – TROPICAL, SAVANNAH

FEEDING – HERBIVOROUS

REPRODUCTION – SEXUAL, INTERNAL FERTILISATION

ANTENNA

COMPOUND EYE

CHITINOUS EXOSKELETON CHARACTERISTIC OF ARTHROPODA

LARGE HIND LIMB MODIFIED FOR JUMPING CHARACTERISTIC OF ORTHOPTERA

TWO PAIRS OF MEMBRANOUS WINGS JOINED TO THORAX CHARACTERISTIC OF INSECTA

MANDIBLES FOR CHEWING VEGETATION

MAXILLARY AND LABIAL PALPS FOR MANIPULATING FOOD

JOINTED APPENDAGE CHARACTERISTIC OF ARTHROPODA

THREE PAIRS OF LEGS CHARACTERISTIC OF INSECTA

SPIRACLE –PORE LEADING TO TRACHEAE AND TRACHEOLES FOR GASEOUS EXCHANGE

SPINES FOR PRODUCING SOUND WHEN LEG IS RUBBED AGAINST WING. CHARACTERISTIC OF ORTHOPTERA

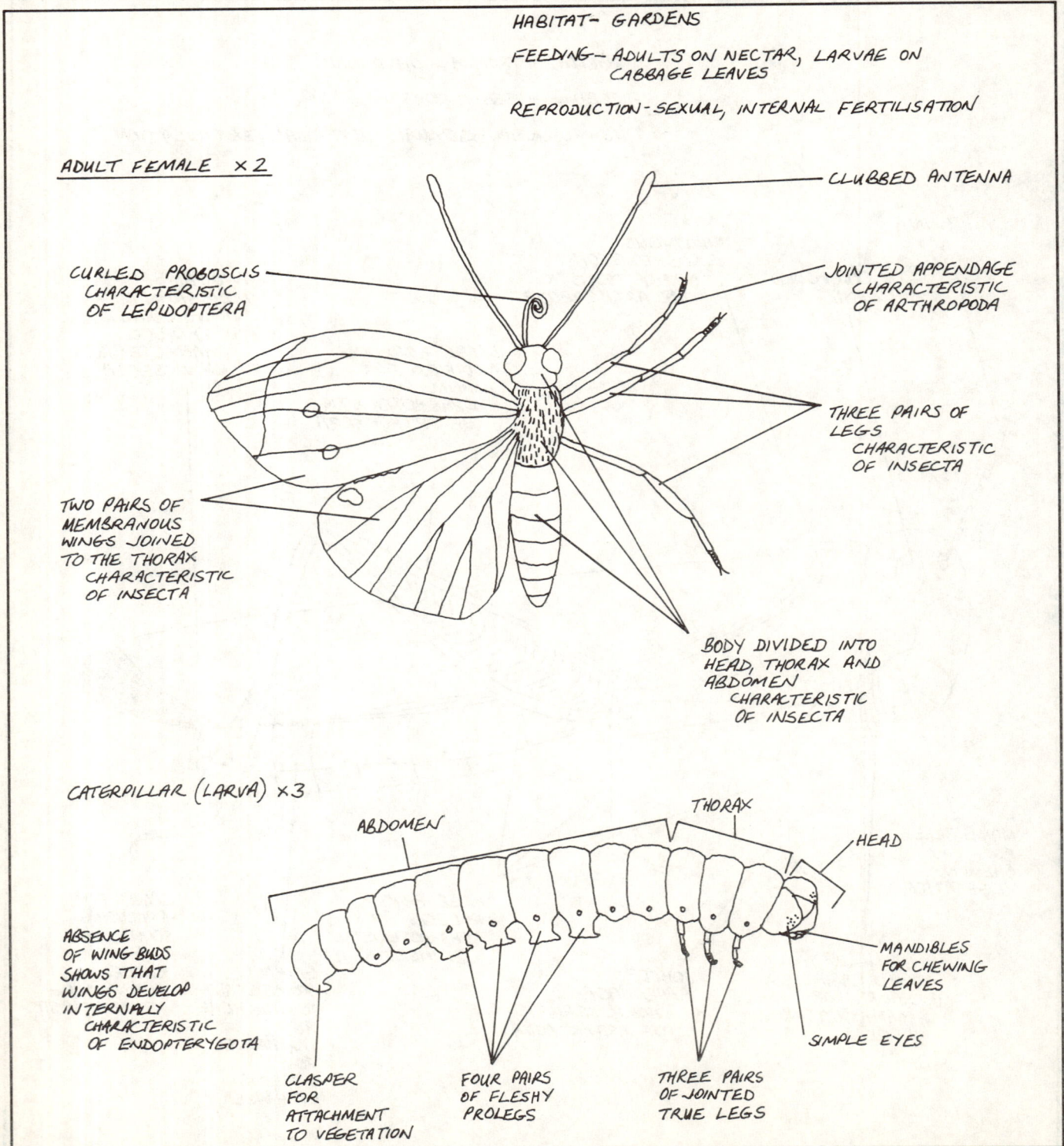

PHYLUM *ARTHROPODA*

CLASS *INSECTA*

SUB-CLASS *ENDOPTERYGOTA*

ORDER *LEPIDOPTERA*

GENUS *PIERIS*

Fig. 1.27

HABITAT- GARDENS

FEEDING— ADULTS ON NECTAR, LARVAE ON CABBAGE LEAVES

REPRODUCTION-SEXUAL, INTERNAL FERTILISATION

ADULT FEMALE × 2

CLUBBED ANTENNA

CURLED PROBOSCIS CHARACTERISTIC OF LEPIDOPTERA

JOINTED APPENDAGE CHARACTERISTIC OF ARTHROPODA

THREE PAIRS OF LEGS CHARACTERISTIC OF INSECTA

TWO PAIRS OF MEMBRANOUS WINGS JOINED TO THE THORAX CHARACTERISTIC OF INSECTA

BODY DIVIDED INTO HEAD, THORAX AND ABDOMEN CHARACTERISTIC OF INSECTA

CATERPILLAR (LARVA) × 3

ABDOMEN

THORAX

HEAD

ABSENCE OF WING BUDS SHOWS THAT WINGS DEVELOP INTERNALLY CHARACTERISTIC OF ENDOPTERYGOTA

MANDIBLES FOR CHEWING LEAVES

SIMPLE EYES

CLASPER FOR ATTACHMENT TO VEGETATION

FOUR PAIRS OF FLESHY PROLEGS

THREE PAIRS OF JOINTED TRUE LEGS

PHYLUM *ARTHROPODA*

CLASS *INSECTA*

ORDER *HYMENOPTERA*

GENUS *APIS (HONEY BEE)*

ADULT WORKER   X6

Fig. 1.28

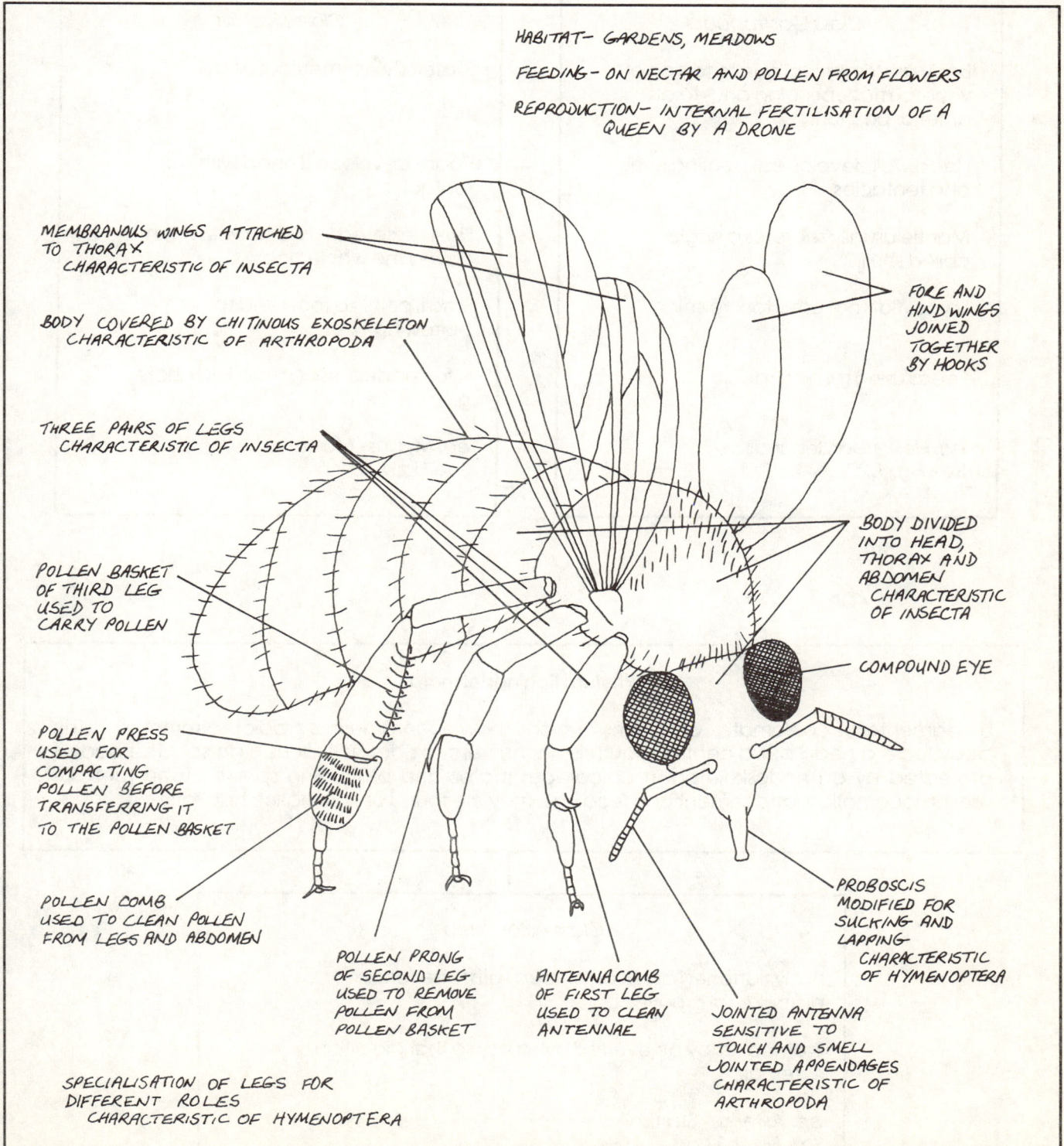

HABITAT – GARDENS, MEADOWS

FEEDING – ON NECTAR AND POLLEN FROM FLOWERS

REPRODUCTION – INTERNAL FERTILISATION OF A QUEEN BY A DRONE

MEMBRANOUS WINGS ATTACHED TO THORAX CHARACTERISTIC OF INSECTA

BODY COVERED BY CHITINOUS EXOSKELETON CHARACTERISTIC OF ARTHROPODA

THREE PAIRS OF LEGS CHARACTERISTIC OF INSECTA

POLLEN BASKET OF THIRD LEG USED TO CARRY POLLEN

POLLEN PRESS USED FOR COMPACTING POLLEN BEFORE TRANSFERRING IT TO THE POLLEN BASKET

POLLEN COMB USED TO CLEAN POLLEN FROM LEGS AND ABDOMEN

POLLEN PRONG OF SECOND LEG USED TO REMOVE POLLEN FROM POLLEN BASKET

ANTENNA COMB OF FIRST LEG USED TO CLEAN ANTENNAE

JOINTED ANTENNA SENSITIVE TO TOUCH AND SMELL JOINTED APPENDAGES CHARACTERISTIC OF ARTHROPODA

PROBOSCIS MODIFIED FOR SUCKING AND LAPPING CHARACTERISTIC OF HYMENOPTERA

COMPOUND EYE

BODY DIVIDED INTO HEAD, THORAX AND ABDOMEN CHARACTERISTIC OF INSECTA

FORE AND HIND WINGS JOINED TOGETHER BY HOOKS

SPECIALISATION OF LEGS FOR DIFFERENT ROLES CHARACTERISTIC OF HYMENOPTERA

Phylum Mollusca

Unsegmented, triploblastic and coelomate animals although the coelom is very reduced. The basic body plan is bilaterally symmetrical. The body is divided into a head, foot and visceral mass, covered by a mantle which secetes a calcareous shell. Found widely distributed although many are marine.

Class Gastropoda

Body asymmetrical due to torsion of visceral mass, bringing anus to an anterior position.

Head well developed, bearing eyes and tentacles.

Mantle usually secretes a single coiled shell.

Large, flat foot used for creeping.

Feeds using rasping radula.

eg. Helix - Garden snail
See *Fig. 1.29*

Class Bivalvia

Bilaterally symmetrical body.

Poorly developed head without tentacles.

Shell secreted in two halves which covers the whole body.

Small, pointed foot used for burrowing.

Filter feeders, using modified ciliated gills.

eg. Mytilus - Mussel
See *Fig. 1.30*

Phylum Echinodermata

Unsegmented, coelomate organisms which show pentamerous radial symmetry. The body lacks a head but a central mouth is on the ventral side. The anus is dorsal. The body is protected by an endoskeleton of calcareous plates and protruding spines. Tube feet are used in locomotion, attachment and feeding. They are found only in marine habitats.

Class Asteroidea

Body flattened and star-shaped with tube feet in ambulacral grooves.

Stomach may be everted over prey so that digestion is external.

eg. Asterias - Starfish
See *Fig. 1.31*

PHYLUM *MOLLUSCA*

CLASS *GASTROPODA*

GENUS *HELIX*   X 3

Fig. 1.29

HABITAT— DAMP TERRESTRIAL E.G GARDENS, DECIDUOUS WOODLAND

FEEDING— ON VEGETATION USING A RASPING RADULA

REPRODUCTION— HERMAPHRODITE, BUT WITH CROSS—FERTILISATION

CALCAREOUS SHELL TYPICAL OF MOLLUSCA

SINGLE COILED SHELL CHARACTERISTIC OF GASTROPODA

GROWTH LINES

RETRACTILE TENTACLES BEARING EYES CHARACTERISTIC OF GASTROPODA

RETRACTILE CHEMOSENSITIVE TENTACLES

PNEUMOSTOME -PULMONARY APERTURE FOR GASEOUS EXCHANGE

MUSCULAR FOOT LUBRICATED WITH MUCUS CHARACTERISTIC OF GASTROPODA

VENTRAL MOUTH WITH RASPING RADULA CHARACTERISTIC OF GASTROPODA

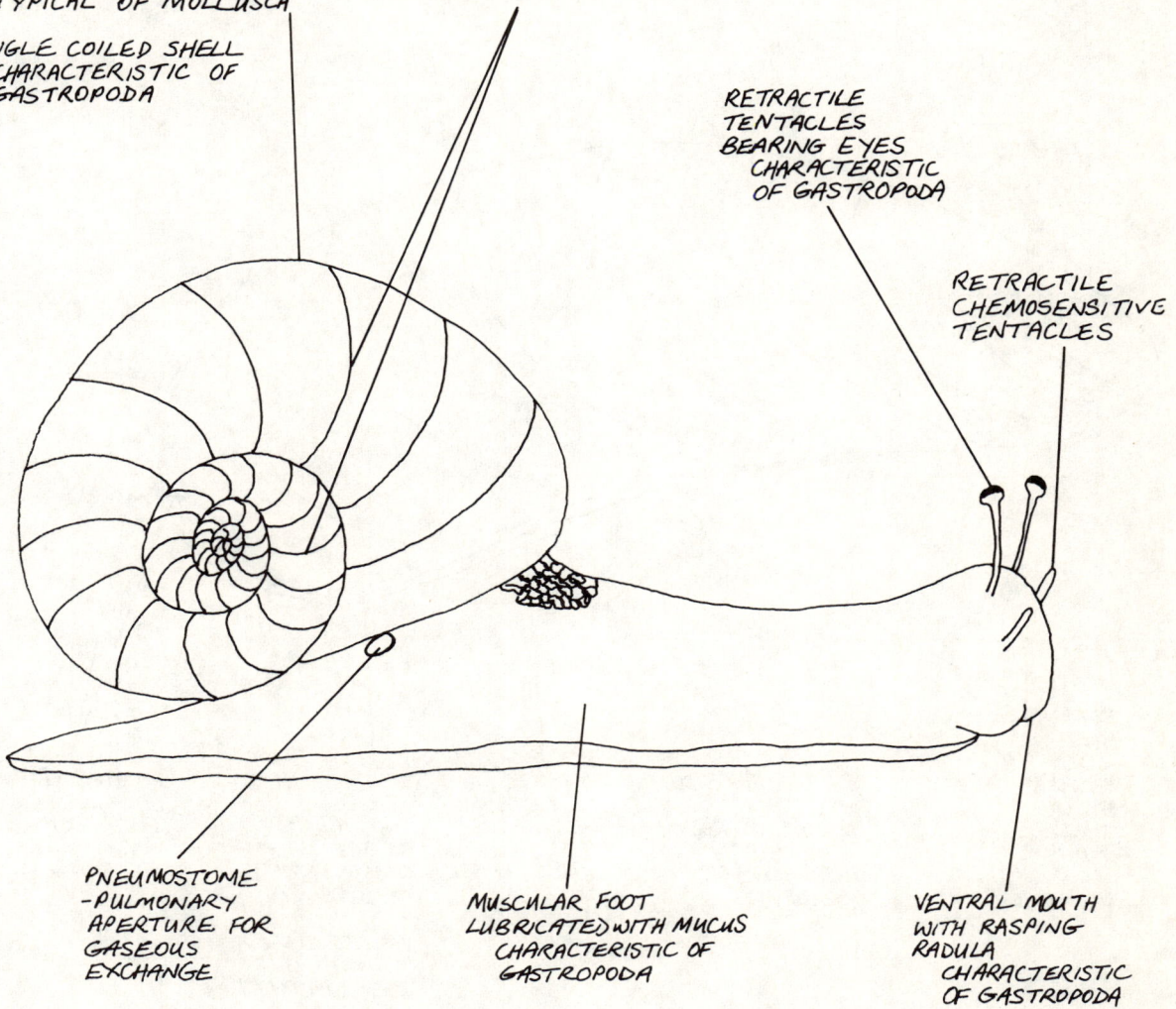

PHYLUM *MOLLUSCA*

CLASS *BIVALVIA*

GENUS *MYTILUS (MUSSEL)*   X 2

Fig. 1.30

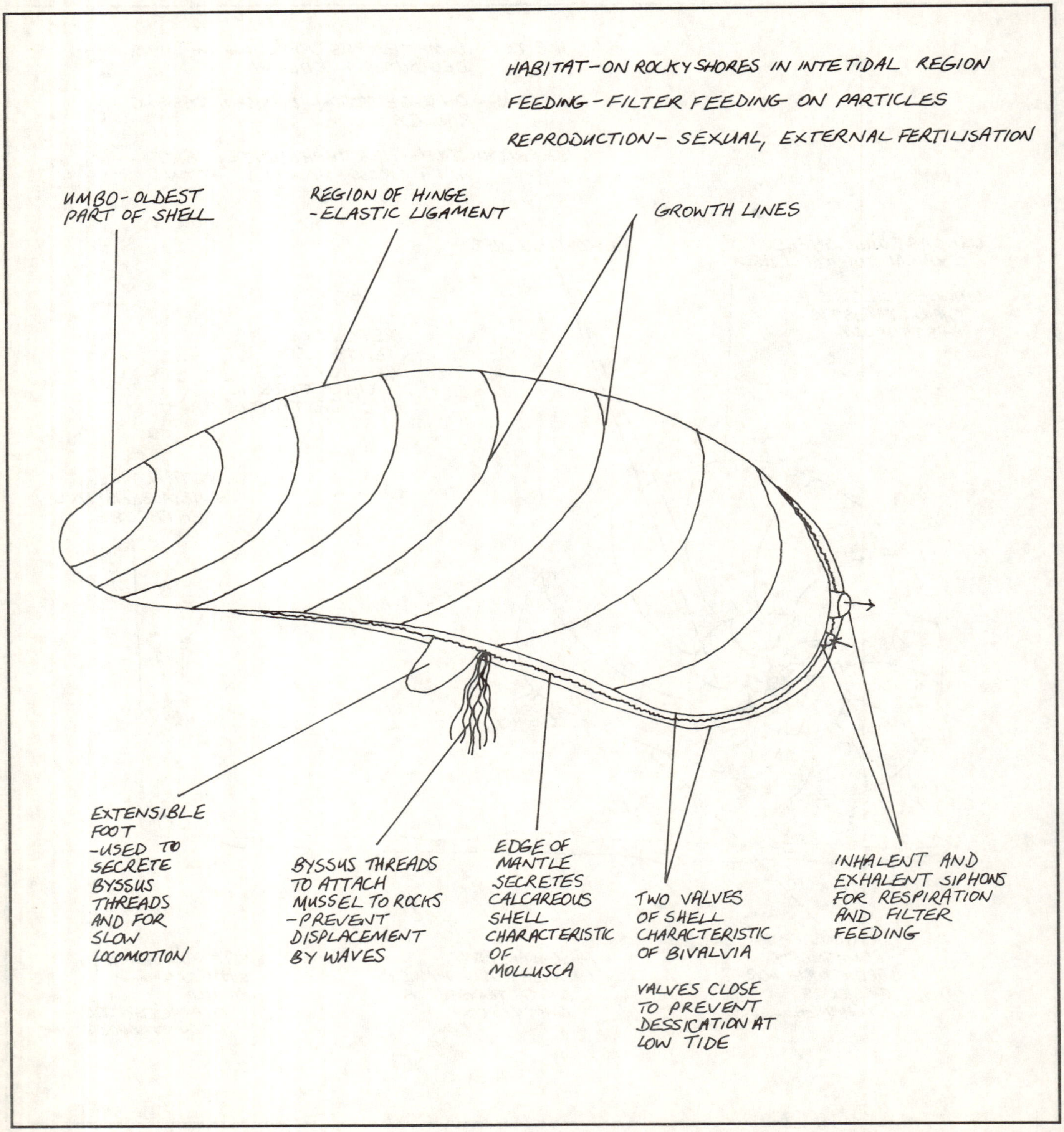

HABITAT—ON ROCKY SHORES IN INTETIDAL REGION

FEEDING—FILTER FEEDING ON PARTICLES

REPRODUCTION— SEXUAL, EXTERNAL FERTILISATION

UMBO— OLDEST PART OF SHELL

REGION OF HINGE —ELASTIC LIGAMENT

GROWTH LINES

EXTENSIBLE FOOT —USED TO SECRETE BYSSUS THREADS AND FOR SLOW LOCOMOTION

BYSSUS THREADS TO ATTACH MUSSEL TO ROCKS —PREVENT DISPLACEMENT BY WAVES

EDGE OF MANTLE SECRETES CALCAREOUS SHELL CHARACTERISTIC OF MOLLUSCA

TWO VALVES OF SHELL CHARACTERISTIC OF BIVALVIA

VALVES CLOSE TO PREVENT DESSICATION AT LOW TIDE

INHALENT AND EXHALENT SIPHONS FOR RESPIRATION AND FILTER FEEDING

PHYLUM *ECHINODERMATA*

CLASS *ASTEROIDEA*

GENUS *ASTERIAS*   X 1

Fig. 1.31

HABITAT– MARINE, IN INTERTIDAL REGIONS

FEEDING– CARNIVOROUS, ON BIVALVES

LOCOMOTION–SLOW, BY MEANS OF TUBEFEET

REPRODUCTION– EXTERNAL FERTILISATION

DORSAL SURFACE

PENTAMEROUS RADIAL SYMMETRY CHARACTERISTIC OF ECHINODERMATA

BODY COVERED WITH CALCAREOUS SPINES CHARACTERISTIC OF ECHINODERMATA

BODY FLATTENED AND STAR-SHAPED CHARACTERISTIC OF ASTEROIDEA

ANUS ON DORSAL SURFACE CHARACTERISTIC OF ECHINODERMATA

VENTRAL SURFACE

VENTRAL MOUTH CHARACTERISTIC OF ECHINODERMATA STOMACH IS EVERTED THROUGH MOUTH INTO BIVALVE FOR EXTERNAL DIGESTION

AMBULACRAL GROOVES CHARACTERISTIC OF ASTEROIDEA (TUBE FEET NOT SHOWN)

LONG SPINES PROTECT TUBE FEET IN AMBULACRAL GROOVE

TUBE FEET USED FOR LOCOMOTION AND FOR PULLING APART VALVES OF BIVALVES CHARACTERISTIC OF ECHINODERMATA

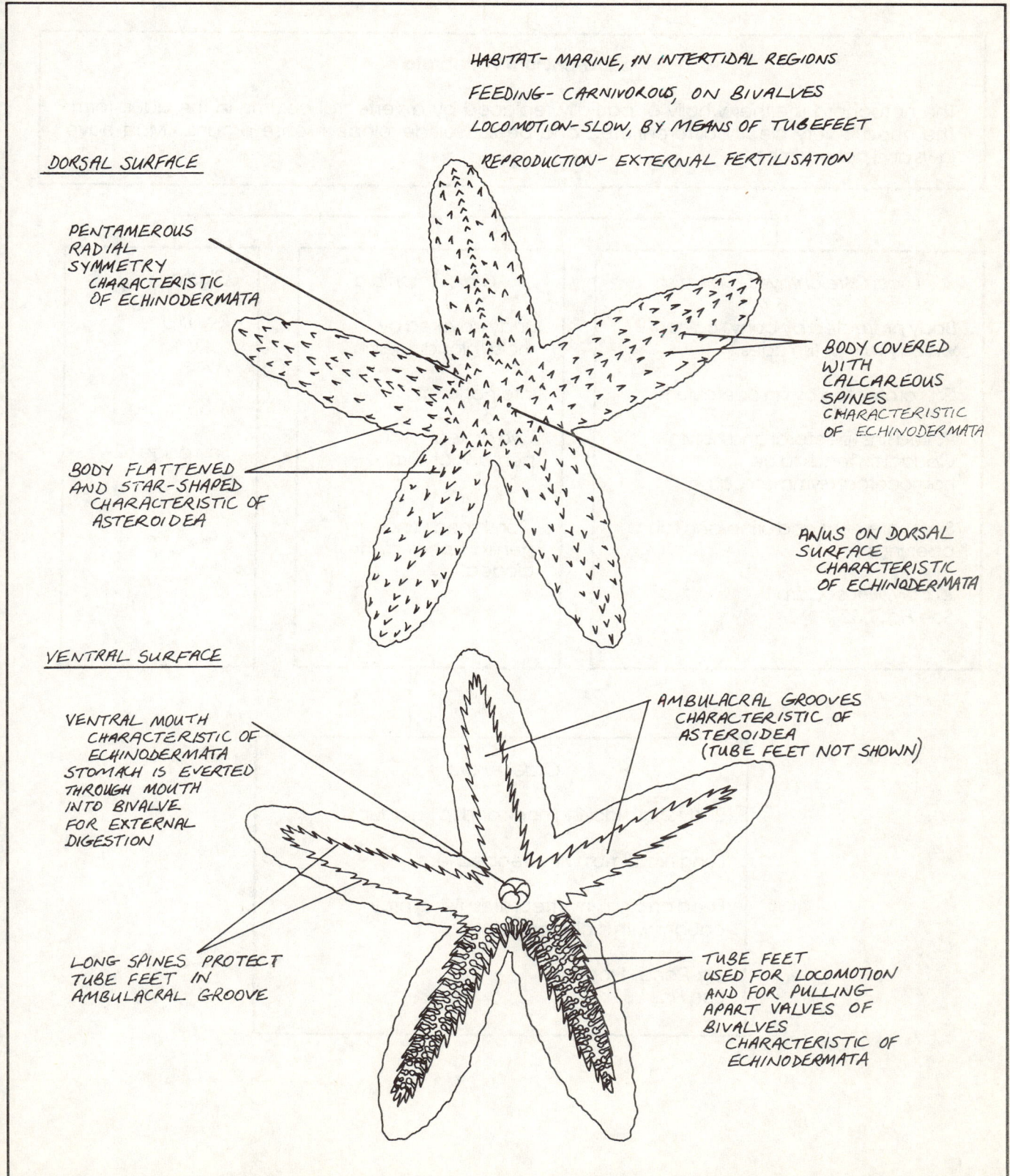

47

Phylum Chordata

The body is basically bilaterally symmetrical, usually with a metamerically segmented post-anal tail. A notochord (skeletal rod) and visceral clefts (gill slits) are usually present at some stage of the life history.

Sub-phylum Vertebrata

The notochord is either wholly or partially replaced by a vertebral column in the adult form. The head is very clearly differentiated and bears well-developed sense organs. Most have jaws and paired limbs.

Class Osteichthyes - Bony fish

Body protected by bony scales which grow as fish ages.

Gills protected by an operculum.

Paired fins (pectoral and pelvic). Caudal fin tends to be homocercal (symmetrical).

Separate anus and urino-genital openings.

eg. Cyprinus - Carp
See *Fig. 1.32*

Class Amphibia

Body covered by moist, glandular skin.

Internal lungs

Two pairs of pentadactyl limbs.

Combined urino-genital opening, the cloaca.

Classes

Reptilia

Aves

Mammalia

See page 52

Order Anura

Body short, lacking neck and tail in adult.

Long hind limbs with webbed feet.

Feed on small invertebrates; flying prey caught with sticky tongue.

eg. Rana - Frog
See *Fig. 1.33*

PHYLUM *CHORDATA*

SUB-PHYLUM *VERTEBRATA*

CLASS *OSTEICHTHYES*

GENUS *CYPRINUS (CARP)*   X0.5

Fig. 1.32

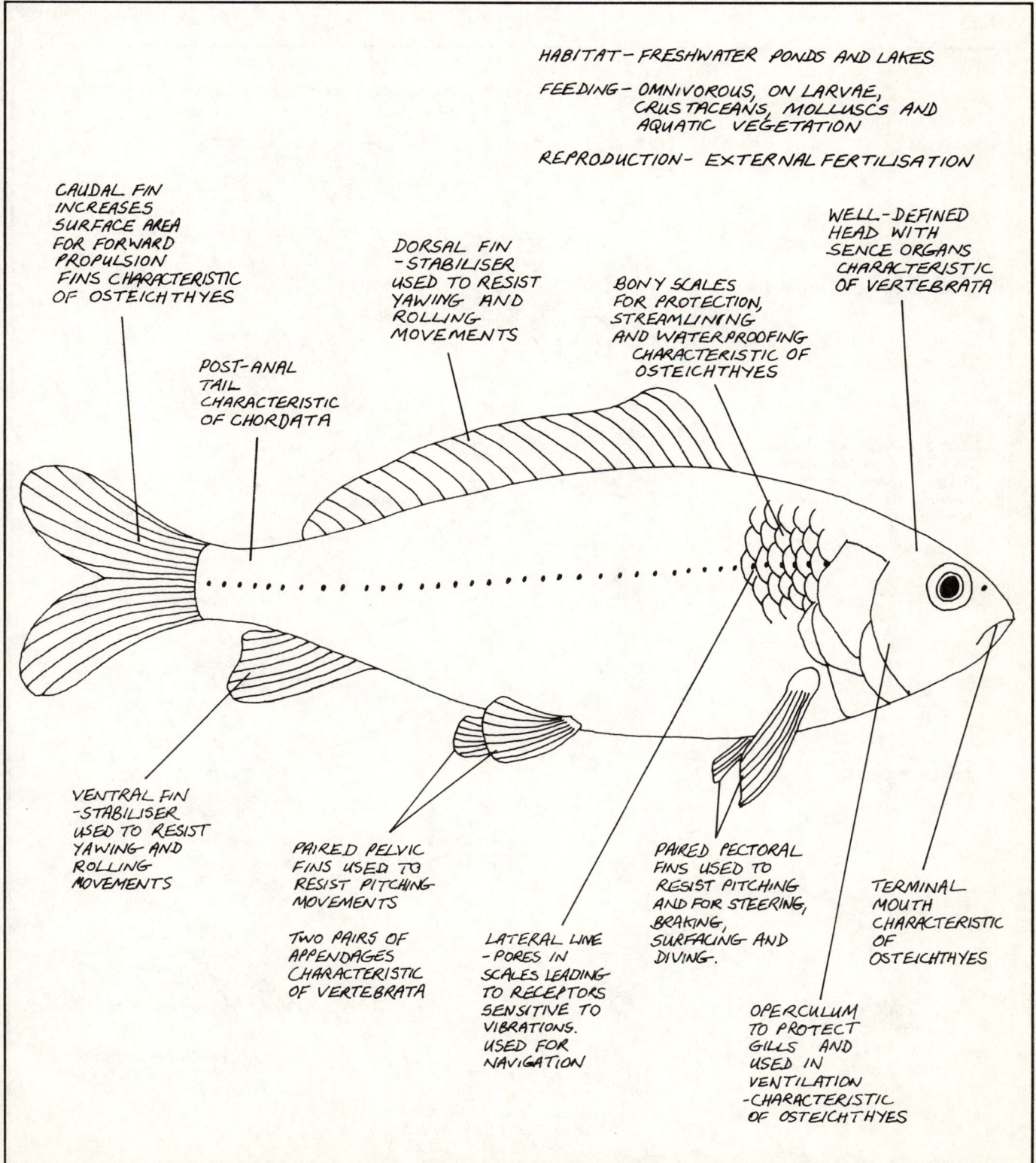

HABITAT — FRESHWATER PONDS AND LAKES

FEEDING — OMNIVOROUS, ON LARVAE, CRUSTACEANS, MOLLUSCS AND AQUATIC VEGETATION

REPRODUCTION — EXTERNAL FERTILISATION

CAUDAL FIN INCREASES SURFACE AREA FOR FORWARD PROPULSION FINS CHARACTERISTIC OF OSTEICHTHYES

POST-ANAL TAIL CHARACTERISTIC OF CHORDATA

DORSAL FIN -STABILISER USED TO RESIST YAWING AND ROLLING MOVEMENTS

BONY SCALES FOR PROTECTION, STREAMLINING AND WATERPROOFING CHARACTERISTIC OF OSTEICHTHYES

WELL-DEFINED HEAD WITH SENCE ORGANS CHARACTERISTIC OF VERTEBRATA

VENTRAL FIN -STABILISER USED TO RESIST YAWING AND ROLLING MOVEMENTS

PAIRED PELVIC FINS USED TO RESIST PITCHING MOVEMENTS

TWO PAIRS OF APPENDAGES CHARACTERISTIC OF VERTEBRATA

LATERAL LINE -PORES IN SCALES LEADING TO RECEPTORS SENSITIVE TO VIBRATIONS. USED FOR NAVIGATION

PAIRED PECTORAL FINS USED TO RESIST PITCHING AND FOR STEERING, BRAKING, SURFACING AND DIVING.

TERMINAL MOUTH CHARACTERISTIC OF OSTEICHTHYES

OPERCULUM TO PROTECT GILLS AND USED IN VENTILATION -CHARACTERISTIC OF OSTEICHTHYES

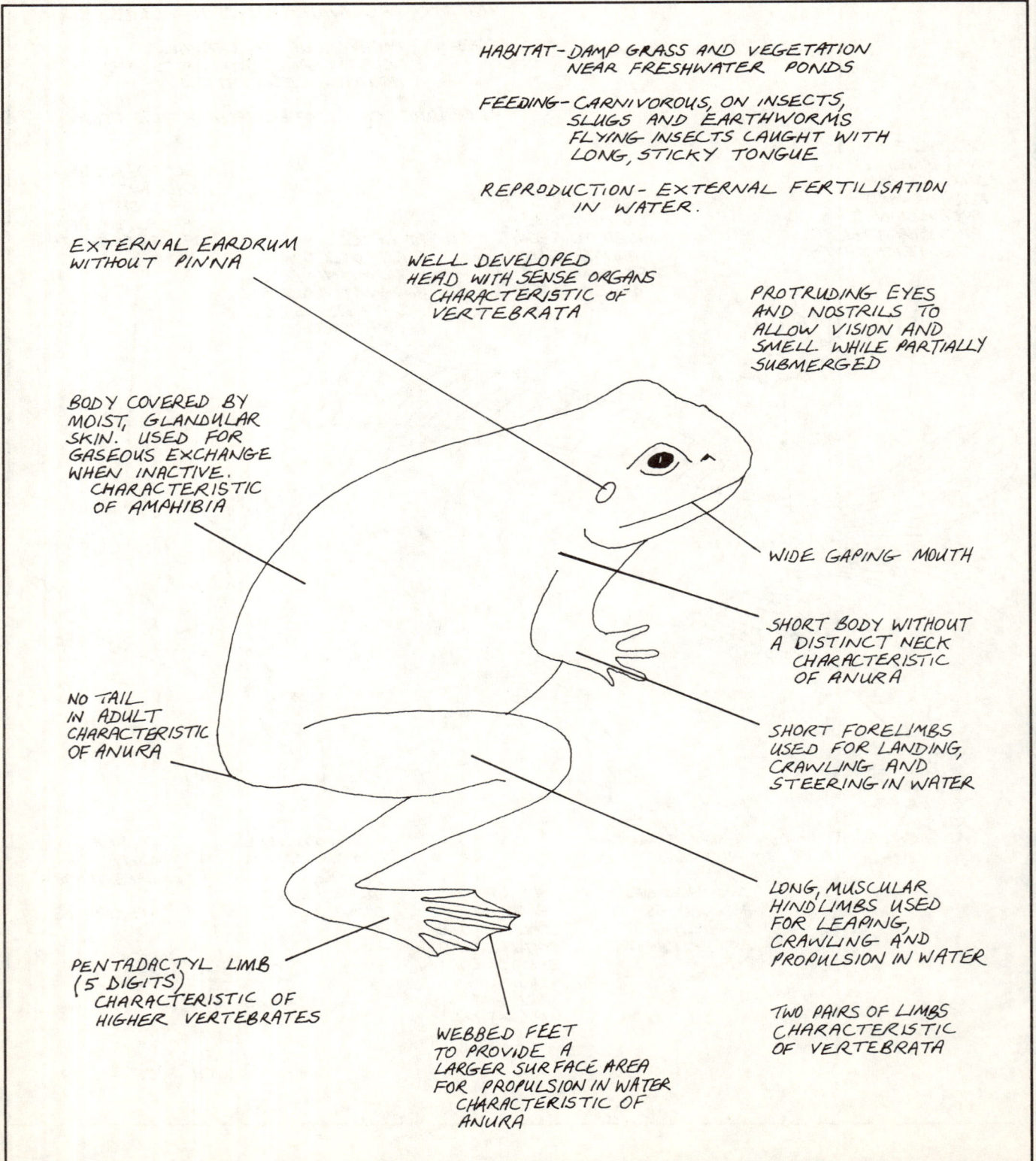

PHYLUM *CHORDATA*

SUB-PHYLUM *VERTEBRATA*

CLASS *AMPHIBIA*

ORDER *ANURA*

GENUS *RANA*   X2

Fig. 1.33

HABITAT - DAMP GRASS AND VEGETATION NEAR FRESHWATER PONDS

FEEDING - CARNIVOROUS, ON INSECTS, SLUGS AND EARTHWORMS. FLYING INSECTS CAUGHT WITH LONG, STICKY TONGUE

REPRODUCTION - EXTERNAL FERTILISATION IN WATER.

EXTERNAL EARDRUM WITHOUT PINNA

WELL DEVELOPED HEAD WITH SENSE ORGANS CHARACTERISTIC OF VERTEBRATA

PROTRUDING EYES AND NOSTRILS TO ALLOW VISION AND SMELL WHILE PARTIALLY SUBMERGED

BODY COVERED BY MOIST, GLANDULAR SKIN. USED FOR GASEOUS EXCHANGE WHEN INACTIVE. CHARACTERISTIC OF AMAHIBIA

WIDE GAPING MOUTH

SHORT BODY WITHOUT A DISTINCT NECK CHARACTERISTIC OF ANURA

NO TAIL IN ADULT CHARACTERISTIC OF ANURA

SHORT FORELIMBS USED FOR LANDING, CRAWLING AND STEERING IN WATER

LONG, MUSCULAR HINDLIMBS USED FOR LEAPING, CRAWLING AND PROPULSION IN WATER

PENTADACTYL LIMB (5 DIGITS) CHARACTERISTIC OF HIGHER VERTEBRATES

TWO PAIRS OF LIMBS CHARACTERISTIC OF VERTEBRATA

WEBBED FEET TO PROVIDE A LARGER SURFACE AREA FOR PROPULSION IN WATER CHARACTERISTIC OF ANURA

STAGES IN THE DEVELOPMENT OF TADPOLES

Fig. 1.33 (continued)

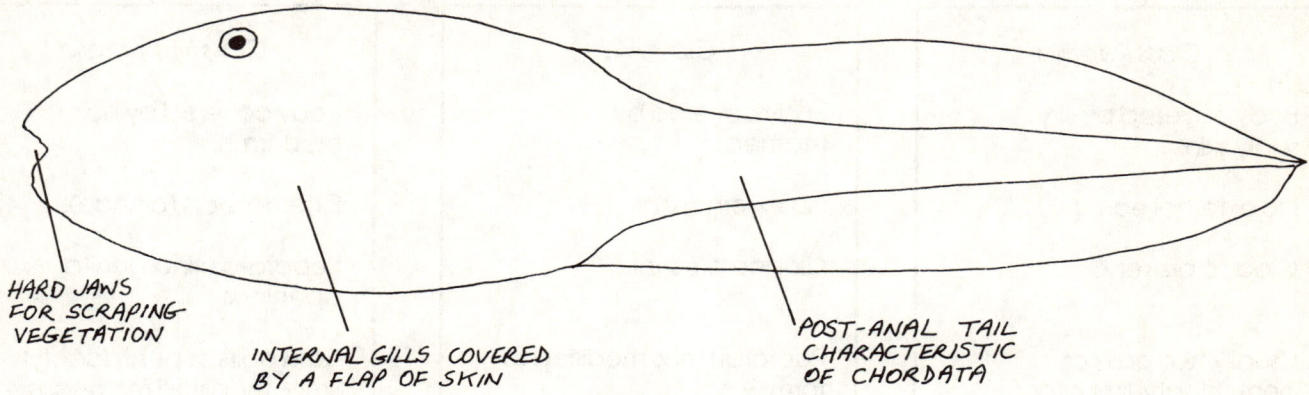

4 WEEKS ×10

HARD JAWS
FOR SCRAPING
VEGETATION

INTERNAL GILLS COVERED
BY A FLAP OF SKIN

POST-ANAL TAIL
CHARACTERISTIC
OF CHORDATA

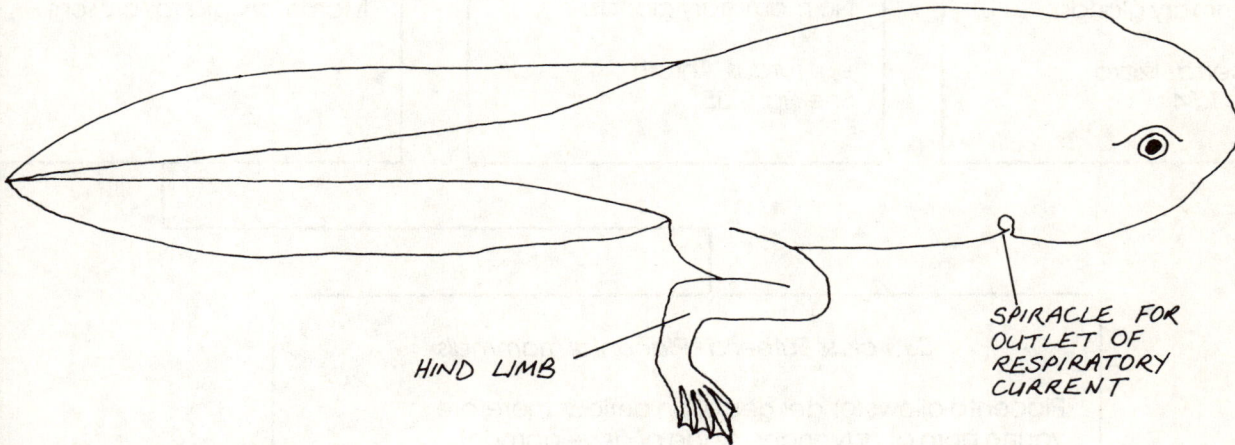

8 WEEKS ×10

HIND LIMB

SPIRACLE FOR
OUTLET OF
RESPIRATORY
CURRENT

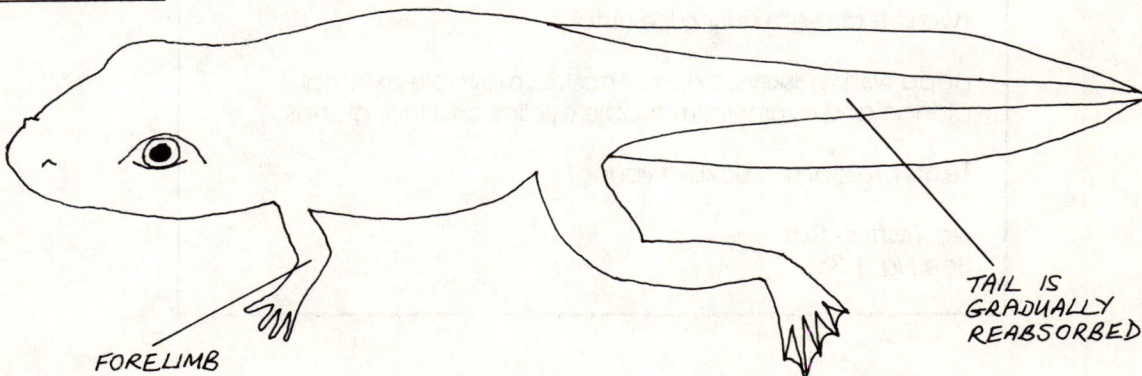

12 WEEKS ×10

FORELIMB

TAIL IS
GRADUALLY
REABSORBED

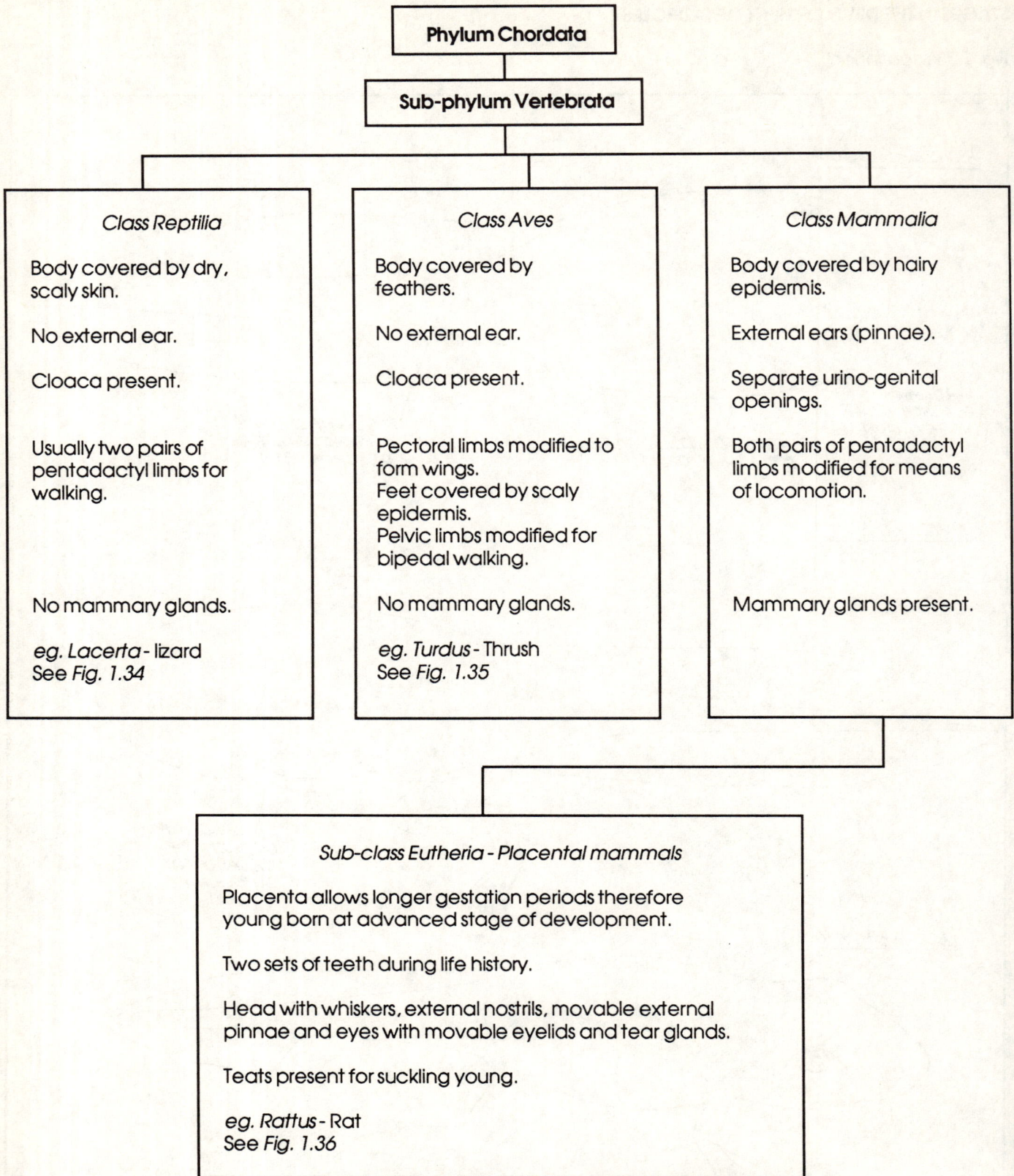

Phylum Chordata

Sub-phylum Vertebrata

Class Reptilia

Body covered by dry, scaly skin.

No external ear.

Cloaca present.

Usually two pairs of pentadactyl limbs for walking.

No mammary glands.

eg. Lacerta - lizard
See *Fig. 1.34*

Class Aves

Body covered by feathers.

No external ear.

Cloaca present.

Pectoral limbs modified to form wings.
Feet covered by scaly epidermis.
Pelvic limbs modified for bipedal walking.

No mammary glands.

eg. Turdus - Thrush
See *Fig. 1.35*

Class Mammalia

Body covered by hairy epidermis.

External ears (pinnae).

Separate urino-genital openings.

Both pairs of pentadactyl limbs modified for means of locomotion.

Mammary glands present.

Sub-class Eutheria - Placental mammals

Placenta allows longer gestation periods therefore young born at advanced stage of development.

Two sets of teeth during life history.

Head with whiskers, external nostrils, movable external pinnae and eyes with movable eyelids and tear glands.

Teats present for suckling young.

eg. Rattus - Rat
See *Fig. 1.36*

PHYLUM *CHORDATA*

SUB-PHYLUM *VERTEBRATA*

CLASS *REPTILIA*

GENUS *LACERTA*   X 1

Fig. 1.34

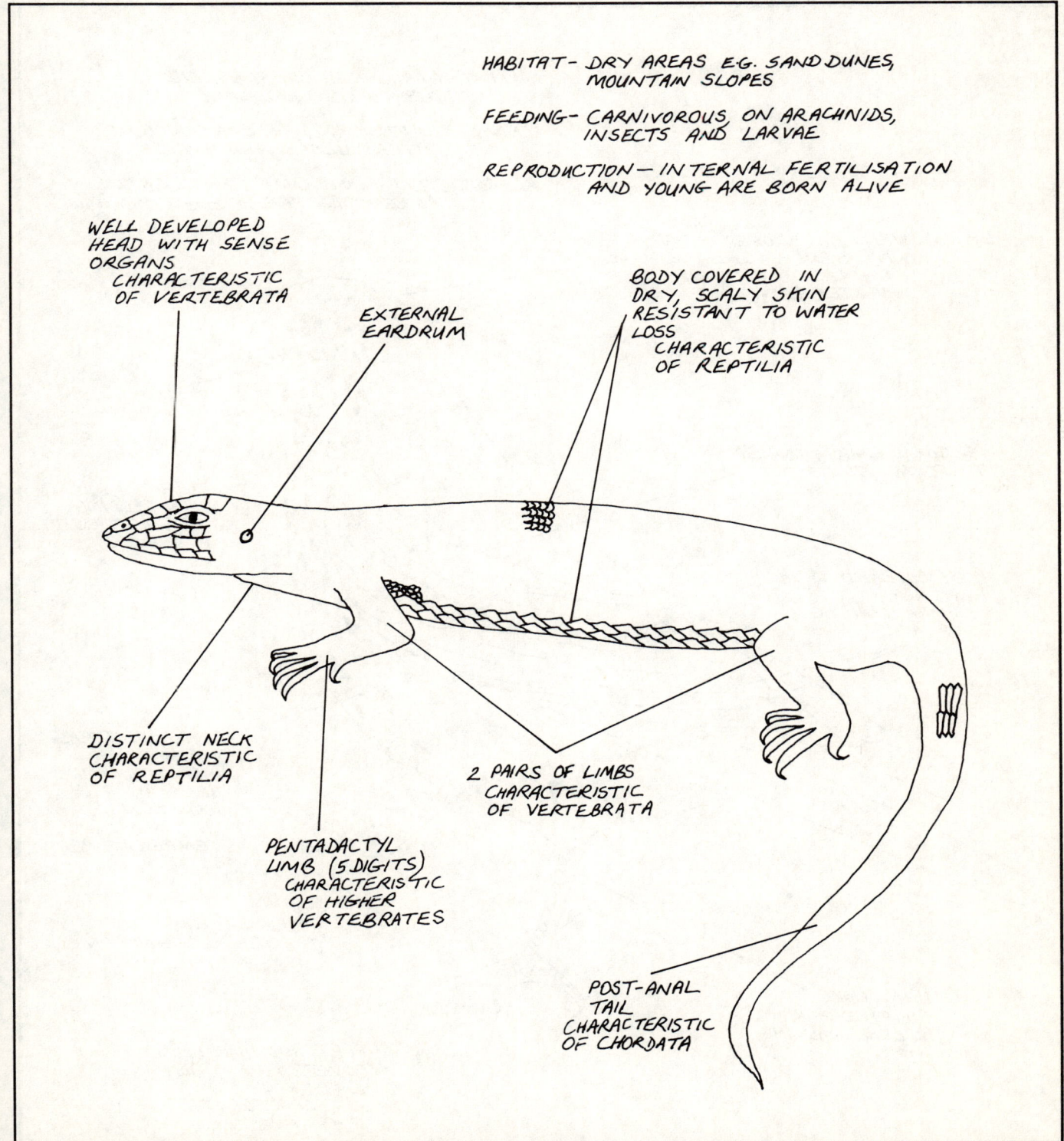

HABITAT – DRY AREAS E.G. SAND DUNES, MOUNTAIN SLOPES

FEEDING – CARNIVOROUS, ON ARACHNIDS, INSECTS AND LARVAE

REPRODUCTION – INTERNAL FERTILISATION AND YOUNG ARE BORN ALIVE

WELL DEVELOPED HEAD WITH SENSE ORGANS CHARACTERISTIC OF VERTEBRATA

EXTERNAL EARDRUM

BODY COVERED IN DRY, SCALY SKIN RESISTANT TO WATER LOSS CHARACTERISTIC OF REPTILIA

DISTINCT NECK CHARACTERISTIC OF REPTILIA

2 PAIRS OF LIMBS CHARACTERISTIC OF VERTEBRATA

PENTADACTYL LIMB (5 DIGITS) CHARACTERISTIC OF HIGHER VERTEBRATES

POST-ANAL TAIL CHARACTERISTIC OF CHORDATA

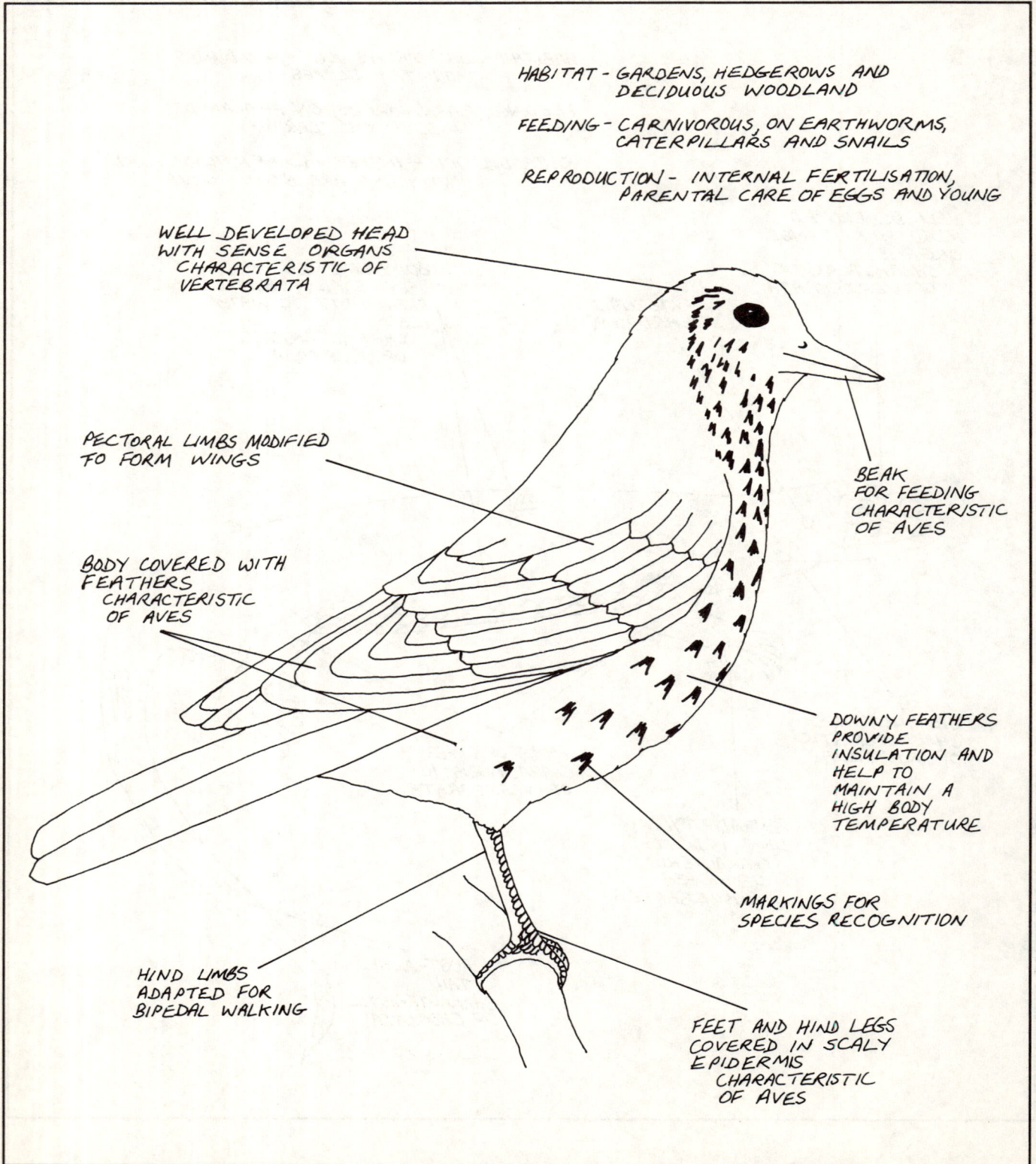

PHYLUM *CHORDATA*

SUB-PHYLUM *VERTEBRATA*

CLASS *AVES*

GENUS *TURDUS (THRUSH)*   X 1

Fig. 1.35

HABITAT - GARDENS, HEDGEROWS AND
DECIDUOUS WOODLAND

FEEDING - CARNIVOROUS, ON EARTHWORMS,
CATERPILLARS AND SNAILS

REPRODUCTION - INTERNAL FERTILISATION,
PARENTAL CARE OF EGGS AND YOUNG

WELL DEVELOPED HEAD
WITH SENSE ORGANS
CHARACTERISTIC OF
VERTEBRATA

PECTORAL LIMBS MODIFIED
TO FORM WINGS

BODY COVERED WITH
FEATHERS
CHARACTERISTIC
OF AVES

BEAK
FOR FEEDING
CHARACTERISTIC
OF AVES

DOWNY FEATHERS
PROVIDE
INSULATION AND
HELP TO
MAINTAIN A
HIGH BODY
TEMPERATURE

MARKINGS FOR
SPECIES RECOGNITION

HIND LIMBS
ADAPTED FOR
BIPEDAL WALKING

FEET AND HIND LEGS
COVERED IN SCALY
EPIDERMIS
CHARACTERISTIC
OF AVES

PHYLUM *CHORDATA*

SUB-PHYLUM *VERTEBRATA*

CLASS *MAMMALIA*

SUB-CLASS *EUTHERIA*

GENUS *RATTUS*   X 1

Fig. 1.36

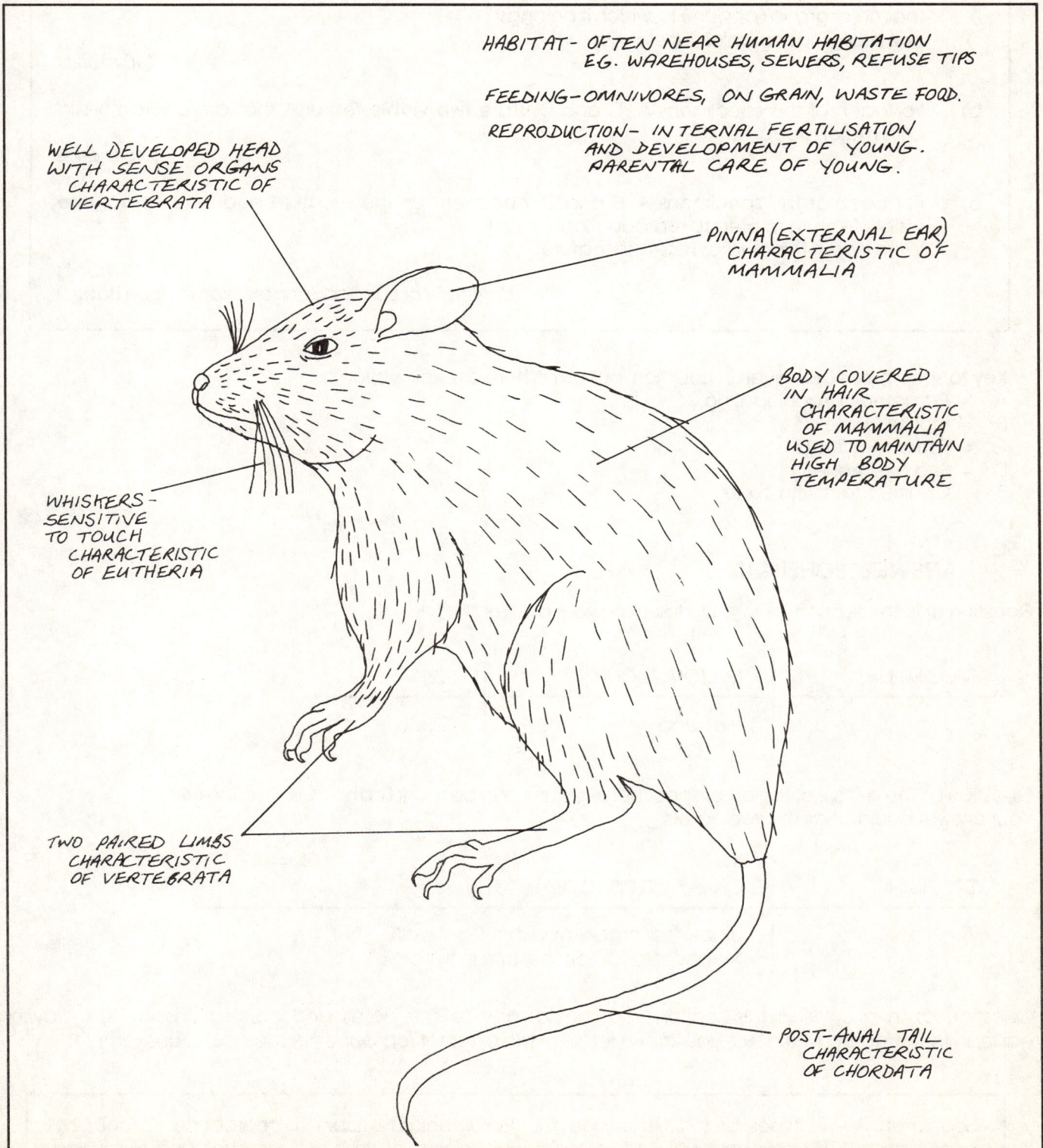

HABITAT- OFTEN NEAR HUMAN HABITATION
E.G. WAREHOUSES, SEWERS, REFUSE TIPS

FEEDING- OMNIVORES, ON GRAIN, WASTE FOOD.

REPRODUCTION- INTERNAL FERTILISATION
AND DEVELOPMENT OF YOUNG.
PARENTAL CARE OF YOUNG.

WELL DEVELOPED HEAD
WITH SENSE ORGANS
CHARACTERISTIC OF
VERTEBRATA

PINNA (EXTERNAL EAR)
CHARACTERISTIC OF
MAMMALIA

BODY COVERED
IN HAIR
CHARACTERISTIC
OF MAMMALIA
USED TO MAINTAIN
HIGH BODY
TEMPERATURE

WHISKERS-
SENSITIVE
TO TOUCH
CHARACTERISTIC
OF EUTHERIA

TWO PAIRED LIMBS
CHARACTERISTIC
OF VERTEBRATA

POST-ANAL TAIL
CHARACTERISTIC
OF CHORDATA

■ CLASSIFICATION QUESTIONS

Questions requiring a detailed knowledge of the main classification features usually follow the same pattern as illustrated by the sample below. When answering questions of this type you should select sub-groups carefully to ensure that you can give visible characteristic features.

EXAM QUESTION 1

a) For each of the specimens A, B, C, D and E, state:
i) the major group (*phylum*) to which it belongs;
ii) **one** sub-group to which it belongs

(10 marks)

b) For each of the specimens A, C and D, state **two visible** features that are characteristic of its major group.

(6 marks)

c) For each of the specimens A, B and C, comment on the structure and functions of **one visible** feature related to reproduction.
Write about thirty words for each feature.

(9 marks)
(University of London Schools Examination Board)

Key to specimens (not given in question, but given here as explanation)
A = *Paramecium* conjugating
B = Mouse (male)
C = Fertile fern frond
D = Sea anemone
E = Conifer shoot with cone

ANSWER TECHNIQUE

Question a) In this section you should tabulate your answer like this:

SPECIMEN	MAJOR GROUP	SUBGROUP
A	Protozoa	Ciliata

Question b) The details of the other specimens' groups can be found in the classification lists.
Your answer could again be tabulated:

SPECIMEN	CHARACTERISTIC FEATURES
A	Unicellular organism without cell wall Means of locomotion - (cilia in this case)

Question c) In answering this section you should refer to the notes and annotations on the drawings earlier in the chapter. Make sure you know details of the different reproductive methods. For example:

Specimen A - In times of food shortage the *Paramecium* is able to reproduce sexually by conjugation. This process involves two individuals joining at their oral grooves and swapping micronuclei. They then separate and undergo binary fission.

☐ CLASSIFICATION QUESTIONS AND ECOLOGY

Some questions will ask for details of the ecological relationships between the specimens. To prepare yourself for these, it is important to include details of the habitat and method of nutrition on your drawings. It is also important to be familiar with the basic ecological terminology given below.

O   **Ecosystem** - An interacting community of plants and animals and their physical environment, *eg.* Oak woodland

O   **Habitat** - The external environment in which an organism lives, including the physical factors (temperature, light, water availability), *eg.* freshwater pond

O   **Ecological niche** - The role played by an organism in a specific ecosystem. This includes the feeding relationships of the organism and any other effects it may have on the ecosystem, such as control or dispersal of another species, *eg.* a grazing animal which would control the spread of plants.

O   **Producer** - An autotrophic organism capable of using energy to convert inorganic compounds to organic materials. These are usually green photosynthetic plants (the term also includes chemosynthetic bacteria).

O   **Primary consumer** - Herbivorous animals feeding directly on plants, *eg.* oak moth caterpillar.

O   **Secondary consumer** - Carnivorous animals feeding on herbivores, *eg.* blue tit.

O   **Tertiary consumer** - Large carnivorous animals feeding on smaller carnivores, *eg.* owl.

O   **Detritivores** - organisms, *eg.* woodlice which feed on dead animals and plants, breaking them into smaller pieces which are then acted upon by decomposers.

O   **Decomposers** - These include bacteria and fungi which complete the process of decay and aid in the recycling of nutrients.

○ **Food web** - This is a diagram used to represent the feeding relationships between organisms in an ecosystem. The producers are named at either the top or the bottom of the diagram and then arrow headed lines are drawn between two organisms with the arrow leading to the consumer. Relationships between organisms and detritivores and decomposers are shown with a dotted line.

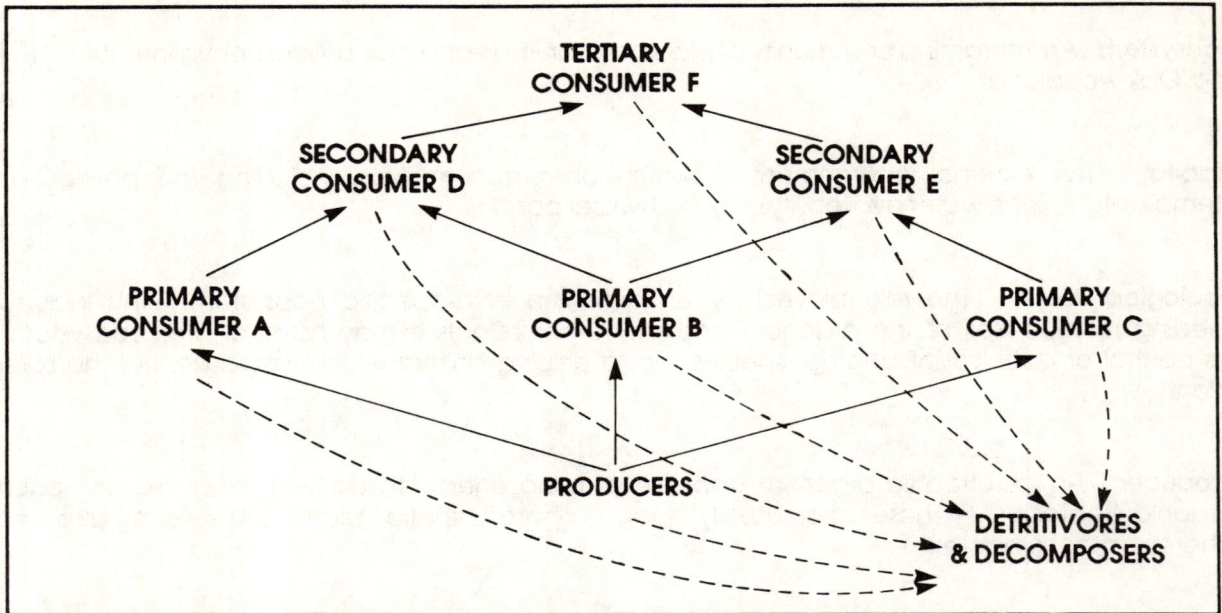

○ **Trophic level** - This term describes an organism's place in a feeding chain with producers existing at the primary trophic level. It is possible for an omnivorous animal to exist at two different trophic levels *ie.* when eating plants it would be at the secondary trophic level but when eating other animals it would be at the tertiary level.

HINTS BOX ✔

ECOLOGICAL RELATIONSHIPS

● State the trophic level of each organism.

● Draw a food web (or chain) to illustrate the feeding relationships.

● Plant/animal relationships include food supply, pollination, symbiosis, seed/fruit dispersal and plants providing habitats for animals.

● Animal/animal relationships include predator/prey, competition, parasitism and symbiosis.

● Refer to the balance of photosynthetic and respiratory gases.

● Refer to cycling of nutrients *eg.* carbon and nitrogen cycles.

EXAM QUESTION 2

a) Specimens A, B, C and D are all found in the same habitat.
i) State what this habitat may be.
ii) Name one other plant and one other animal that may also be found in this habitat

(3 marks)

b) Briefly explain the possible ecological relationships between the four kinds of organism represented by A, B, C and D.

(10 marks)

c) i) State the major group (*phylum*) to which A, B, C and D each belongs.
ii) State the sub group to which A, B, C and D each blongs.
iii) For each of the specimens B and D, give **two** visible features which are characteristic of the **major** group to which each belongs.

(12 marks)
(University of London Schools Examination Board)

Key to specimens
A = Flowering shoot of dead nettle
B = Adult worker bee
C = Snail
D = Earthworm

ANSWER TECHNIQUE

Question a) i) This question shows the importance of noting the habitats on your classification drawings so that you become familiar with them. The examiners will usually choose organisms and habitats that should be reasonably common *eg.* a deciduous woodland or a rocky shore. This particular habitat could be a hedgerow.

ii) Another plant in this habitat could be a primrose; another animal could be a slug.

Question b) For this section you should state the kinds of organisms that A, B, C and D represent. Specimen A is a producer as it is a photosynthetic green plant, B is a primary consumer as it feeds on nectar and pollen from the flowering plant, C is also a primary consumer as it feeds on the plant vegetation and D is a detritivore as it feeds on dead organic material in the soil produced from the death of the plants and animals.

A food web could then be drawn as it is a convenient way of representing the nutritional relationships between the specimens. You should also note any other ecological relationships *eg.* the bee will pollinate the dead nettle and the earthworm will help to maintain soil fertility by mixing and aerating the soil layers by burrowing.

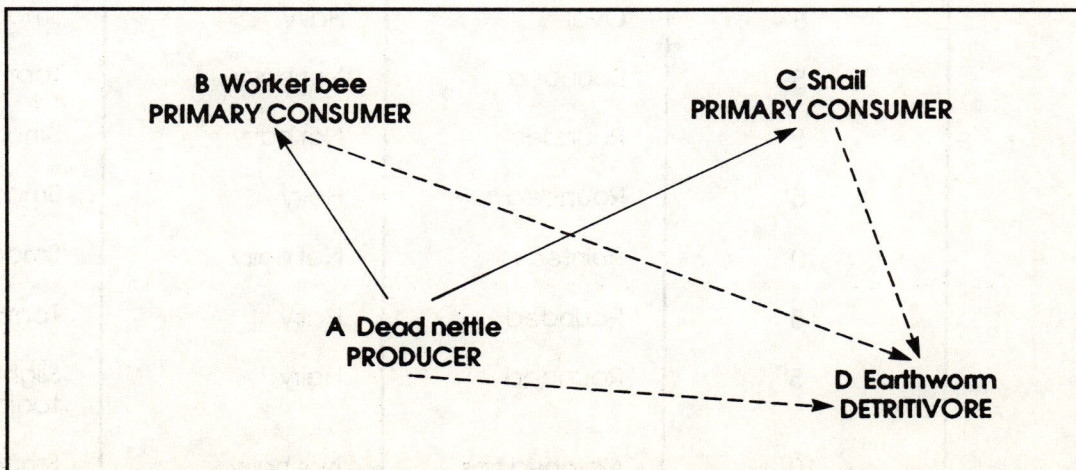

Question c) See classification lists.

CONSTRUCTION OF DICHOTOMOUS KEYS

A key is a tool used to aid identification of a range of similar organisms or parts of organisms. A dichotomous key is one which splits the organisms into two groups initially, rather than separating the organisms individually. Ideally, the two groups should contain the same number of organisms. For the examination you would be expected to construct a simple key based on externally visible characteristics. There are several rules for the construction of a good key:

HINTS BOX ✔

- Select only clearly visible features
- Select features which are common to all members of the same species
- Do **not** use colour as this may vary
- Do **not** use size as this may vary
- Prepare a table of similarities and differences for selected features of the organisms
- When writing the key, arrange it as a series of paired statements with instructions at the end of each statement
- If 6 specimens are to be separated then only 5 pairs of instructions should be used; if 4 specimens then 3 pairs *etc.*.

Example
The following example will illustrate the principles involved:

The leaves labelled A - H on the next page are typical for eight species of the same genus. Construct a key which will identify the species using the reference letters. All the drawings are to the same scale.

Method
Before attempting to construct a key you should compile a table to show the features exhibited by each specimen. To prevent this becoming overlong you should concentrate on the most obvious characteristics:
eg. number of leaf lobes, shape of lobes, presence of hairs on the petiole, toothed or smooth margin.

TABLE OF COMPARISON OF LEAF CHARACTERISTICS FOR SPECIES A TO H

SPECIMEN	NO. OF LOBES	SHAPE OF LOBES	PETIOLE	MARGIN
A	5	Oval	Hairy	Smooth
B	5	Rounded	Not hairy	Toothed
C	5	Rounded	Not hairy	Smooth
D	5	Rounded	Hairy	Smooth
E	10	Pointed	Not hairy	Smooth
F	5	Rounded	Hairy	Toothed
G	5	Rounded	Hairy	Slightly toothed
H	10	Notched tips	Not hairy	Smooth

The leaves, labelled A to H below, are typical for eight species in a particular genus. Construct a key which will identify the species using the reference letters. All the drawings are to the same scale.

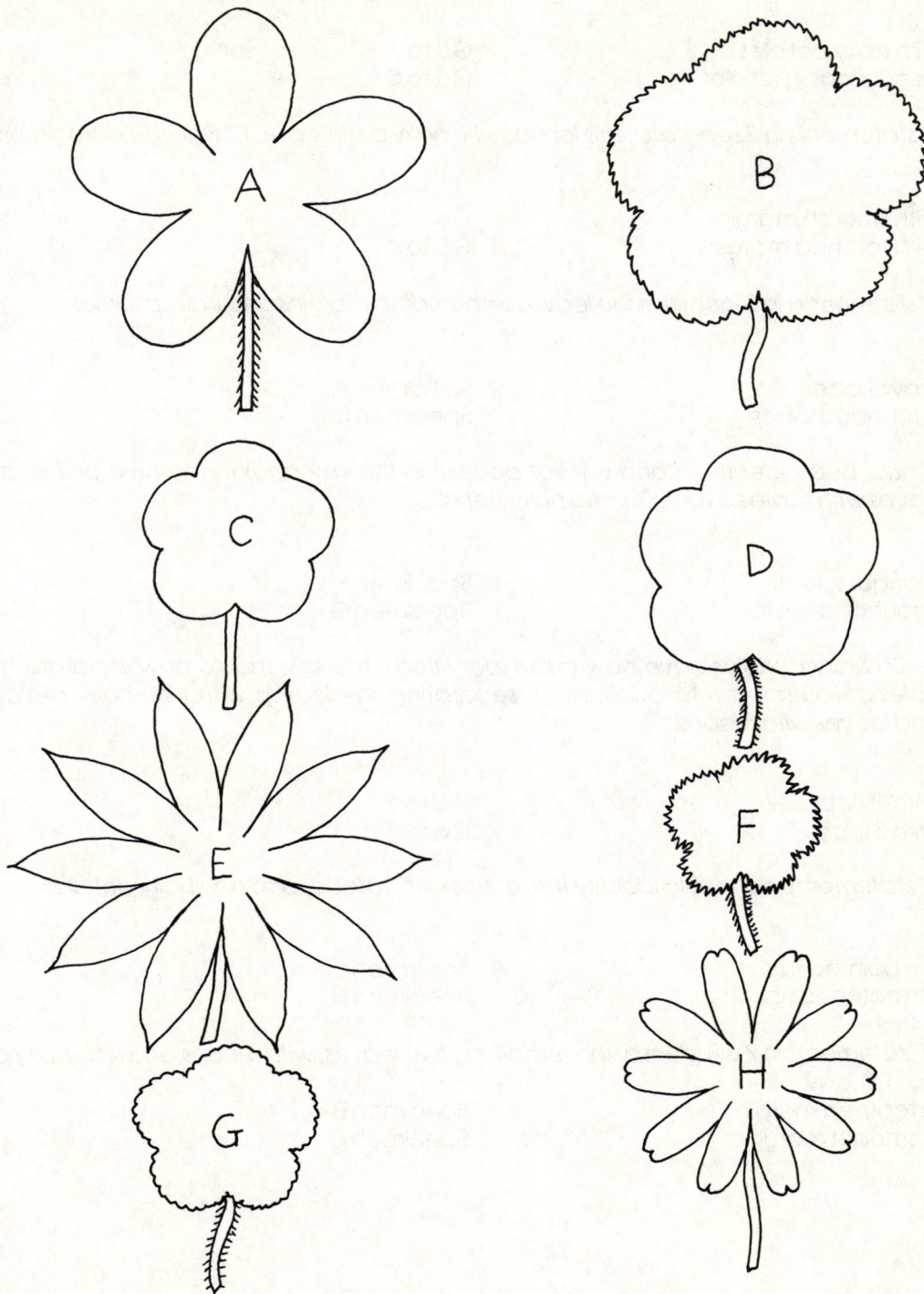

Having compiled a table you should now select a characteristic which can be used to divide the specimens into two groups. From the above table the most obvious feature would be the presence or absence of hairs on the petiole, therefore the first pair of statements should be as follows (The comments in italics are for your guidance and would not normally form part of the key.):

1.   Leaves with hairy petioles   Go to 2
        Leaves without hairy petioles   Go to 5

The next pair of statements in 2 separates the leaves with hairy petioles:- A, D, F and G - into groups.

2.   Leaves with smooth margins   Go to 3
        Leaves with toothed margins   Go to 4

The next pair of statements in 3 identifies the leaves with smooth margins and hairy petioles.

3.   Leaf with oval lobes   Specimen A
        Leaf with rounded lobes   Specimen D

A and D have now been identified and will not appear in the key again. The next pair of statements in 4 identifies the leaves with toothed margins and hairy petioles.

4.   Leaf with angular teeth   Specimen F
        Leaf with rounded teeth   Specimen G

All the leaves with hairy petioles have now been identified. The key should now separate the leaves with non hairy petioles. Statement 5 follows from 1, separating the leaves with non-hairy petioles into leaves with 10 lobes and leaves with 5 lobes.

5.   Leaves with 10 lobes   Go to 6
        Leaves with 5 lobes   Go to 7

The next pair of statements in 6 should identify the leaves with 10 lobes and non hairy petioles.

6.   Lobes with pointed tips   Specimen E
        Lobes with notched tips   Specimen H

The final pair of statements in 7 will identify the remaining two leaves, with 5 lobes and non-hairy petioles.

7.   Leaf with toothed margin   Specimen B
        Leaf with smooth margin   Specimen C

COMPARATIVE MORPHOLOGY QUESTIONS

These questions are mainly designed to test observational skills, although a knowledge of classification will be useful when describing the organisms' features. The drawings in this chapter will help you to become familiar with the characteristic features and their functions and to produce relevant annotations.

You may be asked to produce drawings of either the whole organisms or parts of them; you should refer to the drawing tips 1 - 6 at the beginning of the chapter for help.

HINTS BOX ✔

- When comparing the two (occasionally more) specimens you should ensure that you make comments about the same feature(s) of each specimen, even if this means referring to the presence of a feature on one specimen and the absence on the other.
- Draw only the part of the organism referred to in the question.
- For clarity, the pairs of characteristics could be numbered on the drawings.
- Annotations, if required, should include the functions of the selected characteristics and their relationship to the organism's mode of life.

EXAM QUESTION 3

a) Make drawings of the heads of specimens P and Q and annotate your drawings to show **four visible** differences between the heads.

(15 marks)

b) List **five** other **visible** differences between specimens P and Q.

(10 marks)
(Total 25 Marks)
(University of London Schools Examination Board)

Key to specimens:
P = teleost fish
Q = rat

ANSWER TECHNIQUE

Question a) See the drawings earlier in the chapter. Your drawings should **ONLY** show the head of each animal and be drawn to a sufficiently large scale to illustrate the differences. The annotations on one drawing should be matched by contrasting annotations on the second drawing *eg.* Eye of rat covered by lid, eye of fish not covered by lid.

Question b) The features selected for this section should be different from those used in a) and may refer to the whole specimens. It is easier to present differences in a table. *eg:*

P	Q
Body covered with bony scales.	Body covered with hair.
Paired stabilising fins.	Paired walking limbs.
No claws.	Digits end with claws.
No teats.	Teats present on ventral side.
Laterally flattened body.	Body not flattened.

CHAPTER

TWO

SIMPLE PHYSIOLOGICAL EXPERIMENTS

Experiments form part of every exam board's practical paper. The questions are designed to test a student's ability to:

■ Follow instructions or to design experiments including appropriate controls.

■ Handle apparatus and materials safely.

■ Make and record observations, measurements and estimates.

■ Evaluate and interpret observations and experimental data in the light of biological knowledge.

■ Evaluate methods of investigation and suggest improvements.

These criteria form part of the National Common Core Curriculum and are tested using questions based on the physiology of living organisms. In this chapter we have grouped together all the commonly occurring types of experiment, although their theoretical background covers a wide area of the syllabus.

Each type of experiment is described in a separate sub-section, giving the essential theoretical background as an introduction. Following this, the specific procedures and precautions necessary to carry out the experiments are given. These are then applied to exam questions. These are not intended to be model answers, but rather a guide to tackling the experiment, including hints about writing up the experiment.

Experiments:

Food Tests
Enzymes
Osmosis
Respiration
Photosynthesis
Behaviour
Water uptake

■ TYPES OF EXPERIMENT

○   *Food Tests* - identification of starch, reducing and non-reducing sugars, fats and proteins.

○   *Enzymes* - using amylase, sucrase, catalase and dehydrogenases.   Investigation of effects of pH, temperature, enzyme and substrate concentrations.

○   *Osmosis* - water relations of plant cells; effects of solutions on cells and tissues.

○   *Respiration* - activity of organisms as shown by changes to bicarbonate indicator solution or by direct observation. Use of respirometers.

○   *Photosynthesis* - use of photosynthometers (bubblers).

○   *Behaviour* - woodlice in a choice chamber.

○   *Water uptake* - use of a potometer.

The first three types of experiment tend to be tested more frequently than the others in the practical exam. This is because they involve shorter experiments which can be conducted within the time of the exam and generally give more predictable results.

The section on enzymes and the factors affecting them is more extensive because enzymes are also involved in respiration and photosynthesis. You would be expected to refer to enzyme action in these experiments.

■ EXAM TECHNIQUE

Although each type of experiment has its own set of procedures and precautions, there are several general points which are applicable to all of these questions and which will enable you to perform and write up the experiment under exam conditions. In the exam you can allow up to an hour to complete the question (you may need to start other questions whilst waiting for lengthy reactions to occur). This is usually the longest question on the exam paper so you should start this as early as possible.

HINTS BOX ✔

GENERAL EXPERIMENTAL PROCEDURES

● Read the question carefully before starting any procedure.

● Determine the aim of the experiment to avoid wasting time doing unnecessary procedures.

● If the question requires anything to be left for a period of time - *DO THIS FIRST !*

● Only write what is required by the question; do not give the method if this is part of the instructions or list apparatus unless specifically required.

● Make efficient use of your time - start writing up the method (if required) whilst waiting for reactions to occur.

● Tabulate results; do this on a separate sheet so that time is not wasted copying up rough results.

● Accurately record *all* observations, measurements, timings and special precautions (*ie.* not only basic precautions such as labelling but also those which are specific to the experiment).

● Write in the past tense and third person - *Two test tubes were taken* ...

■ USE AND DESIGN OF CONTROLS

In the exam questions, you may be asked to design a control for the experiment. This is to test your understanding of the underlying principles of the experiment.

A control should prove that any reactions occuring in the experiment are due to the stated cause and not to any other factors. Only one factor should be changed in the control; all others should be exactly the same as in the experiment. This includes volumes, temperature, timings *etc.* depending on the type of experiment. The control will then provide a reference point or comparison for the main experiment.

In many cases, there may be more than one appropriate control. You should choose the one which is easiest and quickest to perform. Read the question carefully to determine the precise factor you are being asked to investigate, as this will assist your choice of control.

It is difficult to generalise about the types of control required by the exam questions because these depend on both the type of experiment and the factors being investigated, but the following table gives suggestions for some typical experiments.

CONTROL BOX	
AIM	**POSSIBLE CONTROL**
1 To show that solution X is an enzyme which breaks down starch.	Boil solution X, allow to cool so that it is at the same temp. as original X. Add to starch and test for breakdown. Boiling will denature the enzyme thus preventing it from hydrolysing starch. This demonstrates that X is an enzyme.
2 To investigate the effect of a range of temperatures on the activity of enzyme X.	*a)* Mix X and substrate and time the reaction at room temperature as a reference point. *b)* Replace X with water to demonstrate that heat alone does not affect the substrate.
3 To investigate the effect of solution Y on onion epidermal cells.	Examine freshly cut epidermis under a microscope and record the appearance of the cells, as a reference point.
4 To investigate the effect of solution Y on strips of potato tuber.	Measure freshly cut strips of potato and record their state of turgidity before immersing them in solution Y, as a reference point.
5 To investigate the effect of living organism X on bicarbonate indicator solution.	Bicarbonate indicator solution alone in the same conditions as in the experiment. This demonstrates that any changes are due to the activities of living organisms.

FOOD TESTS

The tests are used to identify the constituents of biological materials, such as seeds, as well as specially prepared solutions. If seeds or other solid materials are to be used, they should be crushed in a pestle and mortar and then made into a solution. This can then be used as the "unknown" in the tests. (Alternatively, questions could ask for the precise location of food materials in seeds; this would require the dissection of the seed into its various parts before crushing separately.)
(see *Fig. 2.1*)

Food tests may form the basis of whole questions or may be part of other questions such as those involving enzymes. If they are being used in conjunction with an enzyme reaction, do not add the chemical reagent to the enzyme/substrate mixture as this could denature the enzyme. Instead you should withdraw samples from the mixture to use as your "unknown" in the food tests.

In the exam you would be expected to carry out these tests without instructions and, therefore, you must learn them! You would not be asked for the underlying chemistry of the tests but you may be asked to give your reasoning behind the choice of test. You should therefore know why you are carrying out each test.

The most commonly used food tests are given below; it should be realised that these are largely qualitative rather than quantitative. The proportions of reagents given are a rough guide; when writing up your experiments remember to give the exact quantities used.

Before testing any solution make sure that it is well shaken to obtain a representative sample, especially when using suspensions which may settle. To avoid contamination and confusion, a separate pipette should be used for each solution and each test tube should be clearly labelled.

CARBOHYDRATE TESTS

If a carbohydrate is suspected it can be tested by using one of the following 3 tests:
Starch test, reducing sugar test, non-reducing sugar test.

The starch test is the simplest and quickest carbohydrate test and should be carried out first when testing for an unknown carbohydrate.

STARCH TEST

1. Carry out the test on a white spotting tile.
2. To 2-3 drops of unknown, add 2-3 drops of iodine/potassium iodide solution. (iodine reagent)
3. If a blue/black precipitate forms (*ie.* particles collect at the bottom of the cavity), the presence of starch may be inferred.
4. If the solution remains the yellow colour of iodine then the test is negative.

The density of the precipitate formed gives an indication of the concentration of the starch present in the unknown solution.

In this test the iodine reagent forms a complex with the starch, therefore if you are required to use the test as part of an amylase enzyme experiment do not add iodine first as this will prevent the enzymes from working.

REDUCING SUGAR TEST (BENEDICT'S TEST)

1.   Use a test tube.
2.   To 2cm³ of unknown add an equal quantity of Benedict's Reagent.
3.   Heat to approximately 80°C (there is no need to boil).
      Either heat over a low bunsen flame or in a water bath.
4.   If a red/yellow precipitate forms a reducing sugar is present.
5.   A negative result is indicated by the solution remaining blue.

Commonly found reducing sugars include fructose, glucose and maltose but you could not distinguish one from another using this test.

During the course of the test you may observe a variety of colour changes, it is essential that you note down all of these in your results. The first colour change is usually clear blue to a pale green followed by yellow through orange to red. As a rough guide the deeper the precipitate the greater the concentration of reducing sugar. It should be noted that prolonged boiling could cause hydrolysis of any disaccharides in the test mixture, therefore you are advised not to boil the solution.

The use of a water bath for this and the following test has distinct advantages:

○   a controlled temperature is easier to achieve,
○   it allows you to start another test or to begin writing up,
○   it is safer, preventing the spurting out of boiling liquids.
○   it allows you to test more than one solution at a time.

The only disadvantage is that a water bath does take time to set up and reach the required temperature.

NON-REDUCING SUGAR TEST

1.   This should be carried out only **after** the preceeding test, as a solution may contain a mixture of both reducing and non-reducing sugars.
2.   Use a test tube.
3.   To 2cm³ of unknown and 1cm³ of dilute HC1 and boil. (This hydrolyses any disaccharides).
4.   Cool and neutralise the mixture with excess (ie. > 1cm³) NaOH. (Test with litmus paper as the Benedict's Test only works in alkaline conditions. The solution should turn red litmus paper blue).
5.   Repeat the Benedict's Test.
6.   If both reducing and non-reducing sugars are present this will be indicated by the formation of a deeper precipitate than with reducing sugars only.
7.   If the solution remains blue then neither type of sugar is present.

Commonly occurring non-reducing sugars are sucrose and lactose, but these could not be specifically identified.

To determine whether or not both types of sugar are present can often prove difficult. One way to make this slightly easier is to carry out the first test and allow the precipitate to settle, then carry out the non-reducing test on a fresh sample. When the two tubes are compared the second should contain more precipitate if a non-reducing sugar is present as well as a reducing sugar.

PROTEIN TEST

Protein tests are often used during practical exam questions to enable you to identify one of the solutions as an enzyme. All enzymes are proteins, but, it is worth remembering that not all proteins are enzymes.

BIURET TEST

1. Use a test tube.
2. To 2cm³ of unknown add an excess of KOH and shake well.
3. Trickle dilute $CuSO_4$ down the side of the tube.
4. A lilac ring should form if a protein is present.
5. If a light blue ring forms then the test is negative.

LIPID TESTS

Tests for solid fats
There are two tests to check whether a solid contains fat. These are the smear test and the Sudan III Dye test.

SMEAR TEST

A lump of fat rubbed on filter paper will make it translucent when it is held up to light.

The Sudan III Dye test is usually used for seeds *etc.* suspected of having a fat store. Maize fruits are often used for this type of question. You are expected to split the maize fruit in half longitudinally and then test it for the presence of fat.

SUDAN III DYE TEST

1. Immerse the cut seed in dye for 5 minutes.
2. Wash off excess dye in water.
3. A pink stain will indicate areas containing fat.

Test for liquid fat: Emulsion Test
An emulsion test is used to check whether a liquid contains fat.

EMULSION TEST

1. Use a test tube.
2. To 2cm³ of unknown add an equal volume of ethanol and shake it for 30 seconds.
3. Allow to stand, then decant the top layer into water.
4. A milky white emulsion should form if a fat is present.

If any of the above food tests give unclear or unexpected results, you should repeat them.

■ PRESENTATION OF RESULTS

Presentation of the results of your tests must be done clearly and neatly. Look for, and present:

○ colour changes in the solution
○ any other changes *eg.* formation of an emulsion or a precipitate.

Always record results in a table with details of ALL colour changes not just the final appearance. A table containing ticks and crosses alone will not suffice.

EXAM QUESTION 1

Each of the tubes E, F, G and H contains a solution of one or two carbohydrates. Using only the reagents provided, identify as closely as you can the carbohydrate or carbohydrates contained in each tube.

i)   Report on your methods.
ii)   Record all your results and comment on them.

(25 marks)
(University of London Schools Examination Board)

Key to solutions:

E   = 0.1% Starch   F = 1.0% Glucose
G   = 0.1% Glucose +   H = 0.1% Starch +
        1.0% Sucrose   1.0% Glucose

You would not be able to work out the precise concentrations, but would be expected to give an indication of the relative proportions of the carbohydrates in the mixtures based on your interpretation of the densities of the precipitates formed.

✍ ANSWER TECHNIQUE

Section i) Methods

Precise details of quantities used and exact procedures should be given. As mixtures of carbohydrates are included, you should perform all tests on all solutions and record the observed colour changes carefully. These may give an indication of the concentrations of the carbohydrates. You should make no reference to the results or conclusions drawn whilst writing the methods but you can state the expected positive reactions for each test.

Section ii) Results

These should be tabulated, giving precise colour changes. No mention of any conclusions or inferences should be given in the table. The table on page 70 is given to indicate the layout and detail required.

■ TABLE OF RESULTS

This is how your results might be presented:

TEST	SOLUTION	INTERMEDIATE CHANGES	FINAL APPEARANCE
STARCH	E (cloudy)	yellow/brown solution	blue/black precipitate (slight)
	F (clear)	yellow/orange solution	yellow/orange solution
	G (clear)	yellow/orange solution	yellow/orange solution
	H (cloudy)	yellow/brown solution	blue/black precipitate (slight)
REDUCING SUGARS	E	blue solution	blue solution
	F	blue then green solution	red/orange precipitate (dense)
	G	blue then green solution	dull red precipitate (slight)
	H	blue then green solution	red/orange precipitate (dense)
NON-REDUCING SUGARS	E	blue solution	blue solution
	F	blue then green solution	red/orange precipitate (dense)
	G	blue then green solution	red/orange precipitate (dense)
	H	blue then green solution	red/orange precipitate (dense)

Comments

In the question you are asked to identify, as closely as possible, the carbohydrates present in the solutions. Your comments should therefore include references to the type of carbohydrate in each solution (starch, reducing sugars and/or non-reducing sugars). Comments should also refer to the rough proportions of each carbohydrate. This can be inferred from the amount of precipitate formed in each tube; *eg.* Solution H contains more reducing sugars than solution G.

■ USE OF SEEDS IN FOOD TESTS

Questions may require the investigation of food materials in seeds.
The seeds could be dicotyledonous such as peas, beans and peanuts or monocotyledonous such as maize, barley and wheat. Dicotyledonous seeds consist of two large hemispherical cotyledons and a small embryo enclosed in a seed coat or testa. The embryo includes the plumule (immature shoot) and the radicle (immature root). See *Fig. 2.1*.
Monocotyledonous seeds have an outer testa with a large endosperm, a single cotyledon (seed leaf) and an embryo. The embryo plumule is enclosed in a sheath or coleoptile and the radicle is enclosed in a similar sheath the coleorhiza.
It is important that you know the parts of the seeds and their functions so that you can relate this to the food materials they may contain.
The following table gives the likely food materials contained in the various seed parts:

TABLE OF SEED STRUCTURES AND FOOD MATERIALS

STRUCTURE	FOOD MATERIAL
Testa (seed coat)	Mainly cellulose
Dicotyledonous Cotyledon	Mainly protein Fat in some seeds *eg.* peanuts Some sugars in actively germinating seeds
Endosperm	Mainly starch Fat in some seeds
Embryo	Protein

To test for the foodstuffs, the seeds have to be dissected into their various parts. These must then be crushed separately in a pestle and mortar and made into solutions. You should use the same amount of crushed material in each solution to obtain comparative results in the food tests.

■ USE OF SEEDS AS ENZYME SOURCES

Seeds may be used as enzyme sources in physiological experiments. You need to be able to relate the site of the enzyme to the functions of the seed structures. Only germinating seeds will show enzyme activity; if they have been killed *eg.* by boiling, the enzymes will be inactive. Details of the enzymes are given in the next section.

The following table gives the location of enzymes in seeds:

ENZYME	LOCATION IN SEEDS
Amylase & Sucrase	Cotyledons of germinating Dicotyledonous seeds Endosperm of germinating Monocotyledonous seeds
Catalase & Dehydrogenases	Moderate concentrations in cotyldons and endosperm High concentrations in embryos

DIAGRAMS TO SHOW SEED STRUCTURES

FIG 2.1

L.S. DICOTYLEDONOUS SEED - PEA   X 10

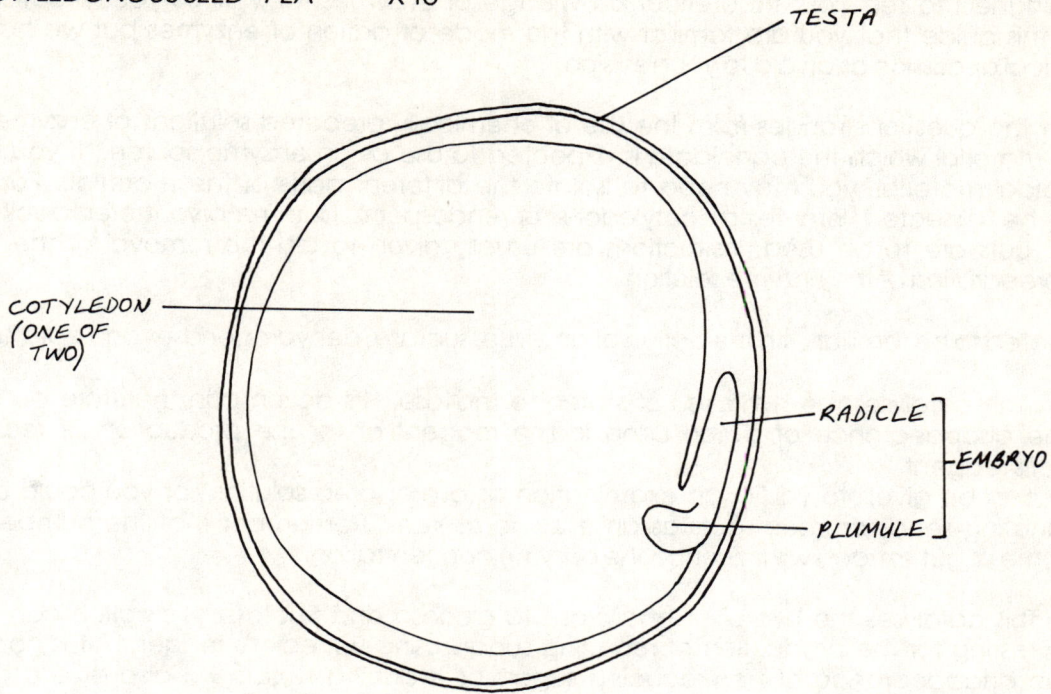

TESTA

COTYLEDON
(ONE OF
TWO)

RADICLE
PLUMULE
— EMBRYO

L.S. MONOCOTYLEDONOUS SEED - MAIZE   X 10

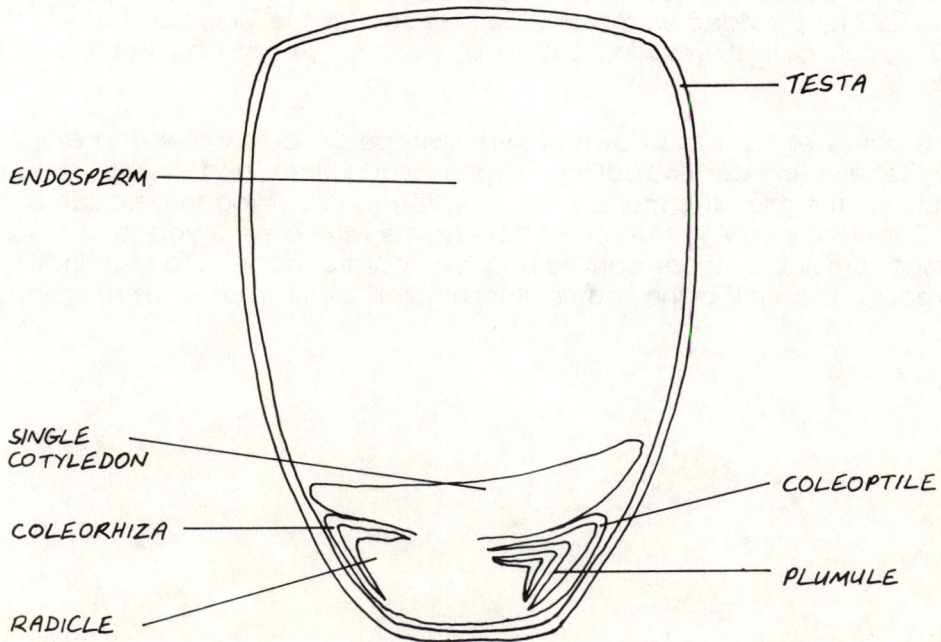

TESTA

ENDOSPERM

SINGLE
COTYLEDON

COLEOPTILE

COLEORHIZA

PLUMULE

RADICLE

ENZYME EXPERIMENTS

These are designed to test your theoretical knowledge of enzymes, as well as your practical skills. It is assumed by this guide that you are familiar with the mode of action of enzymes but we have included some theoretical discussion as an aid to your revision.

The nature of the questions ranges from the use of chemically prepared solutions of enzymes to the use of biological material which the candidate is expected to use as an enzyme source. If you are required to use biological material, you may need to isolate the different parts of the material. For example; a seed should be dissected into testa, cotyledons or endosperm and embryo (refer back to *Fig. 2.1*) Where insect guts are to be used, instructions are usually given to aid the removal of the gut and the subsequent preparation of the enzyme solution.

You are expected to be familiar with the action of amylase, sucrase, dehydrogenases and catalase.

❑ **Amylase**   This catalyses the hydrolysis of starch to maltose. Its action can therefore be detected by testing for the disappearance of starch using iodine reagent or for the production of reducing sugars using Benedict's reagent.
The amylase can be given to you in an examination as a prepared solution, or you could be expected to use germinating seeds or insect guts as an enzyme source. Remember that the number and size of seeds (or volume of gut extract) will influence the enzyme concentration.

❑ **Sucrase**   This catalyses the hydrolysis of sucrose to glucose and fructose. Its action can therefore be detected by testing for the production of reducing sugars using Benedict's reagent. It is not appropriate to test for the disappearance of non-reducing sugars as reducing sugars will also give a positive result with the non-reducing sugar test. Sucrase can be given as a prepared solution or it can be found in insect guts or plant storage tissues such as onion bulbs and carrot tap roots.

❑ **Dehydrogenases**   These are a group of enzymes catalysing the oxidation (by removing hydrogen) of substrates and transferring the hydrogen atoms to co-enzymes. Their activity can be detected by using artificial hydrogen acceptors which change colour on reduction. You are given these colour changes in the exam question. Commonly used acceptors are methylene blue which becomes colourless when reduced and tetrazolium chloride which becomes pink. Dehydrogenase enzymes are involved in many metabolic processes including the Krebs' TCA cycle of aerobic respiration and therefore you are usually provided with biological material as the enzyme source. You may be given whole organisms *eg.* an actively respiring culture of yeast or germinating seeds and they can also be found in fresh milk.

❑ **Catalase**   This catalyses the breakdown of hydrogen peroxide to water and oxygen. Its activity can be detected by effervescence (indicating oxygen production) and a rise in temperature as the reaction is strongly exothermic. It is found in all living tissues as hydrogen peroxide is a toxic by-product of metabolism. Questions involving the use of this enzyme may expect you to refer to differences in the activity of the tissues provided. These can include liver, potato, apple and germinating seeds. A lack of catalase activity could indicate that the tissue is either naturally inert (*eg.* seed testa) or had been killed.

ENZYME EXPERIMENTS

Questions on enzyme experiments examine the effects of temperature, pH, substrate and enzyme concentrations and inhibitors on the activity of enzymes.

■ TEMPERATURE

All enzymes have minimum, optimum and maximum temperature for their activity; the precise range depends upon the source of the enzyme. The effect of temperature on any reaction is to double its rate for every $10^{\circ}C$ due to increased kinetic energy and the consequent increased rate of collisions of reactants. This is also true of enzyme reactions until the optimum is reached; then the vibrations within each enzyme become too severe for the hydrogen bonds and disulphide bridges to be maintained. Once these are broken the specific 3D shape is lost, disrupting the active site of the enzyme and activity ceases. The enzyme is said to be denatured.

The experiments generally require the use of a water bath which can be set up using a container of water on a tripod above a bunsen burner. You should start by heating the water to the lowest temperature required as it is easier to increase the temperature gradually. The temperature should be monitored using a thermometer. If the temperature rises too much, add cold tap water for quick cooling.

⚠ Precautions

When investigating the effect of temperature on the rate of an enzyme catalysed reaction the following precautions should be observed:

❑ Choose a range of temperatures which are above and below the expected optimum. (Around $40^{\circ}C$ for most enzymes you will use.)
❑ Allow the enzyme and substrate solutions to reach the required temperature before mixing. This is to ensure that the reaction occurs at the specified temperature. Do not heat hydrogen peroxide as this is unstable and breaks down spontaneously.
❑ All other factors should be kept constant (enzyme and substrate concentration and pH).

■ pH

The pH scale is used to measure the acidity or alkalinity of a solution and is a measure of the concentration of hydrogen ions. A pH of 7 is neutral, below is acid and above is alkaline.

Each enzyme works within a narrow pH range and has its own optimum. Amylase, sucrase, catalase and dehydrogenases all work best in slightly alkaline conditions. Extremes of pH, on either side of the optimum, denature the enzyme by disrupting the hydrogen bonds and the electrostatic charges on the active sites.

If you are warned not to spill any solutions onto your skin or clothing you can infer that the experiment is investigating the effects of varying pH. The "unknown" solution could be an acid or an alkali. To determine the nature of the solution you could use litmus paper, if this is provided. Alkalis turn red litmus blue and acids turn blue litmus red.

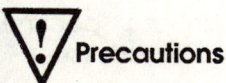

⚠ Precautions

The following precautions should be observed:

❑ The acid or alkali should be added to the enzyme before mixing with the substrate. This is to ensure that the reaction proceeds at the specified pH.
❑ If you are given a range of solutions, you should pipette the same volume of each to separate enzyme samples. This is to keep a constant ratio between the enzyme and the "unknown" solutions.
❑ If investigating the effect of pH on the action of sucrase you should ensure that the solution is alkaline before testing with Benedict's reagent. (This would also apply to any other enzyme where the breakdown products are reducing sugars.)

■ SUBSTRATE CONCENTRATION

Enzyme activity increases proportionally with increased substrate concentration until the maximum turnover rate is achieved. This is due to increased chances of enzyme and substrate collisions. Once the maximum rate is reached no further increase is possible as the rate is limited by the availability of active sites.

Investigations involving varying substrate concentration may require the preparation of a dilution series. This is a range of concentrations of solutions obtained by progressively diluting a "stock" solution. For example; given a 1M solution of sucrose a dilution series could be prepared in the following way:

10cm³ of sucrose   + 0cm³ distilled water = 1.0M sucrose solution
9cm³ of sucrose   + 1cm³ distilled water = 0.9M sucrose solution
5cm³ of sucrose   + 5cm³ distilled water = 0.5M sucrose solution *etc* ...

These experiments involve mixing each substrate concentration with the enzyme solution, in separate tubes, and then removing samples at regular intervals to test for substrate breakdown or product formation (whichever is quickest).

⚠ Precautions

The following precautions should be observed when carrying out substrate concentration experiments:

❑   The volume and concentration of enzyme should be kept constant throughout the experiment.
❑   Shake the tubes to ensure thorough mixing of the substrate and enzyme.
❑   As the changes in activity may be slight when the concentration is varied, it is often useful to record precise measurements of the amount of product formed. This may require the construction of a colour grading scale to indicate the depth of precipitate formed *eg.* in amylase experiments where iodine reagent is used to test for starch, 10 could be taken to be the deepest black precipitate and 0 could indiate the yellow/brown colour of the iodine reagent. This will then produce numerical results which can be plotted on a graph.
❑   If using food tests to indicate enzyme activity, prepare sufficient substrate/enzyme mixtures to enable you to take more than one sample for testing from each tube.
❑   It may be useful to stagger the time of mixing the enzyme and substrate to allow time for testing.

■ ENZYME CONCENTRATION

Activity also increases in direct proportion to enzyme concentration as more active sites are available. Collisions between enzymes and substrates are also more likely as more enzymes are added; the rate is eventually limited by substrate availability.

In these experiments you may be asked to use a biological enzyme source. You should remember that the size and degree of cutting or crushing of the tissue will affect the concentration of the enzyme. For example, a 1cm³ cube of potato will release less catalase than a 1cm³ cube which has been chopped into pieces.

You may be asked to investigate relative concentrations of a particular enzyme within one specimen *eg.* a germinating pea seedling. In this case you should dissect the seedling into its various parts (see *Fig. 2.1*) before crushing.

If you are given a prepared enzyme solution, a dilution series can be made as above.

Precautions

The necessary precautions for these experiments are:

❑ Substrate concentration and volume should be kept constant throughout.
❑ Shake the tube to ensure thorough mixing of enzyme and substrate.
❑ Record precise measurements of product formation or substrate breakdown (see notes on substrate concentration).
❑ If using food tests to indicate results of enzyme activity, prepare sufficient volumes of enzyme/substrate solution to allow for multiple testing.
❑ Staggered mixing times may be necessary to allow time for testing.

■ INHIBITORS

These influence the rate of an enzyme catalysed reaction in one of two ways:

○ *Competitive inhibition*; substrate and inhibitor have similar molecular structure and therefore both fit into the active site of the enzyme. The degree of inhibition depends upon the concentration of the inhibitor.

○ *Non competitive inhibition*; the inhibitor either blocks the active site or changes the shape of the enzyme. In both cases, small volumes of inhibitor prevent the enzyme from working.

The experiments usually involve the use of non competitive inhibitors given as "unknown" solutions. This may mean that you are unable to distinguish between the effect of an inhibitor and extreme changes of pH as these both cause denaturation of an enzyme. If this is the case you should give both possible causes in your explanations.

Precautions

The precautions necessary for this type of experiment include those given above for enzyme and substrate concentration. Additionally you should allow time (approx 5 mins.) for the inhibitor to affect the enzyme before mixing with the substrate.

EXAM QUESTION 2

a)   Solution J contains **two** carbohydrates. Identify the two carbohydrates as closely as you can.
Record your methods, results and conclusions.

b)   Solutions K and L contain the same enzyme, but at different concentrations.   The enzyme catalyses the hydrolysis of one of the carbohydrates present in solution J.

Carry out an experiment to determine which of the enzyme solutions K or L has the higher concentration.   For your investigation use equal volumes of the enzyme solutions K or L and the substrate solution J.

Write a full report of your methods and note any special precautions taken.
Record your results and explain your conclusions.

(25 marks)
(University of London Schools Examination Board)

Key to solutions:
J   = A mixture of equal volumes of 1% starch and 2% sucrose solutions,
so that the mixture contains 0.5% starch and 1.0% sucrose.
K   = 0.1% amylase solution
L   = 2.0% amylase solution

ANSWER TECHNIQUE

Section a) Method

In this section you would be expected to carry out the carbohydrate tests (starch, reducing sugar and non reducing sugar tests).

Your method should include precise details of the quantities used and exact procedures of the tests.

You should not include results of the tests in this section.

Results

These should be tabulated, giving exact colour changes and amounts of precipitate formed.

Conclusions

You would only be able to identify starch by name; the other carbohydrate would have to be identified by type (in this case, non reducing sugar).

Section b) Method

From the results of part a), you would know that starch and a non reducing sugar are present in solution J. The enzyme in solutions K and L must act on one of these to produce reducing sugars.

To determine which enzyme solution is more concentrated, you would need to prepare two test tubes containing equal amounts of solution J. To one tube the same volume of solution K should be added and to the other, an equal volume of L. These volumes should be sufficient to allow samples to be withdrawn and tested at regular intervals. The test used should be the Benedict's Test for reducing sugars.

Special Precautions

These should be specific to this experiment and not include basic procedures such as labelling of test tubes which should appear in your general method for any experiment. *eg.* The tubes should be shaken to ensure thorough mixing of the solutions, both initially and before taking samples for testing.

Results

Tabulate these, giving exact timings, colours of solutions and densities of precipitates.

Conclusions

You should state the solution which gives the fastest production of reducing sugars and hence must be the most concentrated.

The account should end with a theoretical discussion of the effects of enzyme concentration on rates of reaction.

EXAM QUESTION 3

Catalase is an enzyme which catalyses the breakdown of hydrogen peroxide with the evolution of oxygen gas as shown by effervescence.

a) Investigate the distribution of catalase **in the different parts** of germinating pea seedlings, labelled A, by crushing the tissues and adding a few drops of hydrogen peroxide solution.

(3 marks)

b) Investigate the effect of preheating the seeds on catalase activity. Place seeds, labelled B, in a test tube and transfer the test tube to a water bath maintained at 40°C for 3 minutes. Then remove the test tube. Cool and gently crush the seeds, add a few drops of hydrogen peroxide solution and observe carefully any effervescence which may occur. Repeat the experiment at water bath temperatures of 50°, 60° and 80°C.

(7 marks)

c) Investigate the effect of varying the duration of heating at 50°C by heating pea seeds for 2, 4 and 6 minutes at 50°C.

Report and comment on ALL of your results, stressing any precautions taken to obtain comparable results.

(6 marks)
(Total 16 marks)
(Oxford and Cambridge Schools Examination Board)

Key to specimens:
A = germinating pea seeds with radicles about 5mm long.
B = pea seeds soaked overnight.

✍ ANSWER TECHNIQUE

Section a)

For this section the different parts of the seed would have to be separated *ie.* testa (seed coat), cotyledons and embryo including radicle. (see *Fig. 2.1*)

These would then be crushed and placed in separate test tubes and a few drops of hydrogen peroxide added. (The number of drops should be the same for each sample to maintain constant substrate concentration). Catalase activity could then be measured by noting any temperature changes and also by comparing the degree of effervescence.

Results

Tabulate to indicate the activity of the different parts of the seed in terms of degree of effervescence and temperature changes.

Comments

Hydrogen peroxide is produced as a result of metabolic activity and therefore those tissues which produce more effervescence are more active. The testa is simply an inert protective coat whereas the cotyledons and embryo are both sites of activity. The cotyledons are the food store and this is broken down during germination giving slight activity. The embryo is more active as it is growing and cells are dividing.

Section b) Precautions

This part of your answer should include details of the method which are not given in the instructions, *eg.*

The same number of seeds should be used for each temperature to maintain a constant enzyme concentration. You should ensure that the seeds are cooled to the same temperature before adding them to the hydrogen peroxide. This is because hydrogen peroxide is very unstable and may breakdown due to the influence of heat.

Results

These should be presented in a table.

Comments

A theoretical discussion of the effects of temperature on the rate of an enzyme catalysed reaction should be included. Reference should also be made to the optimum temperature for the reaction (or nearest to optimum, as this is difficult to ascertain from a simple experiment.)

Section c)

Although short exposure to high temperatures may speed the reaction, prolonged heating will denature the enzymes. In this section the examiners will be looking for reference to this phenomenon.

Results should again be presented in a table.

OSMOSIS EXPERIMENTS

Questions on osmosis can involve either:

      ○ observation of plant epidermal cells, or

      ○ measurements of lengths (or masses) of plant tissues.

The organs used include potato tubers, onion bulbs and leaves. The prepared tissues are placed in unknown solutions of varying concentration.

As with all physiology based experiments these require a knowledge of the theoretical aspects of the topic. All exam boards now agree on the use of water potential terminology. This explains the movement of water molecules across differentially permeable membranes in terms of their kinetic energy.

■ DEFINITIONS AND EQUATIONS FOR OSMOSIS EXPERIMENTS

The following is a list of definitions and equations that you will require:

● *WATER POTENTIAL* - This is represented by the symbol Ψ
Pure water is taken to have a water potential value of 0. The presence of any solutes lowers its potential, hence all solutions will have negative values.

● *OSMOSIS* - This is the nett movement of water molecules from a region of higher water potential to a region of lower water potential across a differentially permeable membrane.

● *OSMOTIC POTENTIAL* (Ψ_o) - This is represented by the symbol Ψ_o and is a measure of the concentration of a solution. This is determined by the number of solute particles present. Ionic solutions will have a lower Ψ_o than non ionic solutions of the same molarity because the molecules dissociate into ions thus increasing the number of solute particles.

● *PRESSURE POTENTIAL* (*TURGOR PRESSURE*) (Ψ_p) - This is represented by the symbol Ψ_p and is a measure of the pressure exerted by the cell wall on the cell contents. As the cell becomes turgid this pressure tends to force water out of a cell and is therefore given a positive value.

● *EQUATION TO CALCULATE WATER POTENTIAL OF A CELL* (Ψ_w)
The water potential of a cell is the tendency of water molecules to enter or leave a cell by osmosis:

$$\Psi_w = \Psi_o + \Psi_p$$

Numerical values are given in terms of pressure measured in Pascals (Pa).

If the overall value is 0 then the cell is fully turgid as there is no nett movement of water molecules in either direction. A negative value will indicate a degree of plasmolysis.

■ EXPERIMENTS INVOLVING DIRECT OBSERVATION OF EPIDERMAL CELLS

These experiments require you to obtain strips of epidermis by peeling the lower epidermis from onion bulb scales or from leaves of other plants.

Obtaining strips from onions

The easiest way to obtain several samples of the same size is to cut a square "window" in the side of the onion bulb. This cut should pass down through several layers which can then be levered out and separated before removing the epidermis.

Fig. 2.2

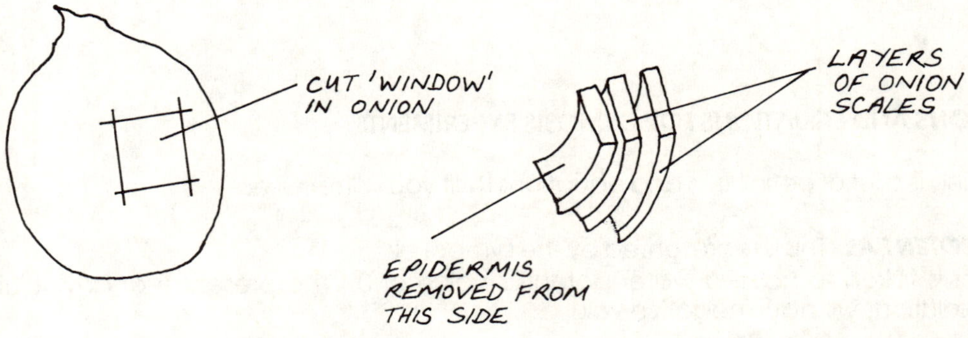

The strips should be placed immediately in watch glasses or mounted on slides in the solutions as directed in the question. This will prevent the strips dehydrating. Dehydration would cause the cells to become plasmolysed to such an extent that the results would be inaccurate.

Obtaining strips from leaves

You may be asked to obtain strips either from the underside of the leaf blade or from the petiole (leaf stalk). The lower side of the leaf may be recognised by the presence of ridges formed by the veins. This is more obvious on a dicotyledonous leaf where there is a marked midrib. Additionally, in some leaves the lower surface is dull and the upper surface is shiny.

The easiest way to prepare a strip is to hold the leaf with the lower surface uppermost and then to snap it horizontally, (the break should not extend across the full width of the leaf).

Fig. 2.3

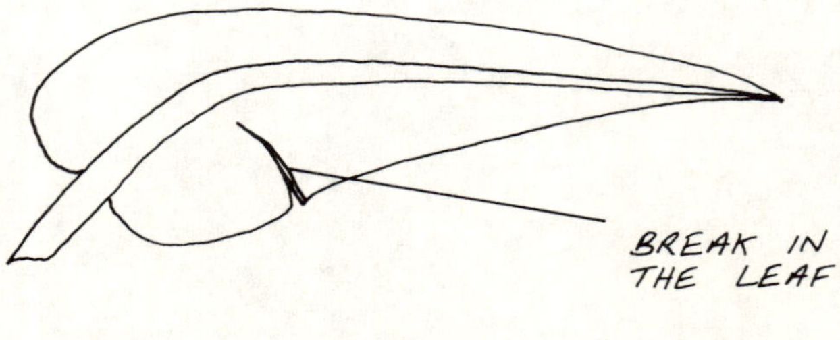

The partially broken leaf should then be wrapped over your finger to reveal a hole in the blade. The edges of this hole will be ragged and it should be possible for you to grasp a piece of lower epidermis in a pair of forceps. A strip can then be removed by steadily pulling the forceps away from you in a single smooth action.

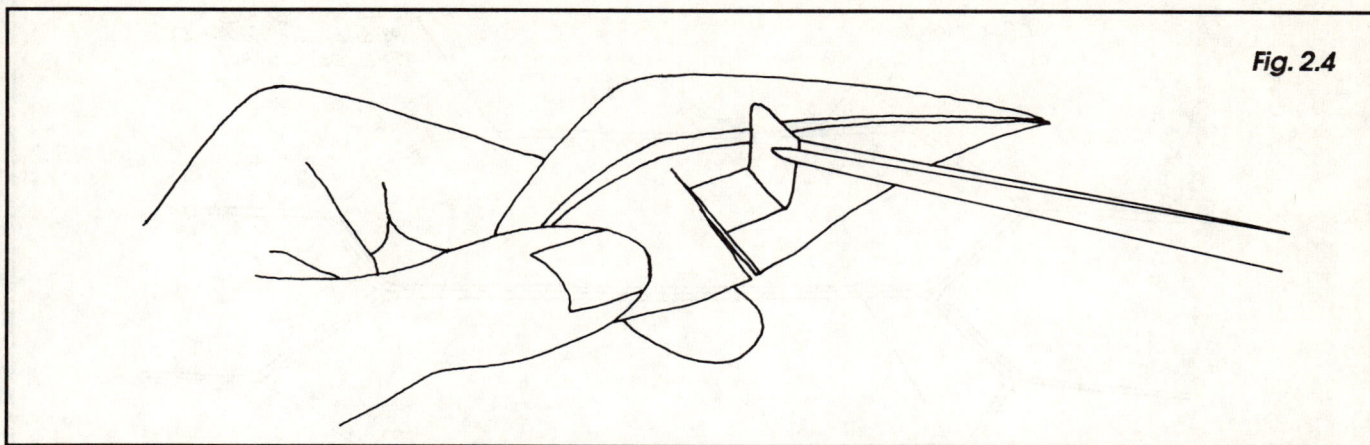

Fig. 2.4

It may be necessary to repeat this several times to obtain a large piece that is free from mesophyll tissue. The strip should be observed under a microscope to check that only one layer of cells is present, at least in some areas, before proceeding with the experiment.

If you are asked to strip coloured epidermis *eg.* on rhubarb petioles, you should remove strips from the most densely coloured areas. Questions often require the use of coloured epidermis because the pigments are found only in the cytoplasm and consequently, changes due to osmosis are more clearly visible.

❏ Observations of osmotic changes

When you are asked to record the changes in epidermal cells caused by different solutions, you should include drawings of a typical group of not more than 6 cells. (see *Figs. 2.5, 2.6* and *2.7*). The whole strip should be scanned under the medium power of the microscope to observe the changes caused by the solution. *DO NOT* draw the first group of cells you see, they could be atypical.

If you are asked to observe the effect of a solution over a period of time, it may be necessary to make more than one drawing to illustrate all the changes. It may also be necessary to add more solution to the slide to prevent the tissue from dehydrating.

INITIAL APPEARANCE OF ONION EPIDERMAL CELLS MOUNTED IN WATER - TURGID CELLS   X 400

Fig. 2.5

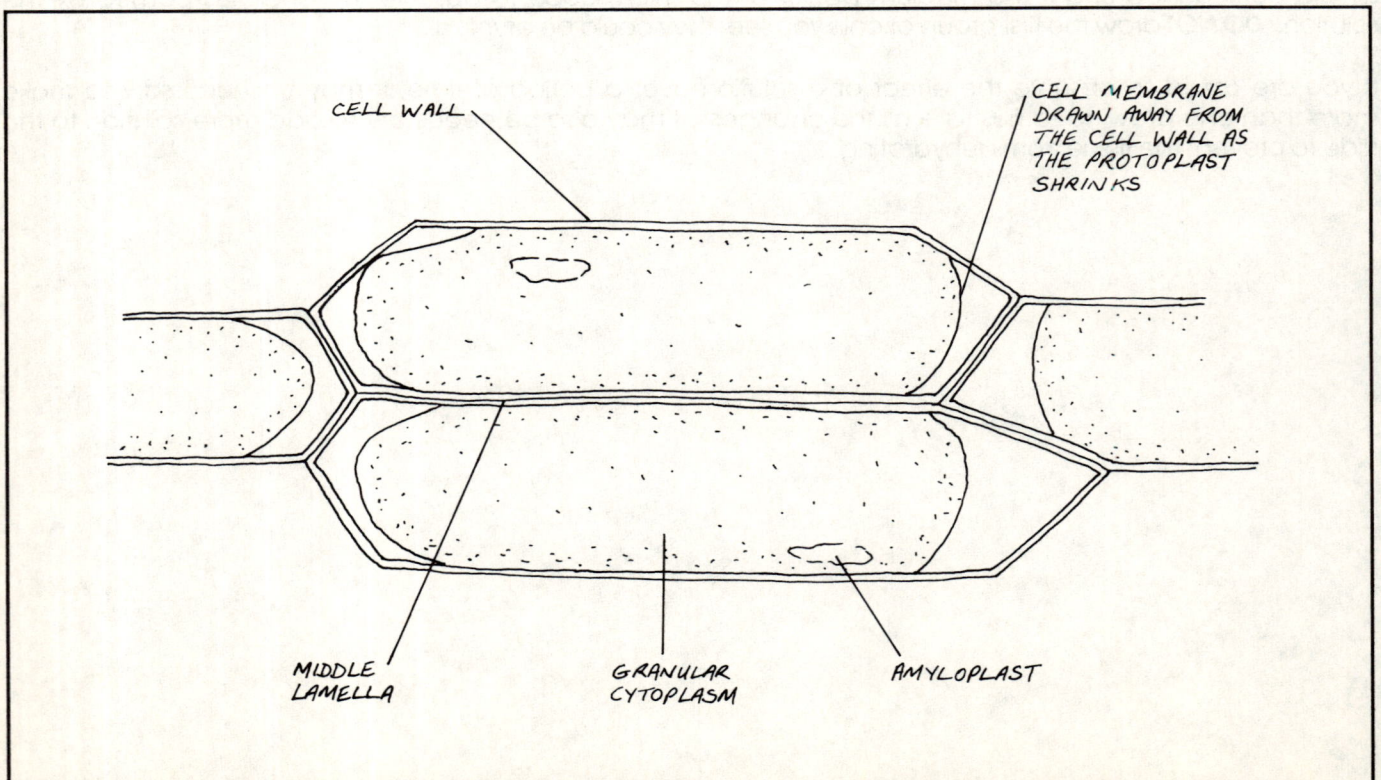

CELL WALL

CELL MEMBRANE PUSHED UP AGAINST THE CELL WALL

MIDDLE LAMELLA

GRANULAR CYTOPLASM

AMYLOPLAST -STARCH STORAGE

ONION EPIDERMAL CELLS AFTER IMMERSION IN A SOLUTION OF LOWER WATER POTENTIAL - INCIPIENT PLASMOLYSIS   X 400

Fig. 2.6

CELL WALL

CELL MEMBRANE DRAWN AWAY FROM THE CELL WALL AS THE PROTOPLAST SHRINKS

MIDDLE LAMELLA

GRANULAR CYTOPLASM

AMYLOPLAST

ONION EPIDERMAL CELLS AFTER IMMERSION IN A SOLUTION WITH A VERY LOW WATER POTENTIAL - CELLS SHOWING COMPLETE PLASMOLYSIS X 400 *Fig. 2.7*

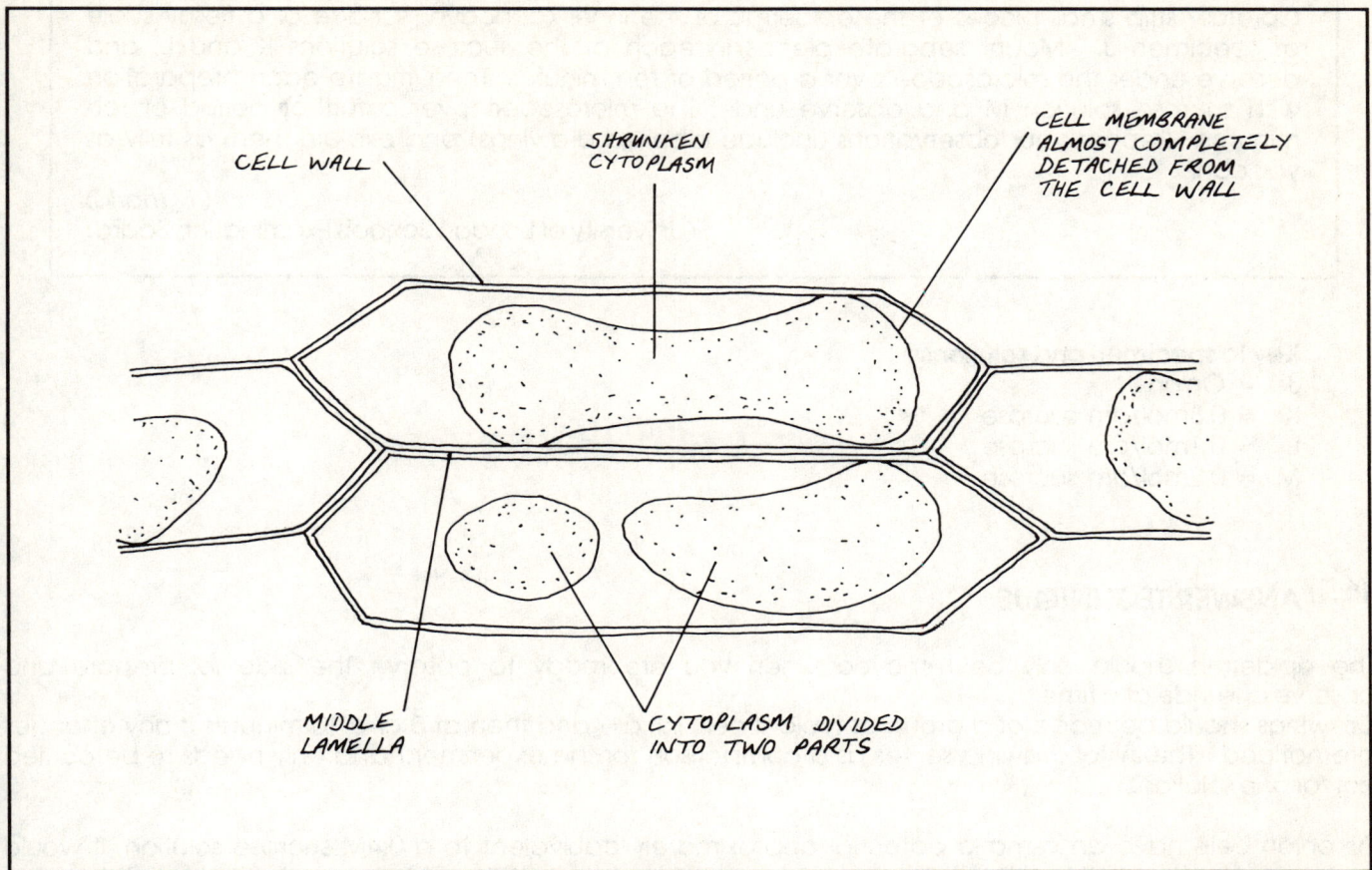

☐ **Slide assessment**

You may be asked to leave your epidermal slide preparation for assessment at the end of the examination. The examiners would be looking for the following qualities:

● A suitable sized portion of epidermis has been used.

● The strip has been well mounted with no air bubbles.

● The coverslip has been well positioned over the strip.

● The slide is clean and the stage of the microscope is free from liquid.

● If a stain has been used, the cytoplasm should be clearly distinguishable from the cell wall.

EXAM QUESTION 4

Carefully strip small pieces of the epidermis of the inner (concave) surface of a fleshy scale of specimen J. Mount separate pieces in each of the sucrose solutions K and L, and observe under the microscope over a period of ten minutes. Then irrigate each preparation with sucrose solution M and observe under the microscope over a further period of ten minutes. Record your observations (include labelled drawings) and explain them as fully as you can.

(17 marks)
(University of London Schools Examination Board)

Key to specimen and solutions:
J = Onion
K = 0.8mol/dm sucrose
L = 0.1mol/dm sucrose
M = 0.2mol/dm sucrose

ANSWER TECHNIQUE

The epidermis should only be removed when you are ready to observe the slide *ie.* prepare and observe one slide at a time.
Drawings should be made of a group of typical cells initially and then at 5 and 10 minutes if any changes are noticed. The initial drawing serves as a comparison for the experiment and only needs to be carried out for one solution.

As onion cells have an osmotic potential approximately equivalent to a 0.4M sucrose solution, it would be expected that solution K would cause plasmolysis because it has a lower water potential than the cells. Water is lost from the cells causing a reduction in the volume of the cytoplasm. Solution L should cause an increase in turgidity as it has a higher water potential than the cells.
Drawings should be large, clear and well labelled. (see *Figs. 2.5, 2.6* and *2.7*) Written explanations should include a theoretical discussion of osmosis and refer to the relative water potentials of the solutions.

To irrigate the epidermis with solution M, you could leave the coverslip in place and add drops of M at one side and draw them through with filter paper. This should be repeated several times to ensure a complete change of solution.

Solution M should cause return to turgidity of cells previously in K and slight plasmolysis of those in L, as it has a water potential which is higher than L but lower than K.

■ EXPERIMENTS INVOLVING CHANGES IN LENGTH OR MASS OF PLANT TISSUES

The principle of these experiments is that osmotic changes to individual cells will affect whole lengths of tissue. An increase in the turgidity of the cells will cause an increase in overall length (or mass) of the tissue, whereas plasmolysis will cause an overall decrease in length (or tissue mass). The changes will only be observed in living tissues; those which have been killed by boiling will not change in length as their membranes are no longer differentially permeable.

These experiments require you to cut "chips" of tissue from storage organs such as potato tubers and beetroot. There are several general precautions to observe when cutting the chips and placing them in the "unknown" solutions.

⚠ Precautions

❑   In order to cut equally sized chips, you should first cut a slice of the required length and thickness. This slice can then be further cut into chips of the required width.
❑   The chips should be carefully measured and the lengths (or masses) recorded in a table.
❑   Ideally, three chips should be placed in each solution to obtain an average change in length (or mass).
❑   The skin should be removed from the chips, as this is impermeable and would prevent gain or loss of water.
❑   The chips should be handled as little as possible, as bruising and grease from the fingers will affect the permeability of the tissues and hence the results.
❑   The chips should be immersed as soon as possible after cutting to prevent dehydration.
❑   The chips should be totally immersed in the solution to ensure that all cells are equally affected.
❑   The dishes containing the chips and solutions should be covered to prevent evaporation which would affect the concentration of the solution.
❑   At the end of the experiment, or before transferring the chips to a second solution, you should measure the chips and again record the results in a table. Changes in length (or mass) should be calculated.
❑   If the chips are to be transferred into a second solution they should be blotted thoroughly before the transfer to remove the original solution.
❑   As well as measuring the lengths (or masses) of the chips, you should note their texture and degree of rigidity.

The questions either ask you to measure changes in length or ask you to investigate changes in turgidity.

EXAM QUESTION 5

a)   Use the apparatus provided, as illustrated in the diagram, to measure the effects of solutions C, D and E on the turgidity of strips of tissue cut from the potato tuber supplied. Solutions D and E are equi-molar.

Cut three strips of tissue approximately 30 x 5 x 5mm (the exact size is not critical, provided the strips are identical). Immerse one strip in solution C, one strip in solution D and the other in solution E for 20 minutes, then remove each strip and blot gently to remove the surface liquid. Insert a pin in the end of the strips as indicated in the diagram, using the locatng pin to position the strip. Record the position of the pin at the end of the strip against the graph paper. Record your results and pin the graph paper to your script.

(2 marks)

(During the period of immersion of the strips, you are advised to go on to the second part of the question.)

b)   Carefully peel off a small strip of the coloured epidermis, free from **the underlying tissue**, from the rhubarb petiole provided and mount a small piece in solution C on a slide. Leave for about 10 minutes and then observe the cells carefully under the microscope.

Mount a similar piece of epidermis in solution D. Leave for about 10 minutes and then make a **labelled** drawing of FOUR adjoining cells as seen under high power. **Annotate** your drawing to comment on the differences between cells immersed in solution C and those in solution D.

(7 marks)

c)   Leave your preparation of cells in solution D under the low power of the microscope at the end of the examination.

(3 marks)

d)   (i) Give a full account of your experiments in parts a) and b), stressing any precautions taken to obtain accurate results.
      (ii) Comment on and give a full explanation of your results. For solutions C and D, relate your observations in Experiment a) to those observed in Experiment b).

(10 marks)
Total 22 marks
(Oxford and Cambridge Schools Examination Board)

Key to solutions:
C = Tap water
D = 0.8M sucrose
E = 0.8M calcium nitrate

See *Fig. 2.8* for a diagram of the apparatus provided.

DIAGRAM OF APPARATUS PROVIDED FOR EXAM QUESTION 5

Fig. 2.8

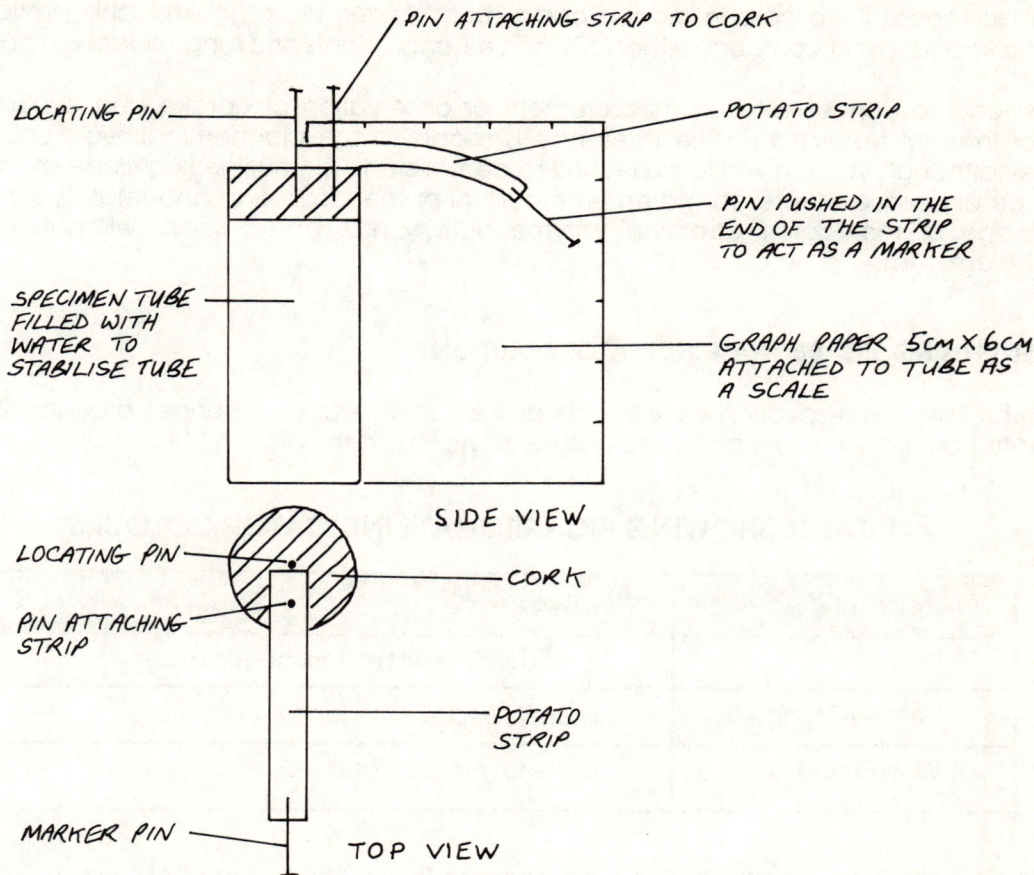

PIN ATTACHING STRIP TO CORK

LOCATING PIN

POTATO STRIP

PIN PUSHED IN THE END OF THE STRIP TO ACT AS A MARKER

SPECIMEN TUBE FILLED WITH WATER TO STABILISE TUBE

GRAPH PAPER 5CM X 6CM ATTACHED TO TUBE AS A SCALE

SIDE VIEW

LOCATING PIN

CORK

PIN ATTACHING STRIP

POTATO STRIP

MARKER PIN

TOP VIEW

✍ ANSWER TECHNIQUE

For our discussions we shall be concentrating on the behaviour of the potato tuber strips.

b) Here the drawings should be made similar to those given in the previous question (see *Figs. 2.5, 2.6* and *2.7*) and annotations should explain the changes in terms of relative water potentials.

d) (i) The method for part a) is clearly set out in the instructions, therefore you should concentrate on giving precautions not mentioned in the question. These should include the following:

The handling precautions mentioned at the beginning of this section.
The pin should be inserted to the same extent in each strip to exert a constant downward force on the strips.
The graph paper should be vertical to ensure accurate marking.

d) (ii) The results of part a) should show that solution C caused the strip to be approximately horizontal whereas D and E both caused drooping, with E having a greater effect. As the question states that these two are equi-molar, your explanation should suggest that E is ionic whilst D is not and therefore E has a lower water potential (see osmotic potential definition). All the changes in the strips should be explained in terms of osmosis and water potentials. You should also mention that turgidity is an important force in support of unlignified tissues as found in tubers and that loss of water causes the cells to become flaccid and hence the tuber strip droops.

RESPIRATION EXPERIMENTS

Respiration is the process by which all living organisms convert energy in food materials into energy, in the form of ATP, for metabolic activities. Organisms either respire aerobically (in the presence of O_2) or anaerobically (in the absence of O_2). When aerobic organisms respire, they use oxygen to completely oxidise organic foodstuffs to carbon dioxide and water. Anaerobic organisms only partially break down the organic compounds and produce either CO_2 and ethanol (plants and fungi) or lactic acid (animals).

Experiments tend to concentrate on measurement or observation of uptake and evolution of gases as indicators of internal respiration. Little reference is made to the biochemical reactions occurring at a cellular level, although you would be expected to demonstrate an outline knowlege of the process. You would also be expected to refer to the enzyme control of the respiration and relate your observations to your knowledge of the factors affecting enzyme activity; *eg.* boiled seeds will not respire as boiling denatures the enzymes.

■ EXPERIMENTS USING BICARBONATE INDICATOR SOLUTION

This is frequently used in respiration experiments as it is sensitive to pH changes brought about by varying CO_2 concentration. CO_2 in solution is acidic and therefore lowers the pH.

TABLE SHOWING BICARBONATE INDICATOR COLOURS

COLOUR	INFERENCE
Red	in equilibrium with atmospheric gases
Yellow/Orange	more CO_2 present than O_2
Blue/Purple	more O_2 present than CO_2

In the practical exam you are usually given a demonstration of the range of colours together with their pH values. If this is not given you can blow into a small sample of the indicator to see the colour change caused by addition of CO_2.

Varying rates of metabolic activity can be detected with bicarbonate indicator. The rate of change of indicator colour is proportional to the activity of the organisms. Seeds are often used for this type of experiment. Obviously germinating seeds with emerged radicles have the greatest activity and hence cause the most rapid colour change from red to yellow. Seeds that have just been soaked will have a lower activity whilst boiled seeds will show no activity at all.

The indicator can also be used to detect the balance between the respiratory and photosynthetic activity or organisms. Green plants will photosynthesise as well as respire in the light but the rate of photosythesis will exceed that of respiration. Under these conditions red bicarbonate indicator would become blue/purple. Animals, and green plants in the dark, will only respire and produce CO_2. In these conditions red indicator would become yellow/orange.

⚠ Precautions

- ❑ The same number or mass of organisms should be used in comparative experiments. This is because more organisms will produce more CO_2.
- ❑ The same volume of indicator should be used in each tube.
- ❑ The tubes should be stoppered to prevent gain or loss of gases.
- ❑ The tubes should be placed in a water bath. This maintains a constant temperature as this affects the enzyme reactions of respiration.
- ❑ A control tube containing indicator solution but no organisms, should be set up as a reference point.
- ❑ All reactions should be timed, as you are often asked to present your results in terms of rates of reaction.

EXAM QUESTION 6

You are provided with bicarbonate indicator J which is extremely sensitive to changes in carbon dioxide concentration. The indicator has had fresh air bubbled through it so that it is in equilibrium with the normal atmosphere.

CAUTION: Do not breathe near the indicator when its container is open and keep it well stoppered when not is use. Immediately before use the experimental test tubes should be rinsed out with a little of the indicator solution.

a)   Use the bicarbonate indicator J and the apparatus provided to investigate the respiratory activity of the samples of seeds K, L and M.
NOTE: Not all of the apparatus and living material supplied need necessarily be used in your experiment.

b)   Describe your method.

c)   Record your results.

d)   Comment critically on the significance of your results.

(Total 25 marks)
(University of London Schools Examination Board)

The examiners are aware that the results from this type of experiment are not completely predictable and will not put undue emphasis on the achievement of "correct" or "expected" results. Credit will be given for the way in which the experiment has been conducted.

Key to specimens:
K = germinating pea seeds.
L = germinating pea seeds, killed by boiling
M = pea seeds soaked for 24 hours only.

ANSWER TECHNIQUE

Method

Before designing the experiment you should work out the principles involved; germinating seeds will be respiring and therefore you should expect them to give out CO_2. Your experiment should seek to demonstrate this principle.

Precise details of the method used should be given, including the number of seeds used in each tube and the volumes of indicator used.

Observations should be made at regular intervals so that an accurate reaction time can be noted.

Results

These should be tabulated.
The colour of the solutions in each tube should be accurately recorded by comparing with the control.

Comments

The results should indicate that seeds K are respiring fastest and therefore produce the quickest colour change. Seeds M should also produce a colour change but to a lesser degree and at a slower rate but L should not produce any change.
Comments should refer to the reasons for these differences.

As you are asked to comment *critically* on the significance of the results, your comments should include criticism of the experimental technique,
eg. the colour changes recorded are subjective and may be localised around the seeds.

91

■ RESPIROMETERS

The exam boards do not usually require you to use a respirometer in the practical exam but you are expected to know how to set up and use the apparatus. Questions on this may appear on either the theory or practical papers.

DIAGRAM OF A SIMPLE RESPIROMETER

Fig. 2.9

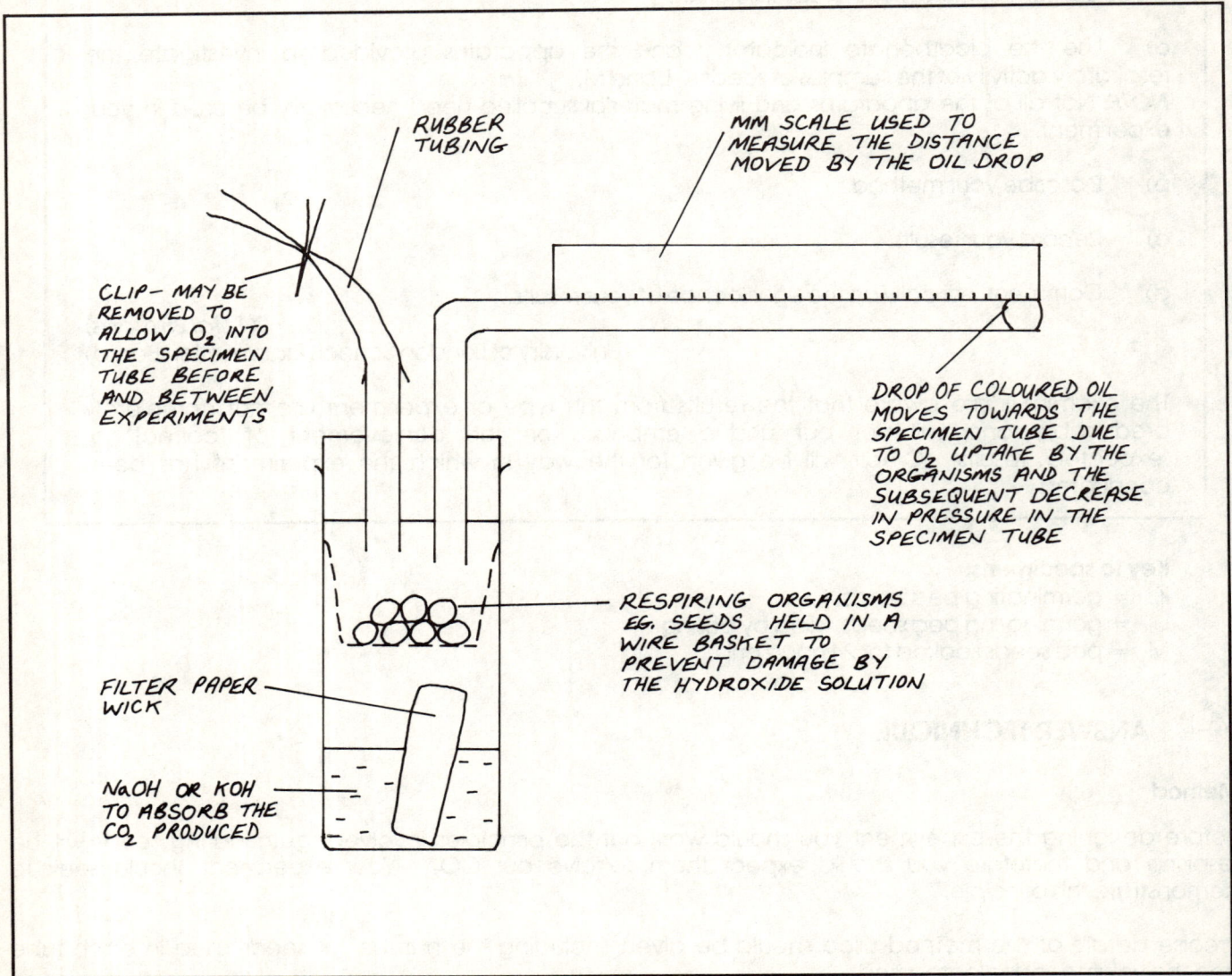

RUBBER TUBING

MM SCALE USED TO MEASURE THE DISTANCE MOVED BY THE OIL DROP

CLIP – MAY BE REMOVED TO ALLOW O₂ INTO THE SPECIMEN TUBE BEFORE AND BETWEEN EXPERIMENTS

DROP OF COLOURED OIL MOVES TOWARDS THE SPECIMEN TUBE DUE TO O₂ UPTAKE BY THE ORGANISMS AND THE SUBSEQUENT DECREASE IN PRESSURE IN THE SPECIMEN TUBE

RESPIRING ORGANISMS EG. SEEDS HELD IN A WIRE BASKET TO PREVENT DAMAGE BY THE HYDROXIDE SOLUTION

FILTER PAPER WICK

NaOH OR KOH TO ABSORB THE CO₂ PRODUCED

❑ Sources of error

1. The bung and clip may not be completely airtight
2. The NaOH/KOH may not absorb all of the CO_2 produced
3. The organisms may have varying rates of activity
4. The capillary tube with the scale may not be absolutely horizontal

■ EXPERIMENTS BASED ON DIRECT OBSERVATION OF VENTILATION MOVEMENTS OF LOCUSTS

The questions give details of how to perform the experiment, therefore marks are awarded for accurate observation and interpretation.

The ventilation mechanism of a locust consists of dorso-ventral squeezing movements of the abdomen. Air is drawn into a tracheal system via spiracles which are pores in the exoskeleton. In the locust, there are muscles controlling the opening and closing of the spiracular valves. The locust is able to control the direction of flow of the respiratory gases. Fresh supplies of air enter via the anterior spriacles and used air exits via the posterior spriacles. The insect does not have to rely on the pumping motions to supply air; some air will simply diffuse into the system.

The rate of the ventilation movements will be affected by changes in CO_2 concentration, temperature and activity of the insect. Increased temperature increases the metabolic rate and therefore the volume of oxygen required for respiration. Increased CO_2 concentration is detected by specific receptors in the "brain" which then causes increased ventilation to expel the CO_2. The oxygen demand of the insect will also be determined by its rate of activity.

⚠ Precautions

❑ Time the ventilation movements to enable you to make comparisons about the rates of respiration in different conditions.
❑ The opening and closing of the spiracles can be observed using a hand lens.
❑ Ventilation movements may not be regular, you should time the intervals between contractions.

EXAM QUESTION 7

You are required to investigate some aspects of ventilation in the locust, using the apparatus shown in *Fig. 1*. Before starting your investigation you are advised to read through all the instructions for the experiment. Construct a Table in the space provided, in which to record your results.

(a) Careful examination of the locust will reveal pumping movements of the abdomen. These are ventilation movements. Occasionally the locust may appear to stop ventilating for brief periods. This is normal. If this occurs during your experiment, wait for the ventilation movements to resume before continuing. Investigate the movements as follows.

   (i) Using the beaker provided, set up a water-bath at 25°C. Place the tube containing the locust in the water-bath as shown in Fig. 1. The water-bath should be maintained at 25°C throughout the experiment. The water level should reach the bung of the tube. Allow 5 minutes for the locust to adjust to the temperature, then count and record in your Table the number of pumping movements (ventilations) in one minute.

   (ii) Count and record in your Table two more readings over one minute periods.

   (iii) Calculate the average of the three results and record it in your Table.

   (iv) With the apparatus still in the water-bath at 25°C, blow gently and steadily through one of the glass tubes for about 15 seconds in order to replace the air in the specimen tube with expired air from your lungs. Remove your mouth from the tube, breathe in, and again blow for about 15 seconds through the apparatus. Repeat once more.

Question continued overleaf

(v)   Plug both glass tubes with a little moist cotton wool to reduce diffusion of gases between the air inside and outside the apparatus, ensuring that the cotton wool can be removed easily later. Allow 2 minutes for the locust to adjust to the new conditions. Then count, and record in your Table, the number of pumping movements over 3 separate, one minute periods, as before. Determine the average number of ventilations per minute and record it in your Table.

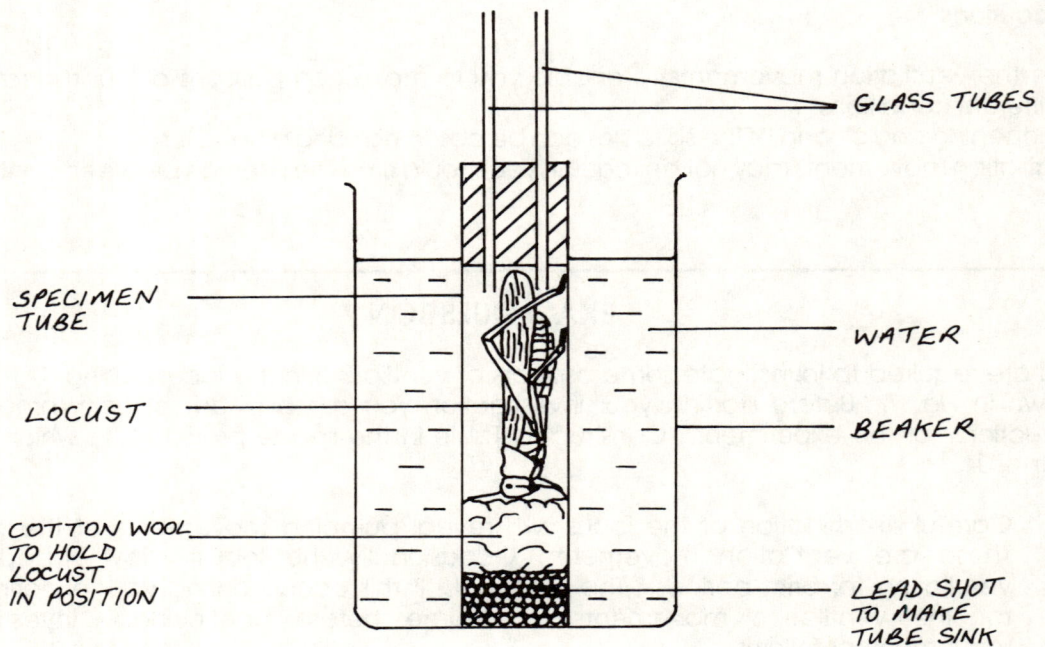

(vi)   Remove the cotton wool plugs from the glass tubes. You are provided with a syringe with a flexible tube attached. Connect the syringe by means of this tube to one of the glass tubes of the apparatus and flush out the expired air by pumping the syringe slowly 5 times. Detach the syringe and flexible tube from the apparatus and allow the locust 3 minutes to adjust to the new conditions. Then count, and record in your Table, the number of pumping movements over 3 separate, one minute periods, as before. Determine the average number of ventilations per minute and record it in your Table.

Fig. 1

(b) (i)   What difference did you observe in the average ventilation rate when normal atmospheric air was replaced by expired air?

    (ii)   What difference did you observe in the average ventilation rate when expired air was replaced by normal atmospheric air?

    (iii)   Calculate the percentage change in ventilation rate when normal atmospheric air was replaced by expired air. Show your calculations.

    (iv)   Suggest 3 factors which could have been responsible for bringing about the observed change on transfer to expired air.

    (v)   Suggest the mechanism by which **one** of these factors might have its effect.

(60 minutes)

(20 Marks)

(University of Cambridge Local Examinations Syndicate)

✍ ANSWER TECHNIQUE

Section (a) **Table of Results**

Conditions	Ventilations per minute			
	Count 1	Count 2	Count 3	Average
25°C Atmospheric air	A	B	C	$\frac{A+B+C}{3} = X$
25°C Exhaled air plugs in glass tube	D	E	F	$\frac{D+E+F}{3} = Y$
25°C Exhaled air flushed out and replaced with atmospheric air	G	H	I	$\frac{G+H+I}{3} = Z$

Section (b) (i) Calculate the change in rate by Y - X *ie.* a positive change. The ventilation rate should have increased.

(ii) Calculate the change in rate by Z - Y *ie.* a negative change. The ventilation rate should have decreased.

(iii) Change in rate = Y - X   % change = $\frac{Y - X}{X} \times 100$

(iv) Increased concentration of CO_2, decreased concentration of O_2, increased temperature of expired air.

(v) Increased CO_2 concentration detected by respiratory centre in the brain which stimulates increased ventilation rates via the nervous system.
Increased temperature or decreased O_2, could also be detected by receptors in the brain and stimulate increased ventilation rates.

■ **EXPERIMENTS BASED ON OBSERVATION OF** *DAPHNIA* **HEART BEAT**

These experiments are included in this section as the heart beat rate of *Daphnia* is influenced by its respiratory activity. This is controlled by enzymes, therefore changes in temperature and pH, and the presence of inhibitors, will all affect the heart rate.

You may be asked to investigate the effect of one of the following factors:

○ Temperature; using water baths or iced water

○ Chemicals which affect the metabolic rate *eg.* aspirin and alcohol solutions.

⚠ Precautions

Before beginning the experiment, you should be able to locate the heart of a *Daphnia*; this is a transparent, pulsating organ towards the rear of the animal just below the head region. (see *Fig. 2.10*)

❑ Select a large active specimen; this should make the heart easier to observe.
❑ Pipette the specimen onto the slide in a drop of water.
❑ Allow five minutes to elapse before counting the heart beats; this should allow the specimen to become adjusted to its new environment and hence have a more regular heart rate.
❑ Count the heart beat for 15 seconds and multiply by 4 to give the rate per minute. This allows more accurate counting as the rate is generally very rapid. You should repeat this several times so that an average rate can be recorded. When recording an average, do not forget to record all individual results as well.
❑ All counts should be carried out as quickly as possible as the heat from the microscope lamp could affect the results.
❑ If you are required to investigate the effect of further factors, you should use the same specimen. Transfer it to its new environment using a wide pipette and again allow a period of equilibration.

EXAM QUESTION 8

Investigate the effect of iced water on the activity of the specimen D. Observe the organism first in water at room temperature and then in the iced water provided. Record and discuss your methods and observations.

(25 marks)
(University of London Schools Examination Board)

Key:
D = *Daphnia* sp.
Apparatus: microscope, cavity slides, beaker, ice and dropping pipettes.

✍ ANSWER TECHNIQUE

With this type of experiment the examiners are testing your observational skills as well as your ability to design experiments. More marks will be awarded for the way in which you carry out the experiment than for "correct" results.

Method

Discussions of your method should include the precautions taken to ensure minimal experimental error as listed above.

Observations

The results should indicate a decrease in heart rate as the animal is exposed to iced water. Your discussion should make reference to the dependence of the metabolic rate on the external temperature. You should also relate this to enzyme activity.

DIAGRAM TO SHOW THE LOCATION OF THE HEART OF DAPHNIA *Fig. 2.10*

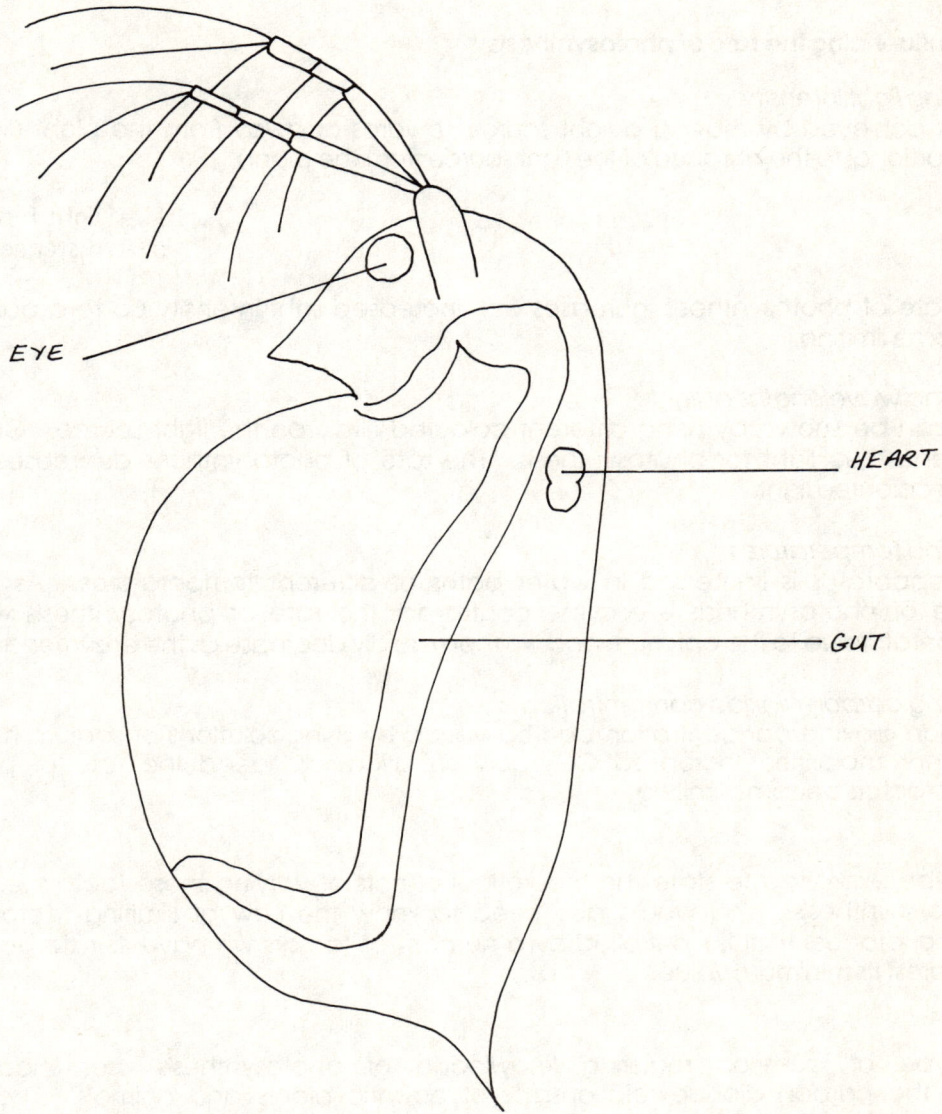

EYE

HEART

GUT

PHYSIOLOGICAL EXPERIMENTS

PHOTOSYNTHESIS EXPERIMENTS

All the exam boards require students to have familiarity with the operation of simple photosynthometers (bubblers). These are designed to measure the rate of photosynthesis of an aquatic plant under varying environmental conditions. The rate is calculated from measurement of the volume of oxygen evolved per unit time or by simply counting the number of bubbles produced per unit time. You would be expected to know how to set up the apparatus and use it to study the effect of a particular factor.

■ Factors influencing the rate of photosynthesis

○ *Varying light intensity*
This is achieved by moving a light source towards or away from the plant (light intensity is inversely proportional to the distance of the light source from the plant)

$$I = \frac{1}{d^2}$$

I = light intensity
d = distance of light source

The rate of photosynthesis increases with increased light intensity up to a point where other factors become limiting.

○ *Varying wavelengths of light*
This can be shown by using different coloured filters on the light source. Green plants use mainly red and blue light for photosynthesis. The rate of photosynthesis decreases if supplied solely with other coloured light.

○ *Varying temperatures*
The apparatus is immersed in water baths of different temperatures. As the light independent stage of photosynthesis is enzyme controlled, the rate of photosynthesis will increase with rising temperature up to the optimum and will then rapidly decrease as the enzymes are denatured.

○ *Varying carbon dioxide concentration*
Carbon dioxide concentration can be varied by using solutions of sodium hydrogen carbonate of different molarities. Increased CO_2 concentration will speed the rate of photosynthesis until the other factors become limiting.

You would be expected to state the theoretical effects of varying these factors *ie.* why each affects the rate of photosynthesis. You would also need to know the Law of Limiting factors. This states that any physiological process that is controlled by a number of factors will have its rate goverened by the factor which is nearest its minimum value.

Another type of question requiring knowledge of photosynthesis uses bicarbonate indicator to investigate the carbon dioxide relationships of aquatic plants and animals. The experiment is usually carried out in both the light and the dark and you would be expected to explain the results in terms of photosynthesis and respiration. In the light, photosynthesis exceeds respiration and the indicator will turn from red to purple as the concentration of CO_2 decreases. In the dark, photosynthesis does not occur and therefore the indicator changes from red to yellow as the concentration of CO_2 increases.

DIAGRAM OF A SIMPLE PHOTOSYNTHOMETER (BUBBLER)   *Fig. 2.11*

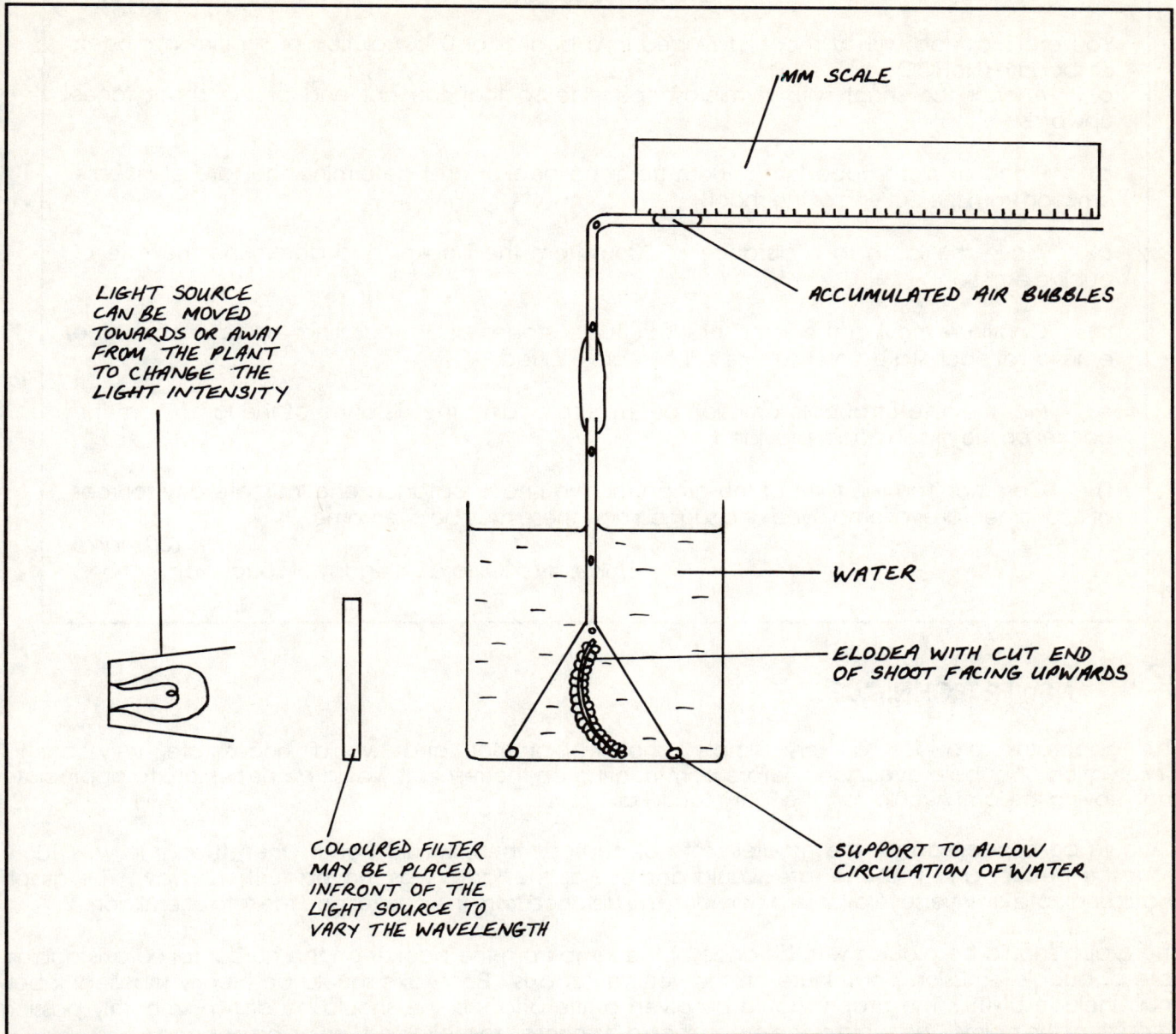

□ **Sources of error**

1.   Air bubbles may be trapped in the leaves, funnel or rubber tubing.
2.   The connections may not be air and water-tight.

EXAM QUESTION 9

You are provided with a shoot of *Elodea* in a beaker of 0.1% solution of sodium hydrogen carbonate ($NaHCO_3$).

a)   Anchor the shoot with a microscope slide so that the cut end of the shoot faces upwards.

b)   Place a microscope lamp 10cm from the beaker and determine the rate of bubble emission from the cut end of the shoot.

c)   Move the lamp to a distance of 20cm from the beaker and determine the rate of bubble emission.

d)   Continue moving the lamp back in 10cm stages and measuring the rate of bubble emission at each state, until no more bubbles are emitted.

e)   Plot the rate of bubble emission per minute against the distance of the lamp from the beaker on the graph paper provided.

f)   Comment on the form of the graph that you have obtaned and indicate any sources of experimental error employed and suggest how these may be overcome.

(30 marks)
(University of Oxford Delegacy of Local Examinations)

ANSWER TECHNIQUE

This apparatus provides a very simple photosynthometer and would necessitate very careful observation of bubble evolution. Before commenting on the results it would be necessary to appreciate that moving the lamp would vary the light intensity as $I = \frac{1}{d^2}$

It would be expected that the greatest rate of photosynthesis would occur when the lamp was 10cm from the beaker and that the rate would decrese as the lamp was moved further away. The graph should indicate an inverse relationship between the distance from the beaker and the rate of emission.

The graph should be plotted with distance of the lamp from the beaker on the horizontal (x) axis against rate of bubble emission per minute on the vertical (y) axis. Each axis should be clearly labelled; labels must include UNITS. The graph should be given a title and the line should be drawn smoothly passing through all the points. The scale of the graph should be chosen to make best use of the paper.
(see **Chapter 6** on drawing graphs)

❑ **Sources of experimental error**

The sources of error are as listed on *Fig. 2.11* with the addition of the following:

1.   The method of estimating the rate is inaccurate, as bubble size may not be uniform and the bubbles are difficult to count. It would be better to collect the oxygen and express the rate as volume of O_2 evolved per minute.
2.   The instructions do not suggest an acclimatisation period before making observations thus the plants may be photosynthesising at varying rates during the observation. Five or ten minutes should be allowed to elapse after moving the lamp.
3.   Only one observation at each distance is suggested but more accurate results would be obtained by making several counts and then taking an average.

BEHAVIOUR EXPERIMENTS

This section covers experiments involving the use of living invertebrates to investigate the effects of varying environmental conditions. The different conditions would be varying light intensity and humidity.

Questions may involve the use of a choice chamber. (see *Fig. 2.12*) This is a circular perspex box which is divided into four compartments. Conditions in each of these compartments can be varied and organisms can be introduced into the chamber via a central hole.

Light intensity can be varied by covering half of the chamber with black paper. Humidity can be changed by placing damp cotton wool in one side and calcium chloride granules or silica gel in the other. The cotton wool is used to prevent the water from spilling into the dehydrating agent.

The effect of each condition on behaviour can be observed by counting the number of organisms in each compartment at regular time intervals and noting any changes in the rate or direction of movement. Hence, the factors influencing their habitat preferences can be determined.

Woodlice are the most frequently used organisms for this type of experiment. Woodlice are found under rotting logs and in other dark and damp crevices; they are detritivores. They are terrestrial crustaceans without a waxy cuticle or any other physical means of conservation of water. They rely on behavioural methods to reduce water loss by evaporation.

Precautions

❑ Select similar sized specimens.
❑ Set up the chamber so that one side is influenced by one condition and the other by the opposite condition. *eg.* dark/light, wet/dry.
❑ Cover with the gauze before replacing the lid. This provides a platform for the organisms.
❑ Seal all the holes in the lid with sellotape and allow the chamber to equilibrate for five minutes before introducing the specimens.
❑ Place the specimens in the chamber via the central hole and reseal.
  This allows the specimens a free choice between the two sides.

EXAM QUESTION 10

Place ten of the specimens labelled X in the choice chamber provided and observe their behaviour relative to damp and dry conditions at five minute intervals over a total period of 30 minutes.

Make a report of, and attempt to explain, your observations.

(25 marks)
(University of London Schools Examination Board)

Key to specimen:
X = woodlice

Apparatus: choice chamber with nylon gauze, cotton wool, calcium chloride granules, sellotape and a spatula. (see *Fig. 2.12*)

DIAGRAM OF A CHOICE CHAMBER SET UP TO INVESTIGATE VARYING HUMIDITY   *Fig. 2.12*
SIDE VIEW

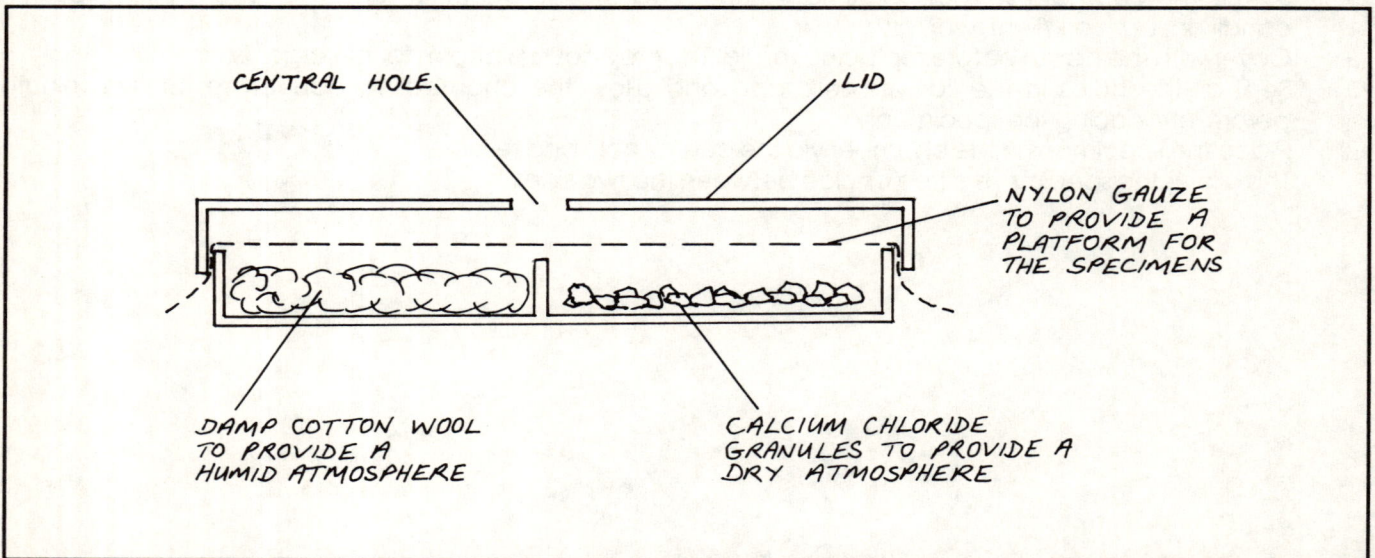

CENTRAL HOLE   LID

NYLON GAUZE TO PROVIDE A PLATFORM FOR THE SPECIMENS

DAMP COTTON WOOL TO PROVIDE A HUMID ATMOSPHERE

CALCIUM CHLORIDE GRANULES TO PROVIDE A DRY ATMOSPHERE

ANSWER TECHNIQUE

In this question you are not asked for an account of your method and, therefore, should not waste time writing this out as it will not gain marks.

Observations

You should make observations of the woodlice movements and behaviour as well as simply counting the numbers of specimens in each half of the chamber. These counts and observations should be presented in a table eg.

TIME MINS.	NOS. OF SPECIMENS WET	DRY	OBSERVATIONS
5	6	4	Woodlice moving rapidly around the edge of the chamber. Waving antennae. Movements seem random with many changes of direction.
10	8	2	Most woodlice moving more slowly. Some clumped together and stationary. Definite slowing over wet area, movement more rapid over dry area.

The table should be continued for the duration of the experiment.

Explanations

These should relate to your knowledge of the specimens' natural habitat.
Each of your observations should be referred to in turn eg.

The distribution of the specimens indicates a marked preference for damp conditions. This would reduce water loss to the atmosphere.
The initial rapid movements are an indication that the woodlice were exploring their new environment to seek out the most favourable areas.
The clumping of the specimens would also help to prevent water loss.
The antennae are used to detect changes in the atmospheric humidity.

WATER UPTAKE EXPERIMENTS

This type of question involves the use of a potometer which is designed to measure the rate of water uptake under varying environmental conditions. The rate of water uptake is directly proportional to the rate of water loss by transpiration and therefore the apparatus can **INDIRECTLY** demonstrate the effects of varying temperature, humidity and air currents on the rate of transpiration.

Questions involving potometers do not usually require their use in the exam; the potometer is provided as a demonstration apparatus but you would be expected to know how to set it up and to be aware of the precautions necessary to obtain accurate results.

DIAGRAM OF A SIMPLE POTOMETER   *Fig. 2.13*

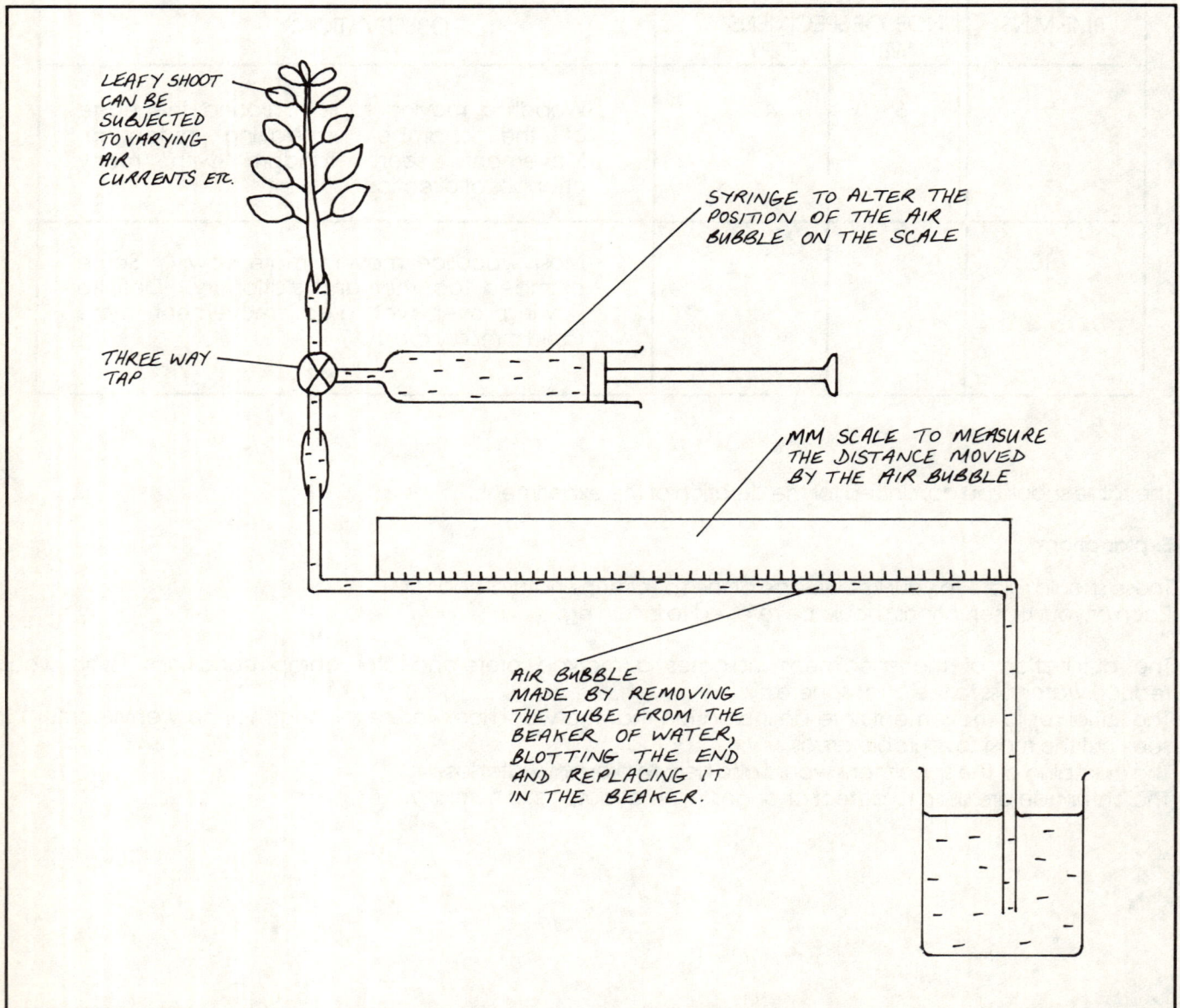

LEAFY SHOOT CAN BE SUBJECTED TO VARYING AIR CURRENTS ETC.

SYRINGE TO ALTER THE POSITION OF THE AIR BUBBLE ON THE SCALE

THREE WAY TAP

MM SCALE TO MEASURE THE DISTANCE MOVED BY THE AIR BUBBLE

AIR BUBBLE MADE BY REMOVING THE TUBE FROM THE BEAKER OF WATER, BLOTTING THE END AND REPLACING IT IN THE BEAKER.

■ SETTING UP AND USING A POTOMETER

1. The shoot should be cut and placed into the rubber tubing under water. This prevents air bubbles forming within the xylem, which would impede the transpiration stream.

2. The whole apparatus should be filled with water.

3. The joints should be sealed with petroleum jelly. This prevents air entering the apparatus.

4. The shoot should be left for ten minutes before any readings are taken. This is to allow it to adjust to the conditions and open its stomata again. These would close as the shoot was handled and cut. An adjustment period should be allowed each time the external conditions are changed.

5. Only one air bubble should be allowed to enter the capillary tube to avoid confusion when taking measurements. Any excess air bubbles could be pushed out using the syringe.

6. The air bubble should be returned to zero before each new reading. Ideally several readings should be taken in each experiment and an average calculated.

7. The rate of water uptake is measured by means of noting the distance moved by an air bubble over a specific time period. The volume of water taken up by the shoot can then be calculated using the following formula:

$$\pi r^2 d$$

where r = radius of the capillary tube in mm
and d = distance moved by the air bubble

Your answer should be expressed in terms of mm. of water taken up per unit time.

■ EXPERIMENTS TO DEMONSTRATE FACTORS INFLUENCING THE RATE OF TRANSPIRATION

○ *Humidity*
This can be varied by enclosing the shoot in a plastic bag and comparing the rate of uptake with that of an exposed shoot. An increase in humidity leads to a decrease in transpiration and hence uptake, because the water potential gradient between the interior of the leaf and the atmosphere is reduced.

○ *Air currents*
These can be created by the use of an electric fan positioned in front of the apparatus. Water uptake should be compared to a shoot in still air. Moving air currents increase the rate of transpiration because they remove the shells of humid air on the leaf surfaces thus creating a steeper water potential gradient.

Note. *Temperature* also affects the rate of transpiration but its effect cannot be measured using a potometer unless the whole apparatus could be placed in a thermostatically controlled chamber.

Light intensity is another factor influencing the rate of transpiration but again this is difficult to investigate as most light sources will also increase the temperature.

EXAM QUESTION 11

Examine the experiment E which has been set up as a demonstration.
a)   Explain carefully:
   i)   what the experiment is designed to measure;
   ii)   the precautions you would take in setting up and carrying out the experiment.

(12 marks)

b)   The following readings were obtained using a similar apparatus:

Time (minutes)	Scale reading (mm)
0	0.0
5	0.5
10	1.1
15	1.7
20	2.1
30	2.4

   i)   Draw a graph of the results.

(4 marks)

   ii)   Explain the results as fully as you can.

(6 marks)

   iii)   What would be the expected effect if a fan had been switched on after the second reading?

(3 marks)
(Total 25 marks)
(University of London Schools Examination Board)

Key:
E   = potometer

ANSWER TECHNIQUE

a) (i) and **(ii)** See the general instructions on page 105.

b) (i) See the graph on page 107.

(ii) When commenting on a graph you should make specific reference to the shape and slope of the graph. You should also calculate rates of change from the graph. It is not enough to make general, descriptive comments. (see **Chapter 6**)

(iii) You should suggest that the rate would be increased and then continue by explaining the effect of increased air movement on the rate of transpiration.

■ GRAPH TO SHOW RATE OF WATER UPTAKE OF A LEAFY SHOOT IN STILL AIR

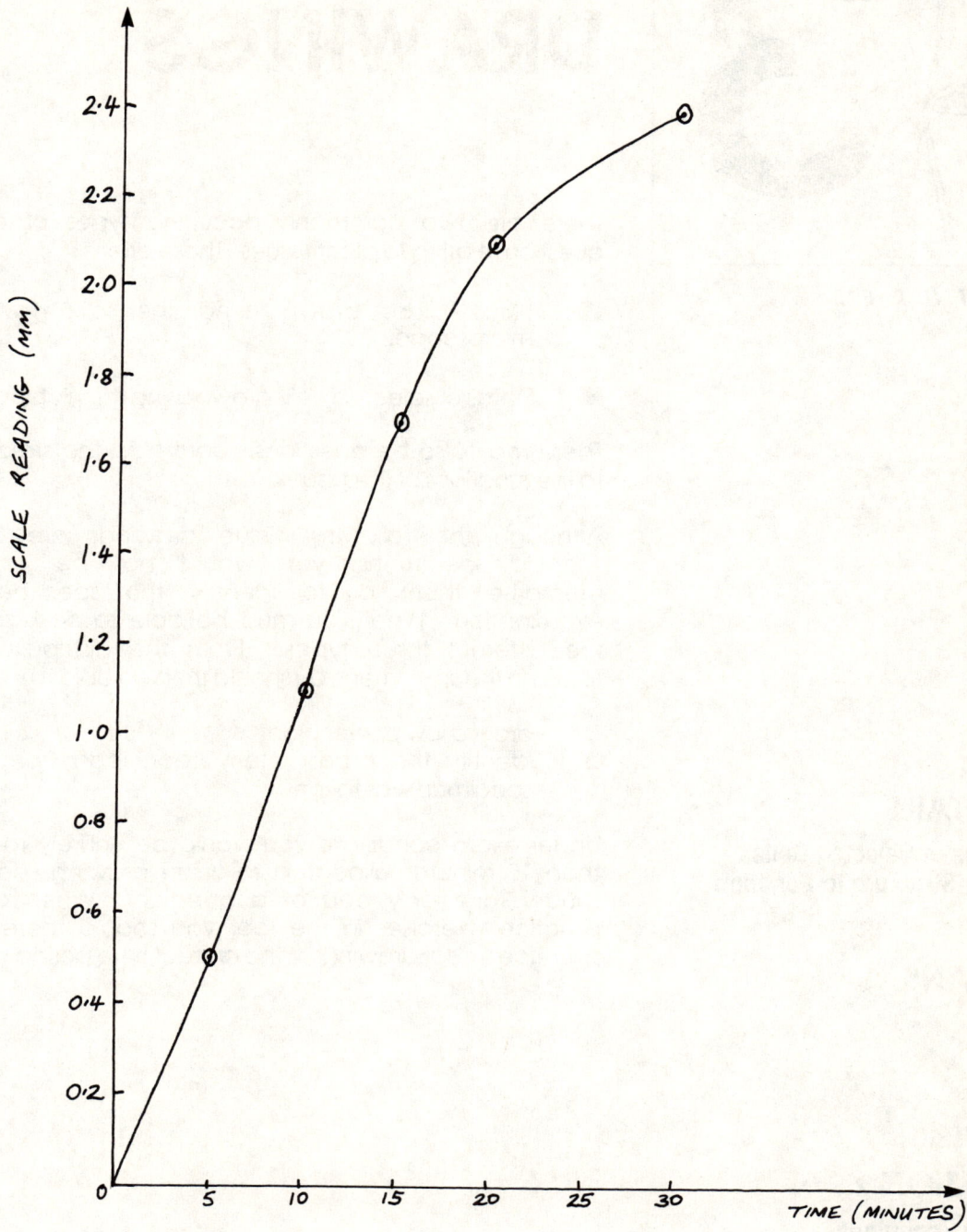

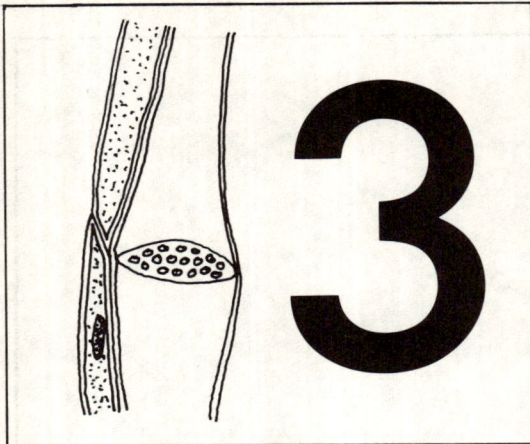

3

PLANT TISSUE DRAWINGS

There are two commonly occurring types of examination question relating to plant tissues. These are:

■ Tissue plans drawn using the low power of the microscope.

■ Detail of selected cells drawn using the high power.

There may also be questions about how the structure relates to the functions of the tissues.

Although the following tissue drawings are taken from specific specimens, you would not be expected to memorise them or to identify the specimen in your examination. What you must be able to do is to recognise the different tissue types. From the distribution of these tissues in the specimen you should then be able to

❏ draw a low power plan
❏ identify the organ (stem, root, leaf) from which the specimen was taken.

Under exam conditions you would be unlikely to have more than 15 minutes allocated to tissue drawings because they usually form only part of a question. When carrying out practice exercises in the lab. you should therefore aim to produce similar drawings in the correct time period.

TISSUE DETAILS

Drawings of Selected Cells
Relating Structure to Function

TISSUE PLANS

Stems
Roots
Leaves

PREPARATION

Staining Techniques
Preparing Temporary Mounts
Calculating Magnification

HINTS BOX ✔

DRAWING TIPS

- Select clear cells which are typical of the tissue type. Do **not** choose those which are broken or obviously distorted.
- Use a sharp H or HB pencil and a clean soft rubber.
- Draw not more than 6 cells. Aim to cover at least half a page.
- Leave space for labels and annotations where appropriate.
- Do not shade or use colour.
- Make all drawings, label lines and labels in pencil for ease of correction.
- Do not cross label lines.
- Give each drawing a title and magnification or scale.
- Each tissue type should be on a separate sheet.

The table below will help you to identify the tissues using their distribution and colour. The colours given are those most commonly occurring when using stains such as botanical triple stain.

TABLE SHOWING TISSUE TYPES AND LOCATIONS

TISSUE	LOCATIONS	USUAL COLOUR WHEN STAINED	FIGURE IN TEXT
Parenchyma	Centre of stem (pith) Periphery of stem (cortex) Cortex of root Surrounding main vein of leaf	Light green or blue	3.1
Chlorenchyma	Palisade and spongy mesophyll of leaf Outer cortex of some stems	Light green	3.2
Collenchyma	Outer cortex of stems Supporting vascular tissue in leaves	Green	3.3
Sclerenchyma	Around vascular bundles in stems Outer cortex of some stems Supporting vascular tissue in some leaves	Red	3.4
Xylem	Peripheral bundles in stem Central stele in root Veins in leaves	Red	3.5
Phloem	Peripheral bundles in stems Central stele in root Veins in leaves	Green or blue	3.6

DRAWINGS OF SELECTED CELLS

Pages 109 to 114 show each of the tissues listed in the previous Table. On each page you will find another Table which illustrates how the structure of each tissue relates to its function. Note that the drawings which follow show the detail of selected cells using the high power of the microscope.

PARENCHYMA FROM HELIANTHUS STEM:
TRANSVERSE SECTION (T.S)   X 600

Fig. 3.1

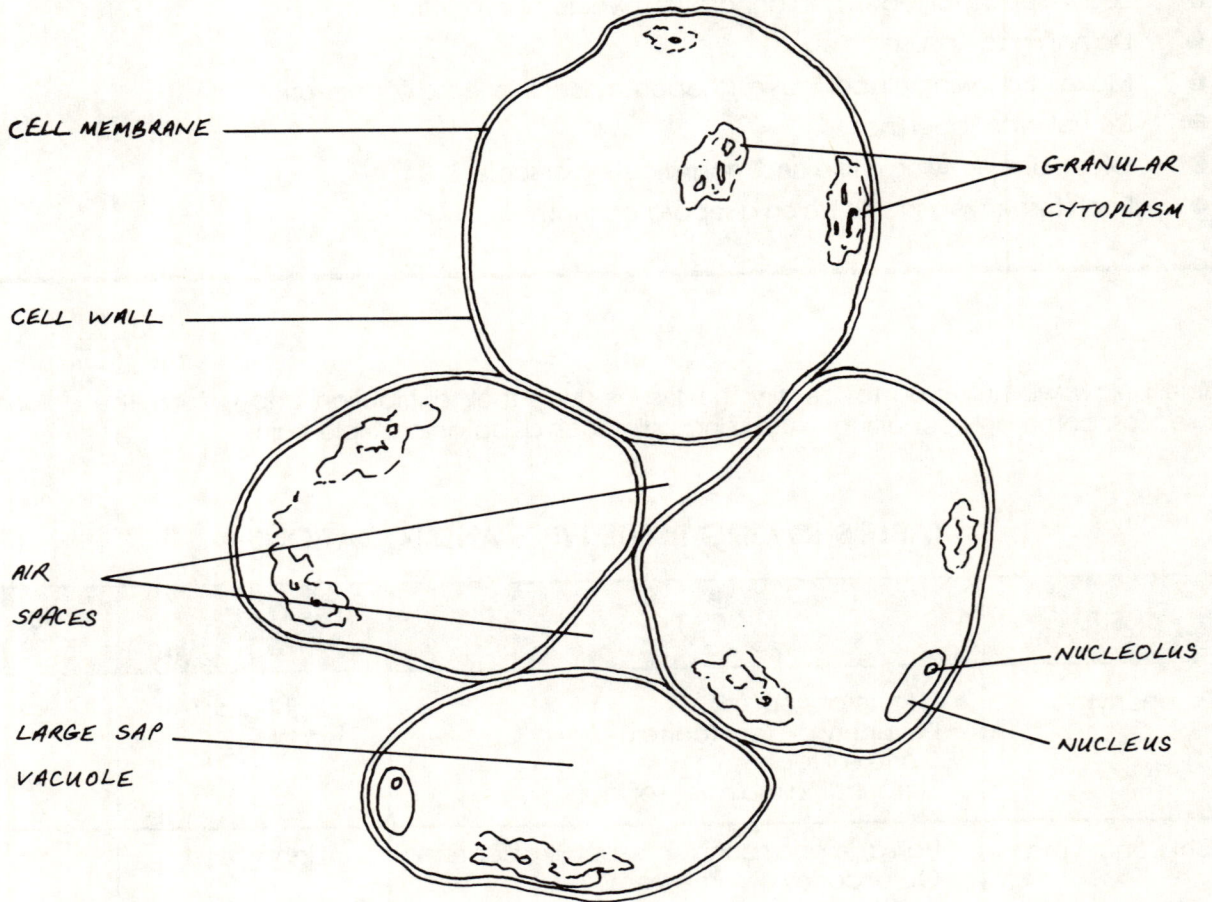

CELL MEMBRANE
CELL WALL
GRANULAR CYTOPLASM
AIR SPACES
NUCLEOLUS
NUCLEUS
LARGE SAP VACUOLE

TABLE SHOWING STRUCTURES RELATED TO FUNCTIONS

STRUCTURE	FUNCTION
Thin cellulose cell walls	Ease of diffusion of gases and dissolved solutes. Allows expansion of turgid cells.
Large sap vacuoles	Support via turgidity. Storage of minerals and some wastes.
Peripheral cytoplasm	Living contents for metabolic activity. May store starch grains (amyloplasts).
Air spaces	Exchange of respiratory gases.
Variable cell sizes	Packing for support

CHLORENCHYMA - PALISADE MESOPHYLL FROM LIGUSTRUM LEAF:
TRANSVERSE SECTION (T.S)   X 600

Fig. 3.2

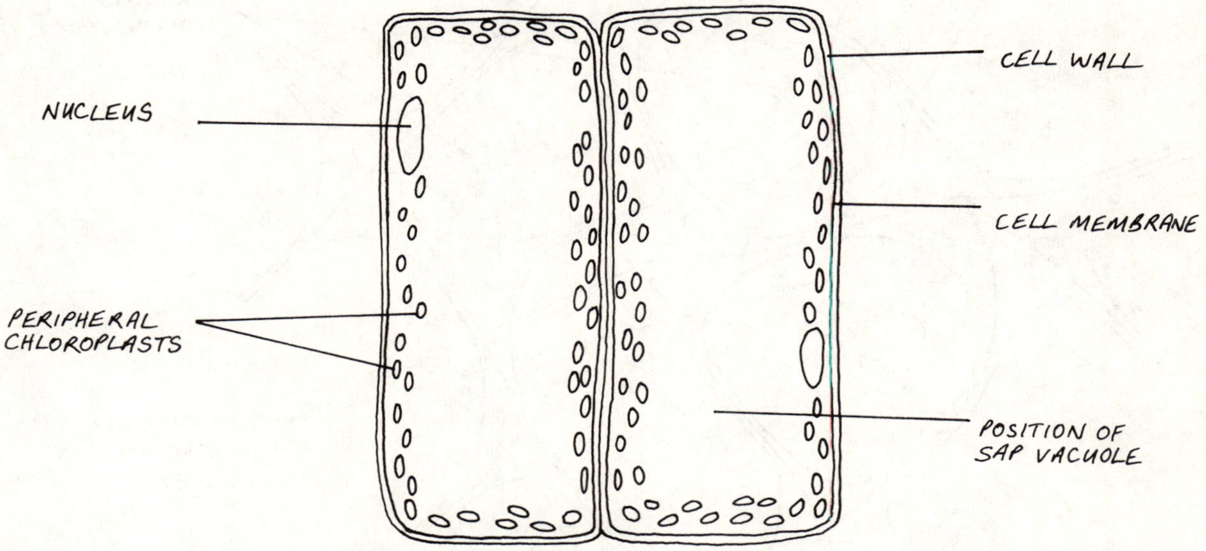

NUCLEUS

CELL WALL

CELL MEMBRANE

PERIPHERAL
CHLOROPLASTS

POSITION OF
SAP VACUOLE

TABLE SHOWING STRUCTURES RELATED TO FUNCTIONS

STRUCTURE	FUNCTION
Large surface area	Maximum absorption of light, CO_2 and H_2O
Peripheral chloroplasts	Sites of photosynthesis
Thin cellulose cell walls	Ease of diffusion of gases and dissolved solutes. Allow passage of light to chloroplasts.
Large sap vacuoles	Support via turgidity. Storage of minerals and some wastes.

COLLENCHYMA FROM LAMIUM STEM:
TRANSVERSE SECTION (T.S)   X 600

MIDDLE LAMELLAE

GRANULAR CYTOPLASM

EXTRA CELLULOSE THICKENING IN CORNERS

NUCLEUS

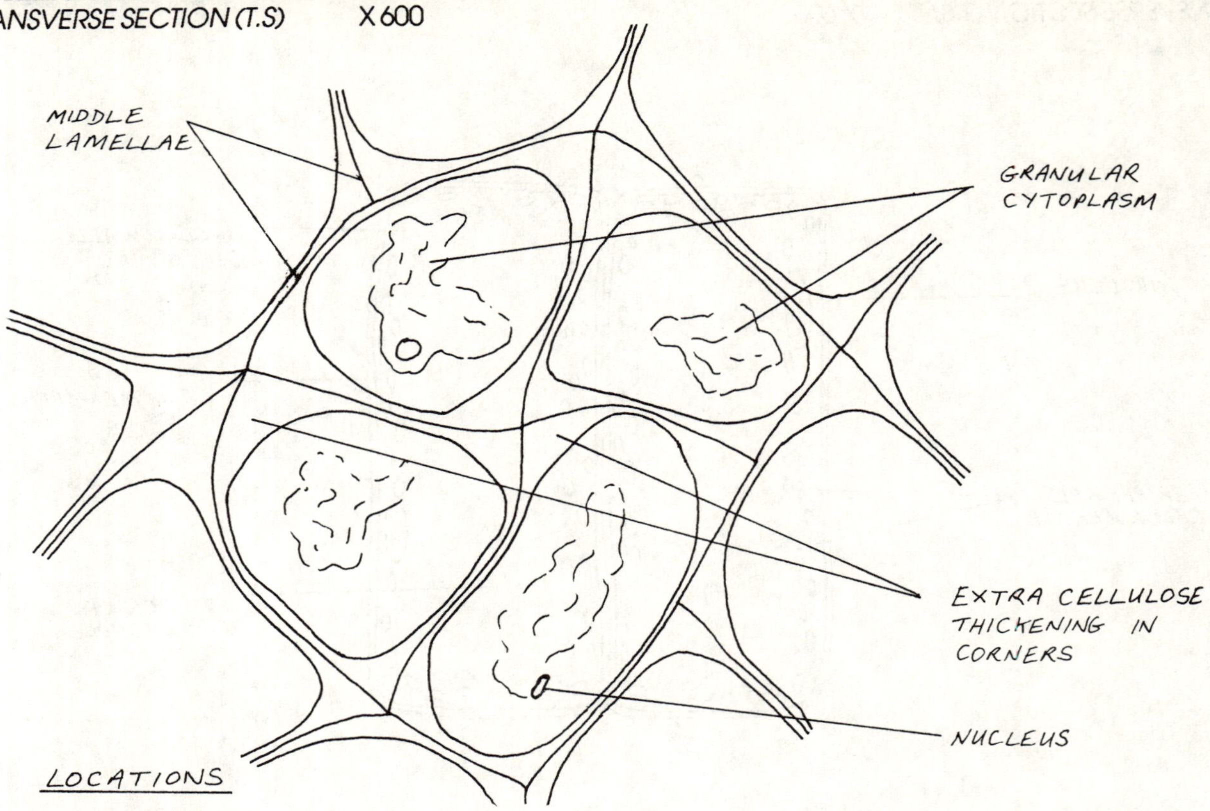

LOCATIONS

STEMS :- OUTER CORTEX, ESPECIALLY STEM CORNERS IN LAMIUM.

LEAVES :- ABOVE + BELOW MIDRIB

STRUCTURES RELATED TO FUNCTIONS

STRUCTURE	FUNCTION
Angular thickening of cellulose	Mechanical support
Sap vacuole	Support via turgidity
Cellulose cell walls	Allow extension of cells during growth

SCLERENCHYMA FIBRES FROM HELIANTHUS STEM:
TRANSVERSE SECTION (T.S)   X 600

Fig. 3.4

LIGNIFIED SECONDARY WALL

HOLLOW LUMEN

PIT

PRIMARY CELLULOSE CELL WALL

MIDDLE LAMELLA

LONGITUDINAL SECTION (L.S.)   X 600

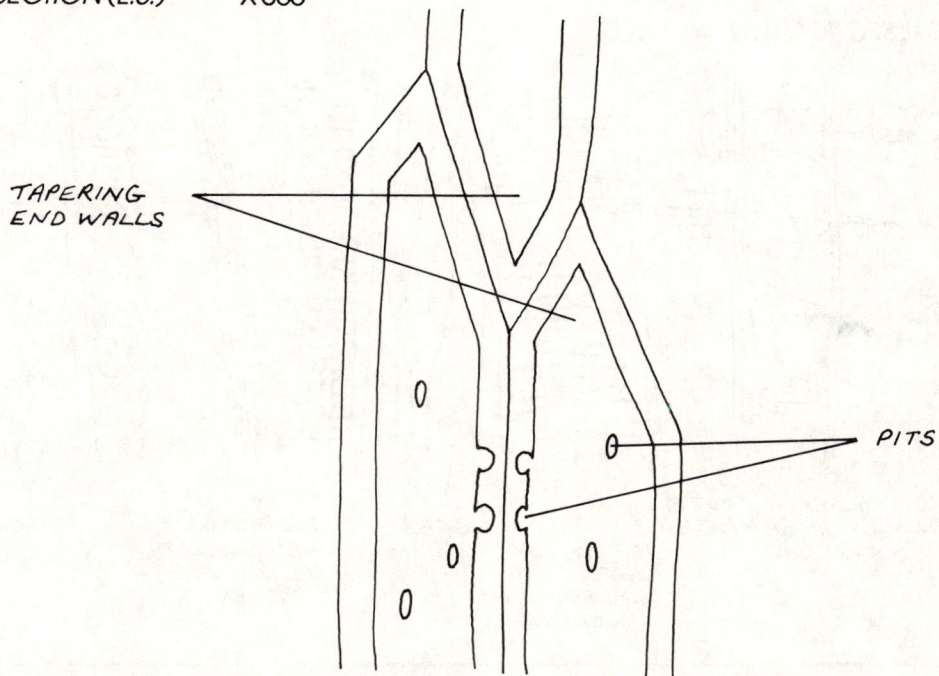

TAPERING END WALLS

PITS

STRUCTURES RELATED TO FUNCTIONS

STRUCTURE	FUNCTION
Lignified with secondary cell wall	Mechanical support
Pits	Lateral transport between cells
Interdigitating, tapering end walls	Extra support and resistance to bending stresses

113

XYLEM
Composite tissue consisting of vessels, fibres, tracheids and parenchyma.

XYLEM FROM HELIANTHUS STEM:
TRANSVERSE SECTION (T.S)   X 600   Fig. 3.5

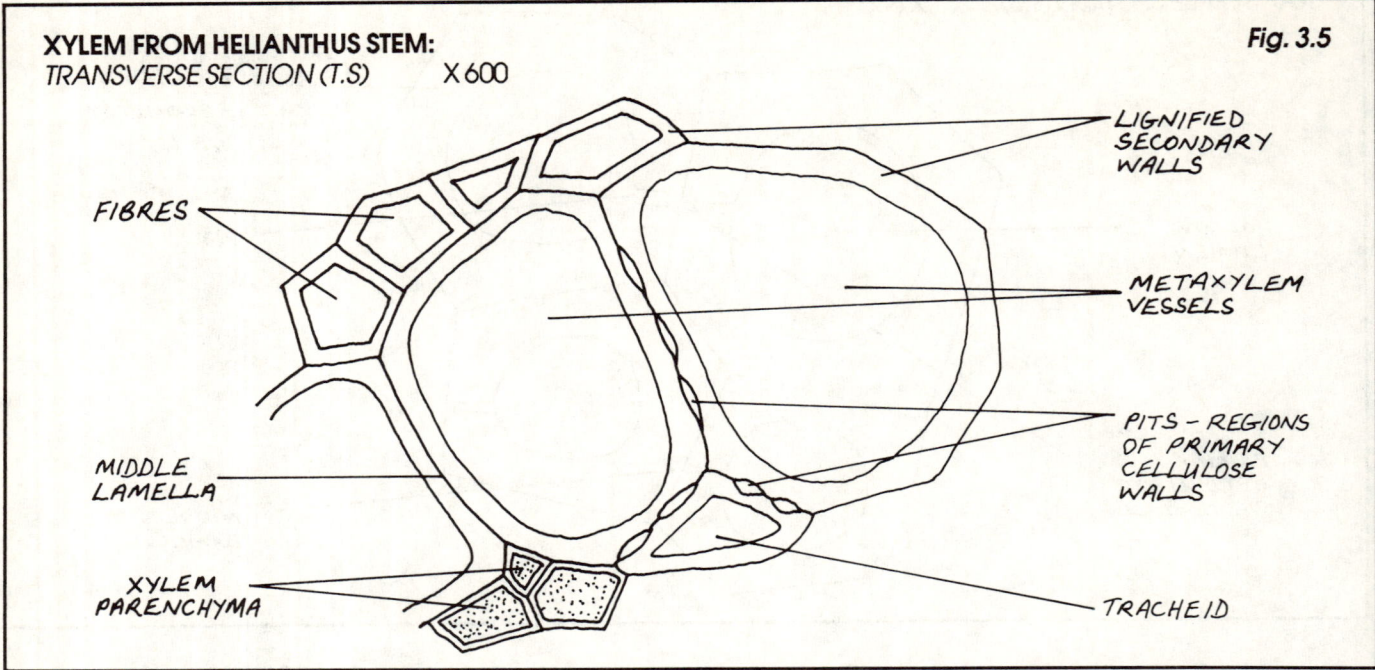

Labels: FIBRES, LIGNIFIED SECONDARY WALLS, METAXYLEM VESSELS, PITS – REGIONS OF PRIMARY CELLULOSE WALLS, MIDDLE LAMELLA, XYLEM PARENCHYMA, TRACHEID

LONGITUDINAL SECTION (L.S)   X 600

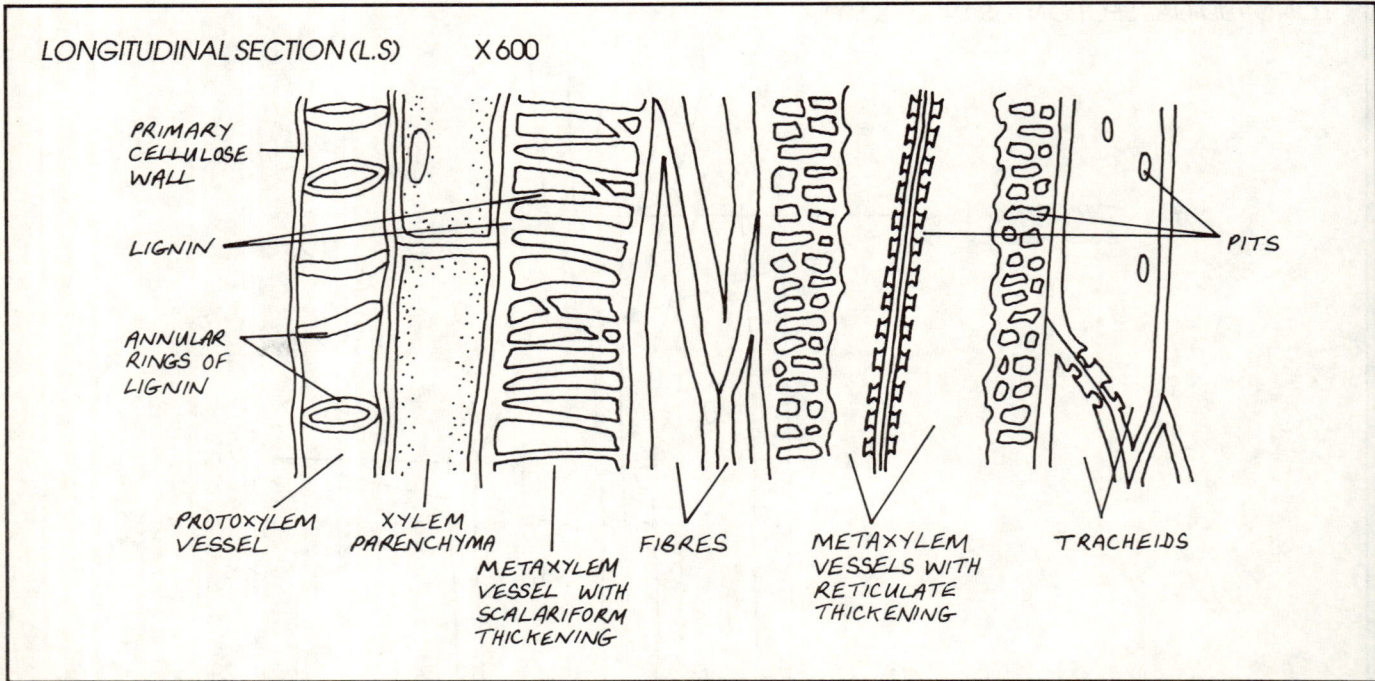

Labels: PRIMARY CELLULOSE WALL, LIGNIN, ANNULAR RINGS OF LIGNIN, PROTOXYLEM VESSEL, XYLEM PARENCHYMA, METAXYLEM VESSEL WITH SCALARIFORM THICKENING, FIBRES, METAXYLEM VESSELS WITH RETICULATE THICKENING, TRACHEIDS, PITS

STRUCTURES RELATED TO FUNCTIONS

STRUCTURE	FUNCTION
Vessel with no end walls	Unhindered transport of water and minerals
Lignified secondary walls	Waterproofing and support
Pits	Lateral transport
Hollow lumen	Free flow of water
Interdigitating fibres	Mechanical support
Tracheids	Transport and support

PHLOEM
Composite tissue consisting of sieve tubes, companion cells and parenchyma.

PHLOEM FROM CUCURBITA STEM:
TRANSVERSE SECTION,　　X 600　　　　　　　　Fig. 3.6

PHLOEM PARENCHYMA

SIEVE TUBES

THIN CELLULOSE CELL WALL

COMPANION CELLS

PORTION OF SIEVE PLATE IN SIEVE TUBE

PERIPHERAL CYTOPLASM

MIDDLE LAMELLA

NUCLEUS AND DENSE CYTOPLASM

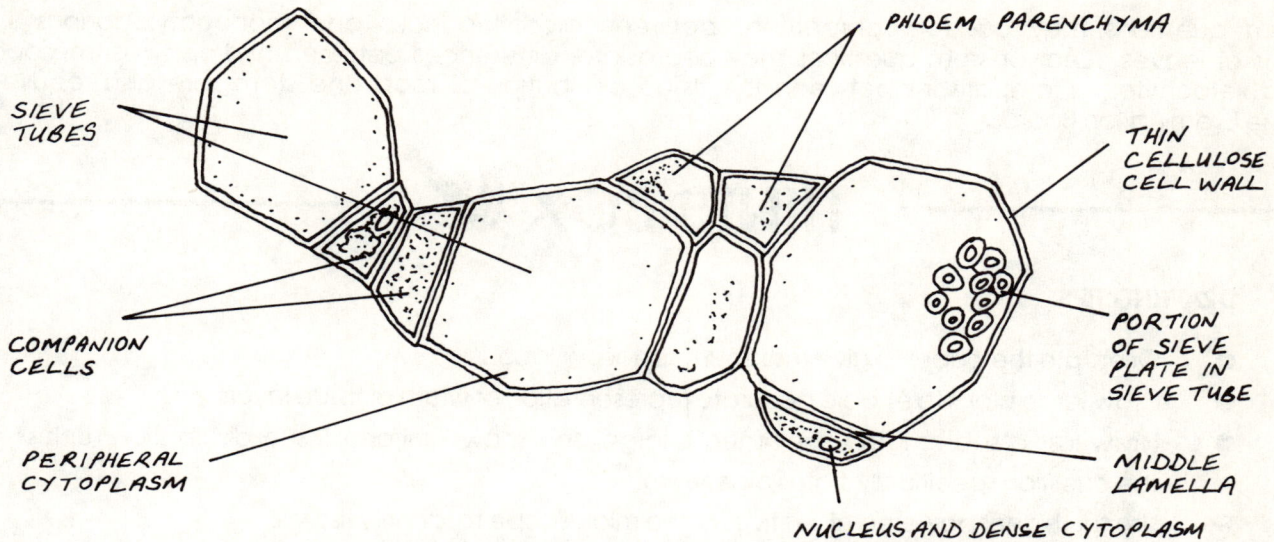

LONGITUDINAL SECTION　　X 600

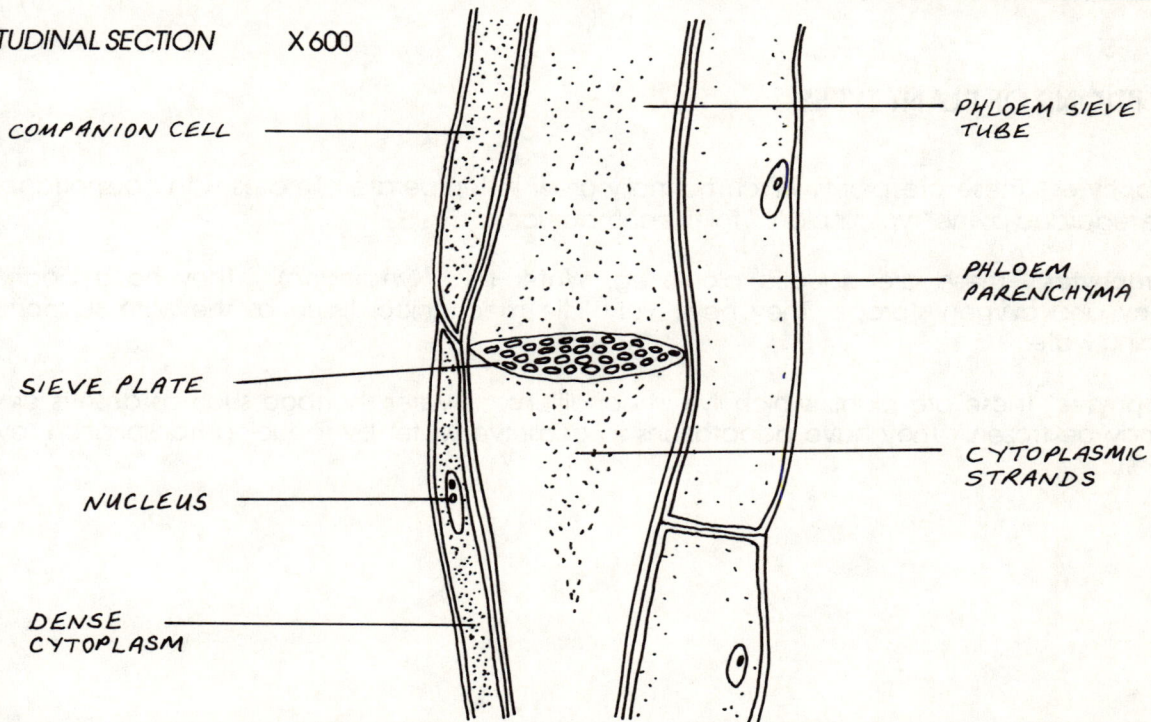

COMPANION CELL

PHLOEM SIEVE TUBE

PHLOEM PARENCHYMA

SIEVE PLATE

CYTOPLASMIC STRANDS

NUCLEUS

DENSE CYTOPLASM

STRUCTURES RELATED TO FUNCTIONS

STRUCTURE	FUNCTION
Sieve tubes with living cytoplasm	Active transport of solutes
Sieve plates	Allow transport between adjacent tubes
Companion cells with dense cytoplasm	Provide ATP from numerous mitochondria for active transport

115

TISSUE PLANS

Tissue plans should be outline maps showing boundaries between tissues without details of cells. Examination questions on tissue plans are designed to test your ability to distinguish between tissues and to represent their distribution accurately, not to test your knowledge of details of cells.

Exam questions may ask for comparisons between dicotyledonous and monocotyledonous stems, roots or leaves. Leaf or stem questions may also ask for differences between hydrophytes, mesophytes and xerophytes. Comparisons between the tissue distribution of roots and stems are also required by some Examination Boards.

HINTS BOX ✔

DRAWING TIPS

- Orientate the paper to give maximum space for labels.
- Draw large plans to enable accurate representation of width of tissue layers.
- Draw just a sector if the specimen is large and shows uniform tissue distribution (unless the question specifically states otherwise).
- Use the higher powered objectives of the microscope to identify tissues.
- Ensure that each tissue type in your plan is clearly delineated.

■ DEFINITIONS OF PLANT TYPES

○ **Mesophytes** These are plants which normally grow in temperate climates with no shortage of water. They are regarded as the "typical plants" for this comparison.

○ **Hydrophytes** These are aquatic plants *eg.* Water Lily (*Nymphaea*). They have adaptations for buoyancy and oxygen storage. They have very little mechanical tissue as they are supported by the surrounding water.

○ **Xerophytes** These are plants which live in conditions of water shortage such as deserts or where the water may be frozen. They have adaptations to conserve water by reducing transpiration (evaporative water loss).

STEMS

DIFFERENCES BETWEEN DICOTYLEDONOUS AND MONOCOTYLEDONOUS STEMS
(Fig. 3.7, Fig.3.8)

DICOTS	MONOCOTS
Peripheral vascular bundles	Scattered vascular bundles
Central pith	No central pith
Secondary thickening is commonly shown	Rarely show secondary thickening
Vascular cambium present	No vascular cambium

DICOT

HELIANTHUS STEM:
T.S. X 40

Fig. 3.7

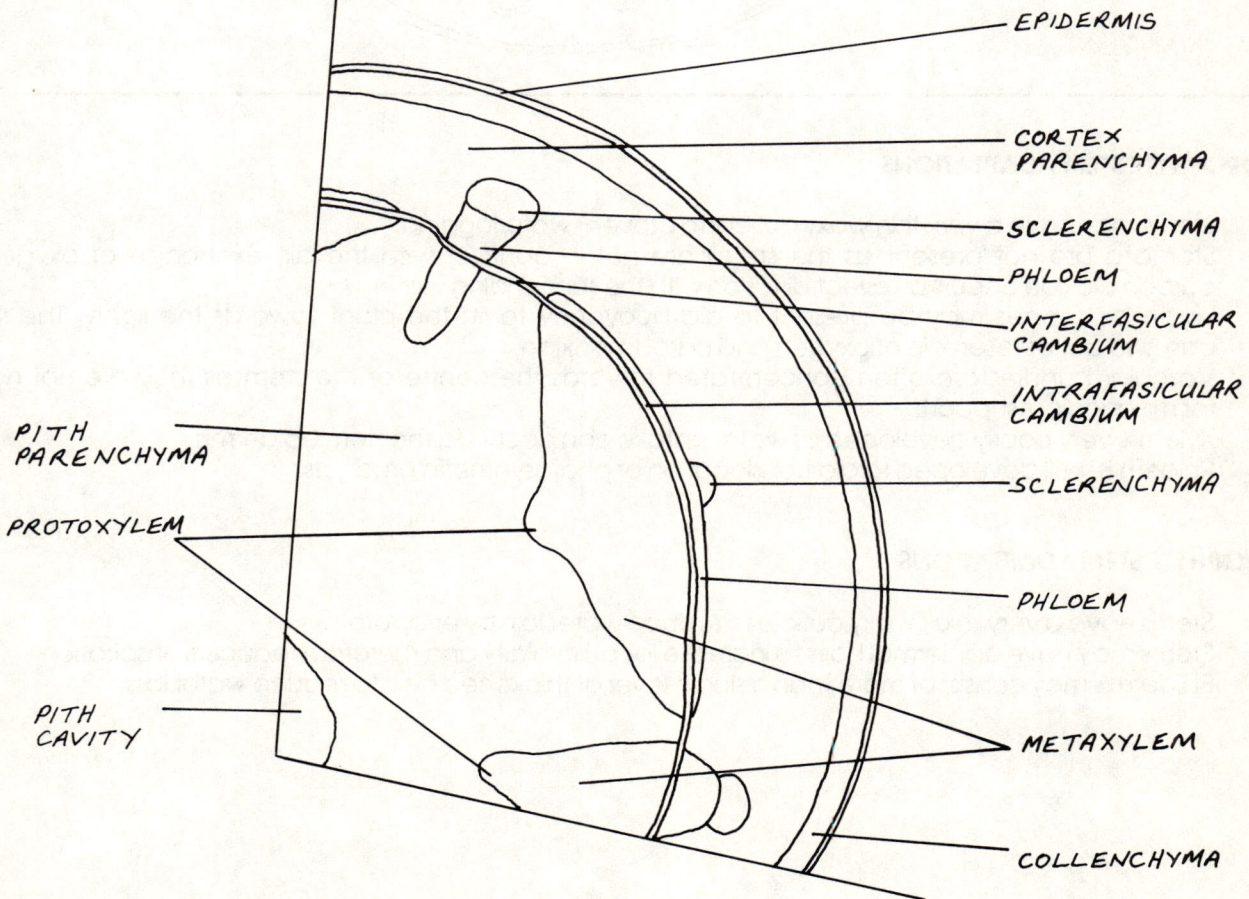

- EPIDERMIS
- CORTEX PARENCHYMA
- SCLERENCHYMA
- PHLOEM
- INTERFASICULAR CAMBIUM
- INTRAFASICULAR CAMBIUM
- SCLERENCHYMA
- PHLOEM
- METAXYLEM
- COLLENCHYMA
- PITH PARENCHYMA
- PROTOXYLEM
- PITH CAVITY

MONOCOT

ZEA STEM: *Fig. 3.8*
T.S.   X 40

EPIDERMIS

PARENCHYMA
– NO CLEAR CORTEX
AND PITH

SCATTERED
VASCULAR
BUNDLES

XYLEM

SCLERENCHYMA
BUNDLE SHEATH
AROUND OUTER
BUNDLES

PHLOEM

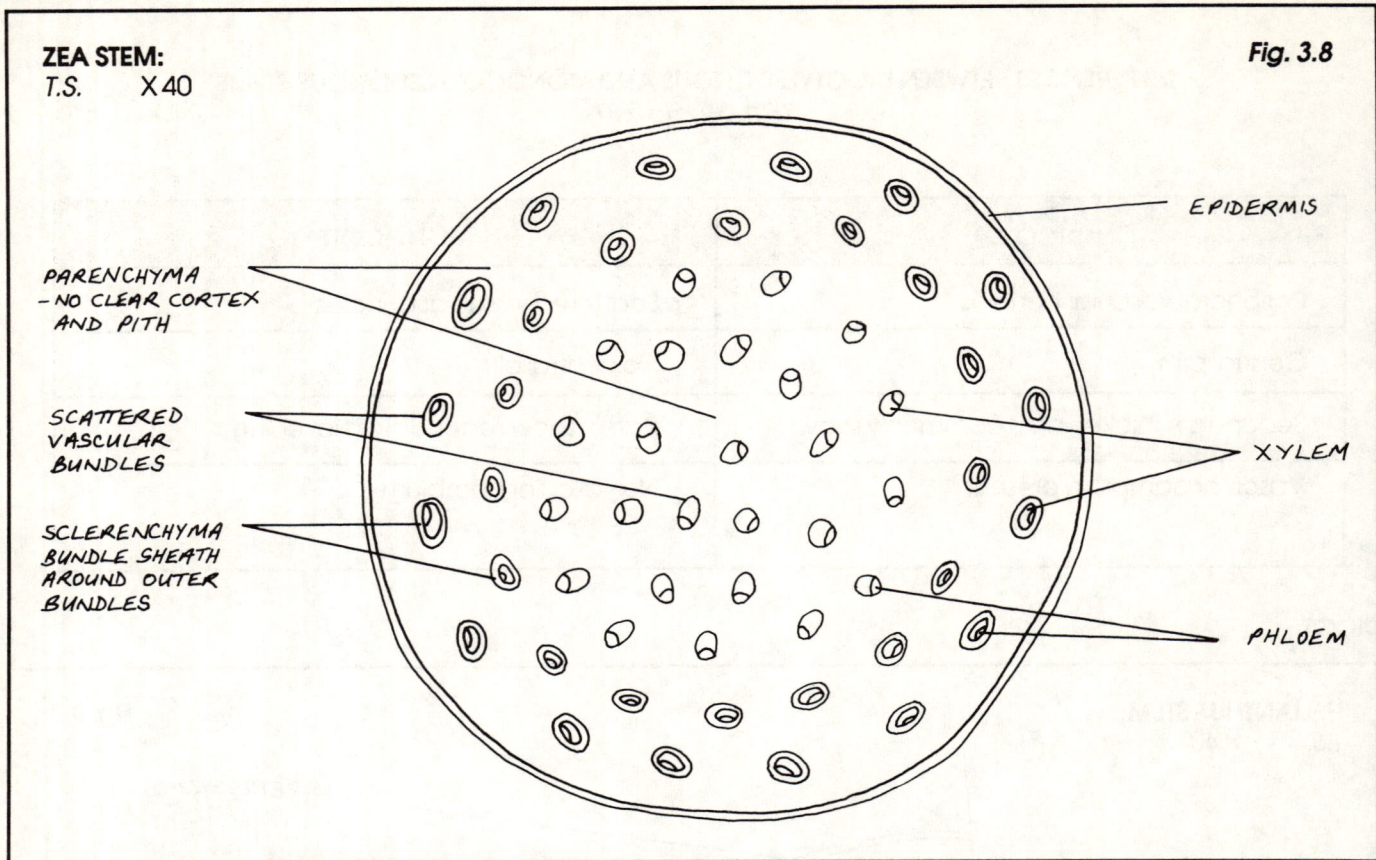

HYDROPHYTE STEM ADAPTATIONS

1   Stems may have a very thin waxy cuticle to prevent waterlogging.
2   Stomata are not present as the stems are not in contact with the air; exchange of oxygen and carbon dioxide occurs by direct diffusion with the surrounding water.
3   Large air spaces may be present to aid buoyancy to lift the plant towards the light. The spaces can also act as reservoirs of oxygen and carbon dioxide.
4   Vascular bundles are often concentrated towards the centre of the stem as they are not needed for mechanical support.
5   Xylem is very poorly developed as water uptake can occur via the stem epidermis.
6   Phloem is well developed to aid translocation of photosynthetic products.

XEROPHYTE STEM ADAPTATIONS

1   Stems have a very thick waxy cuticle to reduce water loss by evaporation.
2   Stems may have epidermal hairs to increase local humidity and therefore reduce transpiration.
3   Epidermis may consist of more than a single layer of thickened cells to reduce water loss.

■ ROOTS

DIFFERENCES BETWEEN DICOTYLEDONOUS AND MONOCOTYLEDONOUS ROOTS
(Fig.3.9, Fig 3.10)

DICOTS	MONOCOTS
Arrangement commonly 4 or 5 pointed star (tetrarch or pentarch)	Xylem arrangement resembles a many pointed star (polyarch)
Poorly defined endodermis	Pronounced endodermis
Cambium usually well defined	Cambium poorly defined

DICOT

RANUNCULUS ROOT:
T.S. X 30 — Fig. 3.9

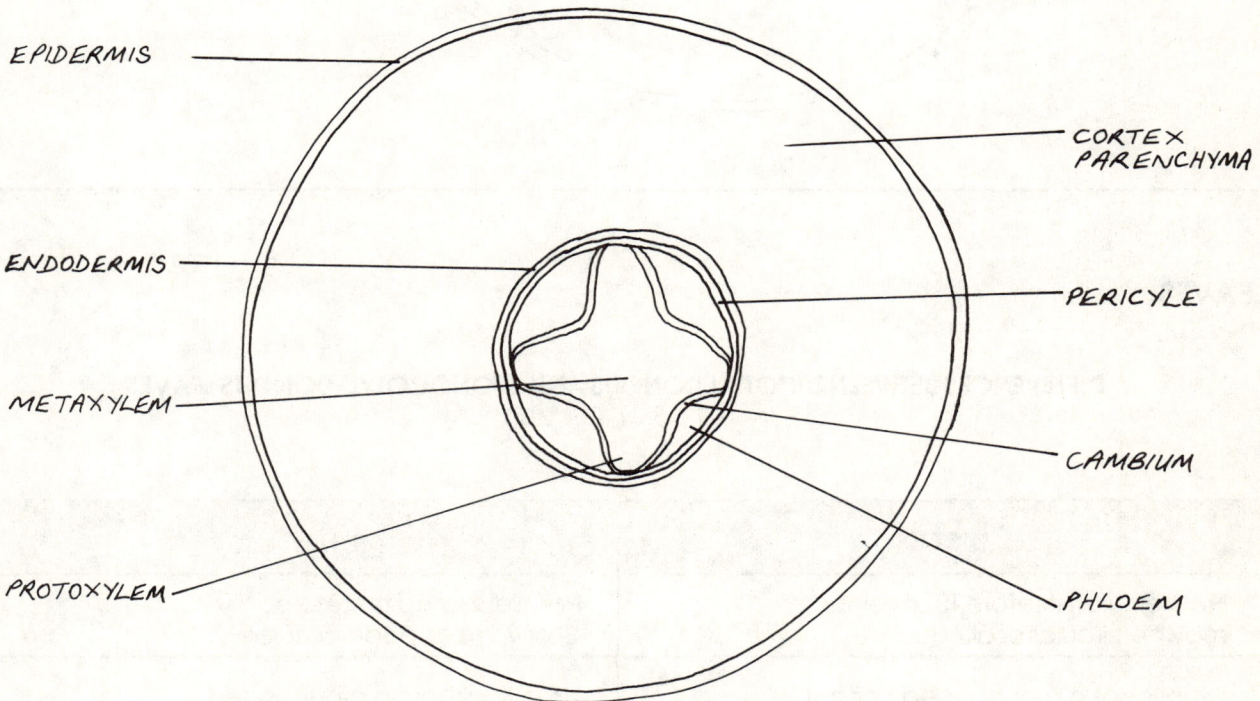

EPIDERMIS, ENDODERMIS, METAXYLEM, PROTOXYLEM, CORTEX PARENCHYMA, PERICYLE, CAMBIUM, PHLOEM

MONOCOT

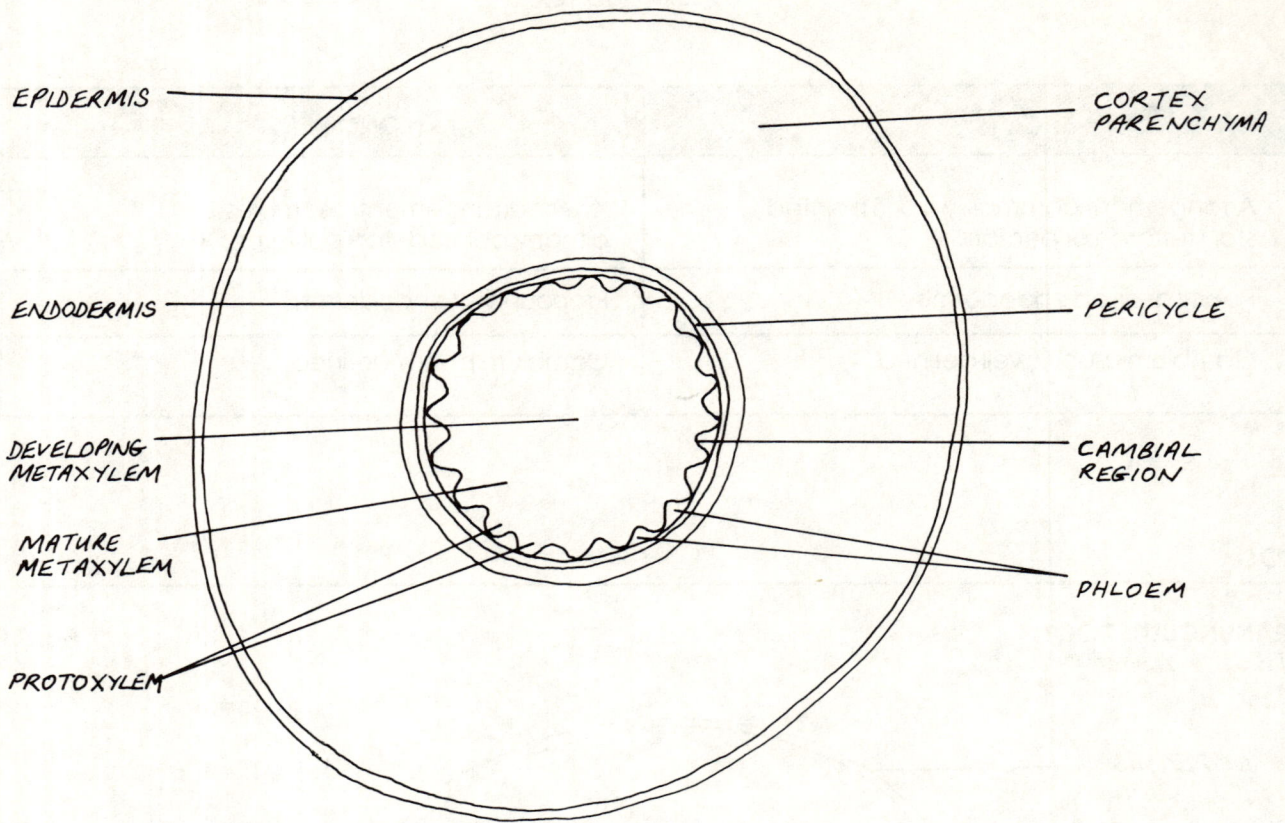

ZEA MAYS ROOT:
T.S. X 30

Fig. 3.10

EPIDERMIS

ENDODERMIS

DEVELOPING METAXYLEM

MATURE METAXYLEM

PROTOXYLEM

CORTEX PARENCHYMA

PERICYCLE

CAMBIAL REGION

PHLOEM

■ LEAVES

DIFFERENCES BETWEEN DICOTYLEDONOUS AND MONOCOTYLEDONOUS LEAVES
(Fig. 3.11, Fig.3.12)

DICOTS	MONOCOTS
Net veined therefore TS of veins may be circular or oblique	Parallel veined therefore TS of veins appears circular
Usually has a pronounced central vein and associated midrib	Usually without a pronounced central main vein
Palisade and spongy mesophyll clearly defined	Mesophyll not always clearly sub-divided

DICOT

LIGUSTRUM LEAF:
T.S.   X 60

Fig. 3.11

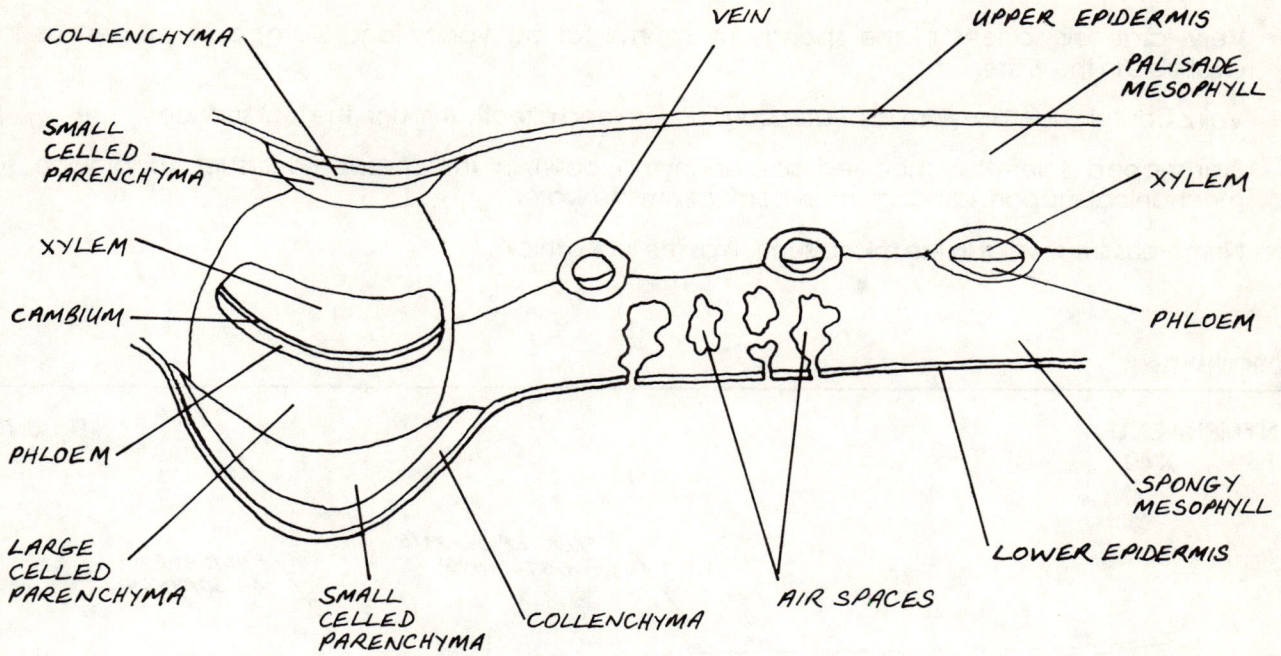

COLLENCHYMA · VEIN · UPPER EPIDERMIS · PALISADE MESOPHYLL · SMALL CELLED PARENCHYMA · XYLEM · CAMBIUM · PHLOEM · LARGE CELLED PARENCHYMA · SMALL CELLED PARENCHYMA · COLLENCHYMA · AIR SPACES · SPONGY MESOPHYLL · LOWER EPIDERMIS

MONOCOT

ZEA LEAF:
T.S.   X 30

Fig. 3.12

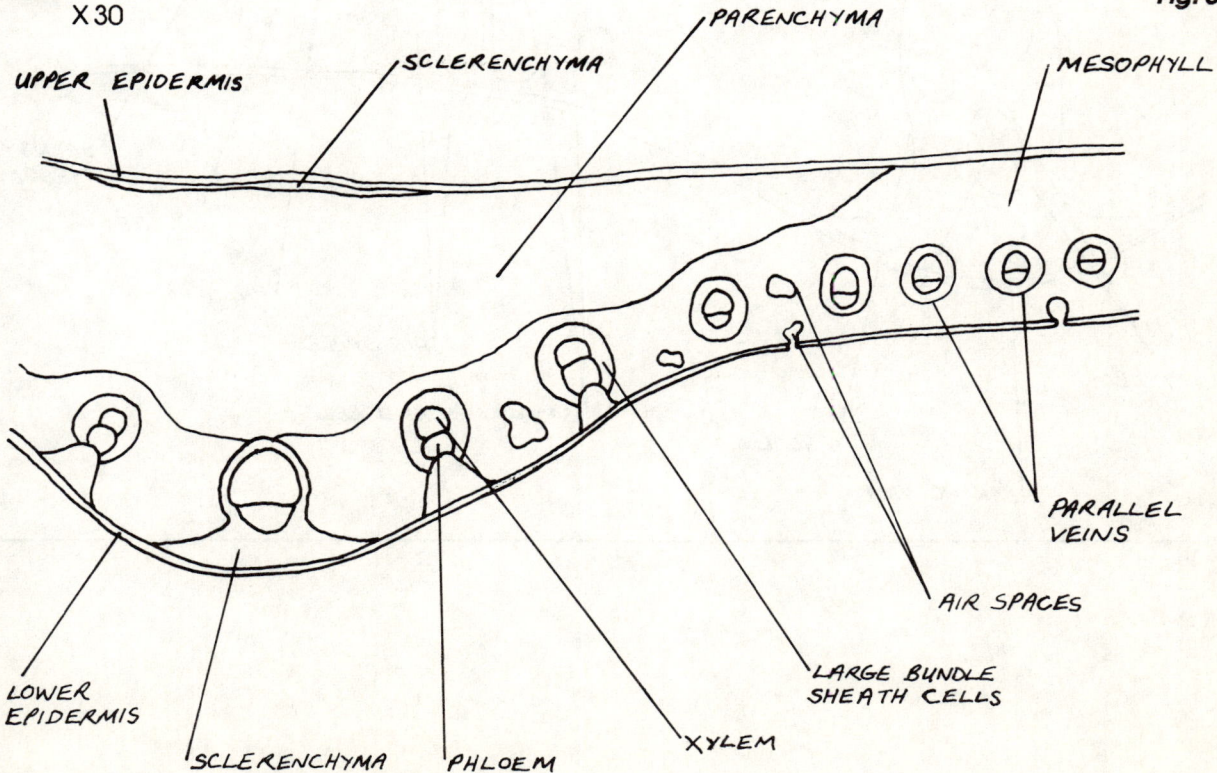

UPPER EPIDERMIS · SCLERENCHYMA · PARENCHYMA · MESOPHYLL · PARALLEL VEINS · AIR SPACES · LARGE BUNDLE SHEATH CELLS · LOWER EPIDERMIS · SCLERENCHYMA · PHLOEM · XYLEM

HYDROPHYTE LEAF ADAPTATIONS

(Fig. 3.13)

1   Stomata on upper epidermis only, to allow gaseous exchange (lower surface is submerged).

2   Very large air spaces in the spongy mesophyll for buoyancy and storage of oxygen as less is available in the water.

3   Veins containing little xylem, as water can be obtained directly through the leaf surface.

4   Star-shaped sclereids (modified sclerenchyma cells) in the mesophyll tissues to provide some mechanical support, although most comes from the water.

5   Numerous small veins in the midrib section as the leaf is thick.

HYDROPHYTE

NYMPHAEA LEAF:
T.S.   X40

Fig. 3.13

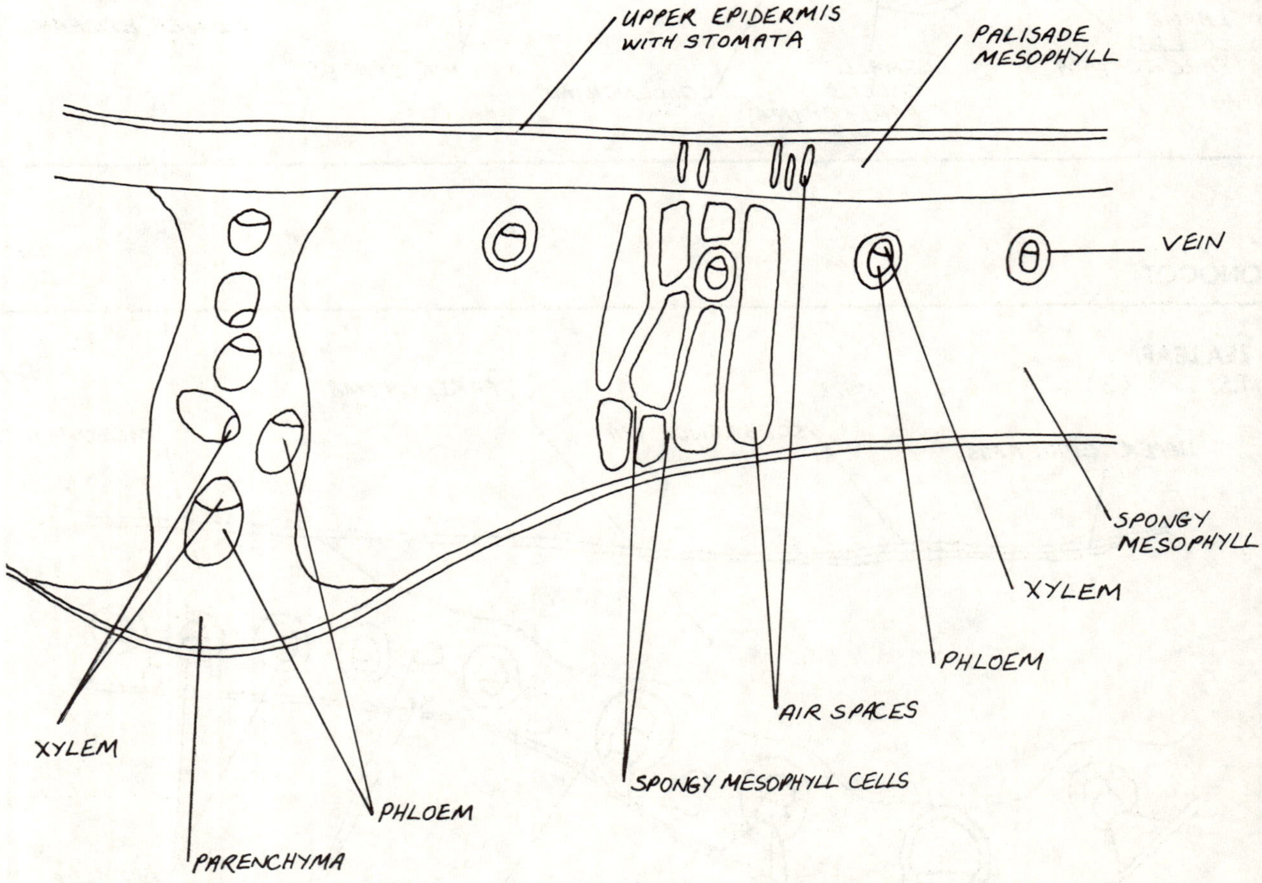

XEROPHYTE LEAF ADAPTIONS

(Fig. 3.14)

1   Thick waxy cuticle on both upper and lower epidermis to reduce transpiration.

2   Thickened epidermal layers to provide additional barriers to water loss.

3   Main vein deep within midrib to reduce loss of water from vascular tissues.

4   Stomata often in sunken chambers with hairs to trap moist air (less likely to be moved away from the leaf surface by air currents).

5   Leaves usually small or rolled up to reduce surface area over which water can be lost.

XEROPHYTE

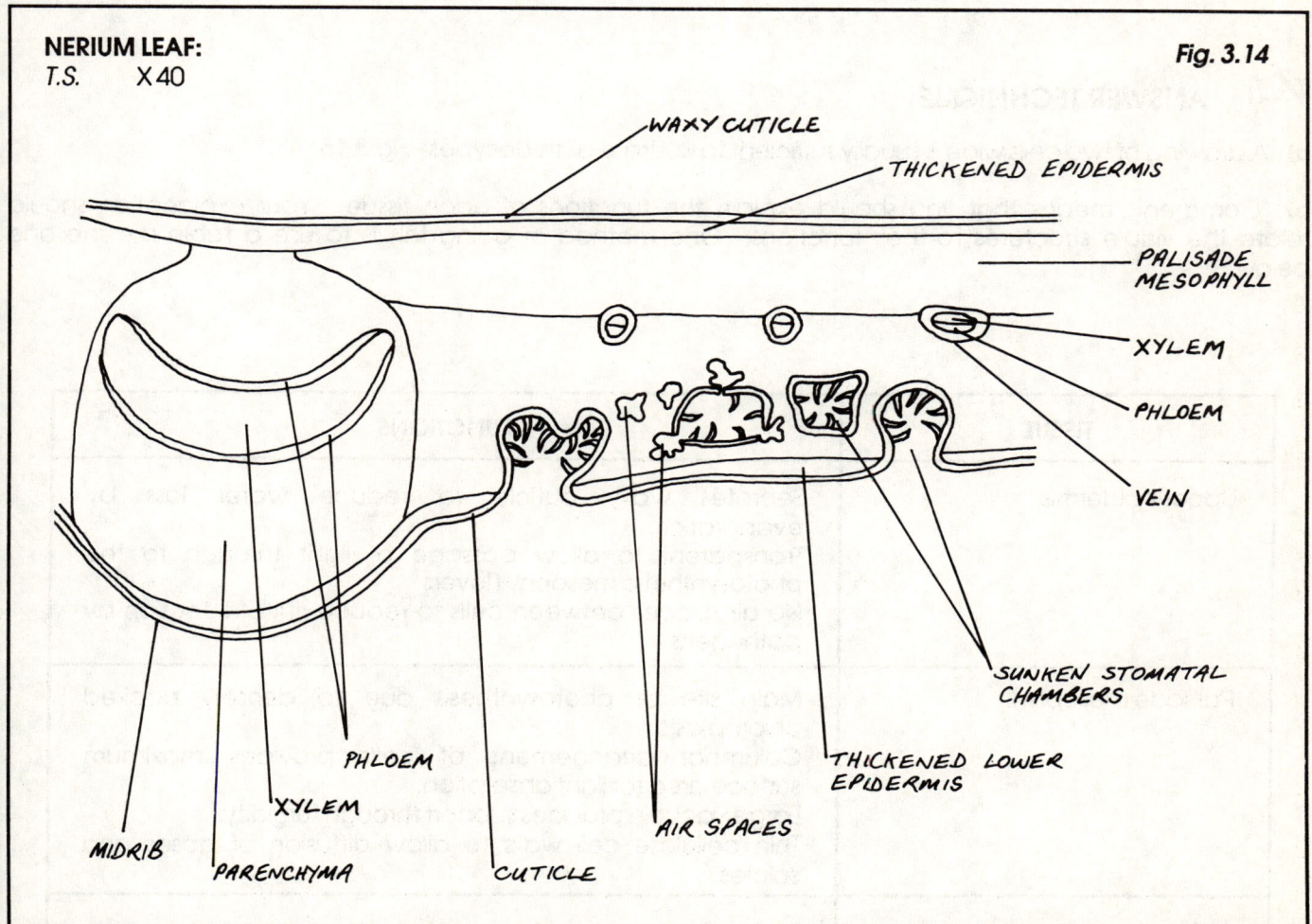

NERIUM LEAF:
T.S.   X 40

Fig. 3.14

WAXY CUTICLE
THICKENED EPIDERMIS
PALISADE MESOPHYLL
XYLEM
PHLOEM
VEIN
SUNKEN STOMATAL CHAMBERS
THICKENED LOWER EPIDERMIS
AIR SPACES
CUTICLE
PHLOEM
XYLEM
PARENCHYMA
MIDRIB

EXAM QUESTION 1

a)   Make a labelled, high power drawing of a narrow section through the lamina of K. Your drawing must include a stoma but not a vein.

b)   Comment on the functions of the tissues you have drawn.

(20 marks)
(University of London Schools Examination Board)

Key:
K   = mesophyte leaf

ANSWER TECHNIQUE

a) A drawing of two cells wide is usually sufficient to illustrate all tissue types - *Fig.3.15.*

b) "Comment" means that you should explain the functions of each tissue. Your explanation should relate the visible structures to their functions. One method of doing this is to use a table like the one below.

TISSUE	FUNCTIONS
Upper epidermis	Secretes waxy cuticle to reduce water loss by evaporation. Transparent to allow passage of light through to the photosynthetic mesophyll layers. No air spaces between cells to reduce risk of infection by pathogens.
Palisade mesophyll	Main site of photosynthesis due to densely packed chloroplasts. Columnar arrangement of cells provides maximum surface area for light absorption. Large vacuole provides support through turgidity. Thin cellulose cell walls to allow diffusion of gases and solutes.
Spongy mesophyll	Main respiratory surface of plant. Increased surface area for gaseous exchange provided by spherically shaped cells. Air spaces between cells allow easy passage of gases. Cells have thin walls to allow rapid diffusion of respiratory gases. Transpiration from sub-stomatal chamber keeps cell surface moist to allow gases to dissolve. Chloroplasts are present therefore some photosynthesis can occur.
Lower epidermis	Main site of entry and exit of gases via stomata. Site of evaporative loss of water, regulated by guard cells.

DETAIL OF LIGUSTRUM LEAF:
T.S.   X 600

Fig. 3.15

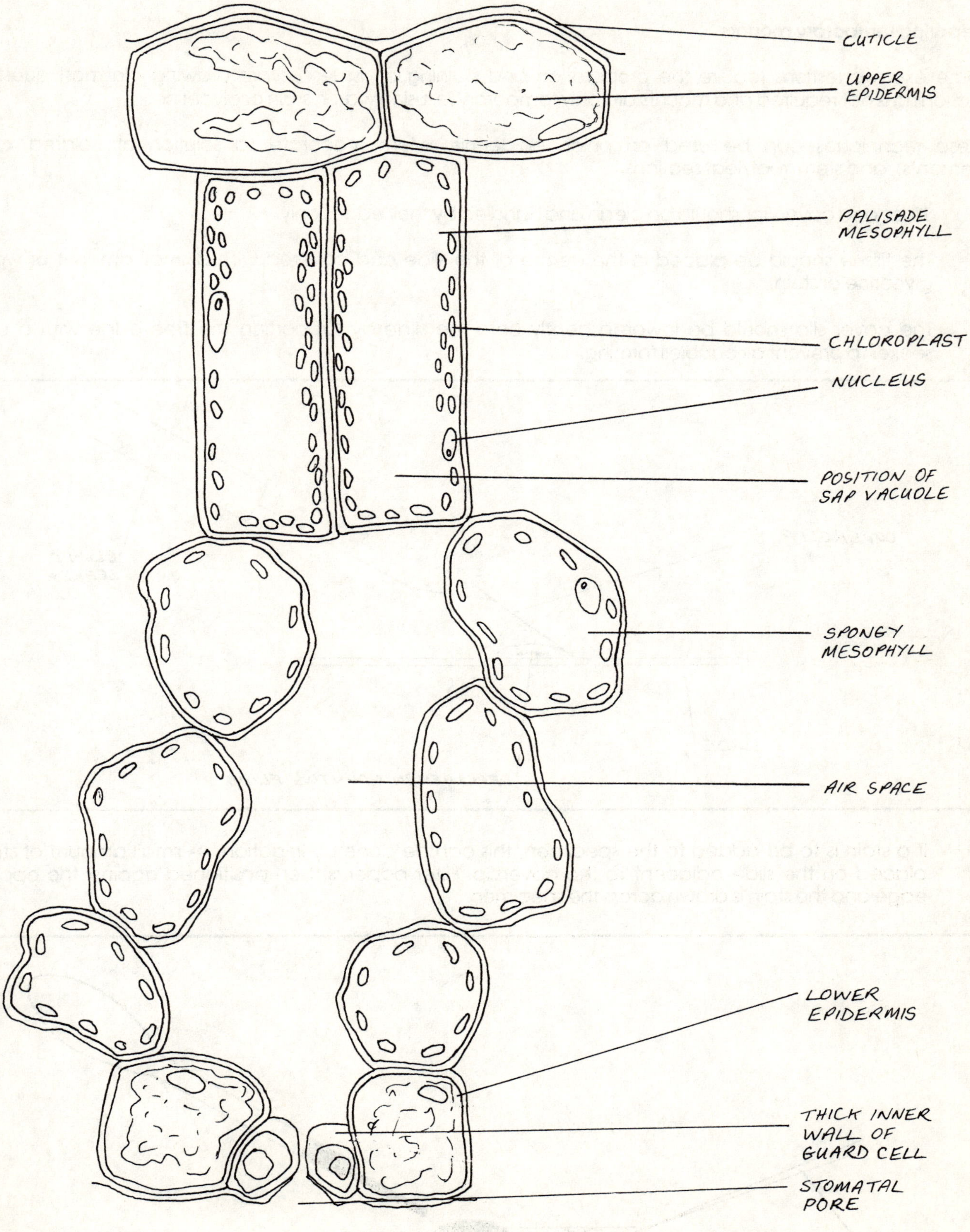

CUTICLE

UPPER EPIDERMIS

PALISADE MESOPHYLL

CHLOROPLAST

NUCLEUS

POSITION OF SAP VACUOLE

SPONGY MESOPHYLL

AIR SPACE

LOWER EPIDERMIS

THICK INNER WALL OF GUARD CELL

STOMATAL PORE

DETAIL OF LIGUSTRUM LEAF:

PREPARATION

■ STAINING TECHNIQUES

Preparing temporary mounts

Some exam questions require the preparation and staining of tissues *before* drawing. In most questions sectioning is not required and mounts are only temporary ie. using water, stain or glycerine.

These techniques can be used on onion epidermis, xylem macerate (a solution of isolated xylem elements), and stem/root/leaf sections.

O   Slides and coverslips should be clean and handled by their edges only.

O   The tissue should be placed in the centre of the slide and covered with a small amount of water, glycerine or stain.

O   The cover slip should be lowered gently onto the slide by supporting the free edge with a blunt seeker to prevent air bubbles forming.

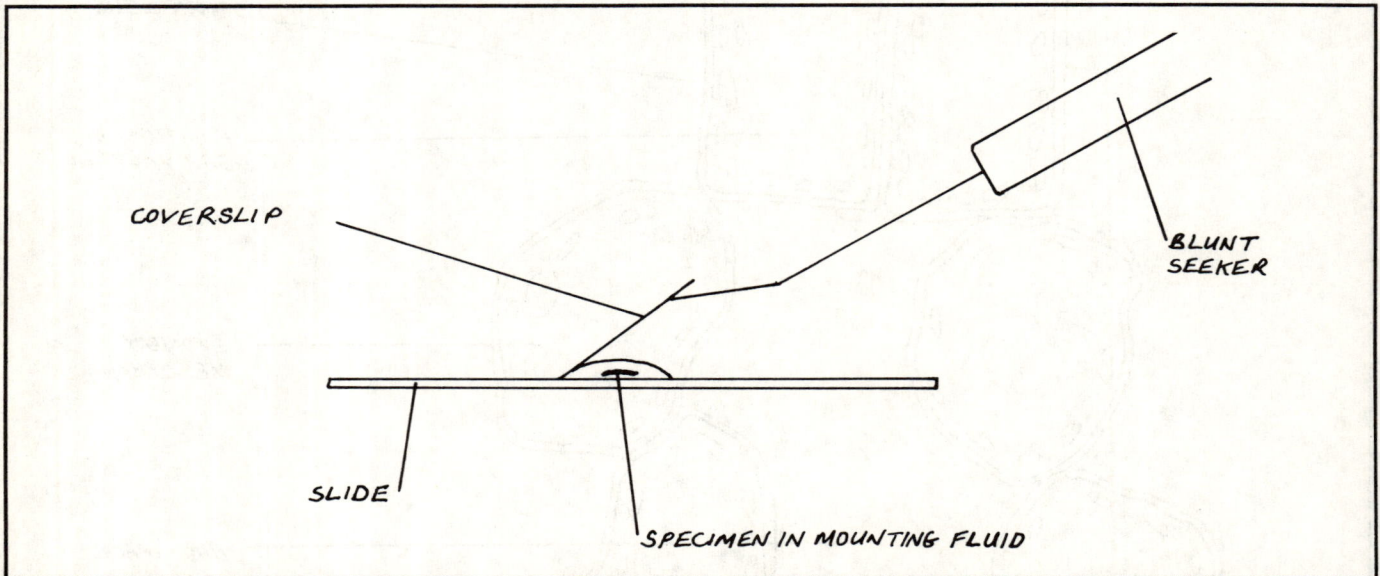

O   If a stain is to be added to the specimen, this can be done by irrigation. A small amount of stain is placed on the slide adjacent to the coverslip. Filter paper is then positioned against the opposite edge and the stain is drawn across the specimen.

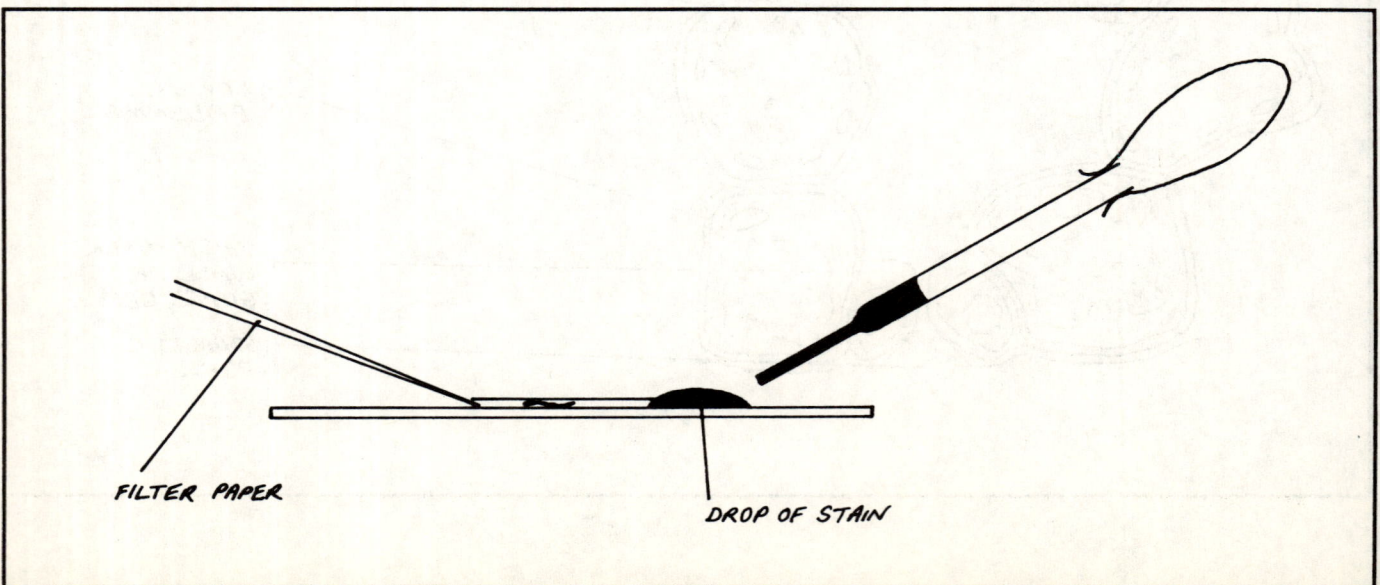

Any excess stain can be removed by repeating the process using water. If a more prolonged immersion is required then the section should be placed in a watch glass.

O   After staining, the slide should be blotted gently and then observed under the microscope.

O   During prolonged observation, the slide may dry out. This can be prevented by either mounting in glycerine or by adding more water or stain.

COMMONLY USED STAINS

STAIN	EFFECT
Aniline chloride	stains lignin yellow
Borax carmine	stains nuclei pink
Methylene blue	stains nuclei blue and helps to distinguish colourless cells from the background
Iodine	stains starch granules blue-black helps to distinguish colourless cells
Phloroglucin + HC1	stains lignin red

EXAM QUESTION 2

Transfer one of the sections X to a drop of stain Y on a microscope slide. Leave the section to stain for one minute and then soak up the excess stain using a small piece of filter paper. Mount the section in dilute glycerine and cover with a coverslip.

a)   Examine your preparation and make a fully labelled, low power plan to show the distribution of the tissues. Indicate clearly, on your plan, the **areas** and **colour** of the tissues stained.

(14 marks)

b)   Compare the distribution of lignified tissues in the preparation X and in the prepared slide Z.

(5 marks)

c)   From which parts of a plant have X and Z been taken? For each of the specimens give two reasons for your answer.

(6 marks)

Leave your slide under the microscope for assessment at the end of the examination.
(University of London Schools Examination Board)

Key to Materials
X   = T.S. Dicotyledonous stem see *Fig. 3.7*
Y   = Aniline chloride
Z   = T.S. Dicotyledonous root see *Fig. 3.9*

ANSWER TECHNIQUE

a)   This is the most valuable part of the question. The sort of plan you might draw is shown in *Fig 3.7*. All the lignified tissues would appear yellow.

b)   X has lignified tissue in the vascular bundles around the periphery (xylem and sclerenchyma) whereas in Z it is only found in the central vascular cylinder (xylem only).

c)   X is from a stem because:

i) There are peripheral vascular bundles.
ii) Sclerenchyma and collenchyma are both present. These tissues do not occur in roots.

Z is from a root because:

i) There is a central vascular cylinder.
ii) Piliferous (root hair) layer is present.

The assessment would include degree and clarity of staining, presence or absence of air bubbles and presentation of slide. The plan would also be compared to the section to determine accuracy.

■ CALCULATION OF MAGNIFICATION OF SPECIMENS

In many questions it is sufficient to give the magnification calculated by multiplying the eyepiece and objective lenses magnifications, *eg.*:

eyepiece lens   = x10
objective lens   = x 40
specimen viewed at a magnification of x 400

If the question requires a more accurate magnification to be indicated on the drawing then a graticule is usually provided. This is a calibrated disc designed to fit inside the eyepiece. When viewing a specimen it is then possible to measure it accurately and then calculate precise magnification by using a ruler on the drawing.

Example calculation

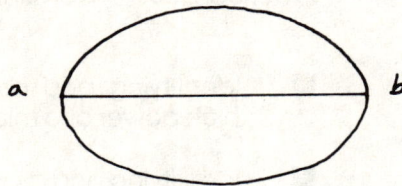

Line a-b = 4 cm on drawing; 2mm on slide

Magnification = $\dfrac{40mm}{2mm}$ = X 20

CHAPTER

FOUR

ANIMAL TISSUES AND ORGANS

The study of animal tissues and organs is included in the syllabus of all Examination Boards. Not all of them regularly set animal histology questions as part of their *practical* papers. This chapter is designed to enable you to answer both practical and theoretical questions on this topic but you should refer to your syllabus for your Board's specific requirements.

Practical questions on animal tissues and organs cover:

■ Identifying and drawing isolated **animal tissues** at the high power of a microscope.

■ Identifying and drawing **mammalian organ** sections.

For both of these types of question you may be expected to give a reasoned explanation of your identification of the tissue or organ section.

■ Identifying isolated parts of the **mammalian skeleton**, usually vertebrae or limb bones.

Tissues

Characteristics
Relating Structure to Functions

Organs

Characteristics
Relating Structure to Functions

Skeleton

Vertebrae & Limb Bones

You should prepare a set of tissue and organ drawings as specified in your exam Board's syllabus.

In this chapter you will find examples of a variety of tissues and organs to aid identification. The Examiners may also ask you how the structure of each tissue/organ is related to its function; each tissue drawing is accompanied by a table of functions.

In the exam you should allow 15 - 20 minutes to complete each drawing and so you should practice timed drawings, without notes, as part of your revision.

ANIMAL TISSUES

The following table should help you to locate the tissues in either isolated slides or organ sections. Use the table in conjunction with the drawings of tissues and organs in this chapter.

TABLE SHOWING ANIMAL TISSUE TYPES AND LOCATIONS

TISSUE	LOCATIONS
Epithelia	Covering surfaces
Squamous	Alveoli of lungs, capillary walls, Bowman's capsule of kidney tubules.
Cuboidal	Thyroid gland follicles, proximal and distal convoluted tubules of kidneys.
Columnar	Villi of ileum, gastric pits of stomach, trachea and oviducts.
Stratified	Skin and vagina
Connective tissues	Bind adjacent tissues.
Areolar	Below the skin (subcutaneous), forming sheaths around nerves.
Adipose	Subcutaneous, around the kidneys and heart.
Fibrous	Ligaments (elastic fibres) attaching bone to bone, tendons (collagen fibres) attaching muscle to bone.
Cartilage	i) fibrous in intervertebral discs ii) elastic in external ear (pinna) iii) hyaline in rings of trachea and ends of bones at joints.
Bone	i) spongy (with marrow channels) in epiphyses (heads) of long bones. ii) compact (with Haversian systems) in shafts of long bones.
Muscular tissues	Associated with moving parts.
Striated (voluntary)	Attached to the skeleton, diaphragm and abdominal wall.
Smooth (involuntary)	Walls of arteries and veins, wall of alimentary canal, hair erector muscles, uterine wall and ciliary muscles.
Cardiac	Walls of heart (atria and ventricles)
Nervous tissues	Central nervous system (brain and spinal cord) and peripheral nerves.

HINTS BOX ✔

ANIMAL HISTOLOGY DRAWINGS

- Scan the slide to find a representative area of tissue - **do not** choose damaged areas.
- Make all drawings, label lines and labels in pencil for ease of correction.
- Give each drawing a title and magnification or scale.
- Draw areas which include the typical features of each tissue type.
- Refer to notes or diagrams for these typical features.
- Use a sharp H or HB pencil and a clean soft rubber.
- Draw only a small representative portion of the tissue.
- Aim to cover at least half a page.
- **Do not** shade or use colour
- Leave space for labels and annotations.
- List the characteristic features of each tissue on its drawing to aid your revision.
- Give examples of the locations of each of the tissues.

■ CHARACTERISTICS OF TISSUES

The following descriptions will help you recognise the various animal tissues.

■ EPITHELIUM
(Figs. 4.1 - 4.6)
Most types of epithelium consist of a single layer of cells on a thin, non-living basement membrane, forming a covering surface. An exception is stratified epithelium which is formed of several layers of cells. The cells in all epithelia are closely packed and small. The types of epithelium are classified according to the shapes of the cells of which they are composed. Examples include

- ○ thin, flat cells form squamous (pavement) epithelium.
- ○ tall, narrow cells form columnar epithelium.

The outer surface of the epithelial cells may be modified to perform a specialised function. Examples include

- ○ tiny microvilli (folds) to increase the surface area for absorption may be found in cuboidal and columnar epithelia.
- ○ cilia to move particles and fluids, may be found on columnar epithelia lining passageways.

TABLE SHOWING STRUCTURE OF EPITHELIAL TISSUES RELATED TO FUNCTIONS

TISSUE	STRUCTURE RELATED TO FUNCTIONS
Squamous	Thin flat cells allowing rapid exchange or passage of materials.
Cuboidal	Tightly packed cells forming a protective yet permeable surface. May have microvilli (brush border) to increase the surface area for absorption.
Simple columnar	Taller cells forming a denser protective layer but still allowing passage of materials.
Columnar with microvilli	Microvilli increase the surface area for absorption.
Ciliated columnar	Cilia beat rhythmically to move particles along passageways.
Glandular	Folded epithelium with specialised secretory cells.
Stratified	Several layers of cells giving greater protection against mechanical damage, invasion by pathogens and water loss.

SQUAMOUS EPITHELIUM: forms a protective layer; very thin, flat cells allow rapid diffusion and exchange of materials.

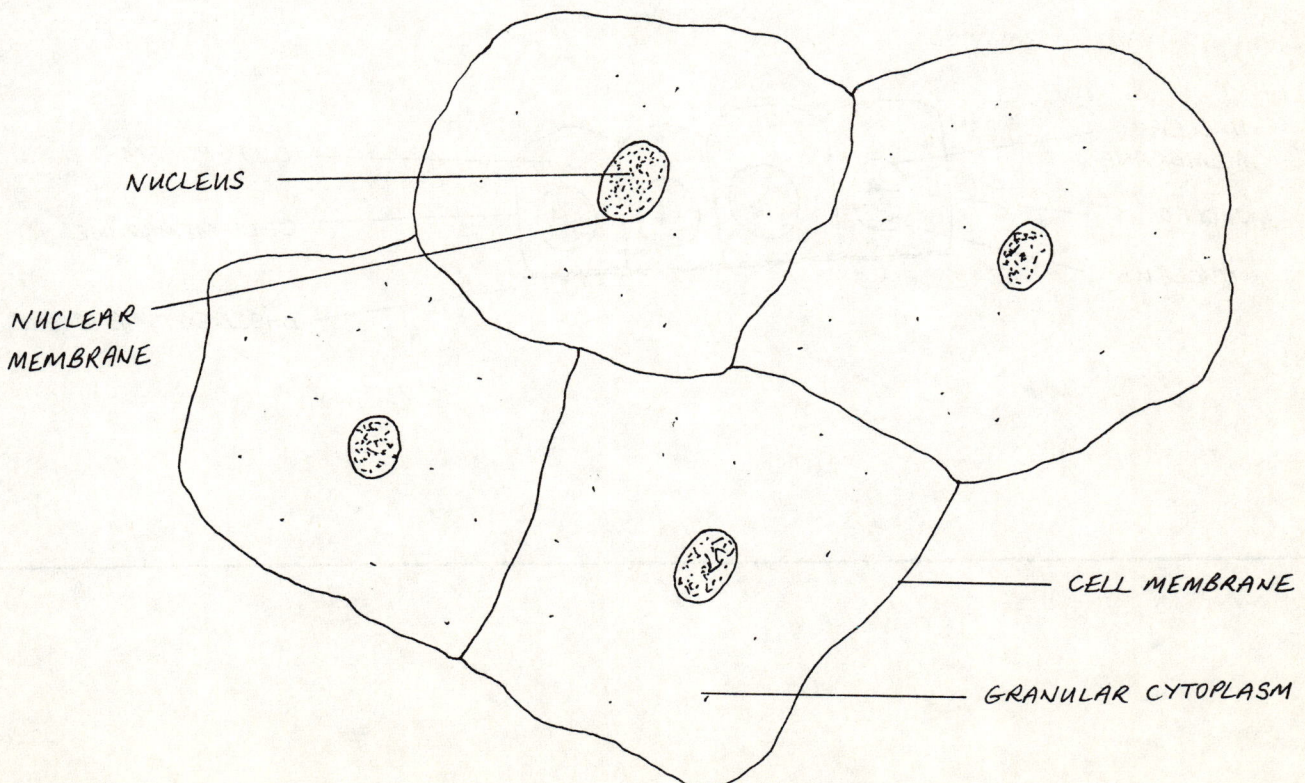

CELLS FROM CHEEK LINING
SURFACE VIEW   X 400   Fig. 4.1

NUCLEUS
NUCLEAR MEMBRANE
CELL MEMBRANE
GRANULAR CYTOPLASM

T.S. LOOP OF HENLÉ (KIDNEY TUBULE)   X 400   **Fig. 4.2**

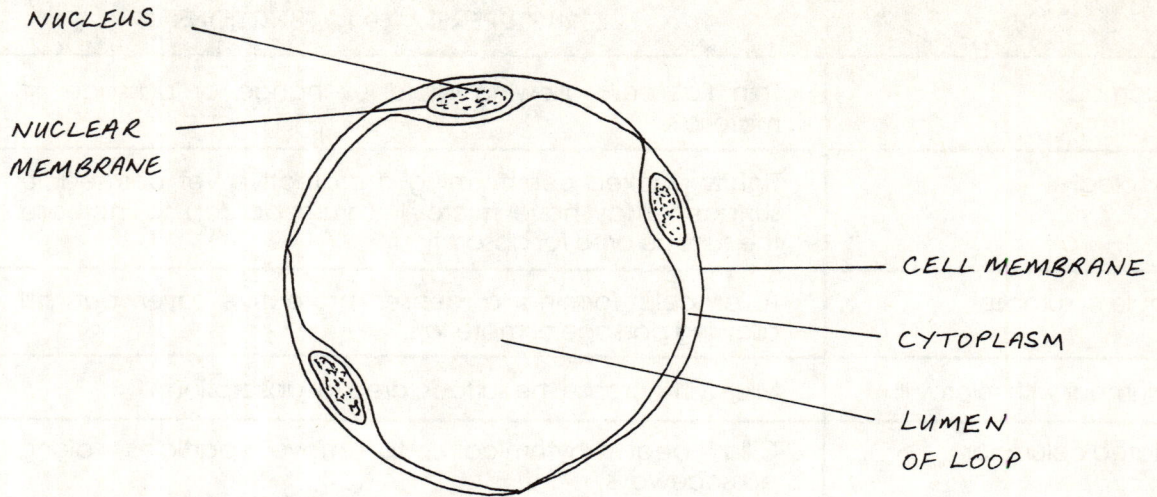

NUCLEUS

NUCLEAR MEMBRANE

CELL MEMBRANE

CYTOPLASM

LUMEN OF LOOP

VERY THIN, FLAT CELLS ALLOWING RAPID DIFFUSION AND EXCHANGE OF MATERIALS

CUBOIDAL EPITHELIUM: forms a protective layer; may have microvilli to increase surface area for rapid absorption

L.S. KIDNEY TUBULE   X 400   **Fig. 4.3**

NUCLEAR MEMBRANE

NUCLEOLUS

NUCLEUS

CYTOPLASM

CELL MEMBRANE

BASEMENT MEMBRANE

SIMPLE COLUMNAR EPITHELIUM: forms a protective but permeable layer

L.S. GALL BLADDER X 400 Fig. 4.4

CELL MEMBRANE

ELIPTICAL NUCLEUS

CYTOPLASM

CILIATED COLUMNAR EPITHELIUM: moves fluids and particles along passageways

T.S. OVIDUCT X 400 Fig. 4.5

CILIA BEAT RHYTHMICALLY

COLUMNAR EPITHELIUM WITH MICROVILLI: provides a large surface area for absorption and active transport

L.S. VILLUS X 100 Fig. 4.6

DARKER EDGE DUE TO MICROVILLI

■ CONNECTIVE TISSUES

The overall function of connective tissues is to bind other tissue types together. Structurally, they all contain the non-cellular components collagen and elastic fibres but each type of connective tissue has its own characteristic arrangement of cells and fibres.

TABLE SHOWING CONNECTIVE TISSUE STRUCTURES RELATED TO FUNCTIONS

TISSUE	STRUCTURE RELATED TO FUNCTIONS
Areolar	Fibroblasts secrete the fibres. Collagen fibres provide strengthening and elastic fibres provide elasticity. Macrophages ingest pathogens. Mast cells secrete heparin (blood anti-coagulant).
Adipose	Large cells for storage of fat. Blood capillaries allow the transport of fats to and from the cells. Collagen fibres provide strengthening.
Hyaline cartilage	Chondrocytes secrete the stiff matrix of chondrin which provides support.
Fibrous cartilage	Chondrocytes secrete chondrin and additional support is provided by collagen fibres.
Compact bone	Osteocytes secrete the bone matrix of calcium phosphate. The matrix is found in concentric rings or lamellae which provides extra strength. The matrix also contains collagen and elastic fibres. The central Haversian canal contains nerves, and blood and lymph vessels which carry nutrients. The radiating canaliculi provide channels to allow exchange of materials between the osteocytes and the vessels.

AREOLAR CONNECTIVE TISSUE *(Fig. 4.7).* This consists of a random network of thick, white, collagen fibres and fine, yellow, elastic fibres with a variety of specialised cells. Star-shaped fibroblasts with long, cytoplasmic processes; irregularly shaped macrophages with granular cytoplasm; and oval mast cells, each with a prominent nucleus.

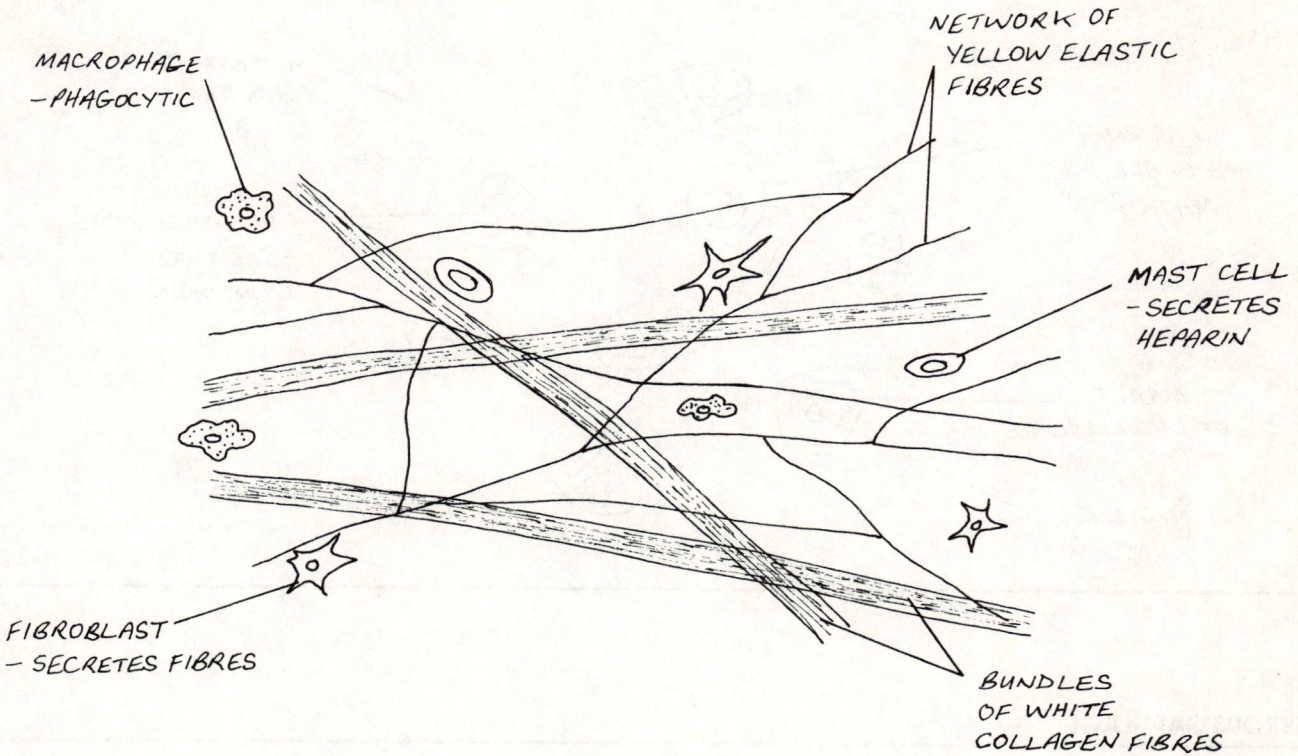

SPREAD FROM BENEATH THE DERMIS   X 400   Fig. 4.7

ADIPOSE TISSUE *(Fig. 4.8).* The cells forming adipose tissue are all fairly large, with most of the cell content being white fat. There is only a small amount of peripheral cytoplasm containing a small nucleus. These are both usually stained pink or purple. There are some spaces between the cells containing fibres, fibroblasts, mast cells and blood capillaries.

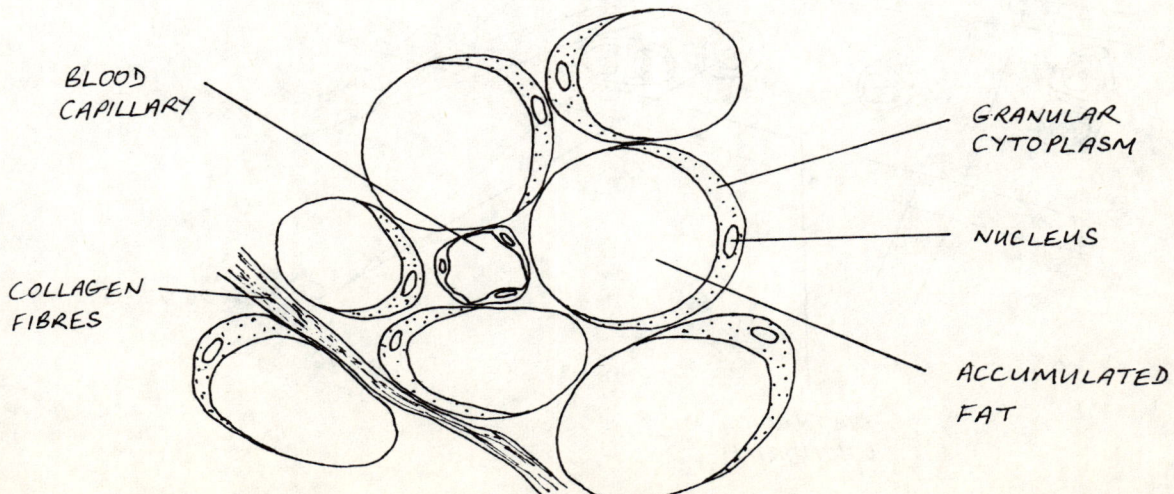

SUBCUTANEOUS FAT   X 400   Fig. 4.8

CARTILAGE (Figs. 4.9 - 4.10). This consists of chondrocytes (cells) and a non-living background matrix. The chondrocytes are often paired in spaces or lacunae within the matrix. There are three different types of cartilage, classified according to the composition of the matrix: hyaline cartilage matrix is just the bluey coloured chondrin; fibrous cartilage matrix contains thick collagen fibres as well; elastic cartilage contains chondrin and thin elastic fibres.

HYALINE CARTILAGE

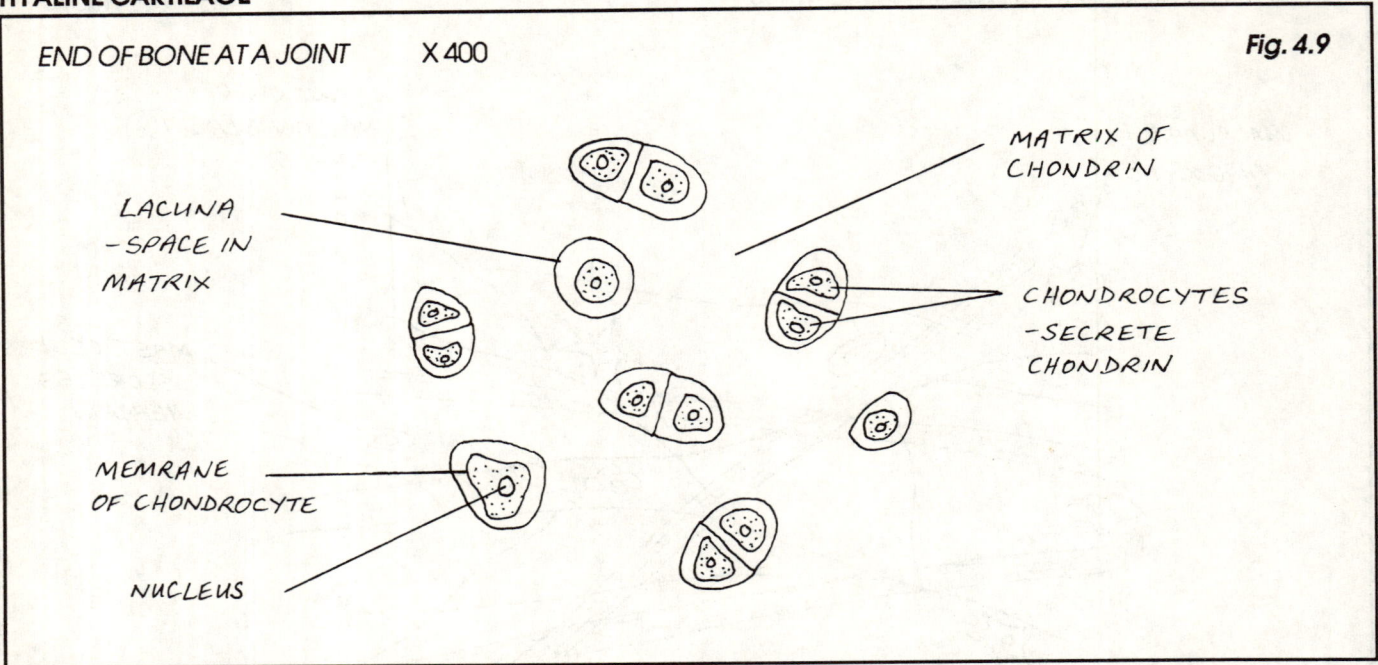

END OF BONE AT A JOINT   X 400   **Fig. 4.9**

MATRIX OF CHONDRIN

LACUNA -SPACE IN MATRIX

CHONDROCYTES -SECRETE CHONDRIN

MEMRANE OF CHONDROCYTE

NUCLEUS

FIBROUS CARTILAGE

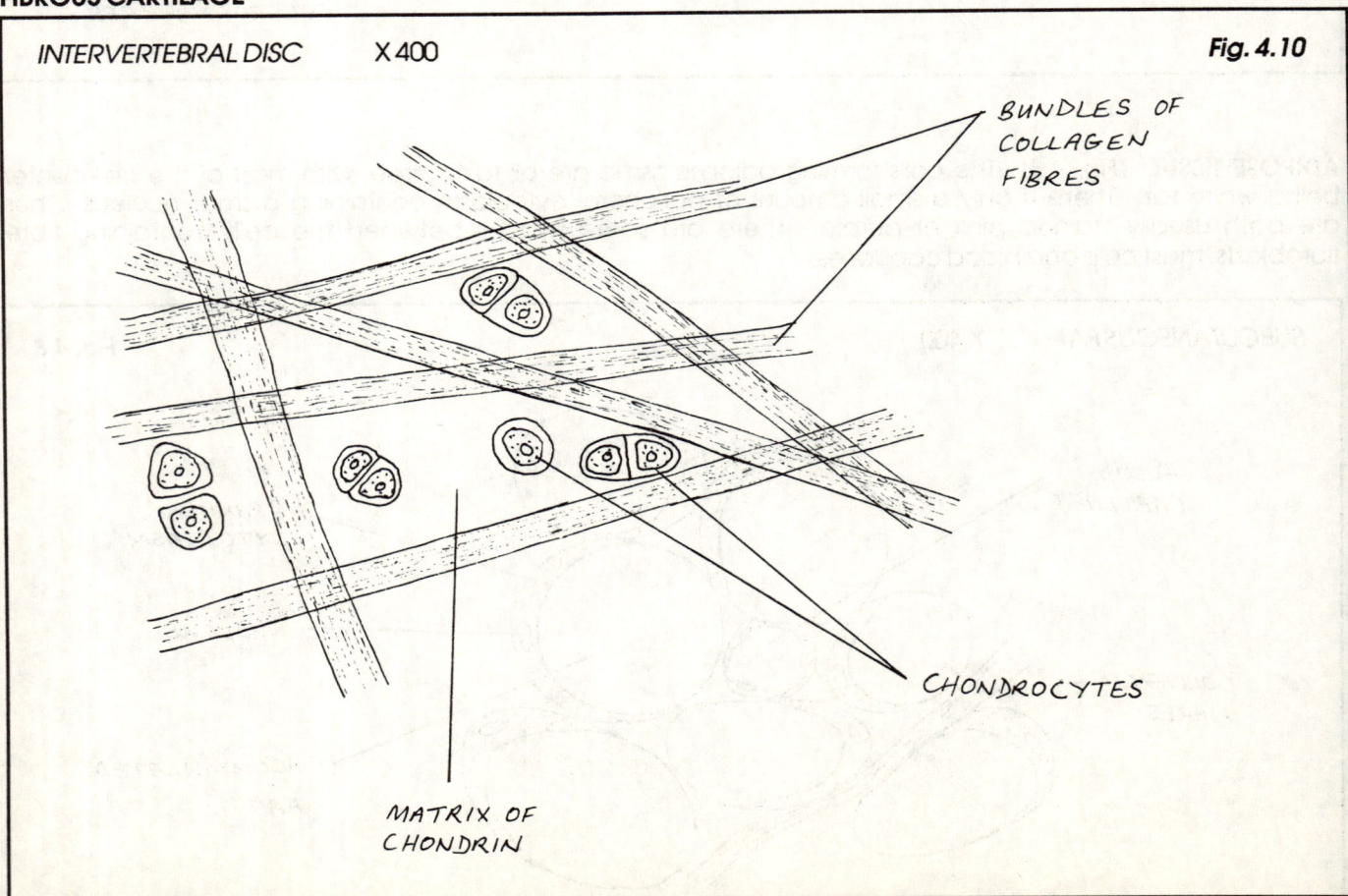

INTERVERTEBRAL DISC   X 400   **Fig. 4.10**

BUNDLES OF COLLAGEN FIBRES

CHONDROCYTES

MATRIX OF CHONDRIN

BONE (Fig. 4.11).

This consists of osteocytes (cells) in lacunae which appear dark in a lighter background matrix. Compact bone is composed of cylindrical Haversian systems (roughly circular in transverse section). The osteocytes are arranged in concentric rings around a central Haversian canal containing blood and lymph vessels. The osteocytes are connected to each other and to the Haversian canal by fine, darkly staining channels (canaliculi). Spongy bone has a much more irregular structure with many large, clear, marrow channels between columns of osteocytes.

COMPACT BONE T.S.   X 400   Fig. 4.11

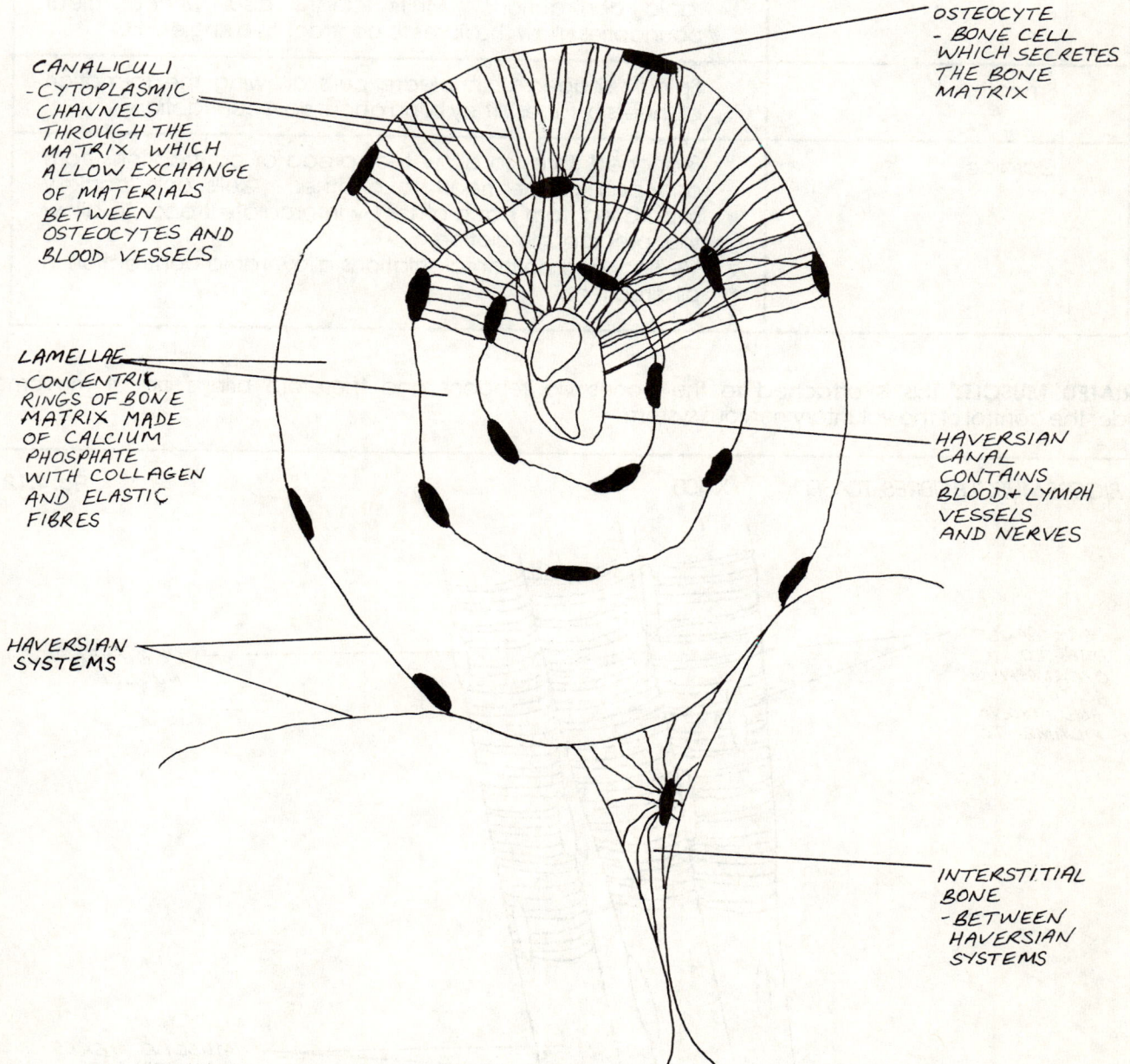

CANALICULI
-CYTOPLASMIC CHANNELS THROUGH THE MATRIX WHICH ALLOW EXCHANGE OF MATERIALS BETWEEN OSTEOCYTES AND BLOOD VESSELS

OSTEOCYTE
- BONE CELL WHICH SECRETES THE BONE MATRIX

LAMELLAE
-CONCENTRIC RINGS OF BONE MATRIX MADE OF CALCIUM PHOSPHATE WITH COLLAGEN AND ELASTIC FIBRES

HAVERSIAN CANAL CONTAINS BLOOD + LYMPH VESSELS AND NERVES

HAVERSIAN SYSTEMS

INTERSTITIAL BONE
-BETWEEN HAVERSIAN SYSTEMS

■ MUSCLE (Figs. 4.12 - 4.15).

All types of muscle tissue stain red and consist of densely packed fibres. Striated (voluntary) muscle has the longest fibres, each with several peripheral nuclei and prominent horizontal stripes. Smooth (involuntary) muscle fibres are spindle shaped, without stripes. Cardiac muscle fibres are branched with both horizontal and vertical stripes.

TABLE SHOWING MUSCLE TISSUE STRUCTURE RELATED TO FUNCTION

TISSUE	STRUCTURE RELATED TO FUNCTION
Striated	Horizontal stripes due to interdigitating actin and myosin filaments. These slide past each other to bring about rapid contraction. Multinucleate cells without clear boundaries allow the fibres to contract as a single unit.
Smooth	Spindle-shaped uninucleate cells allowing the formation of sheets or tubes. They bring about slow contraction.
Cardiac	Branched fibres to allow the spread of contractions from one part of the heart to another. Cells only partially separated from each other by intercalated discs to allow the spread of stimulation. Vertical and horizontal striations allow rapid contraction in all directions.

STRIATED MUSCLE: This is attached to the bones via tendons and therefore brings about movement. Under the control of the voluntary nervous system.

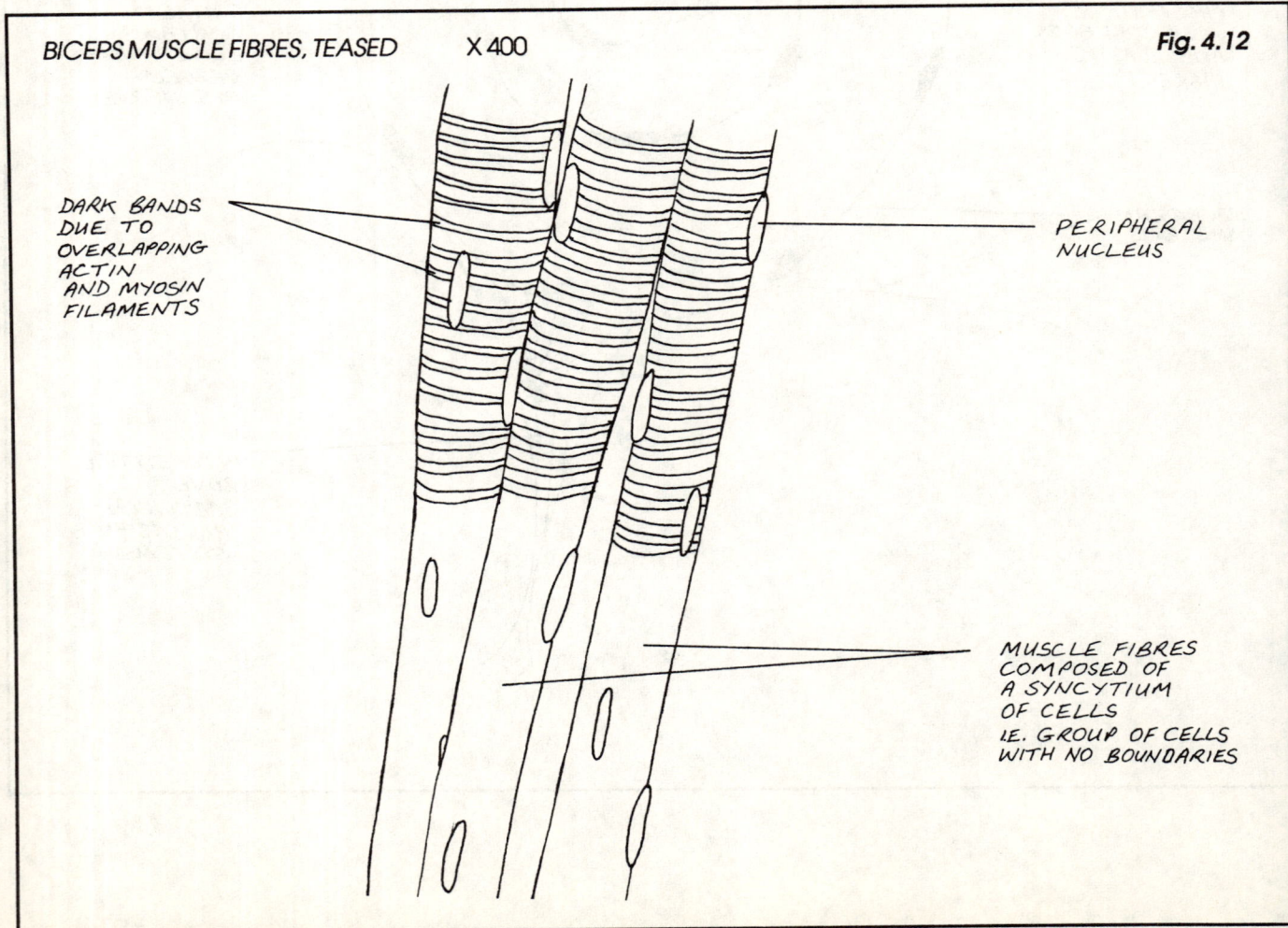

BICEPS MUSCLE FIBRES, TEASED   X 400   Fig. 4.12

DARK BANDS DUE TO OVERLAPPING ACTIN AND MYOSIN FILAMENTS

PERIPHERAL NUCLEUS

MUSCLE FIBRES COMPOSED OF A SYNCYTIUM OF CELLS I.E. GROUP OF CELLS WITH NO BOUNDARIES

SMOOTH MUSCLE: This is myogenic; its rate of contraction is under autonomic nervous system control

SMOOTH MUSCLE FIBRES L.S.   X 400   **Fig. 4.13**

SPINDLE-SHAPED
CELLS ARRANGED
IN SHEETS

CENTRAL
NUCLEUS

CARDIAC MUSCLE: This is myogenic; its rate of contraction is under autonomic nervous control.

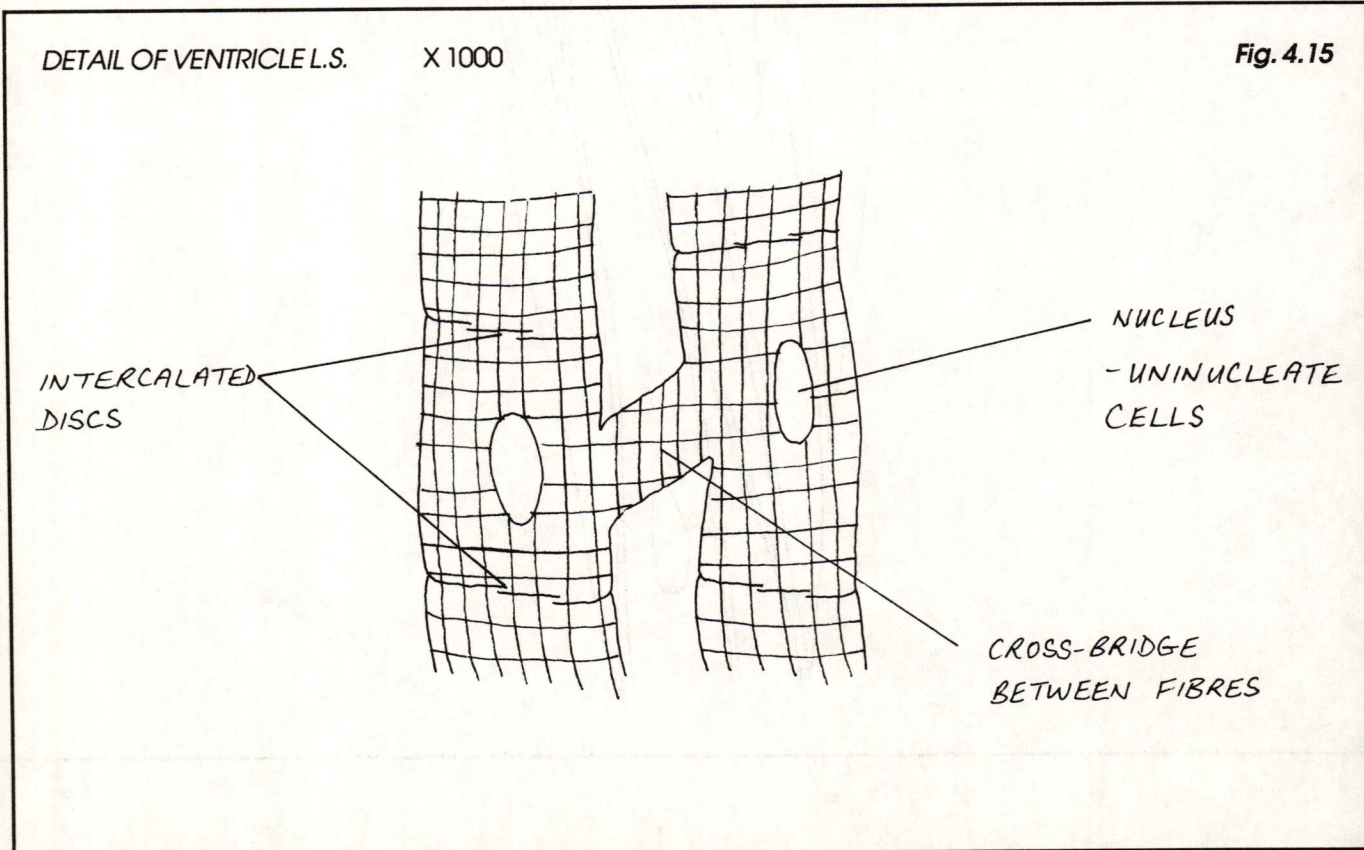

L.S. VENTRICLE   X 600   Fig. 4.14

NUCLEUS

BRANCHED FIBRES

HORIZONTAL AND VERTICAL STRIATIONS

BLOOD VESSELS AND CONNECTIVE TISSUE BETWEEN FIBRES

DETAIL OF VENTRICLE L.S.   X 1000   Fig. 4.15

INTERCALATED DISCS

NUCLEUS - UNINUCLEATE CELLS

CROSS-BRIDGE BETWEEN FIBRES

■ NERVOUS TISSUE

(Figs. 4.16 - 4.17).

This is composed of various types of neurone (nerve cell). Each neurone consists of several cytoplasmic extensions forming dark thin fibres (axons and dendrons) and a cell body (soma) containing a nucleus. The axons and dendrons may be covered by a pale myelin sheath and can be seen most easily in the white matter of the spinal cord. The cell bodies form a dense tissue in the grey matter of the brain and spinal cord.

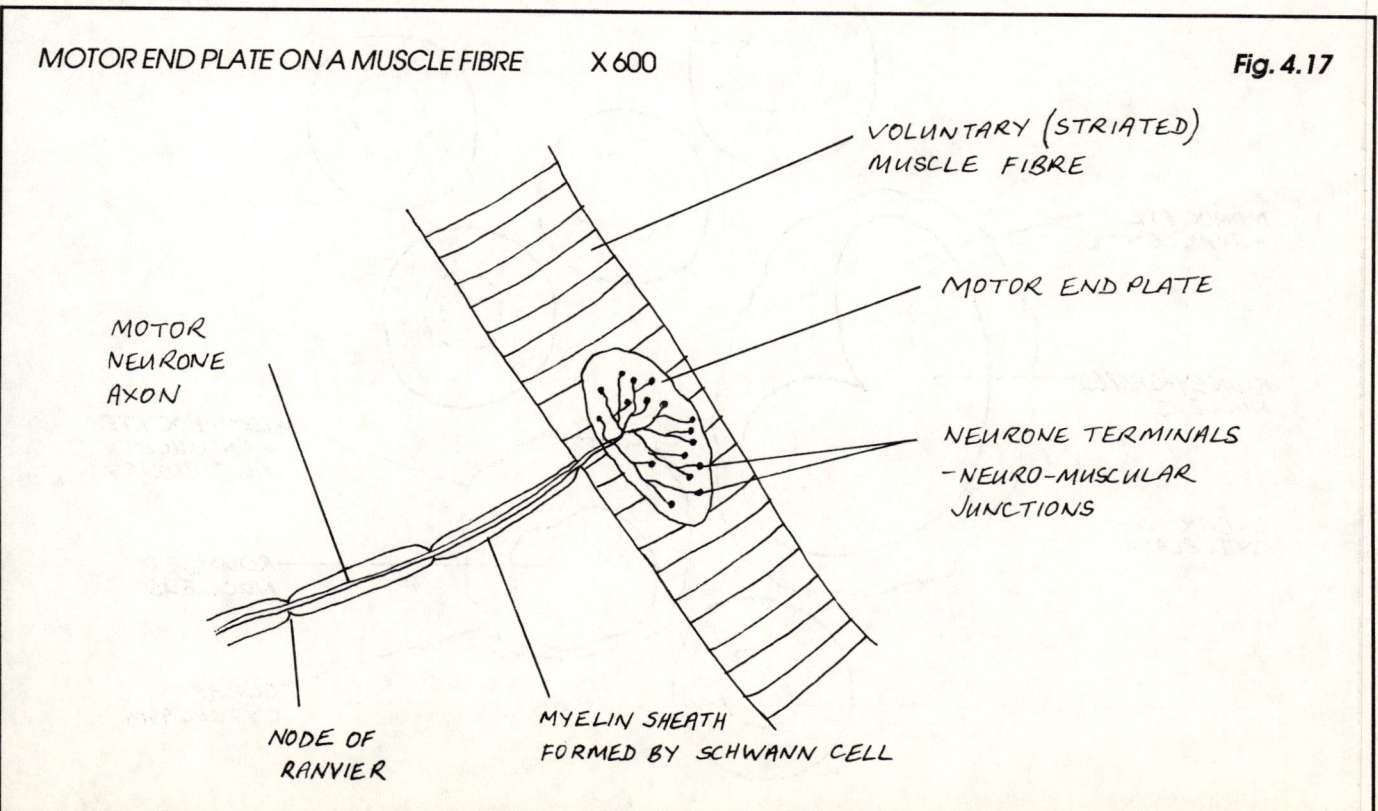

T.S. NERVE   X 400   Fig. 4.16

CONNECTIVE TISSUE SHEATH (EPINEURIUM)
NUCLEUS OF SCHWANN CELL
AXON
MYELIN SHEATH FORMED BY SCHWANN CELL
BLOOD CAPILLARY

MOTOR END PLATE ON A MUSCLE FIBRE   X 600   Fig. 4.17

VOLUNTARY (STRIATED) MUSCLE FIBRE
MOTOR END PLATE
NEURONE TERMINALS - NEURO-MUSCULAR JUNCTIONS
MOTOR NEURONE AXON
NODE OF RANVIER
MYELIN SHEATH FORMED BY SCHWANN CELL

■ BLOOD

(Fig. 4.18).

Blood is a complex, liquid tissue consisting of several different cell types suspended in a clear fluid matrix (plasma).

The majority of the cells are erythrocytes (red blood cells) which do not have a nucleus and appear as biconcave discs.

Leucocytes (white blood cells) are usually stained purple and have an irregular outline. Three main types can be recognised:

○ granulocytes are the most numerous and have a multi-lobed nucleus within a granular cytoplasm

○ lymphocytes have a rounded nucleus and clear cytoplasm; and

○ monocytes have a kidney-shaped nucleus and clear cytoplasm.

Thrombocytes (platelets) are tiny cell fragments, also staining purple, which may be found in some blood smears.

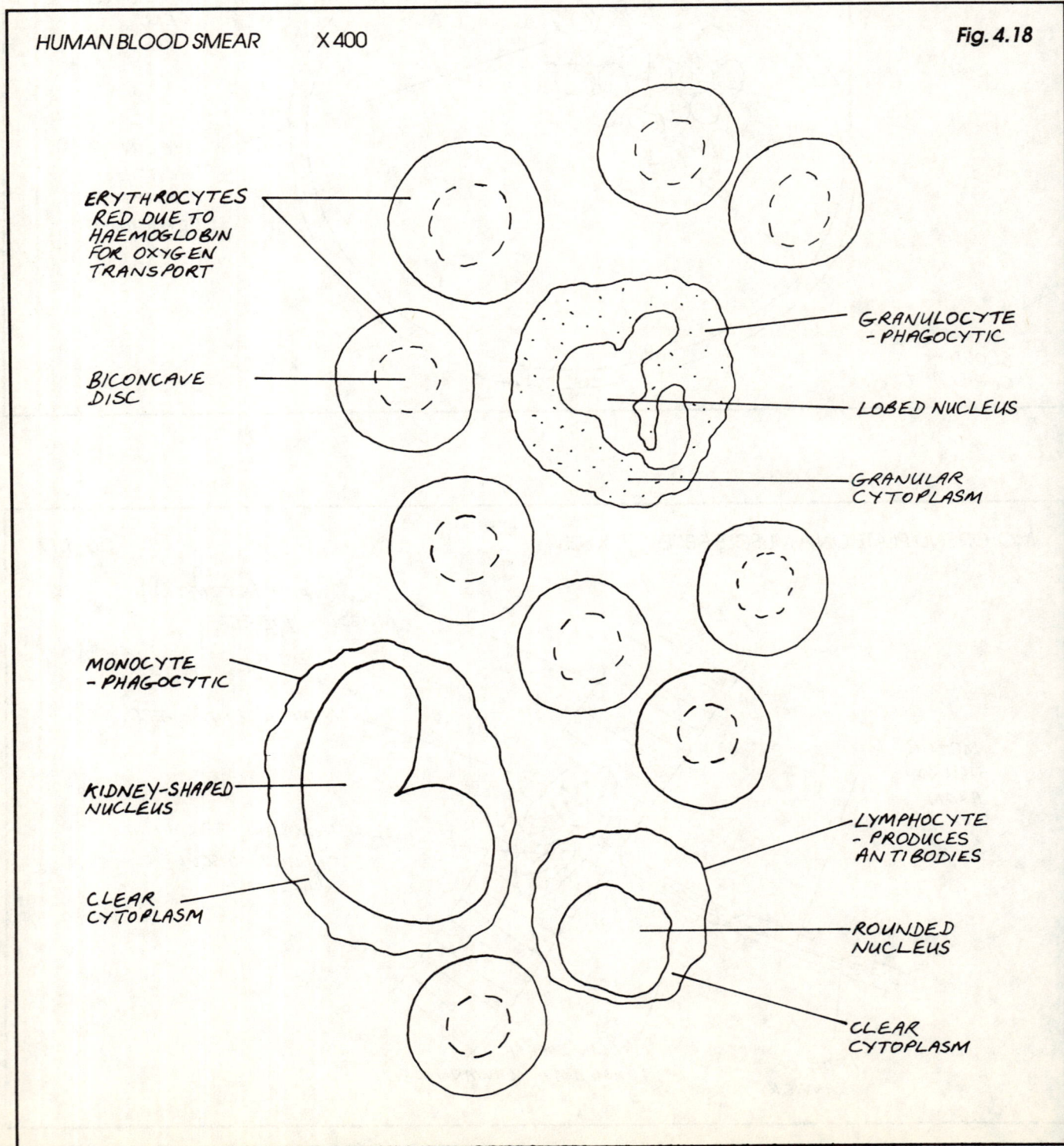

HUMAN BLOOD SMEAR   X 400   Fig. 4.18

ERYTHROCYTES RED DUE TO HAEMOGLOBIN FOR OXYGEN TRANSPORT

BICONCAVE DISC

GRANULOCYTE - PHAGOCYTIC

LOBED NUCLEUS

GRANULAR CYTOPLASM

MONOCYTE - PHAGOCYTIC

KIDNEY-SHAPED NUCLEUS

CLEAR CYTOPLASM

LYMPHOCYTE - PRODUCES ANTIBODIES

ROUNDED NUCLEUS

CLEAR CYTOPLASM

EXAM QUESTION (PART)

b i)   Draw and label a representative region of specimen D.

(8 marks)

ii)   What are the functions of specimen D in the life of specimen A?

(5 marks)
(University of London Schools Examination Board)

Key to Materials:
A = Bony fish
D = T.S. hard bone

ANSWER TECHNIQUE

b i)   For this part of the question, draw a small portion of the slide. Draw only one complete Haversian system, but indicate outlines of adjoining systems to show how they fit together (*Fig. 4.11*). You do not need to draw all the osteocytes and canaliculi. You need only illustrate the pattern of lamellae and interconnections of the canaliculi in a small sector.
Remember that the examiners would be looking for accuracy of drawing and labelling. Your drawing must have a title and show the viewing magnification.

ii)   To answer this, you need to be familiar with all the functions of bone as a tissue and as part of an organ. These are:

● support
● protection (*eg.* bony scales)
● production of blood cells
● muscle attachment
● movement
● storage of calcium and phosphate ions

Each of these functions should be explained and related to the life of the fish.

MAMMALIAN ORGAN SECTIONS

Organs are a collection of tissues, grouped together to perform a specific function. They may be recognised by

● their overall shape
● the types of tissue of which they are composed, and their arrangement.

■ SPINAL CORD
(Fig. 4.19 - 4.20).
This is oval or rounded in transverse section, covered by membrane layers. It has a central, clear hole - the cerebrospinal canal, surrounded by a roughly butterfly-shaped, dense area of grey matter, which in turn is surrounded by white matter. In some sections, the spinal nerve connections may be visible as fibrous, darker regions and it may also be possible to see the swollen dorsal root ganglia on either side of the spinal cord.

T.S. SPINAL CORD (RABBIT)   X 15   Fig. 4.19

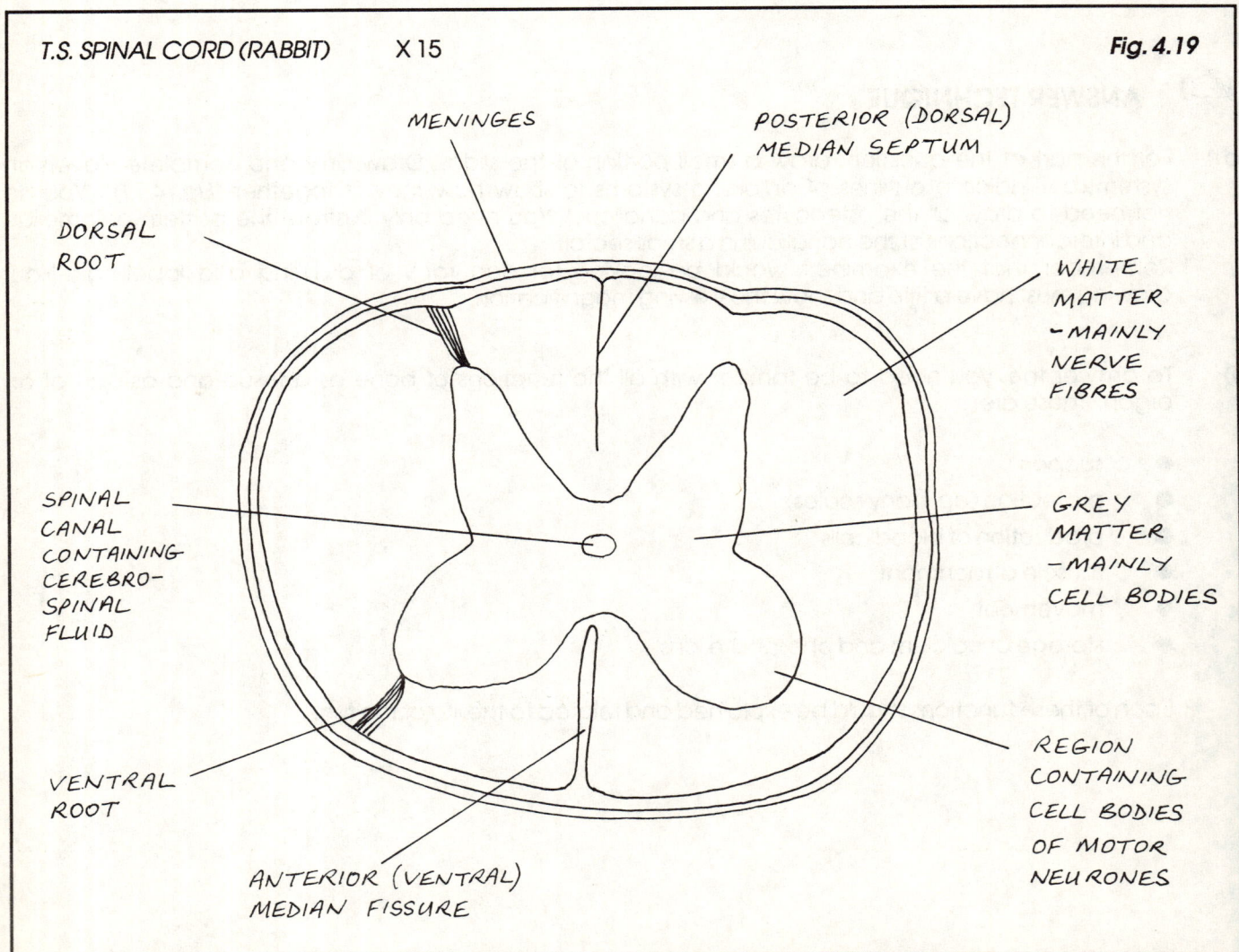

MENINGES

POSTERIOR (DORSAL) MEDIAN SEPTUM

DORSAL ROOT

WHITE MATTER - MAINLY NERVE FIBRES

SPINAL CANAL CONTAINING CEREBRO-SPINAL FLUID

GREY MATTER - MAINLY CELL BODIES

VENTRAL ROOT

REGION CONTAINING CELL BODIES OF MOTOR NEURONES

ANTERIOR (VENTRAL) MEDIAN FISSURE

STRUCTURE OF SPINAL CORD RELATED TO FUNCTION

STRUCTURE	FUNCTION
Meninges	Protective membranes surrounding the spinal cord, containing cerebrospinal fluid.
White matter	White colour due to the high lipid content of the insulating Schwann cells surrounding the neurones. Carries impulses into and out of the CNS.
Grey matter	Grey colour due to the density of the cell bodies of the neurones. Site of synapses between the different types of neurones.
Dorsal root	Carries sensory nerve fibres into the spinal cord.
Dorsal root ganglion	Contains the cell bodies of the sensory neurones.
Ventral root	Carries motor nerve fibres out of the spinal cord.
Spinal canal	Contains cerebrospinal fluid which allows diffusion of nutrients.

NEURONES FROM GREY MATTER OF RABBIT SPINAL CORD   X 400   Fig. 4.20

NUCLEUS

AXON

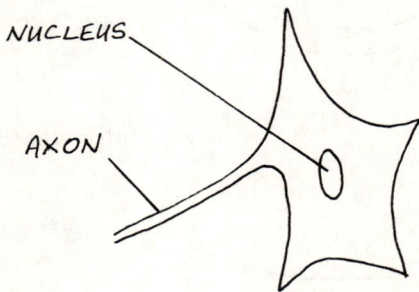

CELL BODY OF MOTOR NEURONE

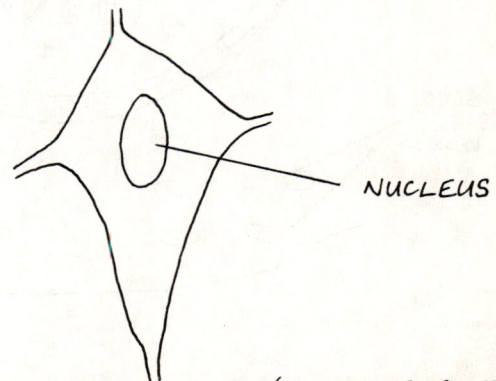

NUCLEUS

PYRAMIDAL CELL (RELAY NEURONE) FROM CEREBRAL CORTEX

■ **ALIMENTARY CANAL**
(Figs. 4.21 - 4.23)
This is circular in transverse section with a wide lumen. Its walls are composed of an innermost mucosa which is specialised differently in the various regions but covered in columnar epithelium:

eg. ● infolding gastric pits in the stomach
 ● finger-like projections (villi) in the ileum.

Below the mucosa is the submucosa, a paler layer containing blood vessels. The outer layers are smooth muscle in circular and longitudinal layers.

L.S. STOMACH WALL   X 40   Fig. 4.21

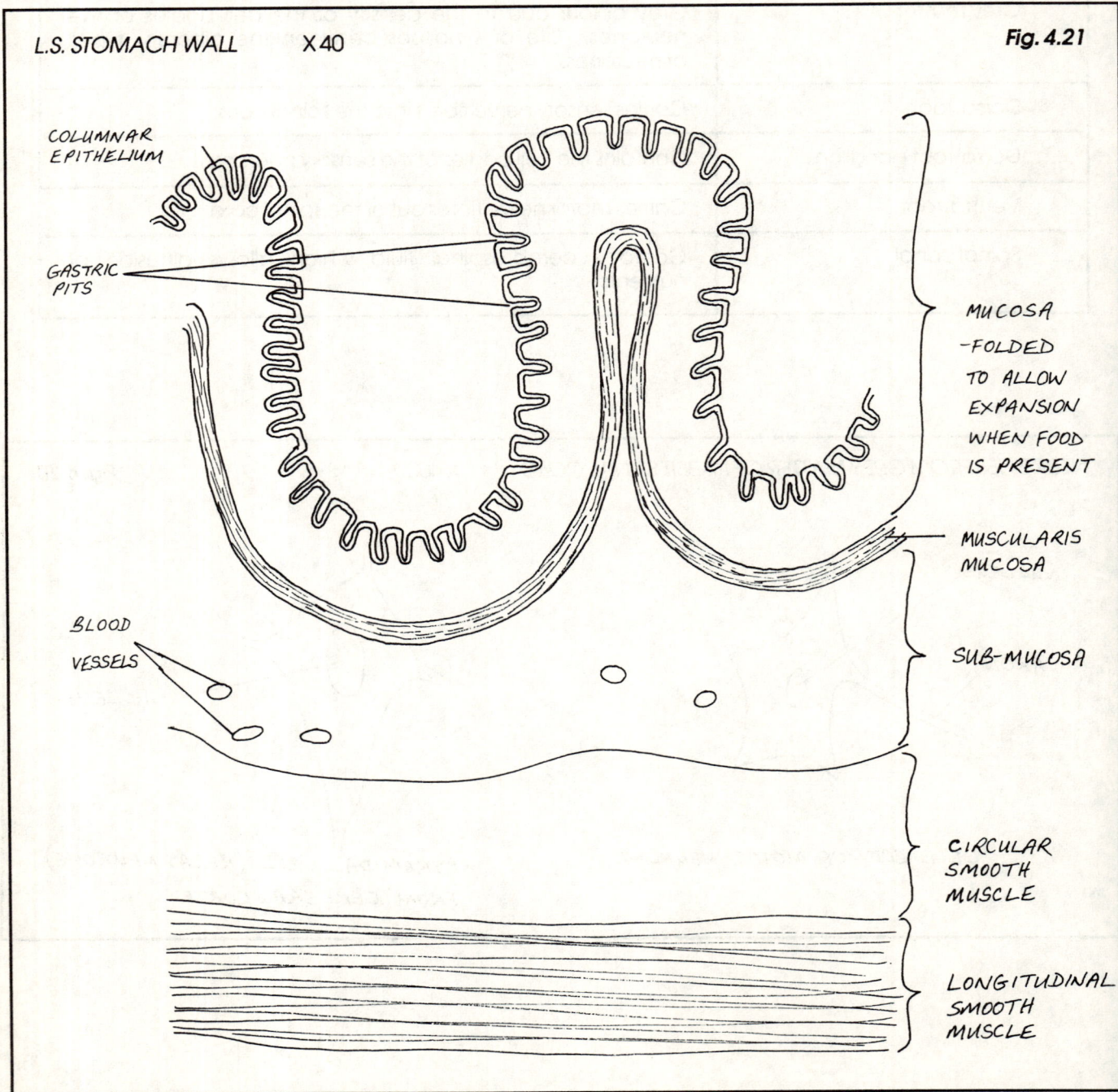

COLUMNAR EPITHELIUM

GASTRIC PITS

MUCOSA -FOLDED TO ALLOW EXPANSION WHEN FOOD IS PRESENT

MUSCULARIS MUCOSA

BLOOD VESSELS

SUB-MUCOSA

CIRCULAR SMOOTH MUSCLE

LONGITUDINAL SMOOTH MUSCLE

ILEUM WALL T.S.   X 14   **Fig. 4.22**

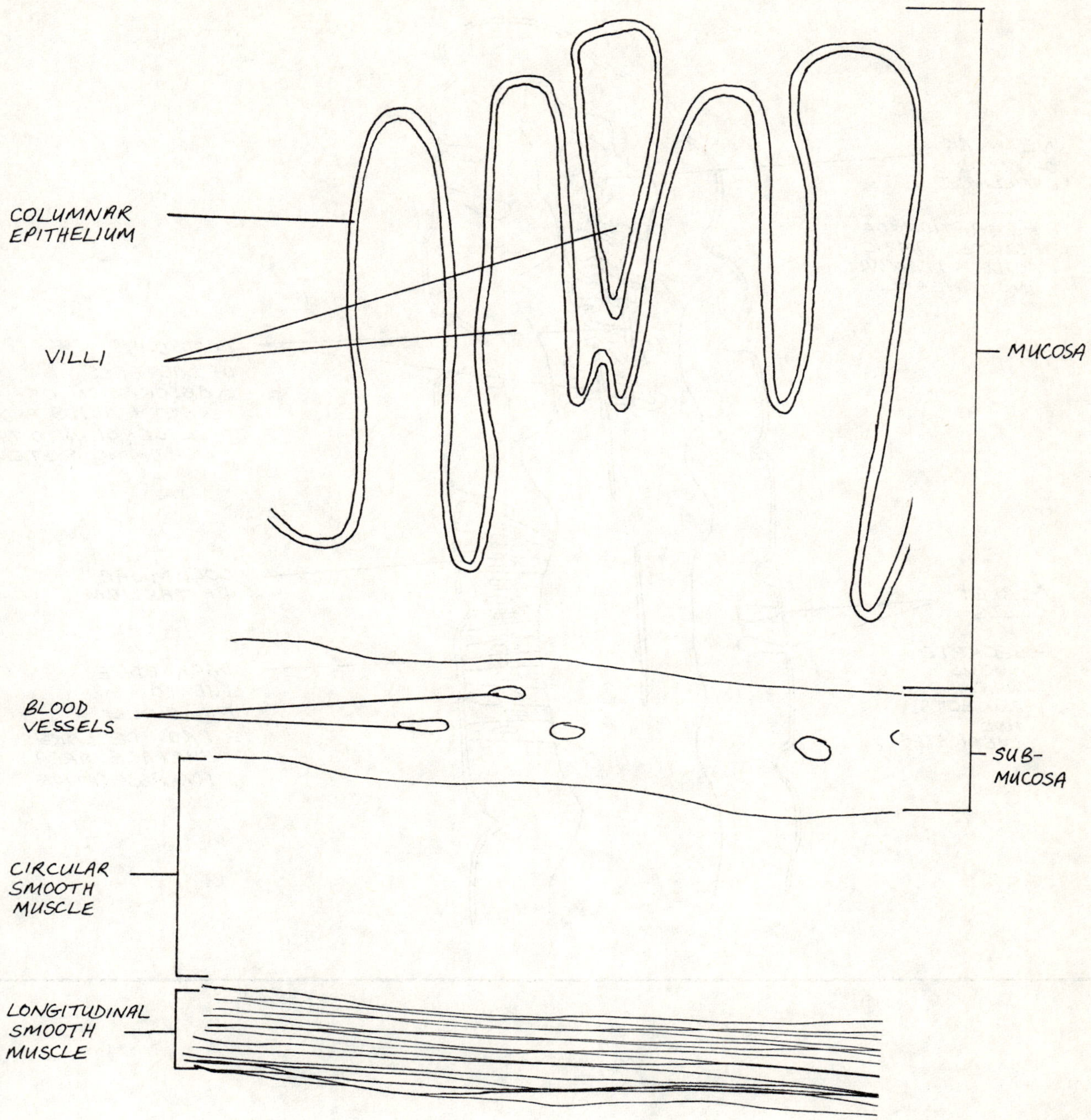

COLUMNAR
EPITHELIUM

VILLI

MUCOSA

BLOOD
VESSELS

SUB-
MUCOSA

CIRCULAR
SMOOTH
MUSCLE

LONGITUDINAL
SMOOTH
MUSCLE

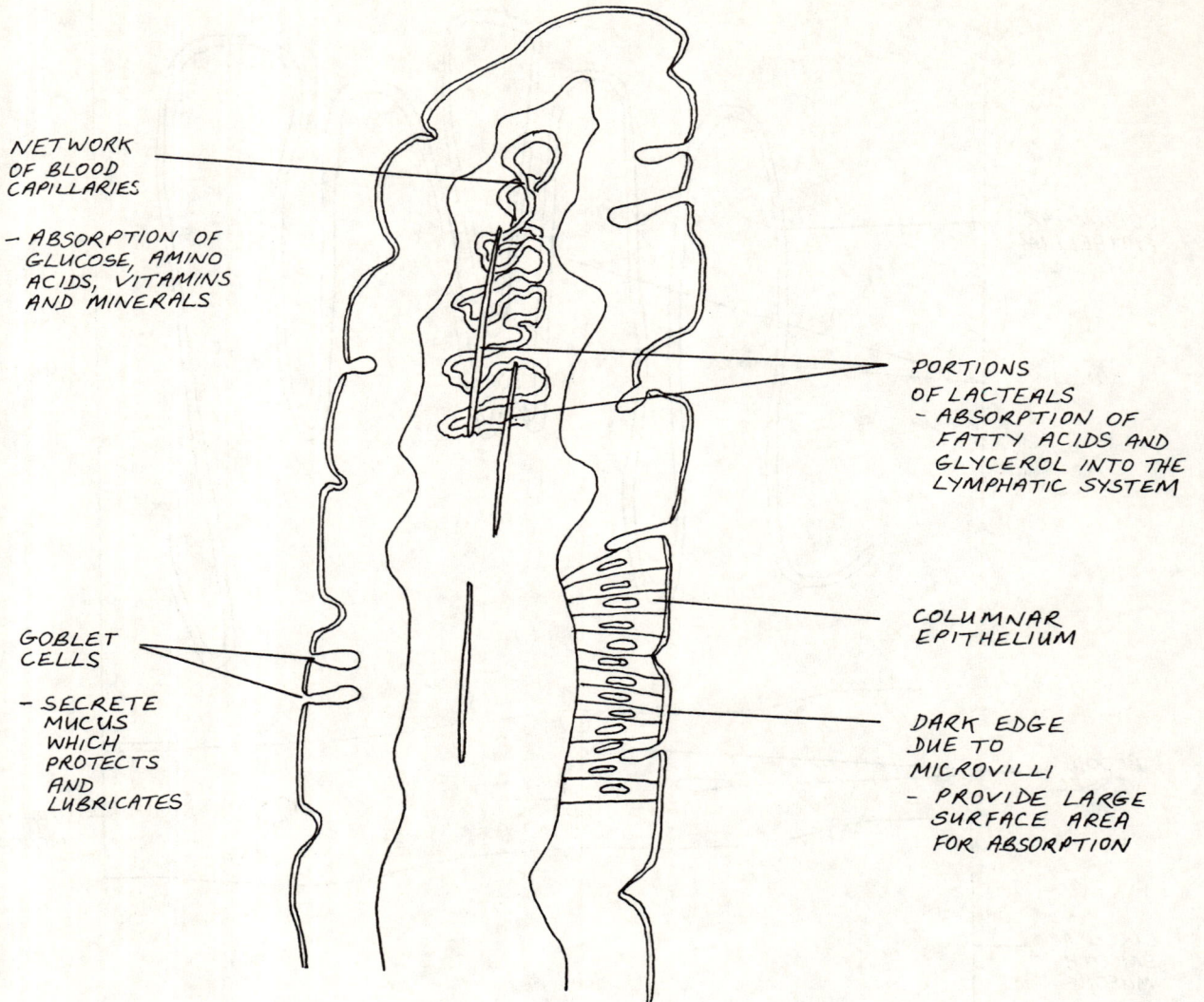

VILLUS DETAIL   X 400   **Fig. 4.23**

NETWORK
OF BLOOD
CAPILLARIES

– ABSORPTION OF
GLUCOSE, AMINO
ACIDS, VITAMINS
AND MINERALS

PORTIONS
OF LACTEALS
– ABSORPTION OF
FATTY ACIDS AND
GLYCEROL INTO THE
LYMPHATIC SYSTEM

GOBLET
CELLS

– SECRETE
MUCUS
WHICH
PROTECTS
AND
LUBRICATES

COLUMNAR
EPITHELIUM

DARK EDGE
DUE TO
MICROVILLI

– PROVIDE LARGE
SURFACE AREA
FOR ABSORPTION

TABLE SHOWING FUNCTIONS OF THE REGIONS OF ALIMENTARY CANAL

REGION	FUNCTIONS
Mucosa	The epithelium is glandular in parts, producing specialised digestive juices, and mucus. The mucosa also contains blood and lymph vessels for absorption and transport of the products of digestion.
Muscularis mucosa	Smooth muscle region which aids movement of the villi to bring them into contact with the semi-digested food.
Sub-mucosa	Contains blood and lymph vessels which transport the products of digestion. The blood vessels connect with the hepatic portal vein which carries nutrients to the liver. Nerve fibres in the sub-mucosa control the peristaltic contractions of the muscles of the alimentary canal and the release of secretions from the glands.
Muscle layers (muscularis externa)	Circular and longitudinal smooth muscles contract alternately to produce the peristaltic movements which move the semi-digested food along the alimentary canal.

The next table will help you to identify the different sections of the alimentary canal which could be given to you in the practical exam.

TABLE SHOWING DIFFERENCES BETWEEN STOMACH, DUODENUM AND ILEUM

STOMACH	DUODENUM	ILEUM
Mucosa with folds (rugae) to allow expansion during food storage.	No folds in mucosa.	No folds in mucosa.
No villi.	Leaf shaped villi projecting into lumen.	Finger like villi projecting into lumen.
Gastric pits forming gastric glands in the mucosa.	Crypts of Lieberkuhn in the mucosa leading to Brunner's glands in the sub-mucosa.	Crypts of Lieberkuhn only.

■ THYROID GLAND
(*Fig. 4.24*)
This is composed of roughly circular, large follicles around blood capillaries. The wall of each follicle is made of cuboidal epithelium. The cavities of the follicles may be darkly staining due to accumulated thyroxine secreted by them.

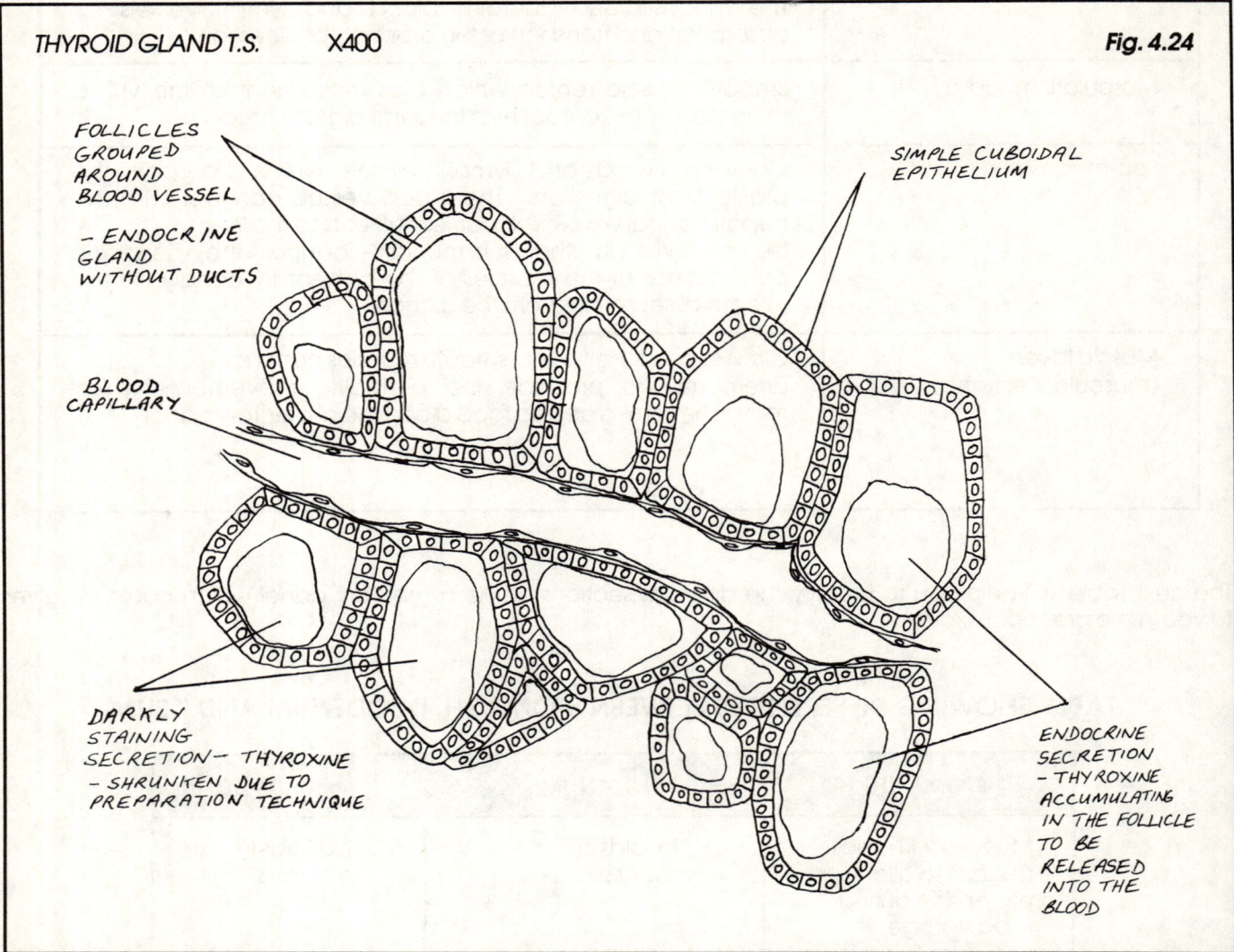

THYROID GLAND T.S.   X400   **Fig. 4.24**

FOLLICLES GROUPED AROUND BLOOD VESSEL

– ENDOCRINE GLAND WITHOUT DUCTS

BLOOD CAPILLARY

SIMPLE CUBOIDAL EPITHELIUM

DARKLY STAINING SECRETION – THYROXINE – SHRUNKEN DUE TO PREPARATION TECHNIQUE

ENDOCRINE SECRETION – THYROXINE ACCUMULATING IN THE FOLLICLE TO BE RELEASED INTO THE BLOOD

■ LIVER
(Fig. 4.25)

This is dark red or purple stained and is composed of chains of cells radiating from central veins in transverse section. It may be possible to see that these collections of cells form hexagonal sections, with small blood vessels at the boundaries between them. The liver cells are very small with tiny channels between the rows of cells.

T.S. LIVER (PIG)   X 100   Fig. 4.25

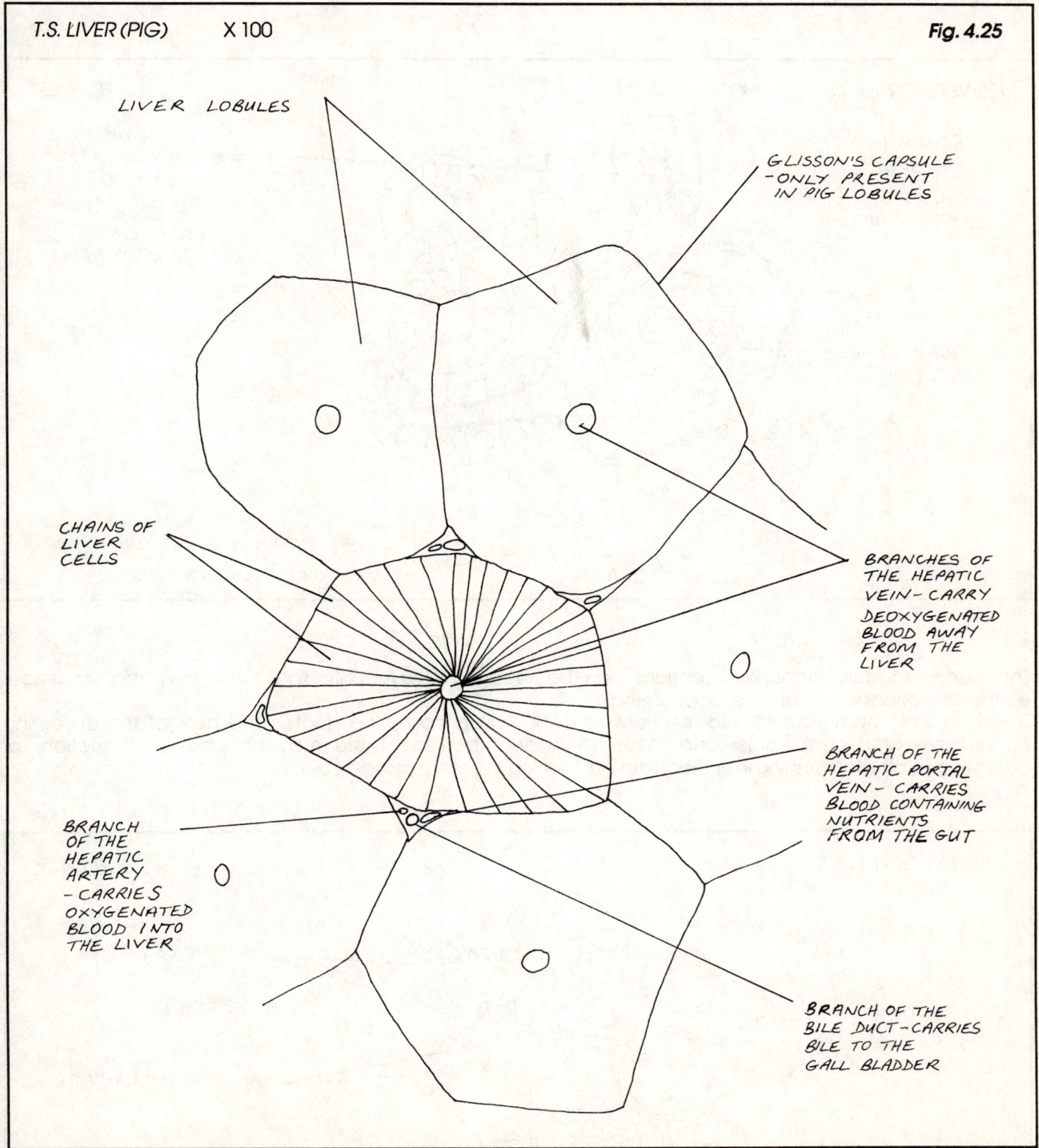

LIVER LOBULES

GLISSON'S CAPSULE - ONLY PRESENT IN PIG LOBULES

CHAINS OF LIVER CELLS

BRANCHES OF THE HEPATIC VEIN - CARRY DEOXYGENATED BLOOD AWAY FROM THE LIVER

BRANCH OF THE HEPATIC PORTAL VEIN - CARRIES BLOOD CONTAINING NUTRIENTS FROM THE GUT

BRANCH OF THE HEPATIC ARTERY - CARRIES OXYGENATED BLOOD INTO THE LIVER

BRANCH OF THE BILE DUCT - CARRIES BILE TO THE GALL BLADDER

MAMMALIAN ORGANS

KIDNEY
(Figs. 4.26 - 4.27)
A transverse section of the kidney cortex may be recognised by the presence of Bowman's capsules and glomeruli. The Bowman's capsules are fairly large; circular in section and composed of squamous epithelium.
Inside each is a dense network of capillaries which appear quite dark. Surrounding the capsules are many smaller circular sections of kidney tubules. These are made of cuboidal epithelium. The proximal portions of the tubules have microvilli, which appear as a "fuzzy" layer next to the lumen. Microvilli are not present in the distal portions of the tubules.

KIDNEY CORTEX T.S.   X400   Fig. 4.26

The kidney medulla transverse sections can be recognised by containing some very thin squamous epithelial sections which are the loops of Henlé.
There are also numerous circular sections of thick walled collecting ducts. The cells of the collecting ducts have prominent nuclei and therefore appear darker. There may also be some sections of collecting ducts seen running in vertical section, forming parallel passageways.

KIDNEY MEDULLA T.S.   X400   Fig. 4.27

154

■ SKIN
(Fig. 4.28)
Vertical sections through the mammalian skin show the stratified epithelium, with the prominent dark red or purple stained cornified layers with spaces between them. There are hairs projecting through the epidermis, originating from horse-shoe shaped follicles deep in the dermis. There are light coloured, irregularly shaped sebaceous glands attached to one or both sides of the shaft of the hairs. Sweat glands appear as a collection of tiny circular tubules in the dermis. Below the dermis is a layer of adipose tissue.

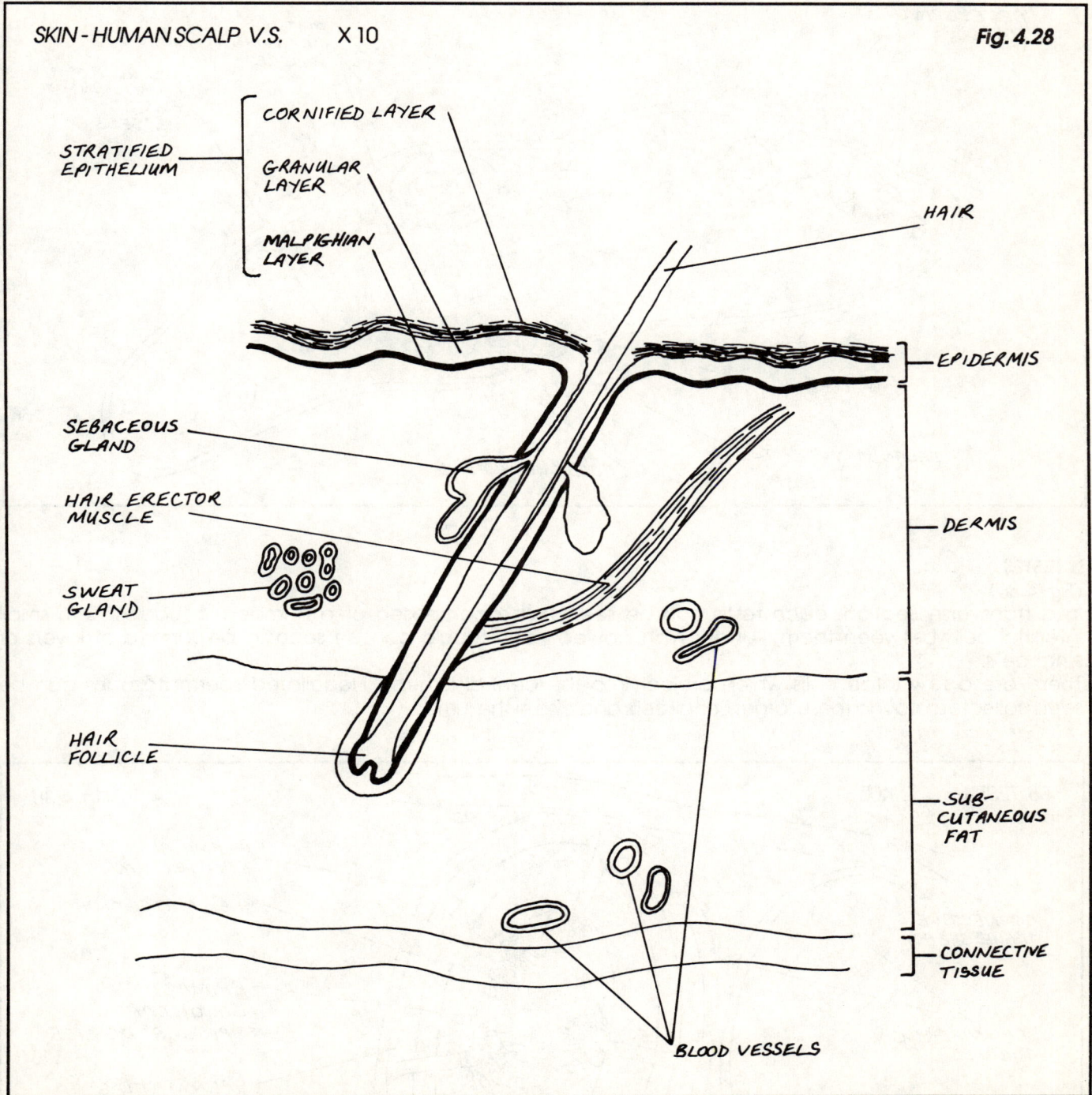

SKIN - HUMAN SCALP V.S.   X 10   Fig. 4.28

■ OVARY
(Fig. 4.29)

This is an elongated, oval structure containing follicles at varying stages of development. Immature follicles consist of a central oocyte, surrounded by very tiny, granular follicle cells. Mature Graafian follicles contain a clear kidney-shaped space around an oocyte at one side, still surrounded by follicle cells. These mature follicles tend to cause bulges in the ovary wall.

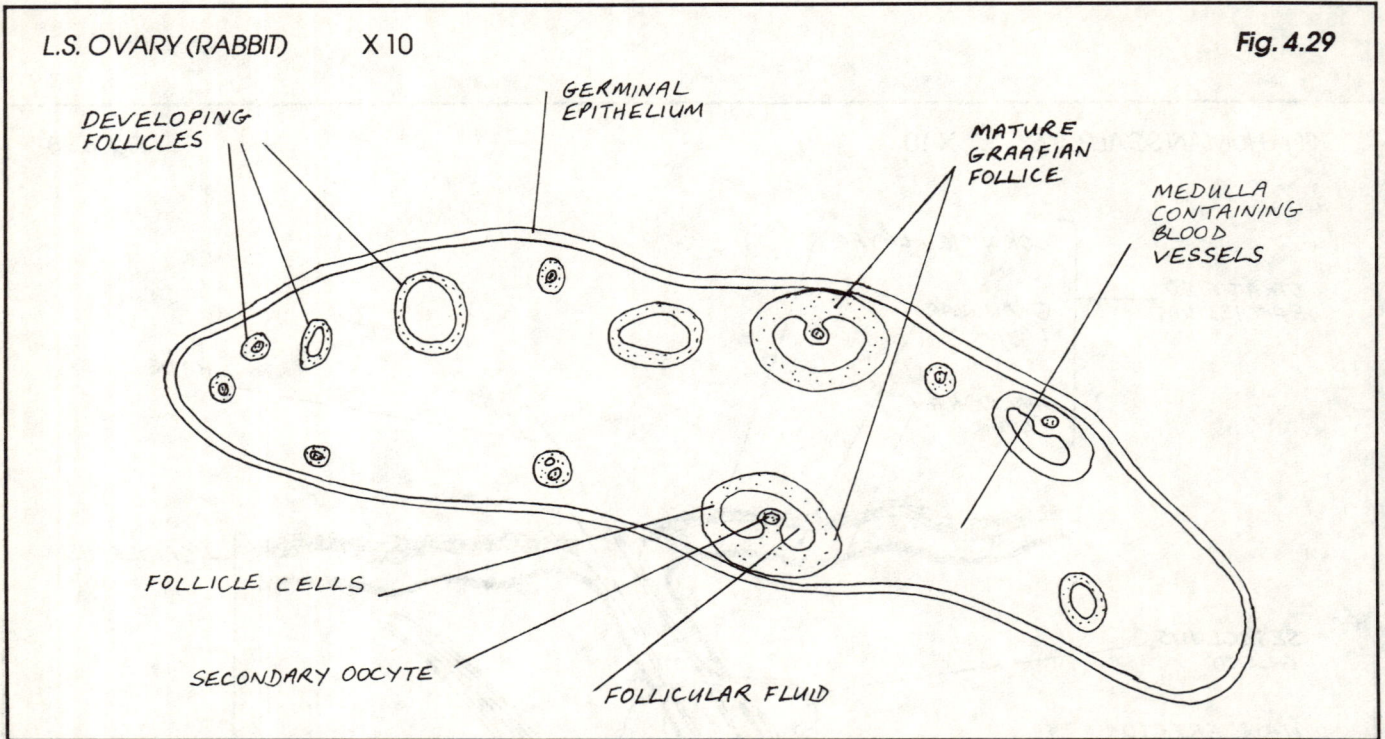

L.S. OVARY (RABBIT)   X 10   Fig. 4.29

DEVELOPING FOLLICLES
GERMINAL EPITHELIUM
MATURE GRAAFIAN FOLLICE
MEDULLA CONTAINING BLOOD VESSELS
FOLLICLE CELLS
SECONDARY OOCYTE
FOLLICULAR FLUID

■ TESTES
(Fig. 4.30)

In a transverse section, each testis can be seen to be composed of a number of tubules, with small interstial cells between them. Under high power, each tubule can be seen to be formed of layers of small cells.

There are a few large cells which project into the central lumen. Flagellated spermatozoans can be seen collected around these larger Sertoli cells and also in the lumen.

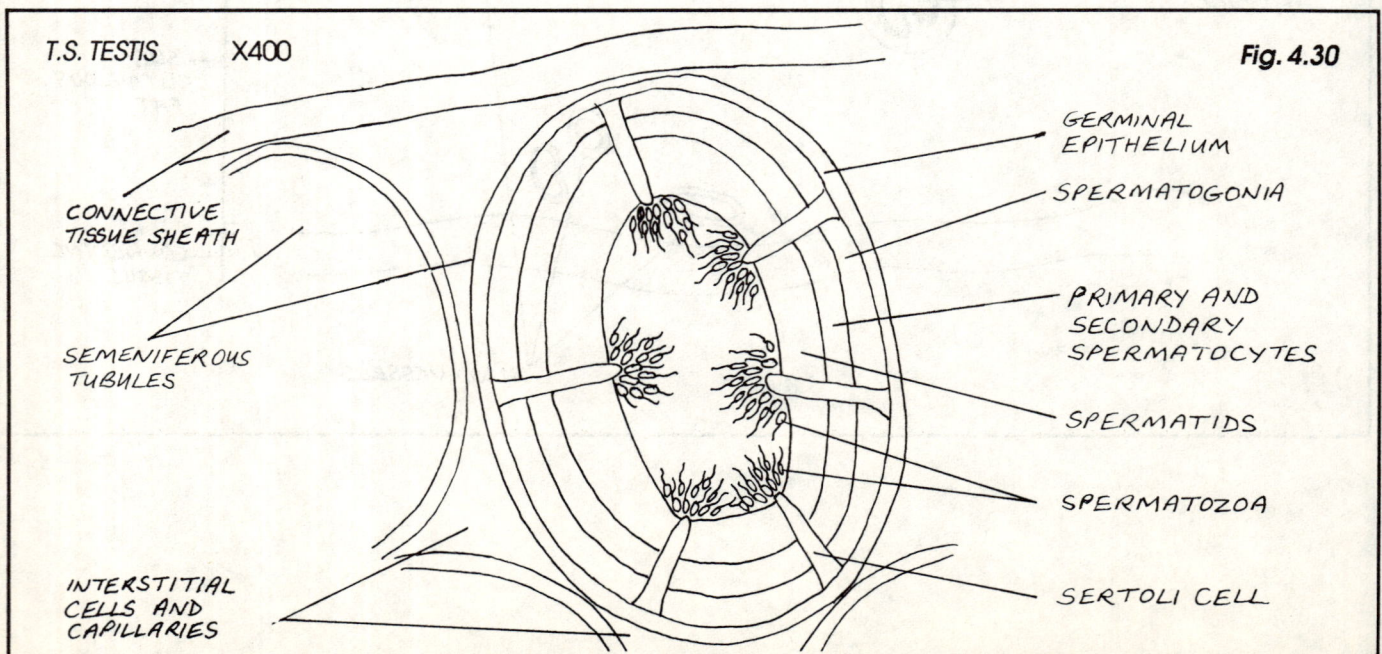

T.S. TESTIS   X400   Fig. 4.30

CONNECTIVE TISSUE SHEATH
SEMENIFEROUS TUBULES
INTERSTITIAL CELLS AND CAPILLARIES
GERMINAL EPITHELIUM
SPERMATOGONIA
PRIMARY AND SECONDARY SPERMATOCYTES
SPERMATIDS
SPERMATOZOA
SERTOLI CELL

■ ARTERIES AND VEINS
(Figs. 4.31 - 4.32)
Arteries are more circular in cross section, veins are more elongated (oval), with a wider lumen. They both have an outer fibrous layer containing collagen and elastic fibres. Inside this is a layer of smooth muscle which is considerably thicker in the arteries. The innermost layer is an endothelium of squamous cells; this layer is folded in arteries and smooth in veins.

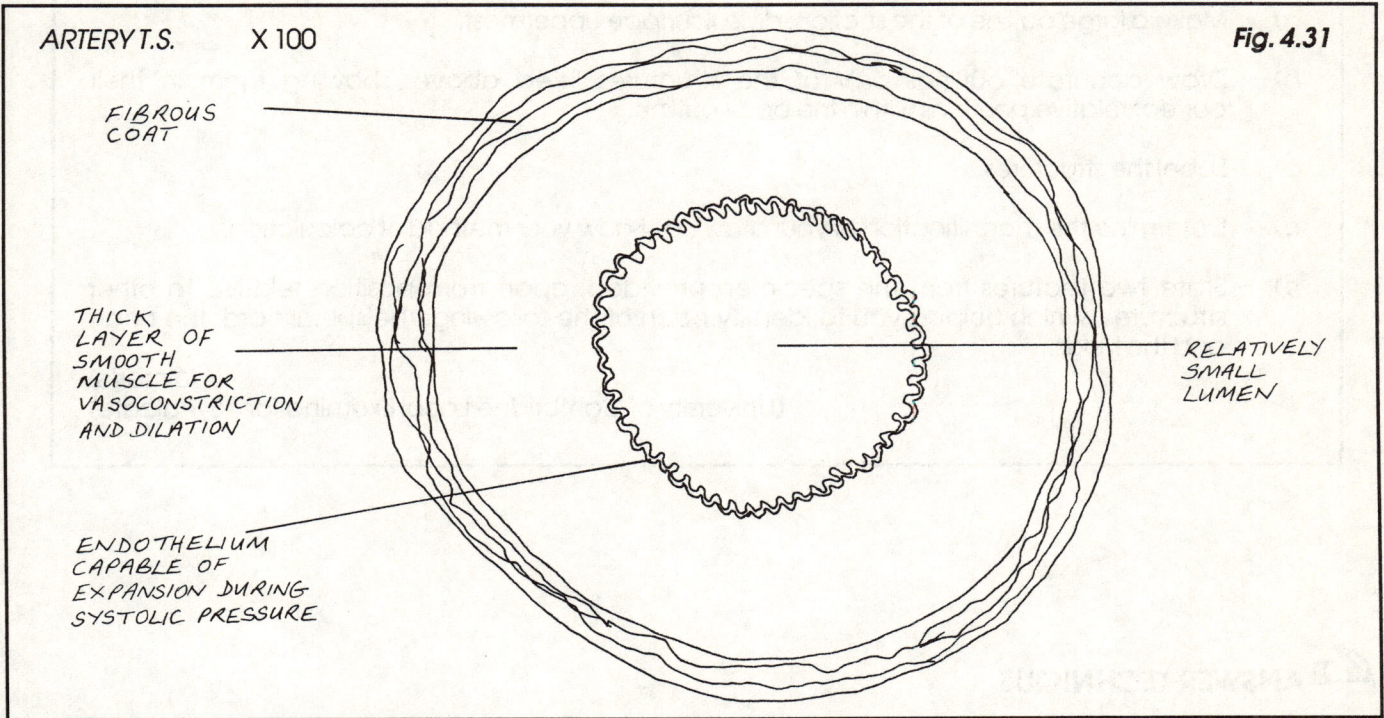

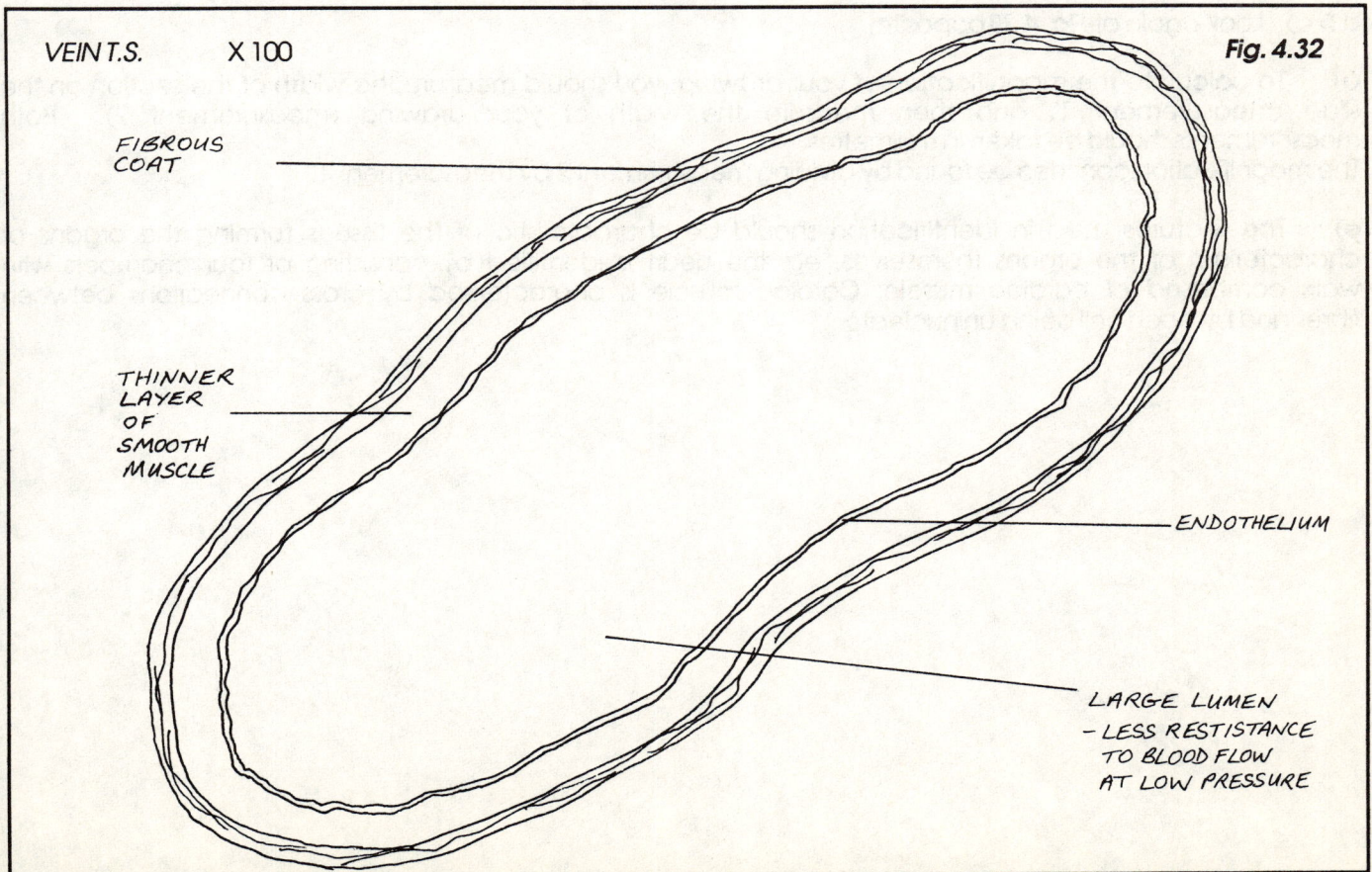

ARTERY T.S.   X 100   Fig. 4.31

FIBROUS COAT

THICK LAYER OF SMOOTH MUSCLE FOR VASOCONSTRICTION AND DILATION

RELATIVELY SMALL LUMEN

ENDOTHELIUM CAPABLE OF EXPANSION DURING SYSTOLIC PRESSURE

VEIN T.S.   X 100   Fig. 4.32

FIBROUS COAT

THINNER LAYER OF SMOOTH MUSCLE

ENDOTHELIUM

LARGE LUMEN - LESS RESTISTANCE TO BLOOD FLOW AT LOW PRESSURE

EXAM QUESTION 2

The slide labelled K8 is a transverse section through the thoracic region of a rat embryo. From your knowledge of the structure of the mammalian body, identify the following structures in K8: spinal cord, ribs, sternum, lungs, heart.

a) Make a large outline of the section, dorsal surface uppermost.

b) Draw accurate outlines only of the structures listed above, showing them in their correct relative positions within the body outline.

c) Label the structures.

d) Determine the magnification of your drawing. Show your method of calculation.

e) State two features from the specimen provided, apart from position relative to other structures, which helped you to identify each of the following: the spinal cord, the heart and the lungs.

(13 marks)
(University of Cambridge Local Examinations Syndicate)

ANSWER TECHNIQUE

a) Look at *Fig. 4.33* opposite. To orientate the section you should be aware that the spinal cord is found towards the dorsal surface and the sternum towards the ventral surface.

b & c) Look again at *Fig. 4.33* opposite.

d) To calculate the magnification of your drawing, you should measure the width of the section on the slide (measurement 1) and then measure the width of your drawing (measurement 2). Both measurements should be taken in millimetres.
The magnification can then be found by dividing measurement 2 by measurement 1.

e) The features used in identification should be characteristic of the tissues forming the organs or characteristic of the organs themselves, *eg.* the heart is identified by consisting of four chambers with walls composed of cardiac muscle; Cardiac muscle is characterised by cross connections between fibres and by each cell being uninucleate.

T.S. THORAX OF RAT EMBRYO   X 10   **Fig. 4.33**

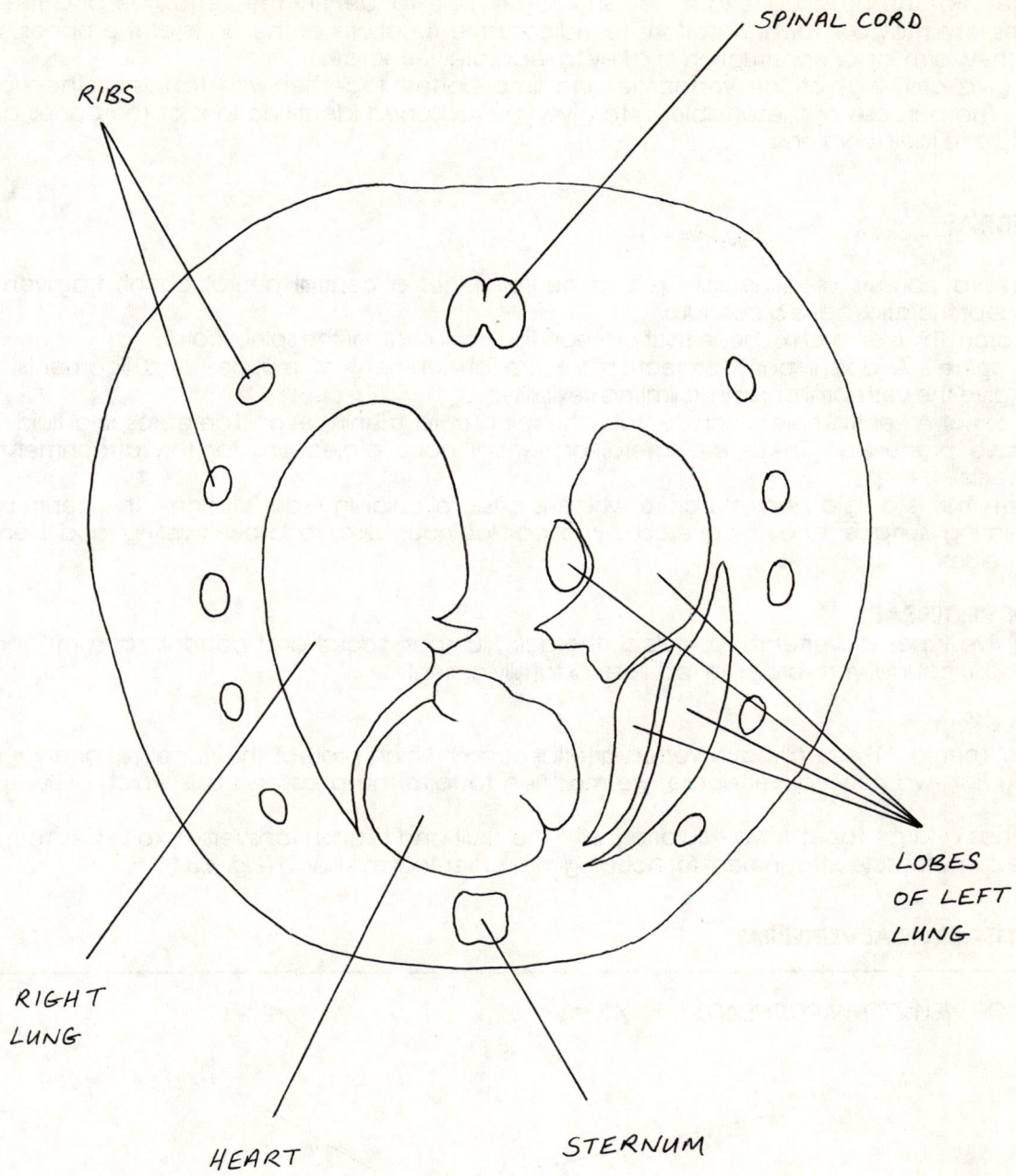

SPINAL CORD

RIBS

LOBES
OF LEFT
LUNG

RIGHT
LUNG

HEART   STERNUM

MAMMALIAN VERTEBRAE AND LIMB BONES

You should be familiar with the major bones of the mammalian skeleton as part of your theory knowledge. For the practical exam, you should be able to identify the vertebrae and the bones of a limb. Questions may ask for annotations to indicate the functions of the parts of the bones, the types of joints that they form, or for construction of a key to separate vertebrae.

Here we give drawings of the vertebrae and limb bones, together with tables of their location and functions. The purpose of these tables is to give you reasoned identifications of the bones and to relate their structure to their functions.

■ VERTEBRAE

Each vertebra consists of a neural arch, a neural spine, a central neural canal, transverse processes and all except the atlas have a centrum.

○ **Neural arch** This is an arch of bone that protects the dorsal side of the spinal cord.

○ **Neural spine** A dorsal bony projection for the attachment of muscles and ligaments. The linking ligaments give the vertebral column its limited flexibility.

○ **Neural canal** A central hole which contains the spinal cord, meninges and cerebrospinal fluid.

○ **Transverse processes** These are lateral or ventral bony projections for the attachment of muscles and ligaments.

○ **Centrum** This is a rigid bony structure which is often circular in cross section. The centrum provides a flat articulating surface and is covered by a cartilaginous disc to allow twisting and bending of the vertebral column.

❑ TYPES OF VERTEBRAE

There are five types of vertebra: cervical, thoracic, lumbar, sacral and caudal. In some mammals (eg. rabbit or man) caudal vertebrae are reduced or totally absent.

○ **Cervical** (neck) These all have vertebrarterial canals which protect the vertebral artery running to the brain. The first two cervical vertebrae are modified to form the atlas and axis which allow movement of the head.

The atlas has a large facet for articulation with the skull and broad transverse processes forming cervical ribs. These allow muscle attachment for nodding movements of the head (*Fig. 4.34*).

ATLAS (FIRST CERVICAL VERTEBRA)

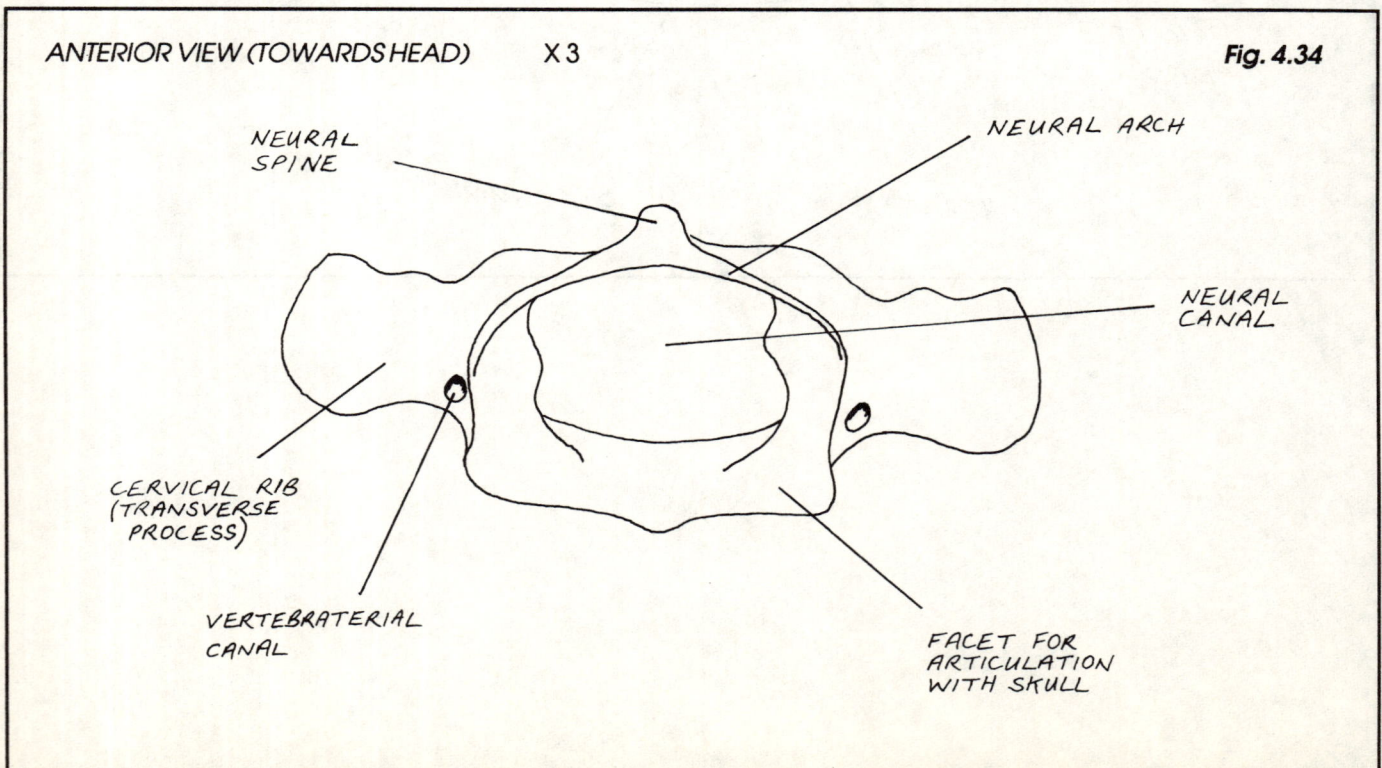

ANTERIOR VIEW (TOWARDS HEAD)   X 3   Fig. 4.34

NEURAL SPINE

NEURAL ARCH

NEURAL CANAL

CERVICAL RIB (TRANSVERSE PROCESS)

VERTEBRATERIAL CANAL

FACET FOR ARTICULATION WITH SKULL

The axis has a small bony peg called the odontoid process which fits into the neural canal of the atlas and allows the head to turn (*Figs. 4.35 - 4.36*).

AXIS (SECOND CERVICAL VERTEBRA)

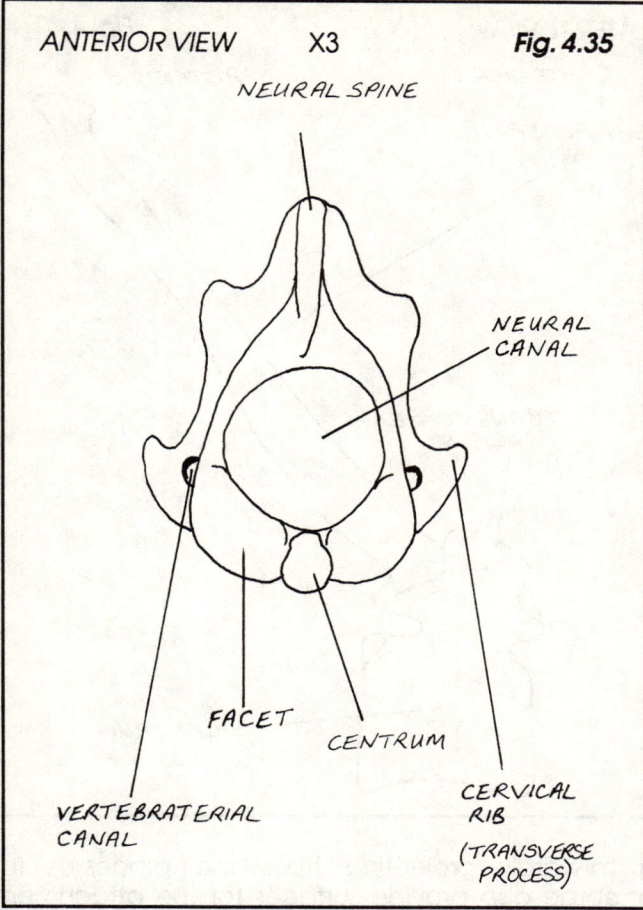

ANTERIOR VIEW   X3   **Fig. 4.35**

NEURAL SPINE

NEURAL CANAL

FACET

CENTRUM

VERTEBRATERIAL CANAL

CERVICAL RIB (TRANSVERSE PROCESS)

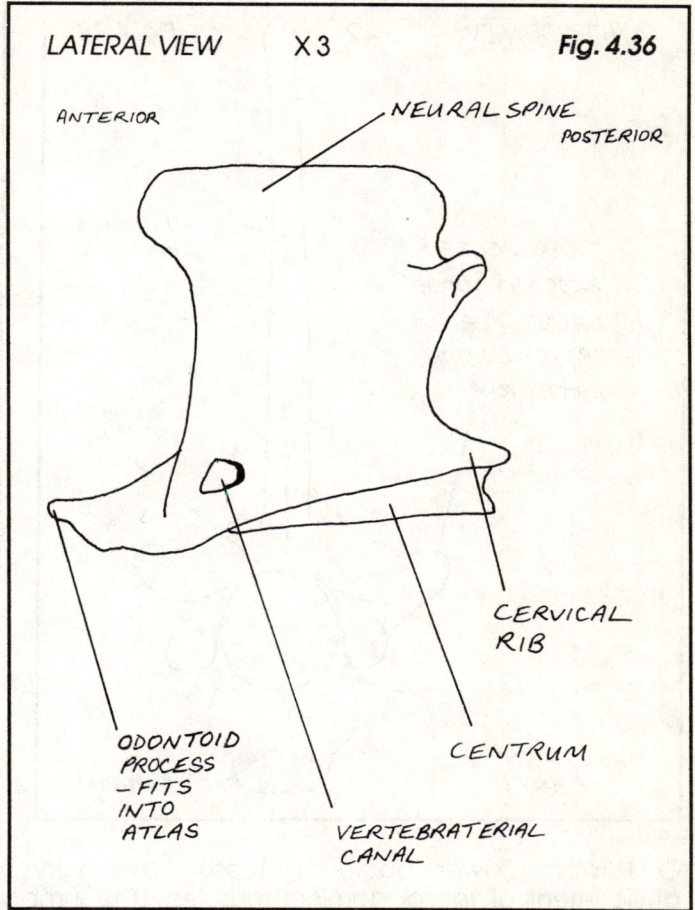

LATERAL VIEW   X3   **Fig. 4.36**

ANTERIOR

NEURAL SPINE POSTERIOR

CERVICAL RIB

ODONTOID PROCESS – FITS INTO ATLAS

VERTEBRATERIAL CANAL

CENTRUM

Other cervical vertebrae have double headed cervical ribs fused to the transverse processes (*Figs. 4.37 - 4.38*).

CERVICAL VERTEBRA

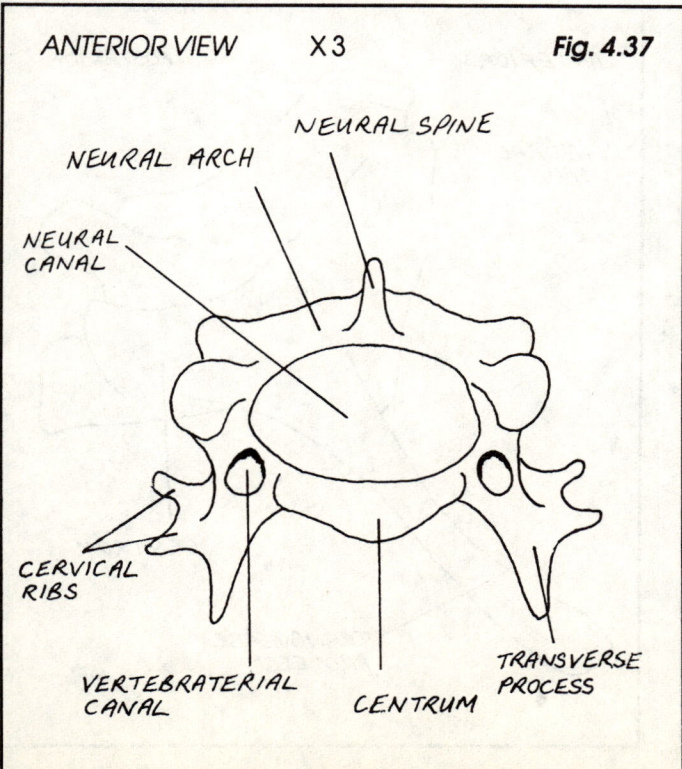

ANTERIOR VIEW   X3   **Fig. 4.37**

NEURAL ARCH

NEURAL SPINE

NEURAL CANAL

CERVICAL RIBS

VERTEBRATERIAL CANAL

CENTRUM

TRANSVERSE PROCESS

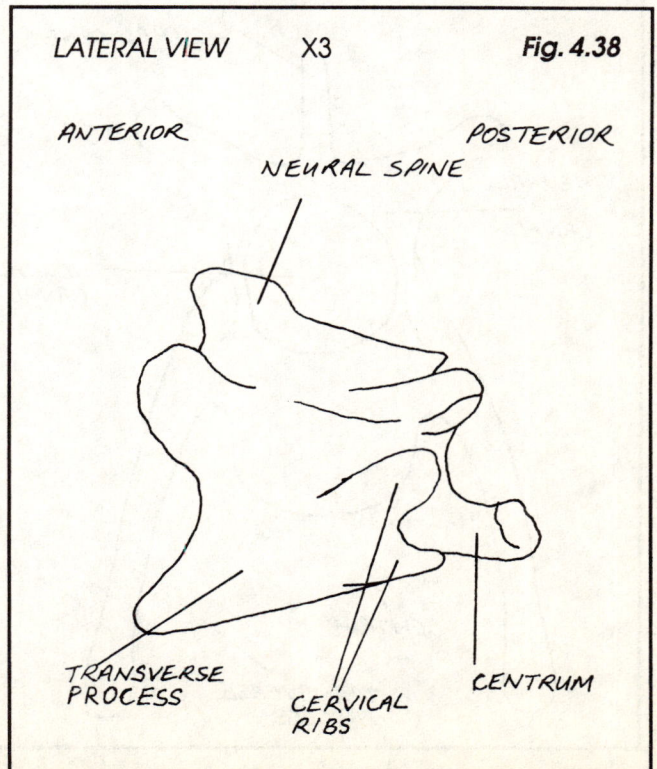

LATERAL VIEW   X3   **Fig. 4.38**

ANTERIOR

POSTERIOR

NEURAL SPINE

TRANSVERSE PROCESS

CERVICAL RIBS

CENTRUM

○ **Thoracic** (chest area)   These are characterised by very long backwardly projecting neural spines. The transverse processes have facets for articulation with the ribs (*Figs. 4.39 - 4.40*).

THORACIC VERTEBRA

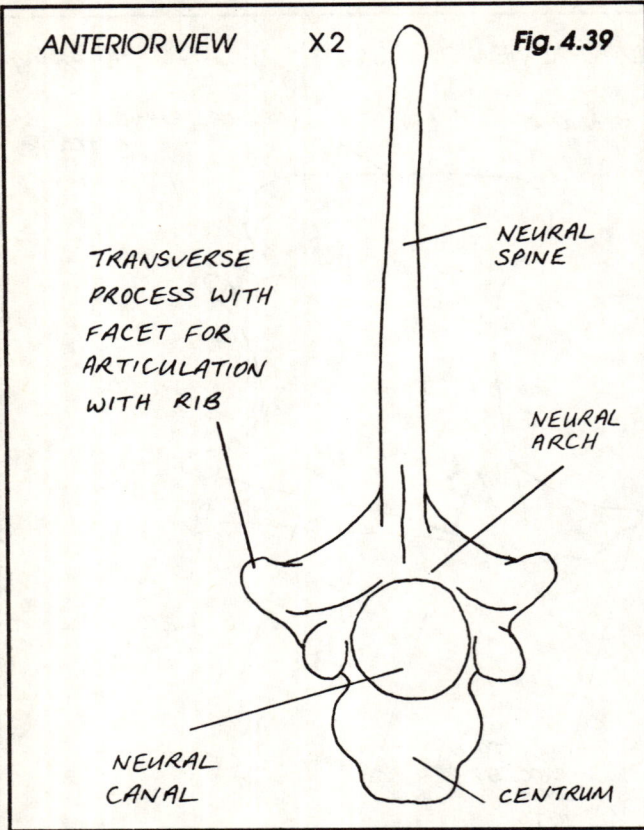

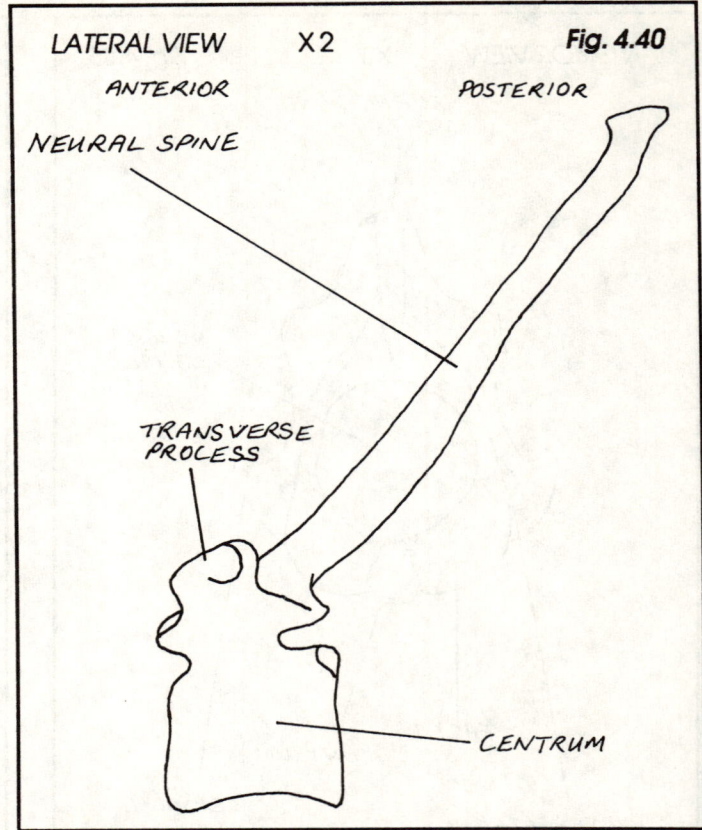

ANTERIOR VIEW X 2 **Fig. 4.39**	LATERAL VIEW X 2 **Fig. 4.40**

ANTERIOR VIEW   X 2   **Fig. 4.39**

TRANSVERSE PROCESS WITH FACET FOR ARTICULATION WITH RIB

NEURAL SPINE

NEURAL ARCH

NEURAL CANAL

CENTRUM

LATERAL VIEW   X 2   **Fig. 4.40**

ANTERIOR   POSTERIOR

NEURAL SPINE

TRANSVERSE PROCESS

CENTRUM

○ **Lumbar** (lower back)   These have very long forwardly projecting transverse processes for attachment of the abdominal muscles.   The lumbar vertebrae also provide surfaces for the attachment of the back muscles (*Figs. 4.41 - 4.42*).

LUMBAR VERTEBRA

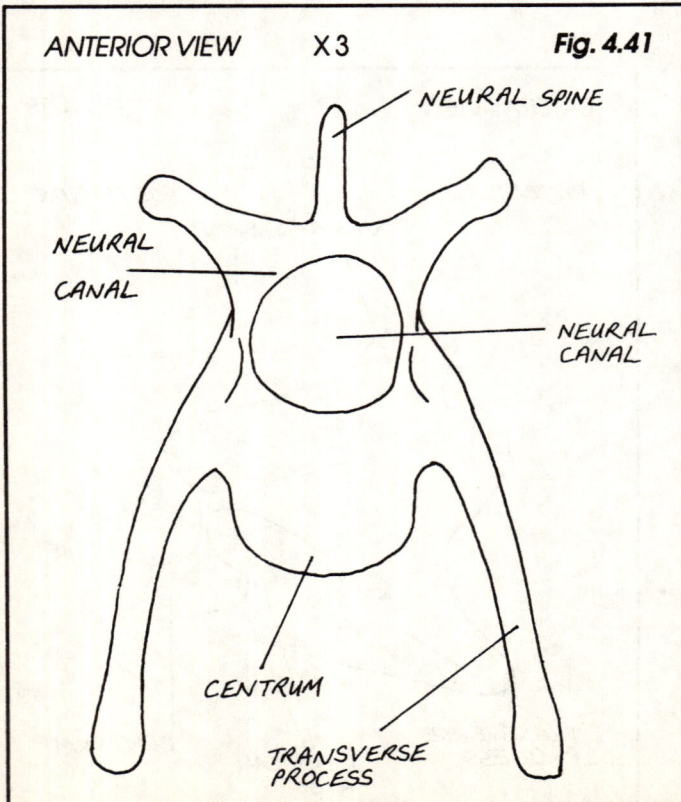

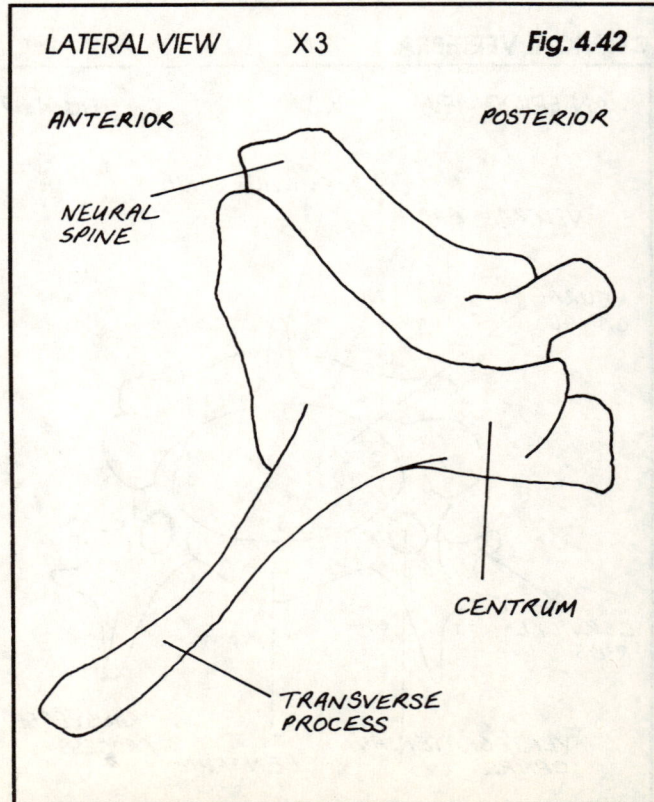

ANTERIOR VIEW   X 3   **Fig. 4.41**

NEURAL SPINE

NEURAL CANAL

NEURAL CANAL

CENTRUM

TRANSVERSE PROCESS

LATERAL VIEW   X 3   **Fig. 4.42**

ANTERIOR   POSTERIOR

NEURAL SPINE

CENTRUM

TRANSVERSE PROCESS

○ **Sacral** (hip region) These are fused to form the sacrum. The transverse processes of the first sacral vertebra have facets for articulation with the ilia of the pelvic girdle (*Figs. 4.43 - 4.44*).

SACRUM

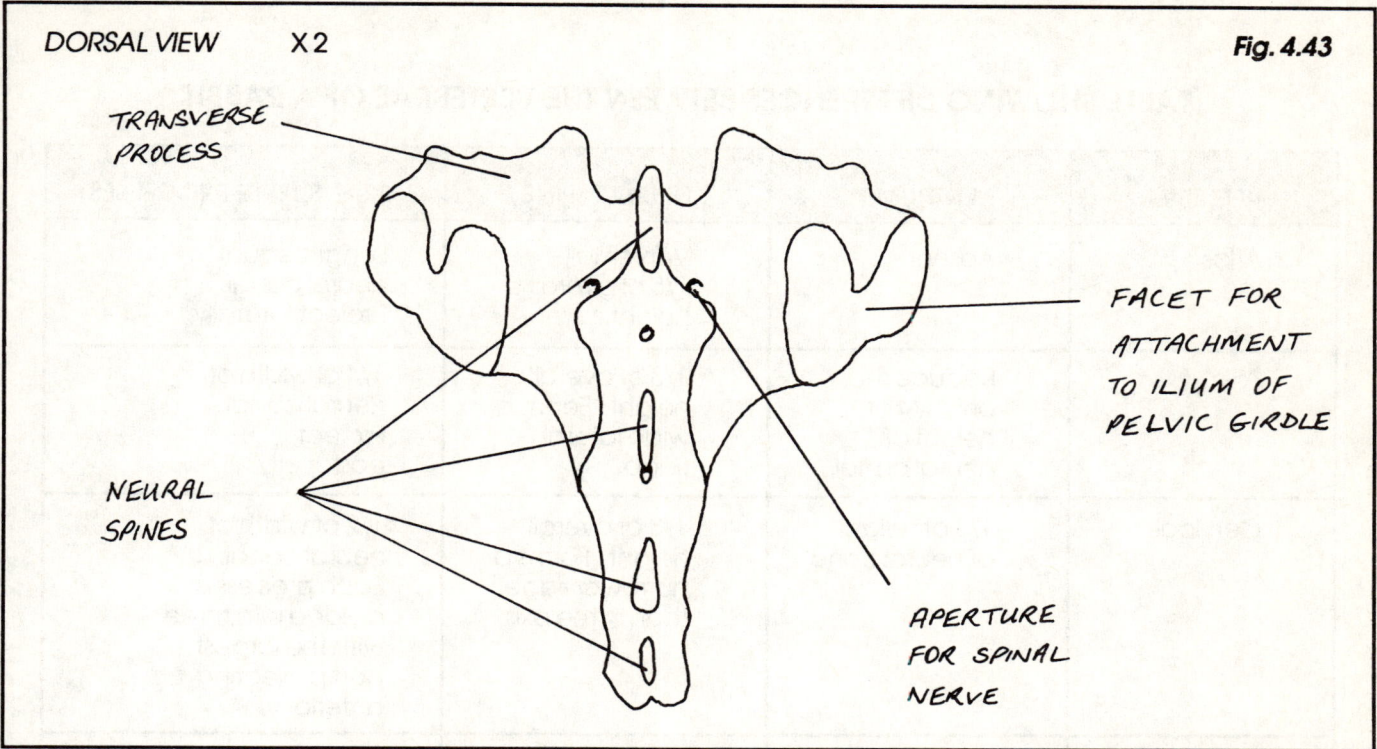

DORSAL VIEW   X 2   Fig. 4.43

TRANSVERSE PROCESS

FACET FOR ATTACHMENT TO ILIUM OF PELVIC GIRDLE

NEURAL SPINES

APERTURE FOR SPINAL NERVE

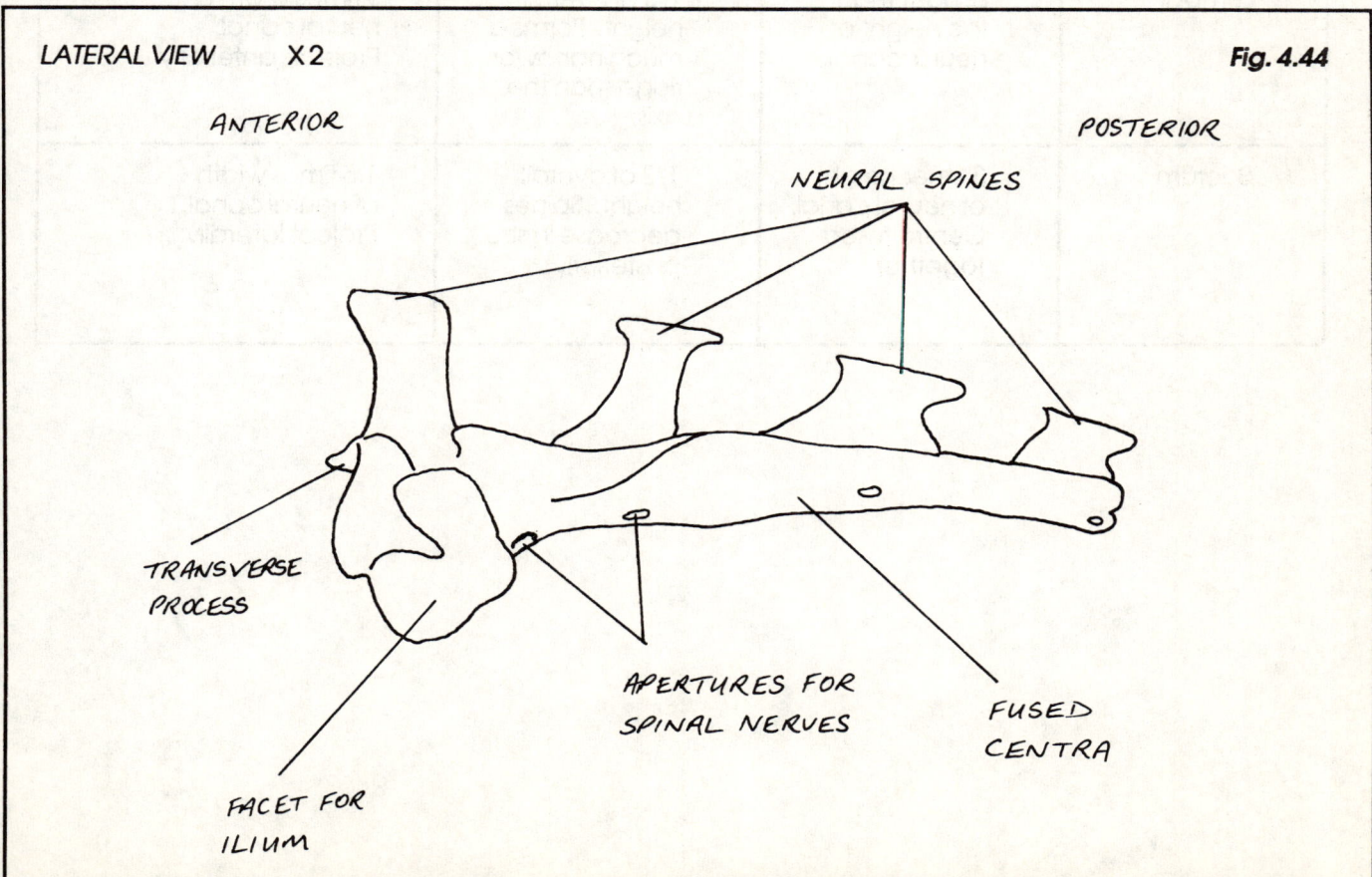

LATERAL VIEW   X 2   Fig. 4.44

ANTERIOR   POSTERIOR

NEURAL SPINES

TRANSVERSE PROCESS

APERTURES FOR SPINAL NERVES

FUSED CENTRA

FACET FOR ILIUM

○ **Caudal** (tail) The number of caudal vertebrae will vary depending on the tail length of the mammal. The size of the vertebrae diminishes along the length of the tail. The processes of the vertebrae also become progressively reduced.

TABLE SHOWING DIFFERENCES BETWEEN THE VERTEBRAE OF A RABBIT

VERTEBRA	CENTRUM	NEURAL SPINE	TRANSVERSE PROCESSES
Atlas	Absent	Very small - 1/5 of overall height.	Length equal to neural canal. Project laterally.
Axis	Reduced - only 1/4 of height of neural canal.	1/3 of overall height. Forms a wide lateral ridge.	1/4 of width of neural canal. Project posteriorly.
Cervical	1/3 of height of neural canal.	1/3 of overall height. Forms a narrower ridge than in the axis.	1/2 of width of neural canal. Each process is divided into three with the largest part projecting anteriorly.
Thoracic	Longer than the height of neural canal.	2/3 of overall height. Projects posteriorly.	Equal to width of neural canal. Projects laterally.
Lumbar	Longer than the height of neural canal.	1/3 of overall height. Forms a much narrower ridge than the axis.	3 times width of neural canal. Projects anteriorly.
Sacrum	3 times height of neural canal. Centra fused together.	1/2 of overall height. Spines decrease in size posteriorly.	1.5 times width of neural canal. Project laterally.

■ LIMB BONES

The bones of the hind limb of a rabbit are shown in *Fig. 4.45*

Each bone consists of two heads, a shaft and projections for the attachment of muscles. The head is formed largely of spongy bone and the outer part of the shaft of compact bone. Spongy bone is light with many marrow spaces whereas compact bone is formed of dense Haversian systems. The use of these two types of bone tissue in the different regions is related to the various stresses placed on the bone.

The shape of the head differs according to the type of joint it forms. The types of joint found in a limb are: ball and socket, hinge and gliding joints.

○ **Ball and socket joint**
 The head of the limb is rounded to articulate with a "socket" in the adjacent bone. The joint allows movement in all planes *ie.* rotational movement. *eg.* the joint between the head of the femur and the pelvis.

○ **Hinge joint**
 The head of one bone is grooved to articulate with ridges on the head of the adjacent bone. This allows movement in one plane *ie.* up and down movement. *eg.* the joints of the phalanges.

○ **Gliding joint**
 These joints are composed of several tightly fitting bones. The heads are smooth to allow limited sliding movements. *eg.* the joints of the tarsals.

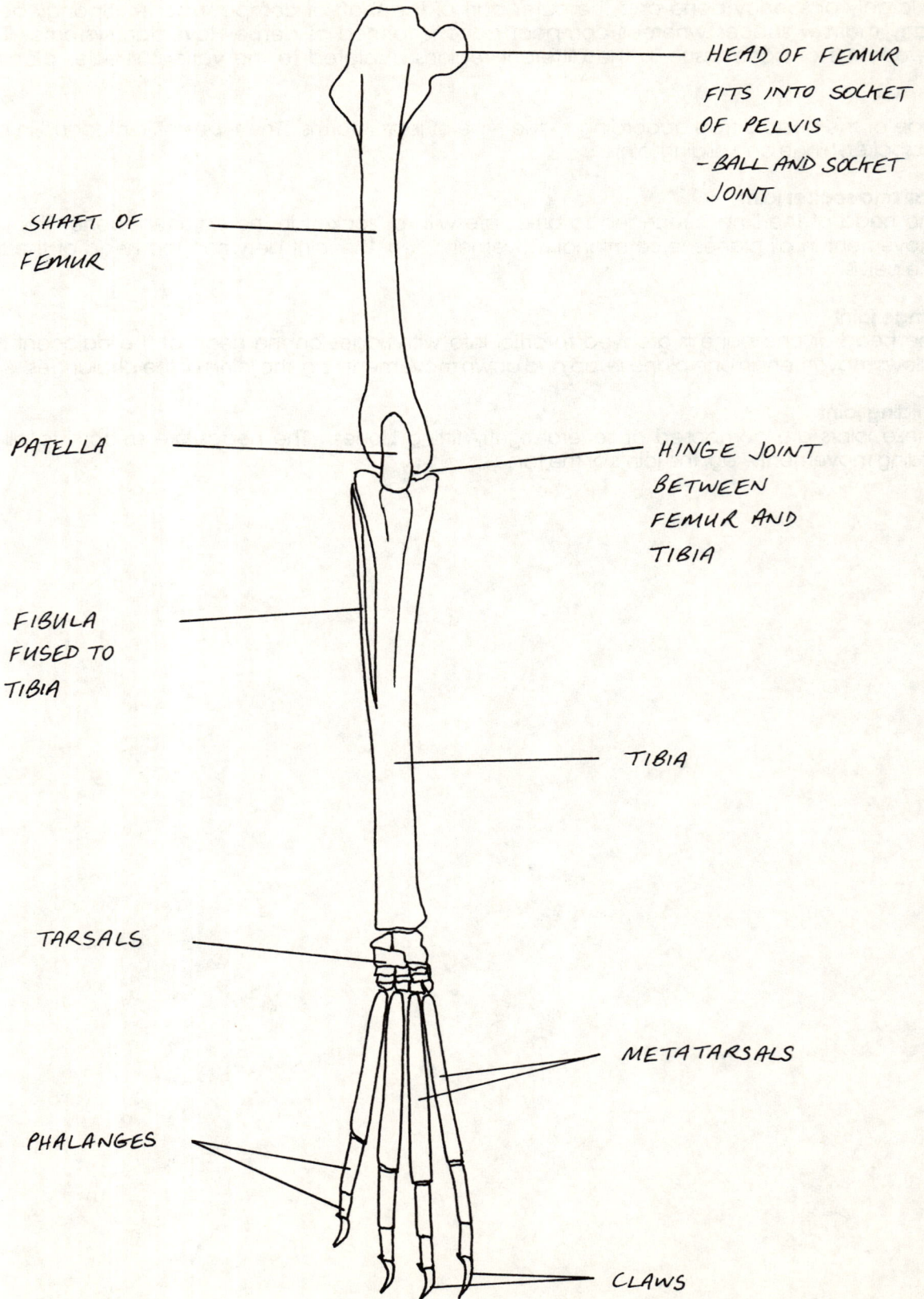

HIND LEG OF RABBIT   X 15   **Fig. 4.45**

HEAD OF FEMUR
FITS INTO SOCKET
OF PELVIS
- BALL AND SOCKET
JOINT

SHAFT OF
FEMUR

PATELLA

HINGE JOINT
BETWEEN
FEMUR AND
TIBIA

FIBULA
FUSED TO
TIBIA

TIBIA

TARSALS

METATARSALS

PHALANGES

CLAWS

EXAM QUESTION 3

Identify specimens E and F. Make labelled drawings of the specimens and indicate the functions of the parts you label. Make a simple plan of the axial skeleton and indicate the position of specimens E and F in relation to the other components.

(20 marks)
(University of Oxford Delegacy of Local Examinations)

Key to Materials:
E = Thoracic vertebra of rabbit
F = Lumbar vertebra of rabbit

ANSWER TECHNIQUE

You should be able to identify a thoracic vertebra by its long neural spine and a lumber vertebra by its long transverse processes. The drawings should be large and clear without any shading (*Figs. 4.39* and *4.41*). You must annotate each part with its functions. The table on page 164 will help you.
The axial skeleton consists of the skull, rib cage and vertebral column (all other bones belong to the appendicular skeleton). Your plan should only be diagrammatic. Do not spend a long time attempting to draw it accurately.

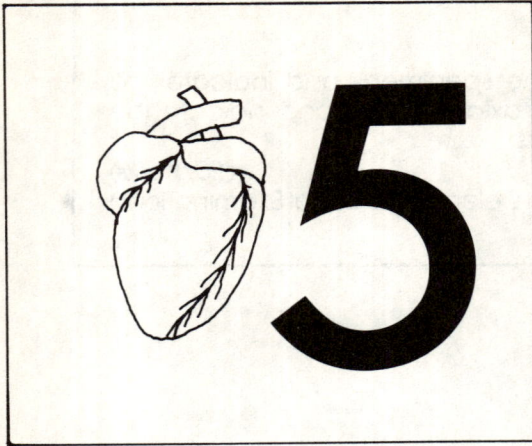

DISSECTION

Dissections form part of the Term-time assessment of several Boards, and some also set dissection questions on parts of organisms in the practical examination. This chapter has therefore been designed for use during practical classes and for final revision if you need to be familiar with dissection techniques.

When dissection questions are set in the practical exam, full instructions are given, so you are not expected to memorise the exact procedures. There are, however, a number of techniques that will make your dissections clearer and more accurate. These should be learned carefully for the assessments.

In this chapter you will find illustrated instructions for the following dissections:

■   Dissecting the abdomen of a mouse to display the alimentary canal and its associated organs and blood vessels.

■   Dissecting the main parts of the male and female urinogenital systems of a mouse, including the renal arteries and veins.

■   Dissecting the neck and thorax of a mouse, showing the pulmonary arteries and veins, dorsal aorta and venae cavae.

■   Dissecting a sheep's heart to show the internal chambers and associated blood vessels.

After each set of instructions a table shows the functions of each part displayed as annotations which form part of the assessment scheme.

Techniques

Preparation
Identifying Structures
Displaying Structures

Dissections

Alimentary Canal
Urinogenital Systems
Neck & Thorax
Mammalian Heart

DISSECTING THE ALIMENTARY CANAL (MOUSE)

■ PREPARATION

1. Lay mouse on its back, stretch the legs out and pin through the feet. Angle the pins away from the mouse.

2. Pinch the skin over the abdomen with forceps and lift up away from the body wall.

3. Snip this skin to make a small hole.

4. Extend this cut longitudinally up to the ribcage and down to the penis/clitoris, keeping the scissor blades horizontal and pulling the skin upwards with forceps (*Fig. 5.1*).

Fig. 5.1

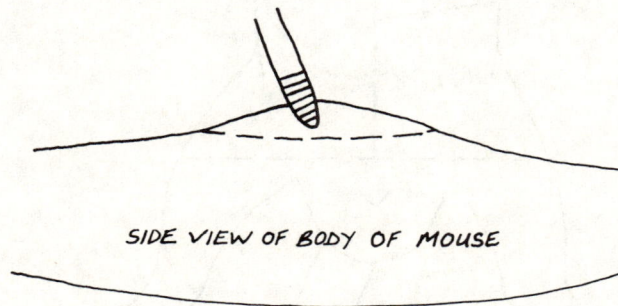

SIDE VIEW OF BODY OF MOUSE

HINTS BOX ✔

DISSECTION TECHNIQUES

● Identify structures as you proceed, especially before removing anything to display underlying systems

● Keep the scissor blades horizontal to avoid cutting underlying structures

● Use a scalpel with the cutting edge facing upwards, making small vertical cuts, to avoid damaging underlying structures

● Use a blunt seeker and blunt forceps to move organs gently without damaging them

● Obscuring fat bodies may be removed by gently pulling or cutting the connective tissue binding them to the organ

● When dissecting a mouse, the systems can be made clearer by submerging the mouse in a tray of water. The structures then float.

● When pinning out to display a system, do *not* pierce stuctures *eg.* the gut or liver, with pins. Instead pin through loops of gut, or use pins as levers to hold the organs to one side

5.   Make horizontal cuts above the ribcage and above the penis/clitoris (*Fig. 5.2*).

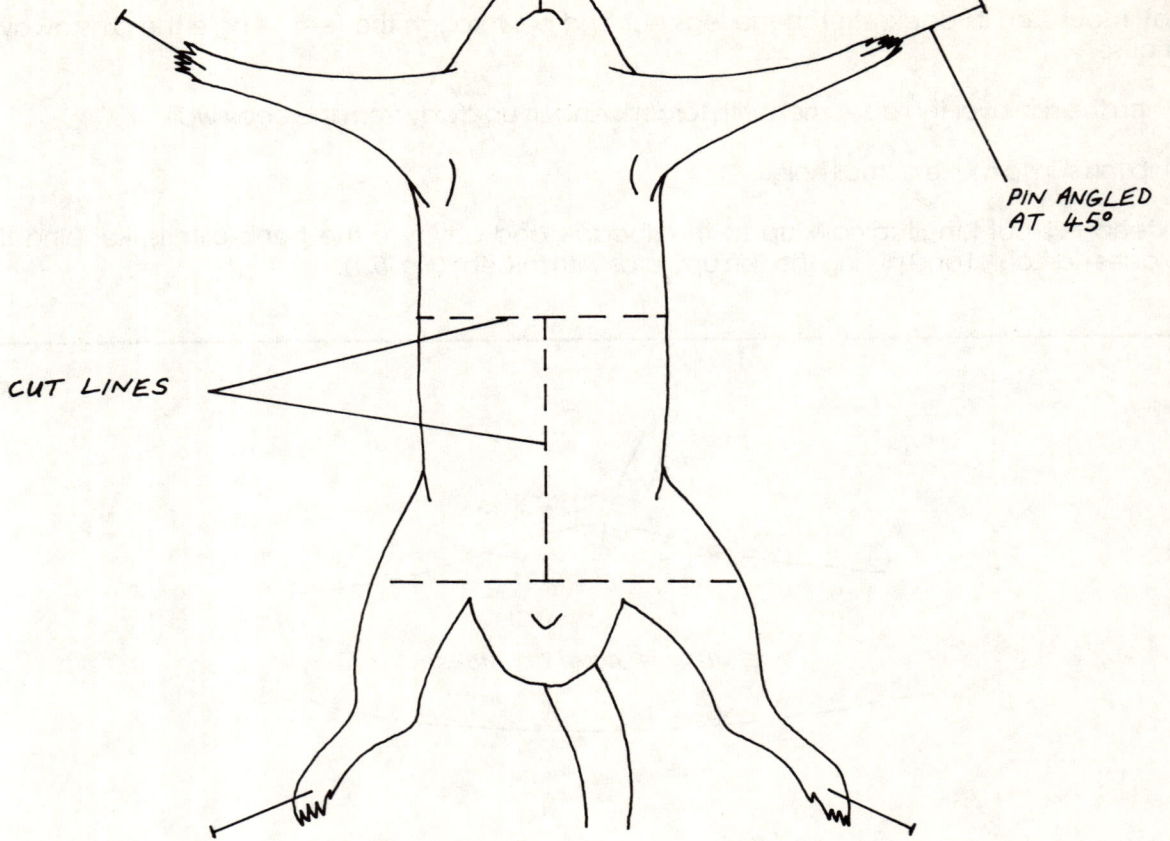

Fig. 5.2

PIN ANGLED
AT 45°

CUT LINES

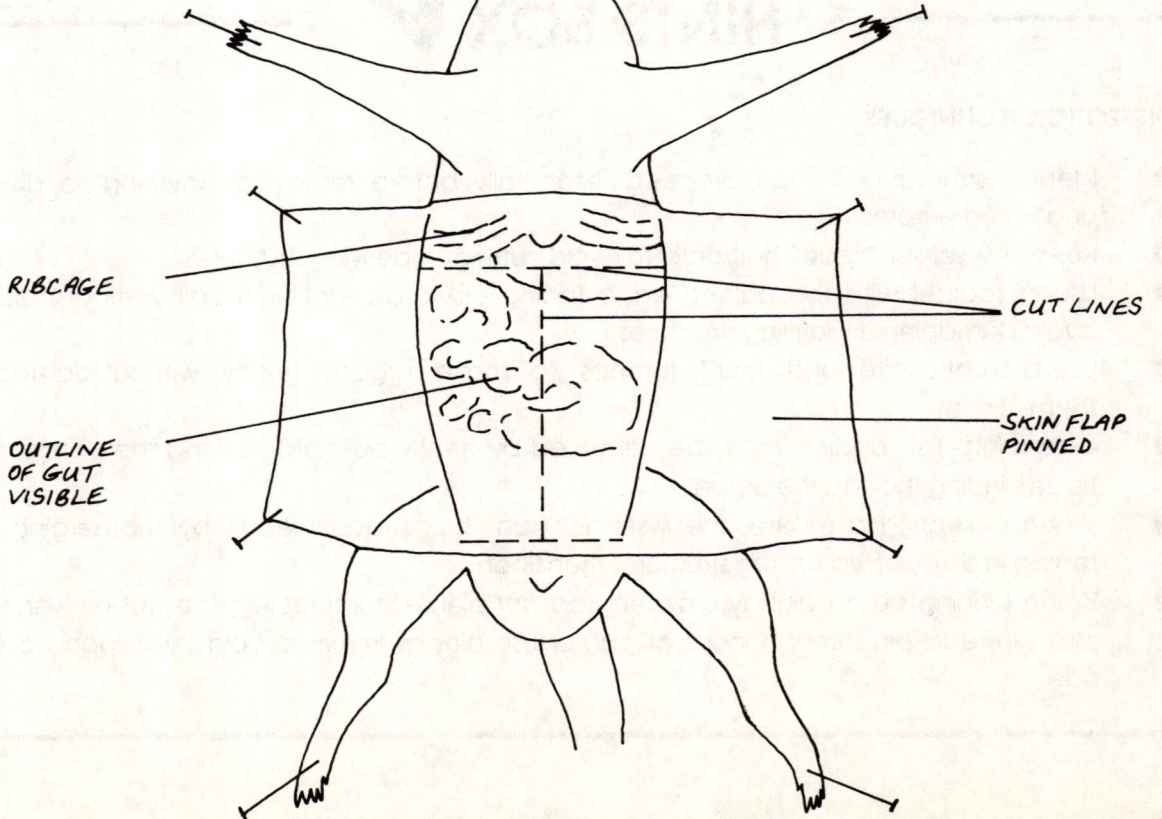

Fig. 5.3

RIBCAGE

CUT LINES

OUTLINE
OF GUT
VISIBLE

SKIN FLAP
PINNED

6. Gently separate the skin from the body wall with a blunt seeker and pin out the skin flaps.

7. Lift the abdominal wall with forceps and snip with horizontally held scissor blades.

8. Continue the cut up to the ribcage and down to the penis/clitoris, keeping the scissor blades horizontal and pulling the abdominal wall away from the gut with forceps (*Fig. 5.3*).

9. Cut along the abdominal wall below the ribs and above the penis/clitoris and pin the flaps to either side.

10. Cover the dissection with water.

■ **IDENTIFYING STRUCTURES**
11. Identify the following in situ (*Fig. 5.4*):

lobes of the liver
stomach
spleen
pancreas
small intestine
caecum
colon

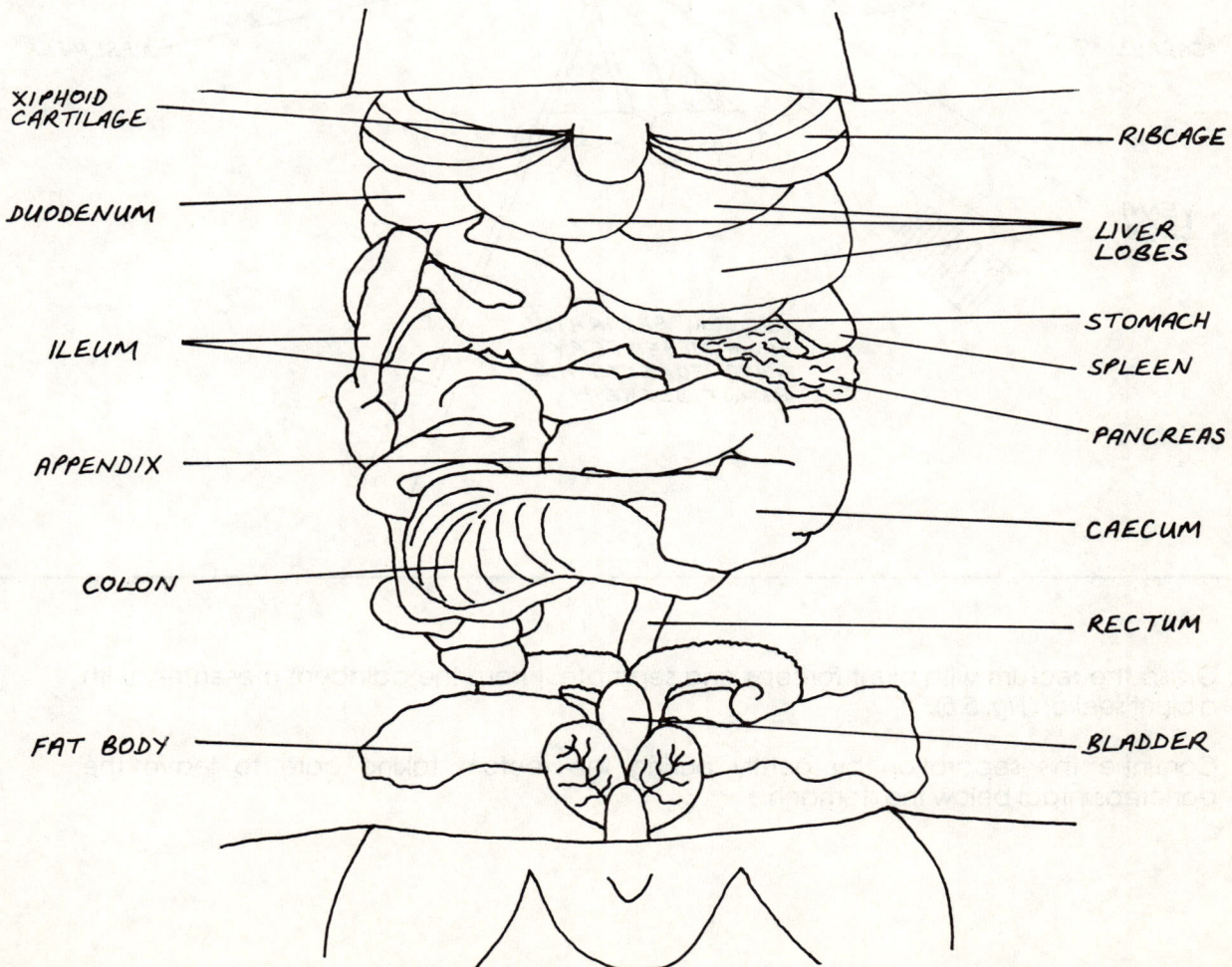

ABDOMINAL CONTENTS IN SITU   X2   Fig. 5.4

12. Gently move the main bulk of the intestines to your left and find the rectum in the mid-line. (*Fig. 5.5*) In females it is above the Y formed by the uterus (*Fig. 5.6*).

MALE

GUT DISPLACED TO THE LEFT TO SHOW THE RECTUM   **Fig. 5.5**

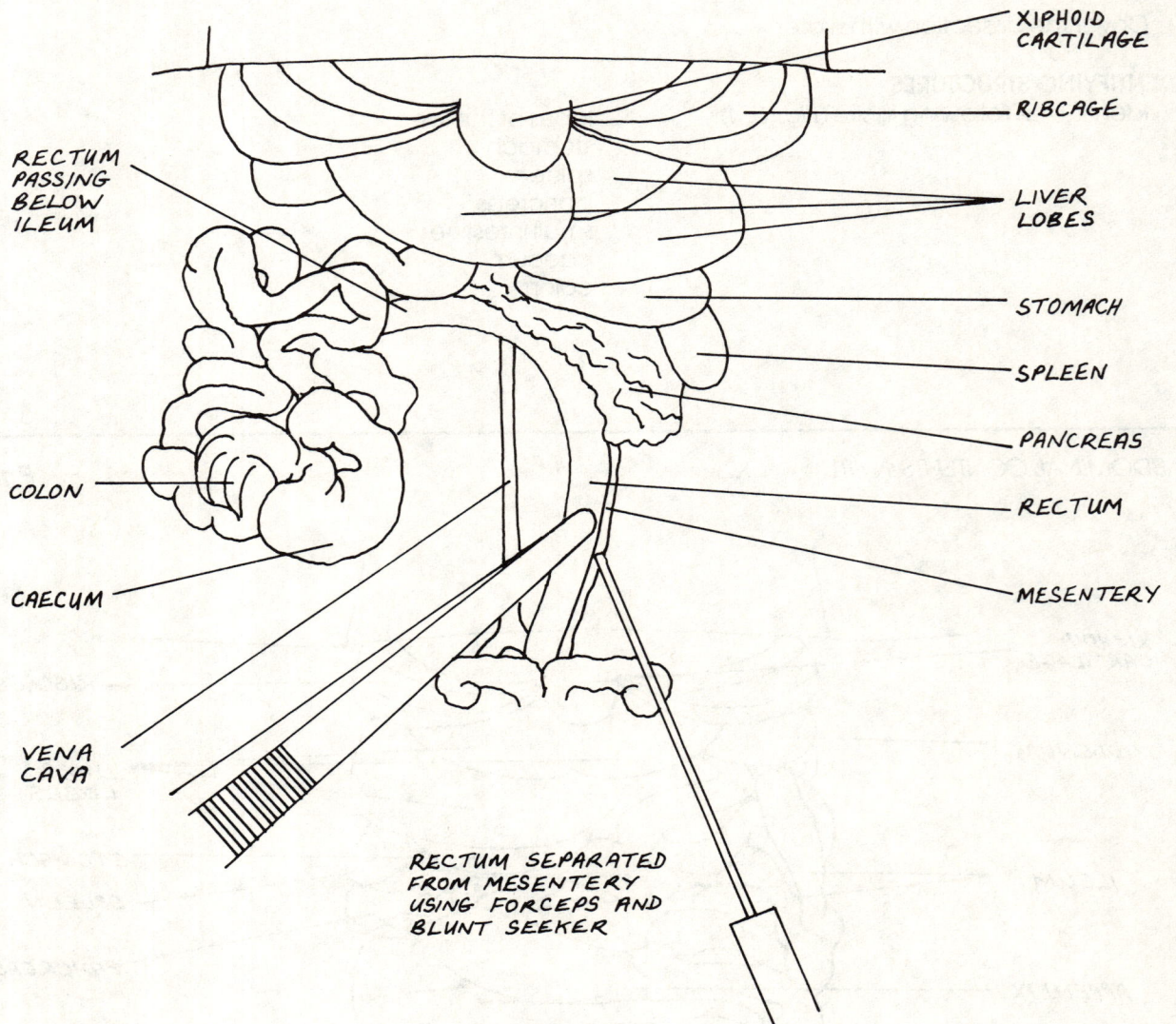

- XIPHOID CARTILAGE
- RIBCAGE
- LIVER LOBES
- STOMACH
- SPLEEN
- PANCREAS
- RECTUM
- MESENTERY
- RECTUM PASSING BELOW ILEUM
- COLON
- CAECUM
- VENA CAVA

RECTUM SEPARATED FROM MESENTERY USING FORCEPS AND BLUNT SEEKER

13. Grasp the rectum with blunt forceps and separate it from the adjacent mesentery with a blunt seeker (*Fig. 5.5*).

14. Continue this separation by gently pulling the rectum taking care to leave the pancreas intact below the stomach.

FEMALE

Fig. 5.6

VENA CAVA

RECTUM

MESENTERY

UTERUS

BLADDER

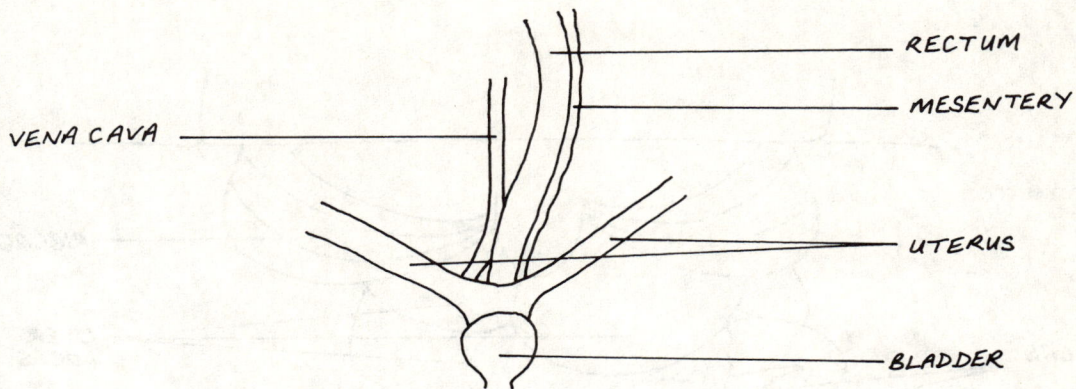

■ **DISPLAYING STRUCTURES**

15. Further gentle pulling and separation of the mesenteries to the right of the rectum causes the gut to untwist so that the whole length of the rectum is visible.

16. Take great care *not* to separate the mesenteries around the caecum or this will damage the hepatic portal vein. This is visible as a dark vessel running up towards the liver amongst the mass of the small intestine.

17. Carefully extend the large intestine and secure with pins. Do *not* pin *through* the gut. Place pins in loops. Ensure that the entrance of the ileum to the caecum and the exit of the colon are both visible.

18.   Gently push any portions of the ileum on the right, under the hepatic portal vein to the left (*Fig. 5.7*).

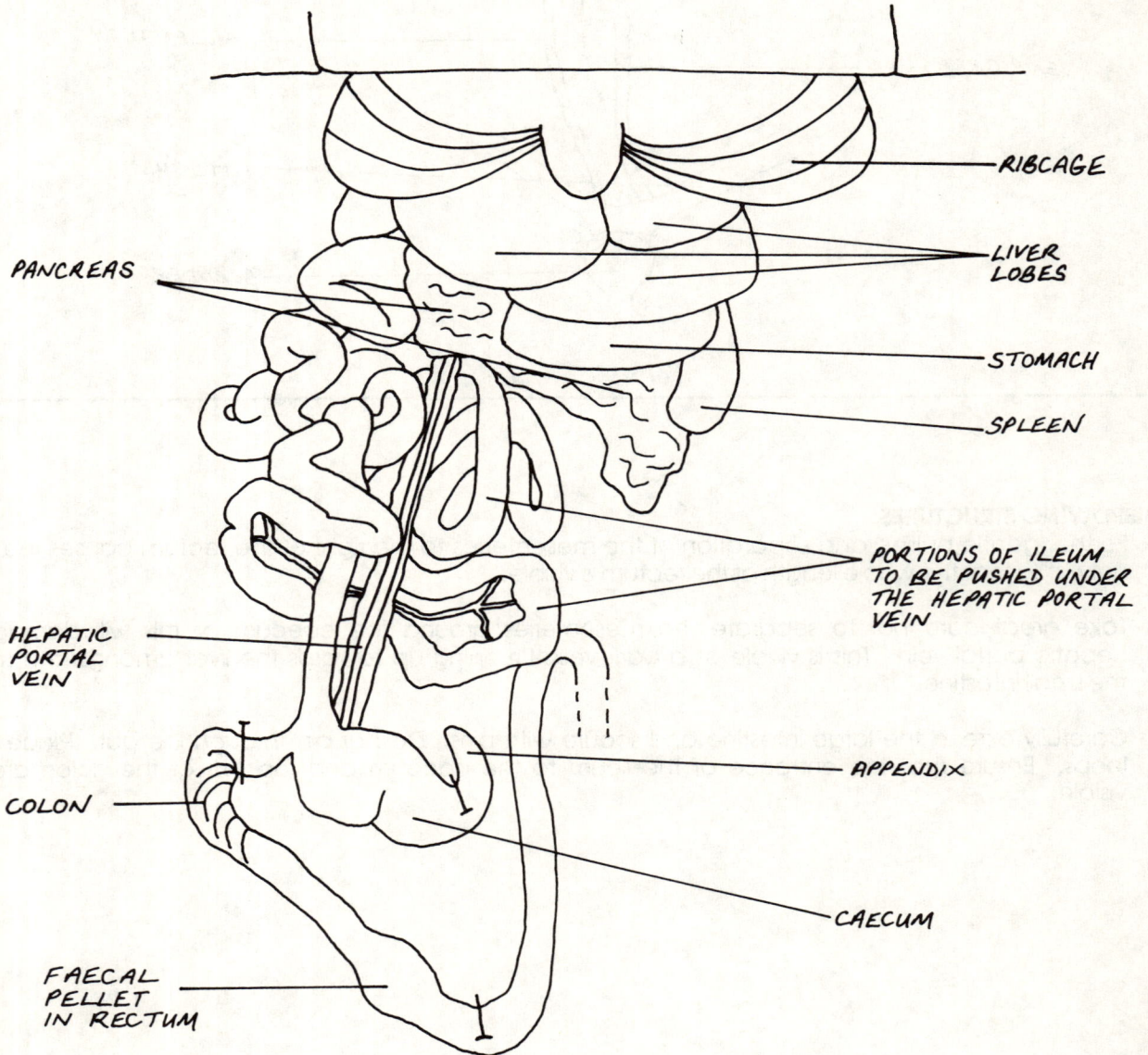

LARGE INTESTINE CLEARED FROM MESENTERY AND PINNED   **Fig. 5.7**

RIBCAGE

LIVER LOBES

PANCREAS

STOMACH

SPLEEN

PORTIONS OF ILEUM TO BE PUSHED UNDER THE HEPATIC PORTAL VEIN

HEPATIC PORTAL VEIN

APPENDIX

COLON

CAECUM

FAECAL PELLET IN RECTUM

19.   Pull the duodenum carefully to the left and extend it and secure with two pins to display the mesenteries and attached pancreas.

20.   Spread out the ileum and secure with pins in the loops to display the mesenteries and their connection to the hepatic portal vein.

21.   Ensure that the stomach and oesophagus are both visible. If they are obscured by liver lobes, hold these back with one or more long pins, making sure that neither the liver nor any underlying structures are pierced.

22. There should now be a clear display of the alimentary canal from the lower oesophagus to the rectum, with associated blood vessels (*Fig. 5.8*).

23. Make a clear, fully labelled drawing of your dissection. Do not shade. Include annotations to give functions of all labelled parts.

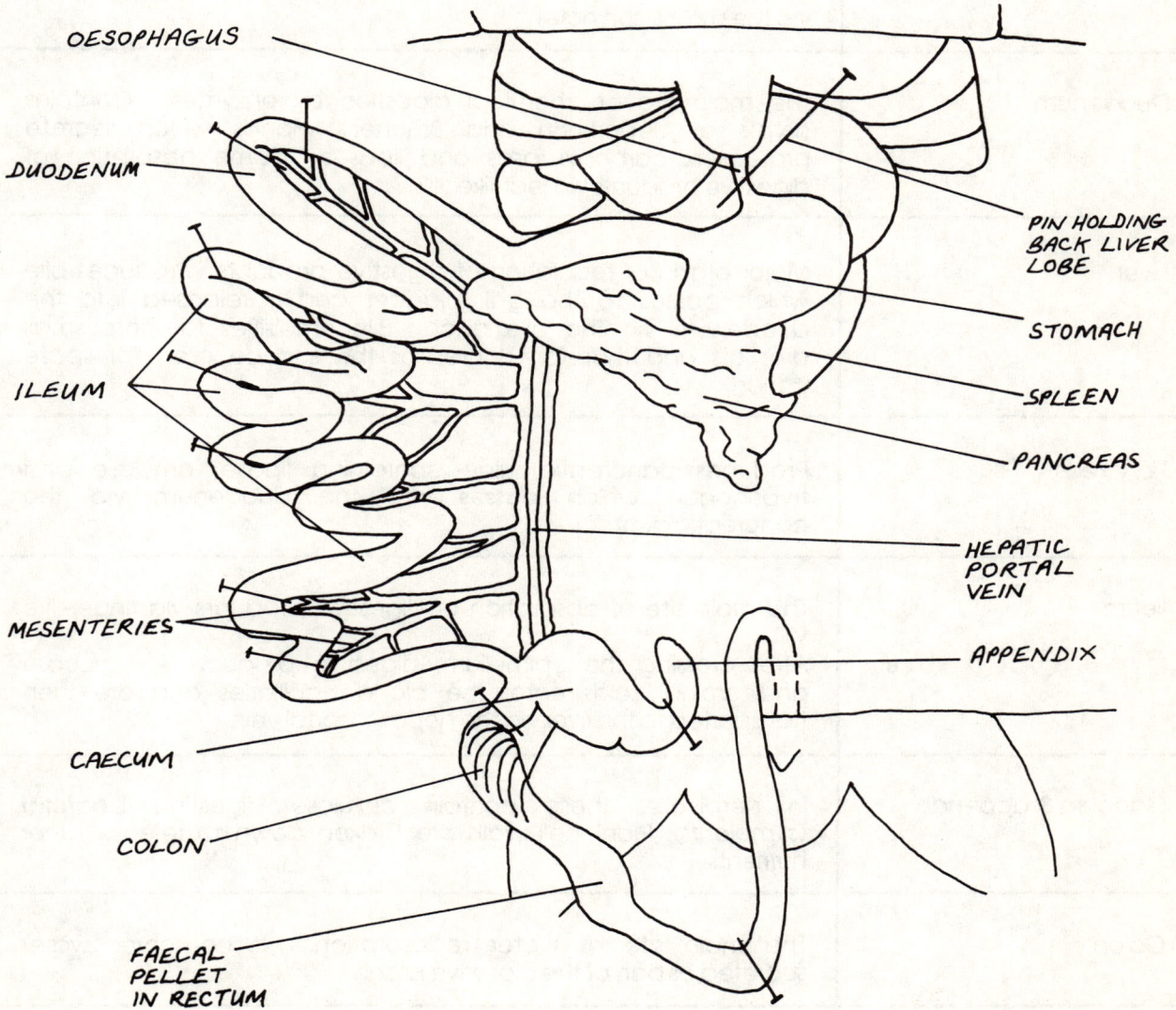

DISPLAY OF ABDOMINAL REGION OF ALIMENTARY CANAL — Fig. 5.8

The following table will help you to annotate your drawing.

TABLE SHOWING FUNCTIONS OF ALIMENTARY CANAL AND ASSOCIATED ORGANS

STRUCTURE	FUNCTIONS
Oesophagus	Carries bolus of food to the stomach by peristaltic contractions.
Stomach	Forms a storage region for food. Secretes gastric juice containing hydrochloric acid and pepsin for protein digestion. The walls of the stomach contract rhythmically to churn the food and provide a means of mechanical digestion. Releases semi-digested food periodically into the duodenum via the pyloric sphincter.
Duodenum	The main site of chemical digestion by enzymes. Contains crypts of Lieberkuhn and Brunner's glands which secrete proteases, carbohydrases and lipases. Some absorption of digestive products via leaf-like villi.
Liver	Major organ of regulation of digestive products. Produces bile which passes to the gall bladder and is released into the duodenum via the bile duct. Bile emulsifies fats into small droplets and therefore increases the surface area for lipase action.
Pancreas	Produces pancreatic juice containing lipase, amylase and trypsinogen which passes into the duodenum via the pancreatic duct.
Ileum	The main site of absorption of digestive products via finger-like villi. After crossing the epithelium, digestive products eg. glucose and amino acids enter the blood capillaries and are then transported to the liver via the hepatic portal vein.
Caecum & appendix	In herbivores these contain cellulose digesting bacteria (symbionts). Plant cell walls are broken down to release other nutrients.
Colon	The main site of water reabsorption. It conserves water secreted as part of the digestive juices.
Rectum	The temporary storage area for undigested material (faeces). Expels faeces by peristalsis via the anus.
Anus	Site of egestion of faeces.

DISSECTING MALE & FEMALE URINOGENITAL SYSTEMS (MOUSE)

■ PREPARATION

1.   Pin, skin and open mouse as instructed for alimentary canal dissection.

2.   Remove alimentary canal, spleen and pancreas by cutting through the oesophagus, hepatic portal vein and associated mesenteries and through the rectum as low down as possible.

MALE URINOGENITAL SYSTEM (for *female* see page 181)

■ IDENTIFYING STRUCTURES

3.   Identify the following (*Fig. 5.9*):

Kidneys, ureters, bladder, vena cava, renal veins, seminal vesicles, preputial glands and penis.

ABDOMINAL REGION WITH ALIMENTARY CANAL REMOVED   Fig. 5.9

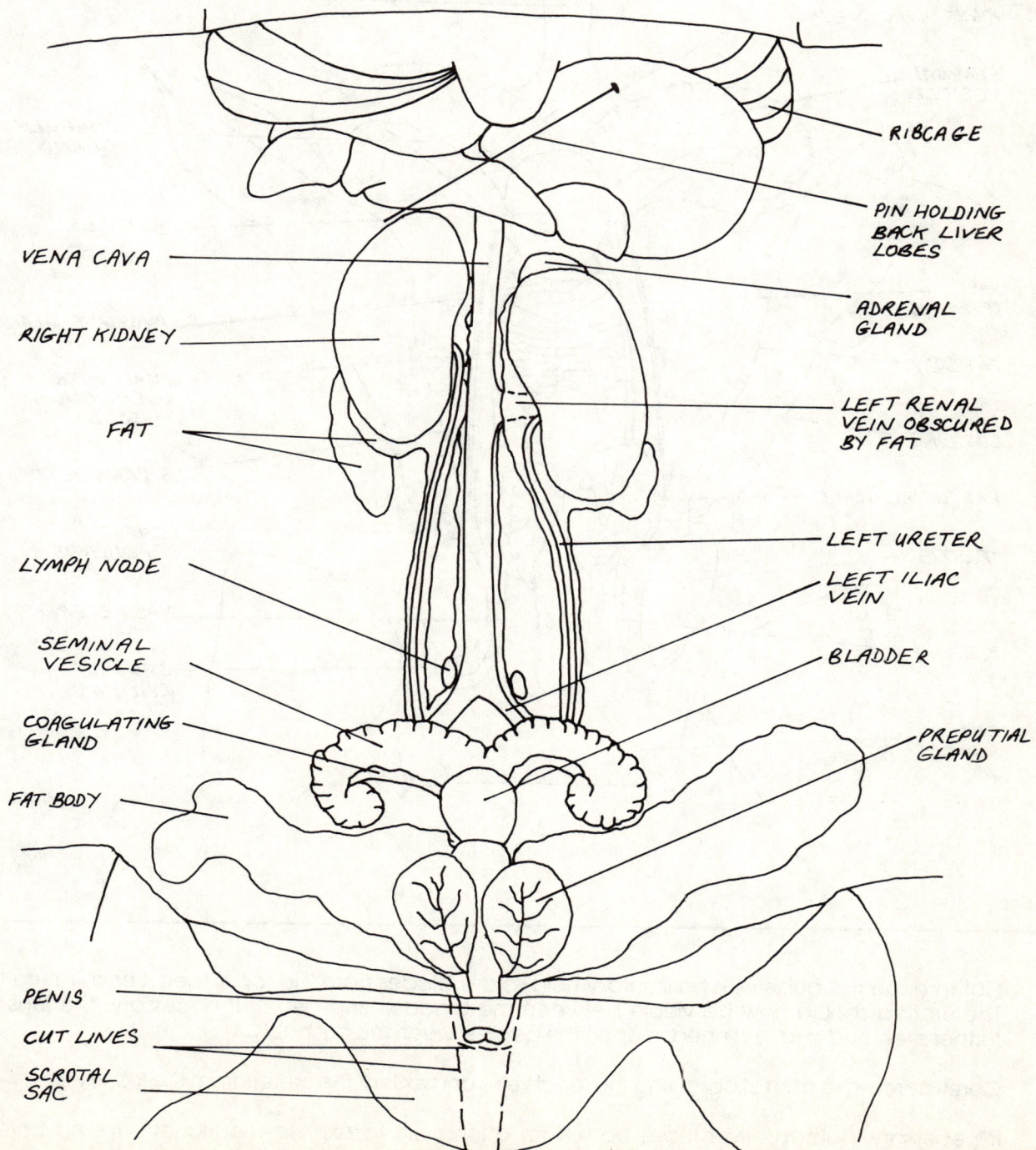

177

■ DISPLAYING STRUCTURES

4. Remove the skin from the penis by cutting down on either side and underneath the penis (*Fig. 5.9*).

5. Cut through the scrotal sacs to expose the testes, ensuring that the body wall is also cut through. Pin the cut walls of the scrotal sacs to either side.

6. Locate the pubis bone between the bladder and the top of the penis. Remove any obscuring fat to view the top of the pubis as a Y shape (*Fig. 5.10*).

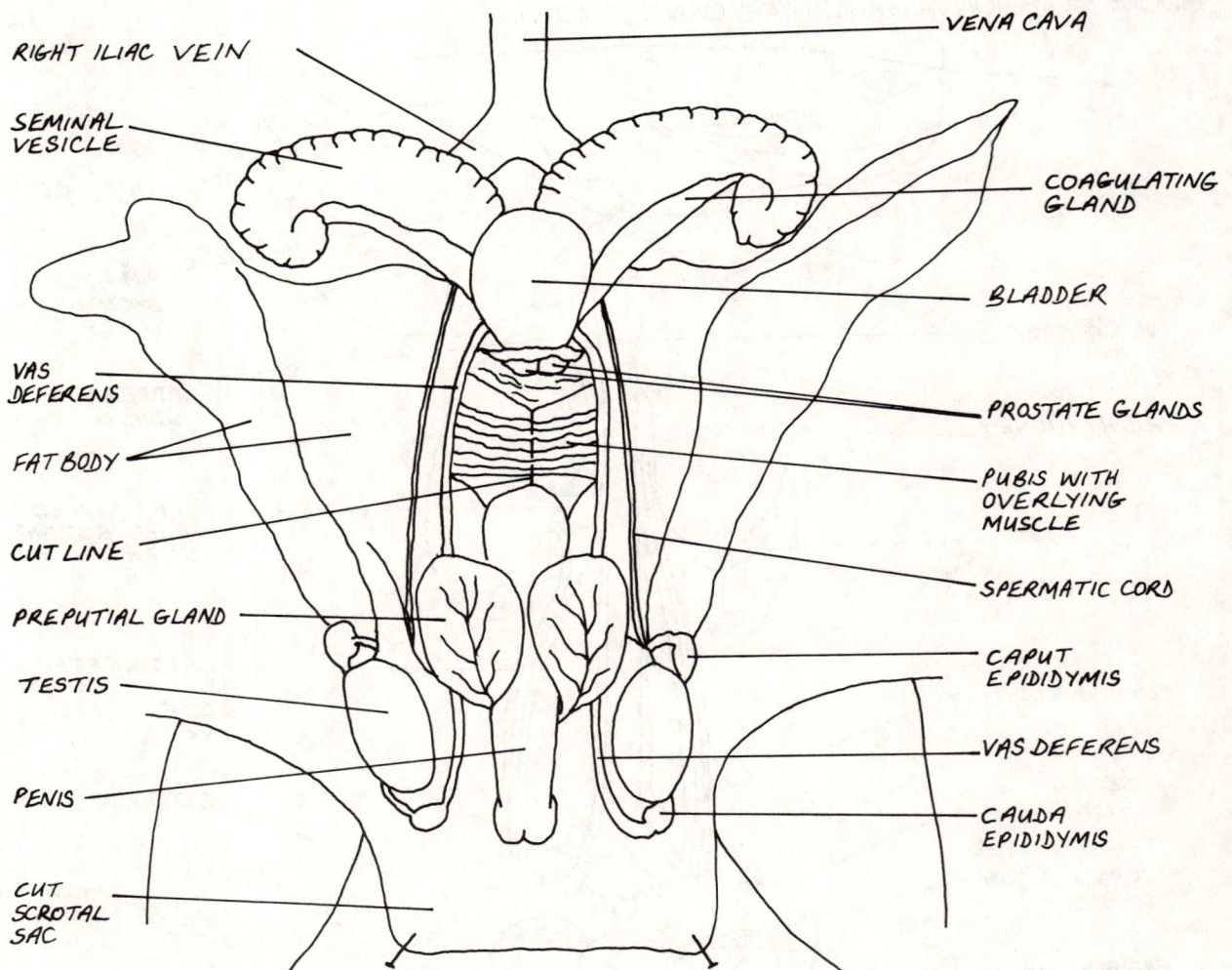

LOWER PORTION OF ABDOMEN, WITH CUT SCROTAL SAC AND SHOWING PUBIS BELOW THE BLADDER

Fig. 5.10

7. Cut through the pubis with horizontally held scissor blades from the top Y (head end) to the tail end. The urethra should now be visible between the bladder and penis. If necessary, the legs can be further stretched and re-pinned to open the gap between the cut pubis.

8. Carefully remove any fat obscuring the renal veins and exits of the ureters from the kidneys.

9. If necessary, hold the liver lobes back with a long pin to expose the kidneys, taking care not to pierce the liver.

10. Pin the fat bodies above the testes to either side in order to expose and display the spermatic cord, testis, epididymis and vas deferens on each side.

11. Secure the seminal vesicles with pins, taking care not to pierce them (*Fig. 5.11*).

12. Make a large, fully labelled drawing of *your* dissection. Add annotations to give functions of each labelled part.

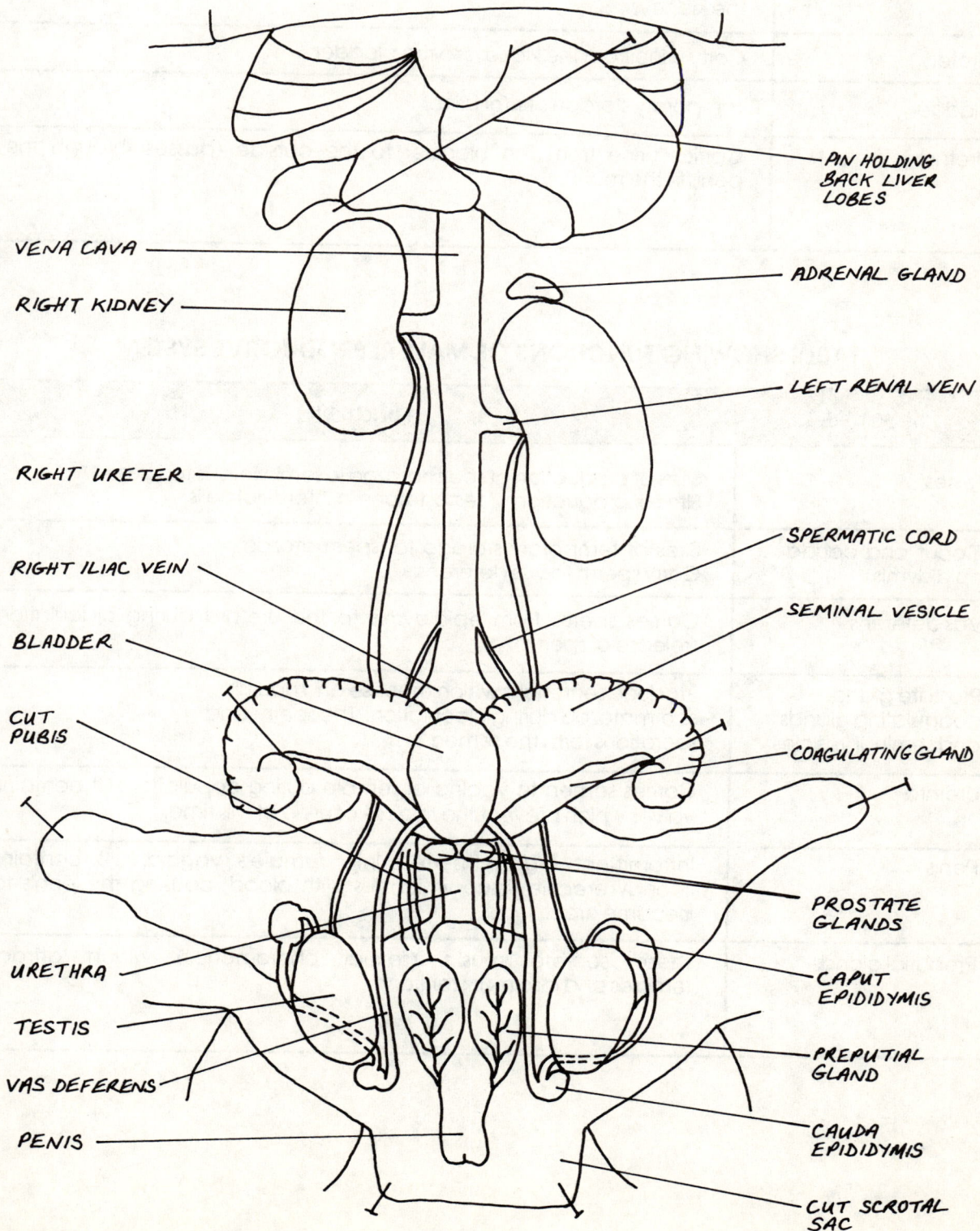

DISSECTION OF THE MALE URINOGENITAL SYSTEM   X3   Fig. 5.11

TABLE SHOWING FUNCTIONS OF URINARY SYSTEM

STRUCTURE	FUNCTIONS
Kidneys	Sites of ultrafiltration of blood and selective reabsorption of useful nutrients and water. Production of urine, containing excretory wastes *eg.* urea and substances in excess *eg.* water.
Renal arteries	Carry oxygenated blood with many wastes into the kidneys.
Renal veins	Carry deoxygenated blood with regulated substances away from the kidneys.
Ureters	Carry urine from the kidneys to the bladder.
Bladder	Temporary storage site for urine.
Urethra	Carries urine from the bladder to the outside (passes through the penis in the male).

TABLE SHOWING FUNCTIONS OF MALE REPRODUCTIVE SYSTEM

STRUCTURE	FUNCTIONS
Testes	Sites of production of spermatozoa in seminiferous tubules. Sites of production of testosterone in interstitial cells.
Caput and cauda epididymis	Sites of temporary storage for spermatozoa. Carry sperm to vas deferens.
Vas deferens	Carries sperm from epididymis to the urethra during ejaculation (release of sperm).
Prostate gland, coagulating glands and seminal vesicles	Produce secretions which mobilise and nourish spermatozoa during ejaculation. The sperm and secretions form the semen.
Urethra	Carries semen to vagina of female during copulation. It contains valves which prevent the release of urine at this time.
Penis	Intromittent organ inserted into female's vagina. It contains spongy erectile tissue which fills with blood, causing the penis to become erect.
Preputial glands	These secrete musks (sexual pheromones) which attract females and also mark territory.

FEMALE URINOGENITAL SYSTEM (for *male* see page 177)

■ **IDENTIFYING STRUCTURES**

3. Identify the following structures (*Fig. 5.12*):

   Kidneys, ureters, bladder, vena cava, renal veins, uterus (forked) and ovaries.

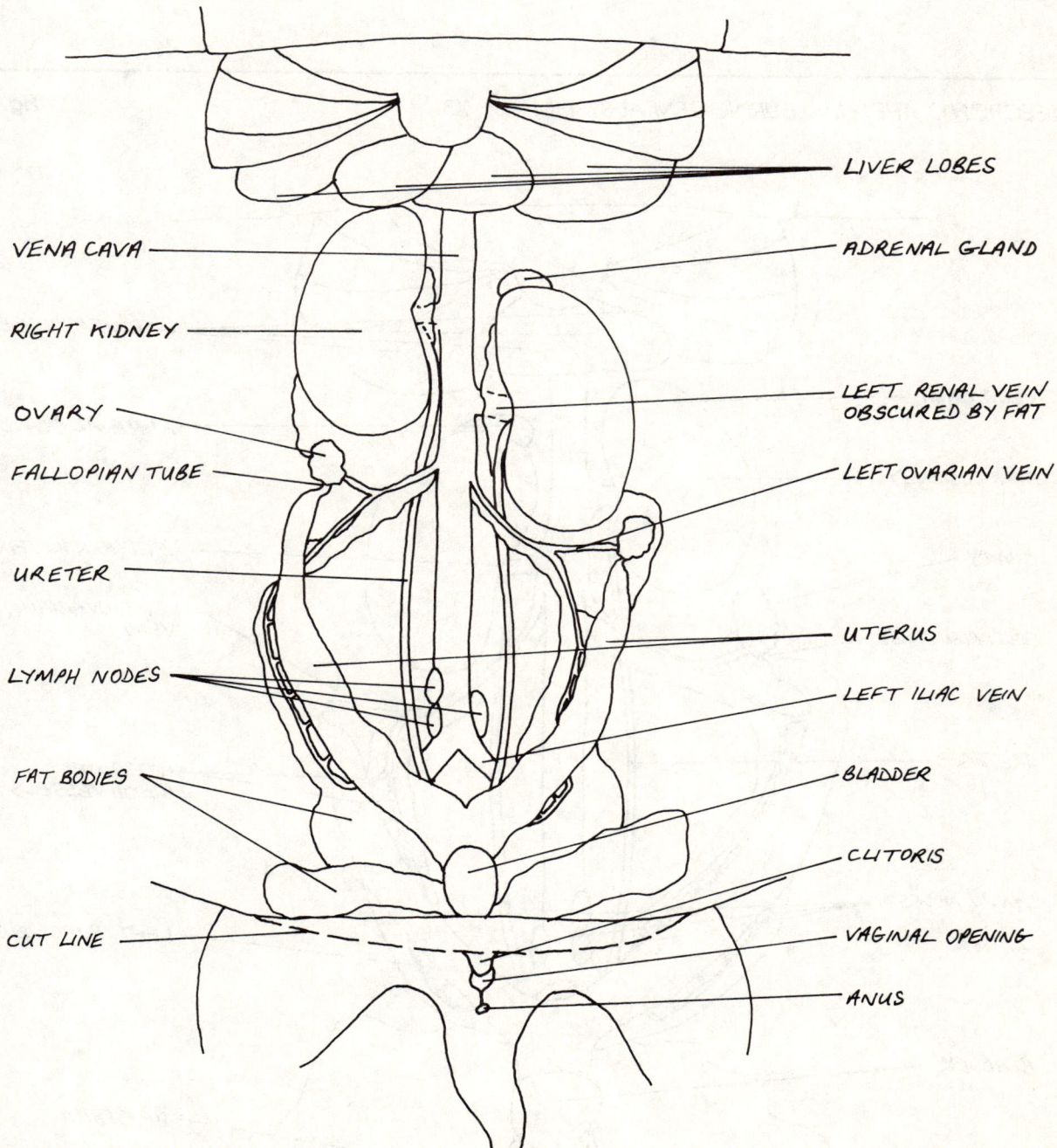

ABDOMINAL PORTION OF FEMALE MOUSE, WITH ALIMENTARY CANAL REMOVED   *Fig. 5.12*

LIVER LOBES

VENA CAVA

ADRENAL GLAND

RIGHT KIDNEY

OVARY

LEFT RENAL VEIN OBSCURED BY FAT

FALLOPIAN TUBE

LEFT OVARIAN VEIN

URETER

UTERUS

LYMPH NODES

LEFT ILIAC VEIN

FAT BODIES

BLADDER

CLITORIS

CUT LINE

VAGINAL OPENING

ANUS

■ **DISPLAYING STRUCTURES**

4. Extend the cuts through the skin and body wall to just above the clitoris (*Fig. 5.12*).

5. Locate the pubis bone between the bladder and the clitoris. Remove any obscuring fat and muscle to expose the Y shaped top of the pubis.

6. Cut through the pubis with horizontally held scissor blades from the top Y (head end) to the tail end. The urethra and underlying vagina should now be visible. If necessary, stretch the legs out further and re-pin to open the gap between the cut pubis.

7.   Carefully remove any fat obscuring the renal veins and exits of the ureters from the kidneys.

8.   If necessary, hold the liver lobes back with a long pin to expose the kidneys, taking care not to pierce the liver.

9.   Pin the forks of the uterus to either side to display the ovarian and uterine blood vessels (*Fig. 5.13*).

10. Make a labelled drawing of your dissection. Add annotations to give functions of each labelled part.

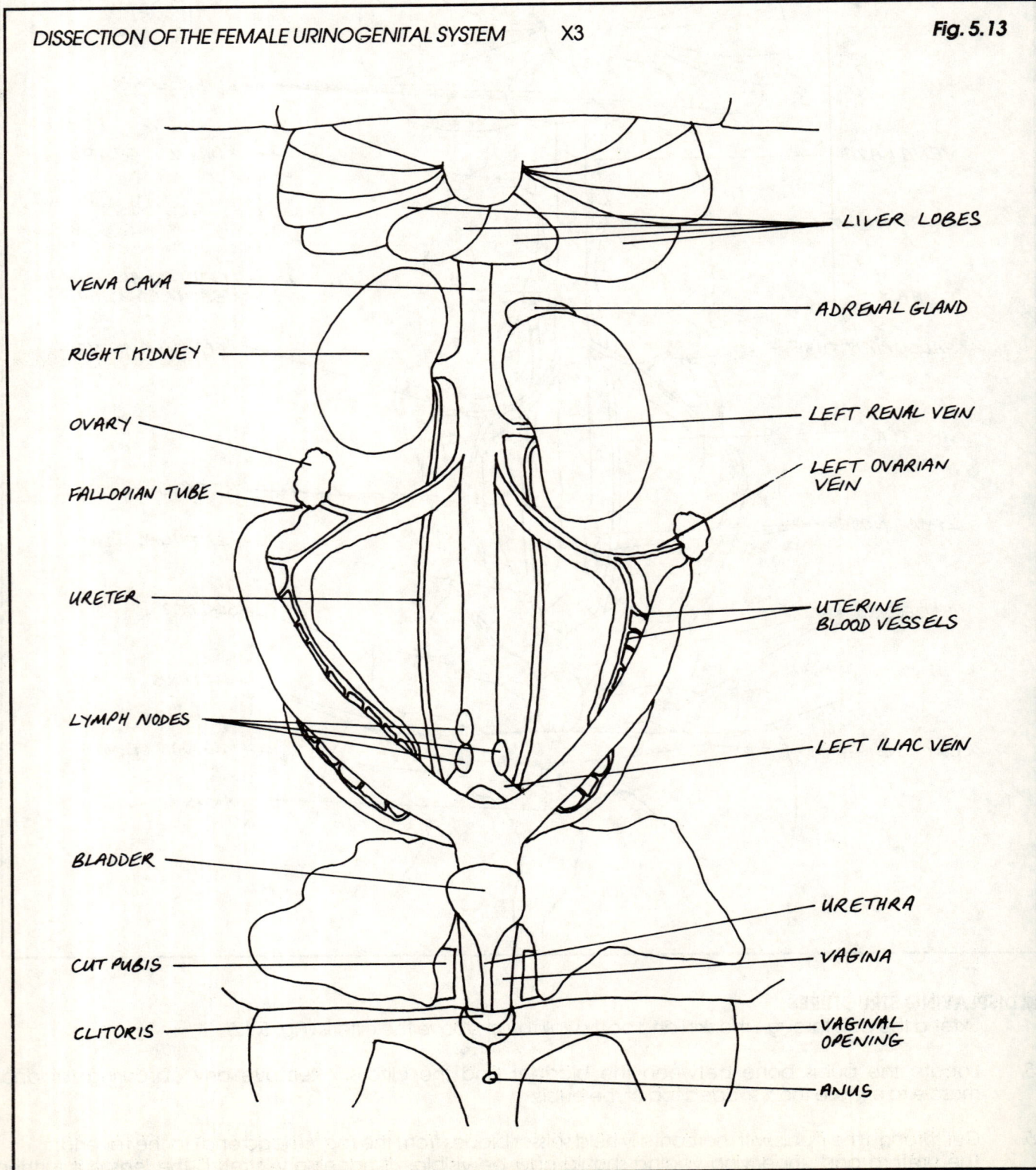

DISSECTION OF THE FEMALE URINOGENITAL SYSTEM   X3   **Fig. 5.13**

TABLE SHOWING FUNCTIONS OF FEMALE REPRODUCTIVE SYSTEM

STRUCTURE	FUNCTION
Ovaries	Sites of maturation of Graafian follicles. Release secondary oocytes during ovulation. Sites of production of oestrogen from follicle cells and progesterone from the corpus luteum.
Oviducts (Fallopian tubes)	Contain ciliated epithelium to draw in secondary oocytes after ovulation. Sites of fertilisation and initial development of zygote and early embryo. The embryo is moved to the uterus by the action of the cilia.
Uterus	Site of implantation of the embryo into the lining (endometrium). Site of development of embryo and placenta. Contains a thick wall of smooth muscle which produces contractions to expel the young.
Clitoris	Contains sensory receptors. Responsible for sexual arousal during copulation.

DISSECTING THE THORAX AND NECK (MOUSE)

PREPARATION

1. Pin mouse as for alimentary canal dissection on page 169.

2. Open the mouse as before but this time extend the skin cut up to just below the lower lip.

3. Make horizontal cuts below the lower lip and above the penis/clitoris.

4. Remove the alimentary canal, spleen and pancreas as for the urinogenital system dissection.

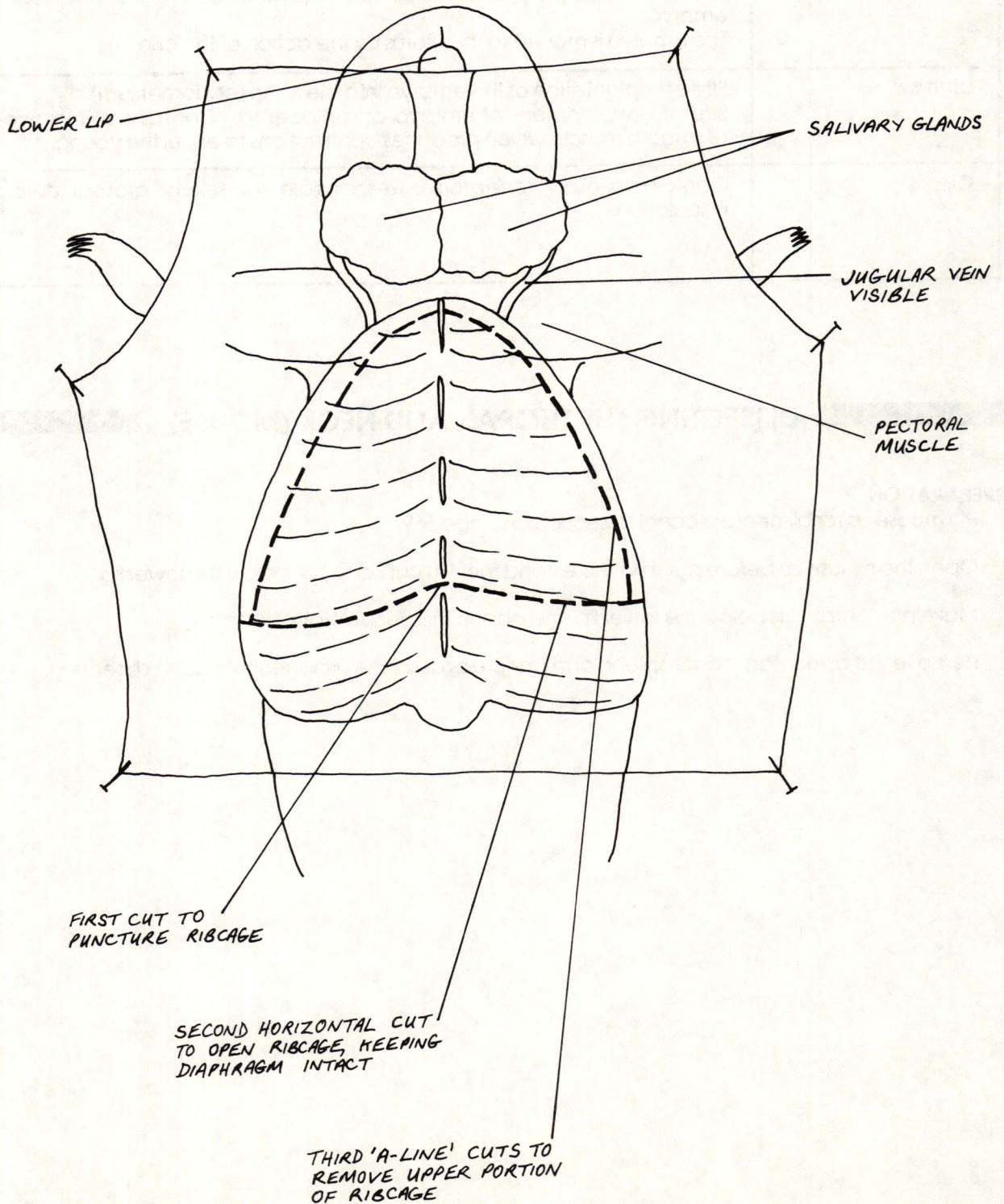

5. Make a small, horizontal cut 2/3 of the way down the sternum to puncture the ribcage (*Fig. 5.14*). Do not penetrate deep into the cavity, to avoid damaging the organs inside.

VIEW OF NECK AND THORAX SHOWING CUTS TO OPEN RIBCAGE

Fig. 5.14

LOWER LIP

SALIVARY GLANDS

JUGULAR VEIN VISIBLE

PECTORAL MUSCLE

FIRST CUT TO PUNCTURE RIBCAGE

SECOND HORIZONTAL CUT TO OPEN RIBCAGE, KEEPING DIAPHRAGM INTACT

THIRD 'A-LINE' CUTS TO REMOVE UPPER PORTION OF RIBCAGE

6.   Ensure that the liver lobes are pulled down free from the diaphragm.

7.   Extend the cut through the ribcage horizontally, taking care to keep the diaphragm intact.

8.   Pull the cut portion of the ribcage downwards to expose the diaphragm. If necessary, secure by tying cotton around the xiphoid cartilage and attaching this to a pin.

9.   Remove the upper portion of the thorax by making 'A-Line' cuts along the sides up to a point at the top of the sternum. Ensure that the jugular veins are not punctured (*Fig. 5.14*).

■ IDENTIFYING STRUCTURES

10.   Identify the thymus gland over the heart and remove this by pulling with forceps, to expose the aortic arch (*Fig. 5.15*). You should also see the ventricles of the heart, the left lung, the lobes of the right lung and the posterior vena cava.

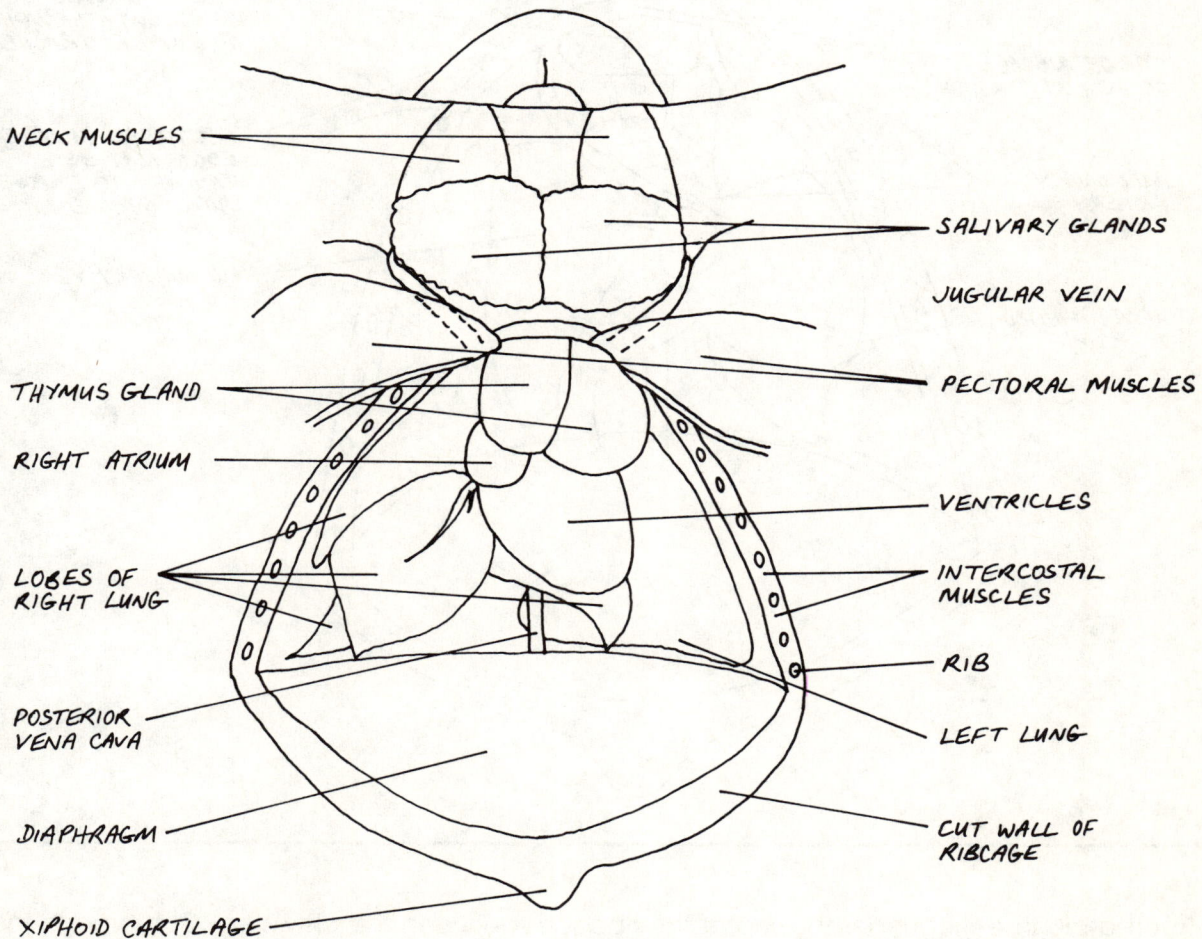

OPEN THORAX SHOWING THYMUS TO BE REMOVED   Fig. 5.15

■ DISPLAYING STRUCTURES

11.   Carefully pin the heart to one side by pinning through the base of the ventricles. Take care not to pierce any underlying structures.

12. Separate the salivary glands using a seeker and pin them upwards, on either side of the head (*Fig. 5.16*).

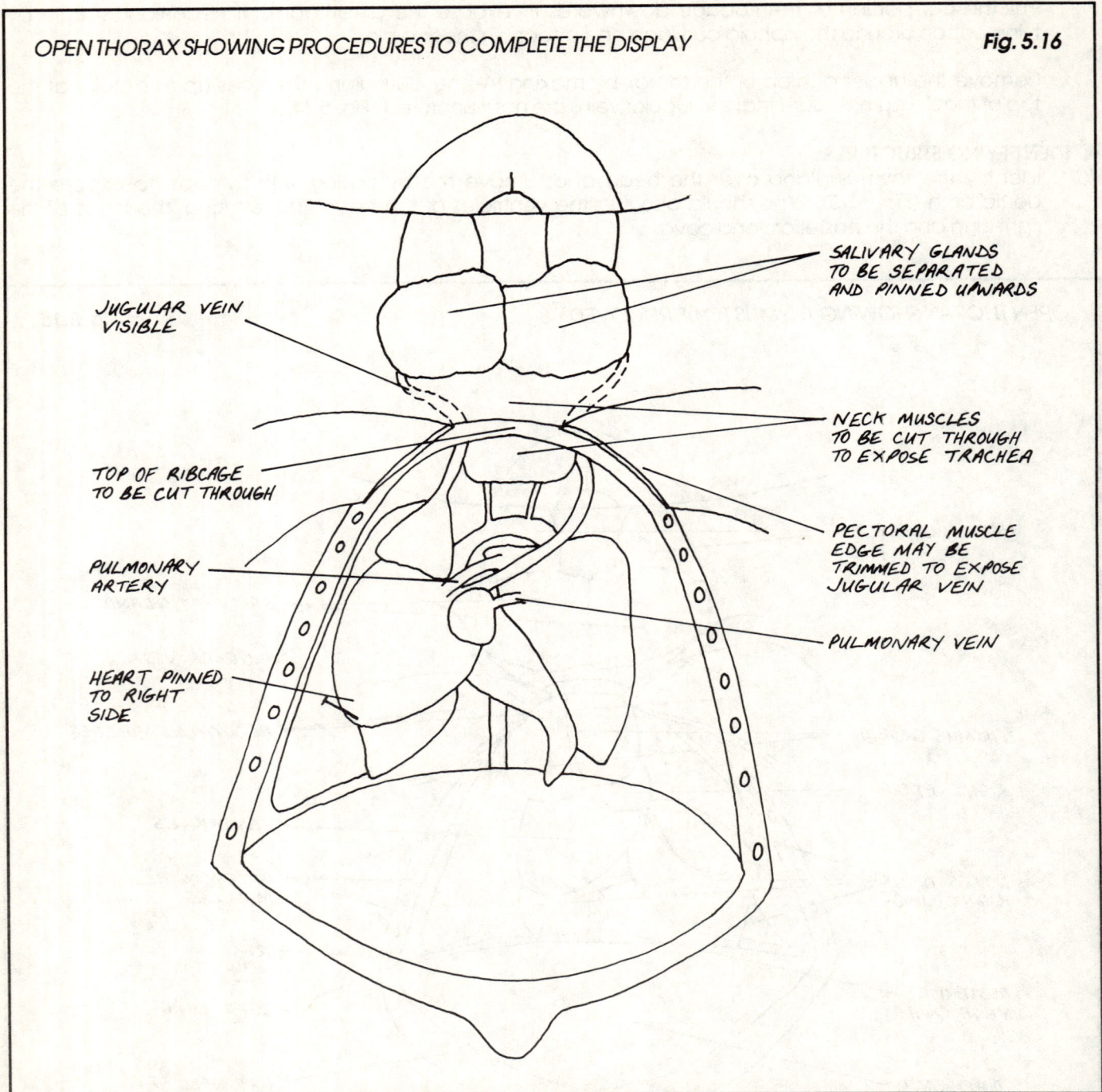

OPEN THORAX SHOWING PROCEDURES TO COMPLETE THE DISPLAY   **Fig. 5.16**

SALIVARY GLANDS
TO BE SEPARATED
AND PINNED UPWARDS

JUGULAR VEIN
VISIBLE

NECK MUSCLES
TO BE CUT THROUGH
TO EXPOSE TRACHEA

TOP OF RIBCAGE
TO BE CUT THROUGH

PECTORAL MUSCLE
EDGE MAY BE
TRIMMED TO EXPOSE
JUGULAR VEIN

PULMONARY
ARTERY

PULMONARY VEIN

HEART PINNED
TO RIGHT
SIDE

13. Insert a blunt seeker under the top of the ribcage, between the clavicles. Cut through the bones, taking care to keep the scissor blades horizontal. Use the seeker as a guide.

14. Cut through the neck muscles, again using horizontal scissor blades to expose the trachea and carotid arteries (*Fig. 5.16*).

15. The jugular veins should be visible running from under the salivary glands, down the neck, under the edge of the ribcage and joining into the left and right anterior venae cavae.

16. Expose the jugulars where obscured by carefully trimming back the cut ends of the clavicles, edge of ribcage and pectoral muscles where necessary. Work on one side at a time (*Fig. 5.16*).

17. The following structures should now be clear (*Fig. 5.17*):

jugular veins, venae cavae (anterior and posterior), aortic arch, carotid arteries, pulmonary vein and artery (on one side), left and right atria, ventricles, lungs, diaphragm, ribs and intercostal muscles, trachea

18. Make a large, labelled drawing of your dissection and add annotations to give functions of parts labelled.

DISSECTION OF THE NECK AND THORAX X4 **Fig. 5.17**

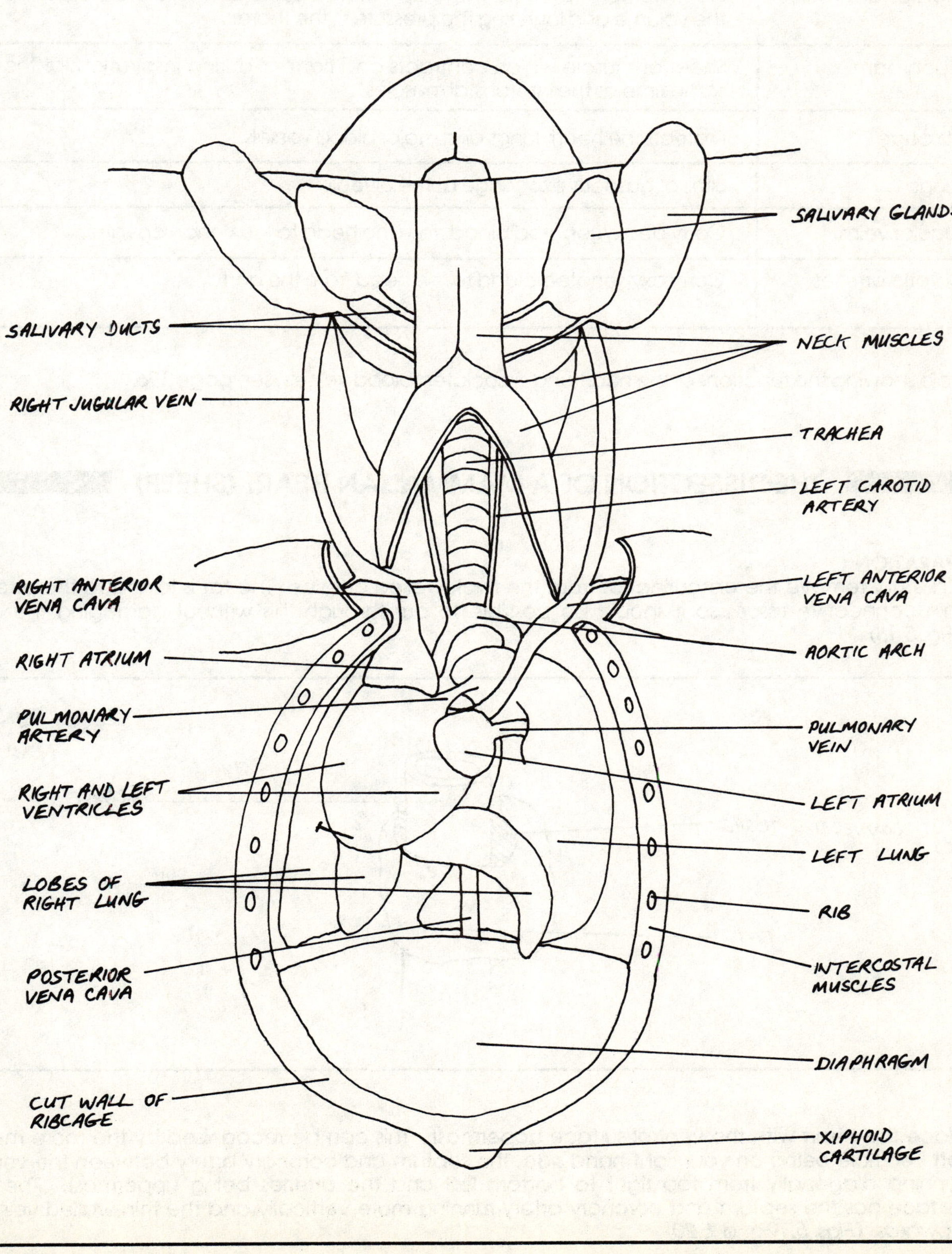

SALIVARY GLANDS
SALIVARY DUCTS
NECK MUSCLES
RIGHT JUGULAR VEIN
TRACHEA
LEFT CAROTID ARTERY
RIGHT ANTERIOR VENA CAVA
LEFT ANTERIOR VENA CAVA
AORTIC ARCH
RIGHT ATRIUM
PULMONARY ARTERY
PULMONARY VEIN
RIGHT AND LEFT VENTRICLES
LEFT ATRIUM
LEFT LUNG
LOBES OF RIGHT LUNG
RIB
POSTERIOR VENA CAVA
INTERCOSTAL MUSCLES
DIAPHRAGM
CUT WALL OF RIBCAGE
XIPHOID CARTILAGE

TABLE SHOWING FUNCTIONS OF STRUCTURES OF THE NECK AND THORAX

STRUCTURE	FUNCTIONS
Salivary glands	Produce saliva containing amylase which is released into the buccal cavity via the salivary ducts.
Trachea	Air passageway from the pharynx (throat) to the bronchi and thence to the lungs. C rings of cartilage prevent it collapsing during the low pressure caused by inspiration.
Intercostal muscles	Contract to pull the rib cage up during inspiration therefore increasing the volume and lowering the pressure in the thorax.
Diaphragm	Sheet of muscle which contracts and flattens during inspiration, at the same time as the intercostal muscles.
Rib cage	Protects the heart, lungs and major blood vessels.
Lungs	Sites of gaseous exchange at the alveoli.
Jugular veins	Carry deoxygenated blood from the head to the venae cavae.
Carotid arteries	Carry oxygenated blood to the head from the aorta.

For a table showing the functions of the heart and associated blood vessels, see page 196.

THE DISSECTION OF A MAMMALIAN HEART (SHEEP)

■ PREPARATION

1. Carefully remove the obscuring fat from the thick-walled arteries. The fat is joined to the arteries by thin connective tissue, so it should be possible to cut through this without damaging the arteries (*Fig. 5.18*).

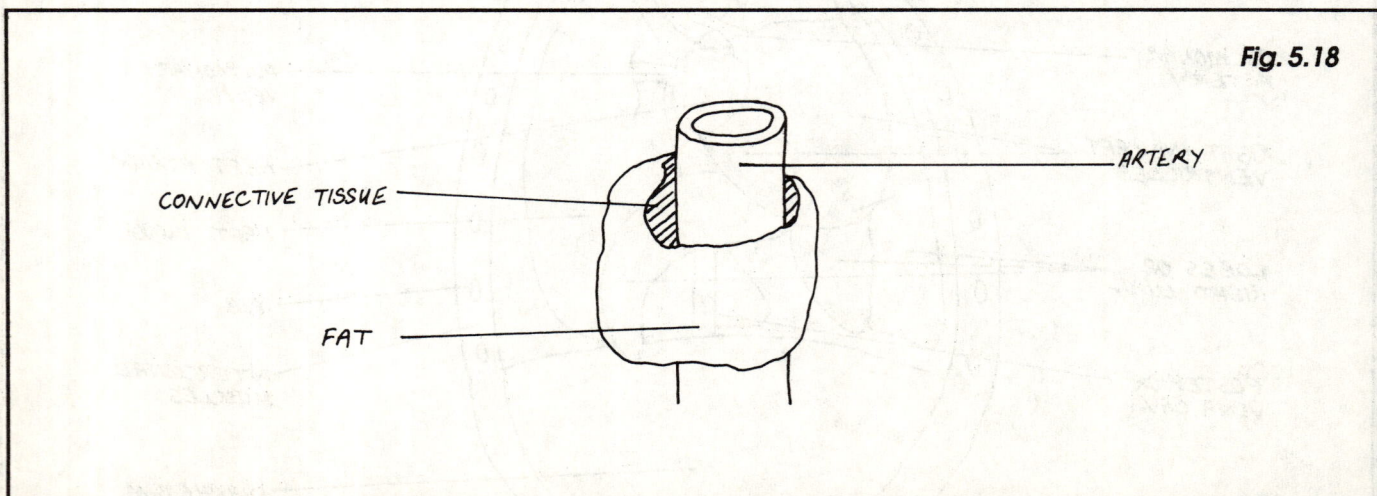

Fig. 5.18

2. Place the heart with the ventral surface uppermost. This can be recognised by the more muscular left ventricle being on your right hand side, the septum and coronary artery between the ventricles running diagonally from top right to bottom left and the arteries being uppermost. The dorsal surface has the septum and coronary artery running more vertically and the thin-walled veins face upwards. (*Figs. 5.19* and *5.20*)

VENTRAL VIEW OF HEART BEFORE CLEARING VESSELS   X 1   **Fig. 5.19**

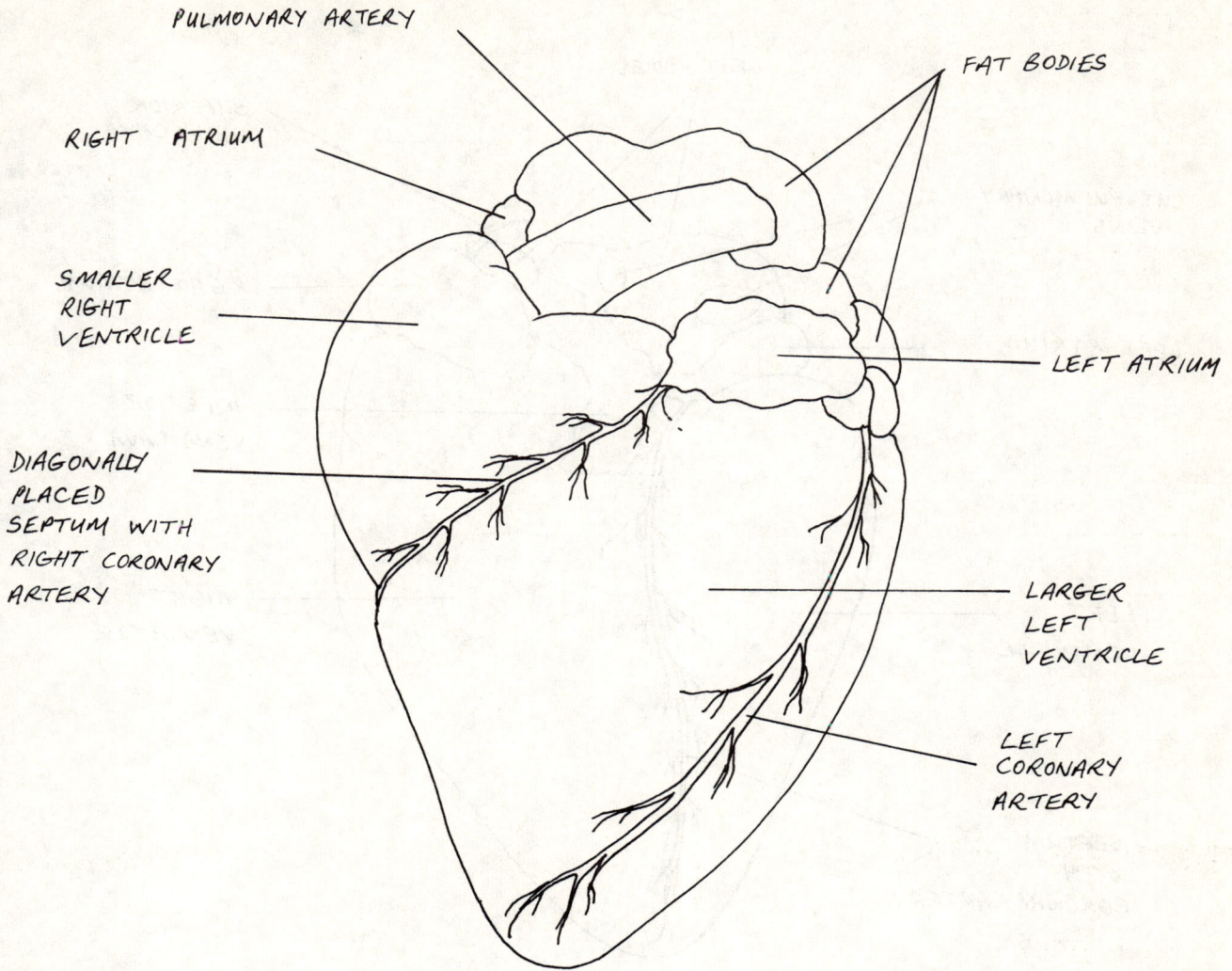

PULMONARY ARTERY

RIGHT ATRIUM

FAT BODIES

SMALLER
RIGHT
VENTRICLE

LEFT ATRIUM

DIAGONALLY
PLACED
SEPTUM WITH
RIGHT CORONARY
ARTERY

LARGER
LEFT
VENTRICLE

LEFT
CORONARY
ARTERY

DORSAL VIEW OF HEART BEFORE CLEARING VESSELS
Fig. 5.20

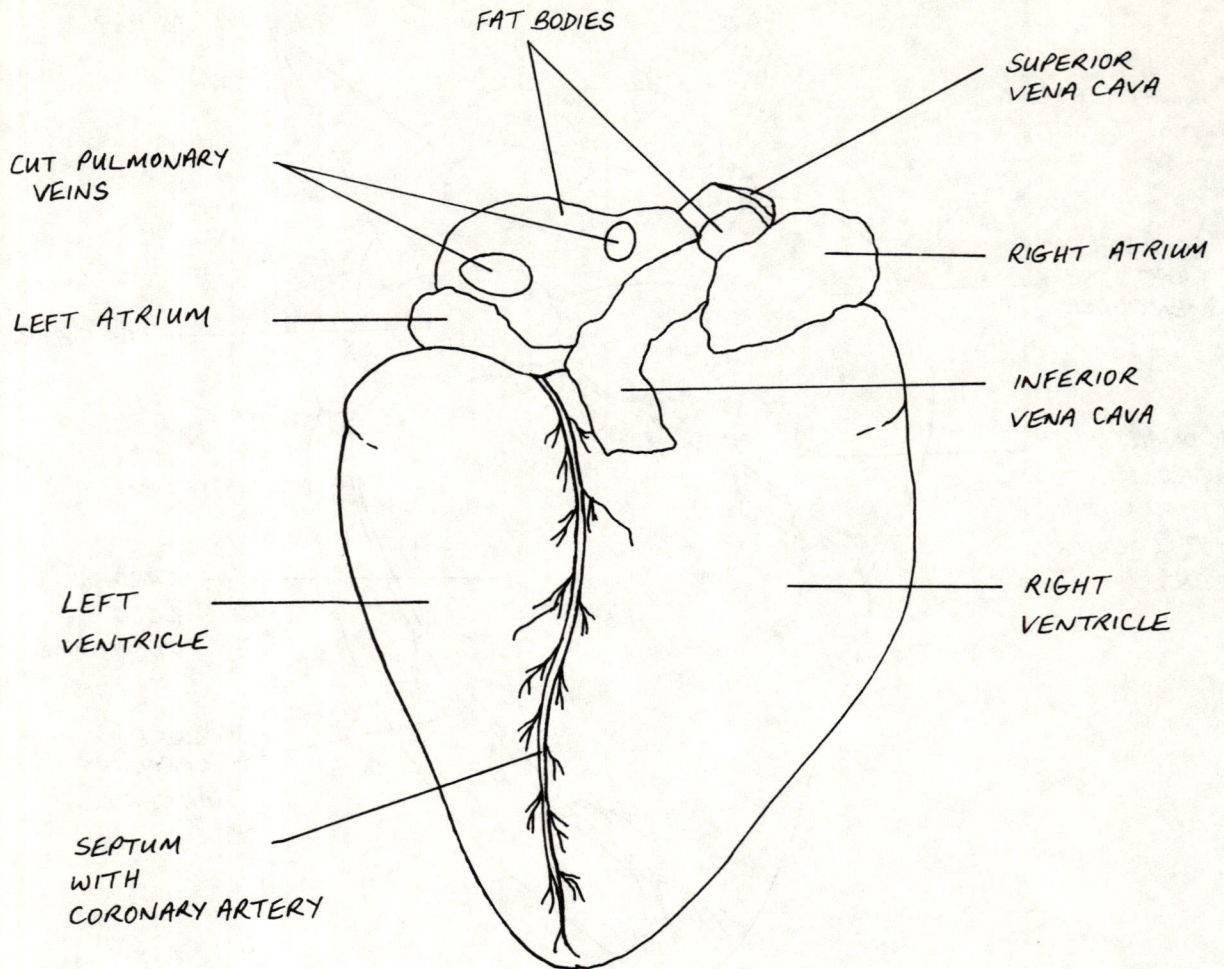

FAT BODIES

SUPERIOR
VENA CAVA

CUT PULMONARY
VEINS

RIGHT ATRIUM

LEFT ATRIUM

INFERIOR
VENA CAVA

LEFT
VENTRICLE

RIGHT
VENTRICLE

SEPTUM
WITH
CORONARY ARTERY

3.   If the arteries have not been cut too short, the ductus arteriosus should be present linking the pulmonary artery to the aorta. Be very careful not to sever this (*Fig. 5.21*).

■ **IDENTIFYING & DISPLAYING RIGHT SIDE STRUCTURES**

4.   Open up the right side of the heart by cutting in to the right ventricle about one centimetre from the coronary vessels on the septum between the two ventricles. Continue the cut parallel to the septum and up through the pulmonary artery (*Fig. 5.21*). Be careful not to cut through the tricuspid valve or tendinous cords.

VENTRAL VIEW OF HEART WITH FAT REMOVED FROM ARTERIES   X 1.5   **Fig. 5.21**

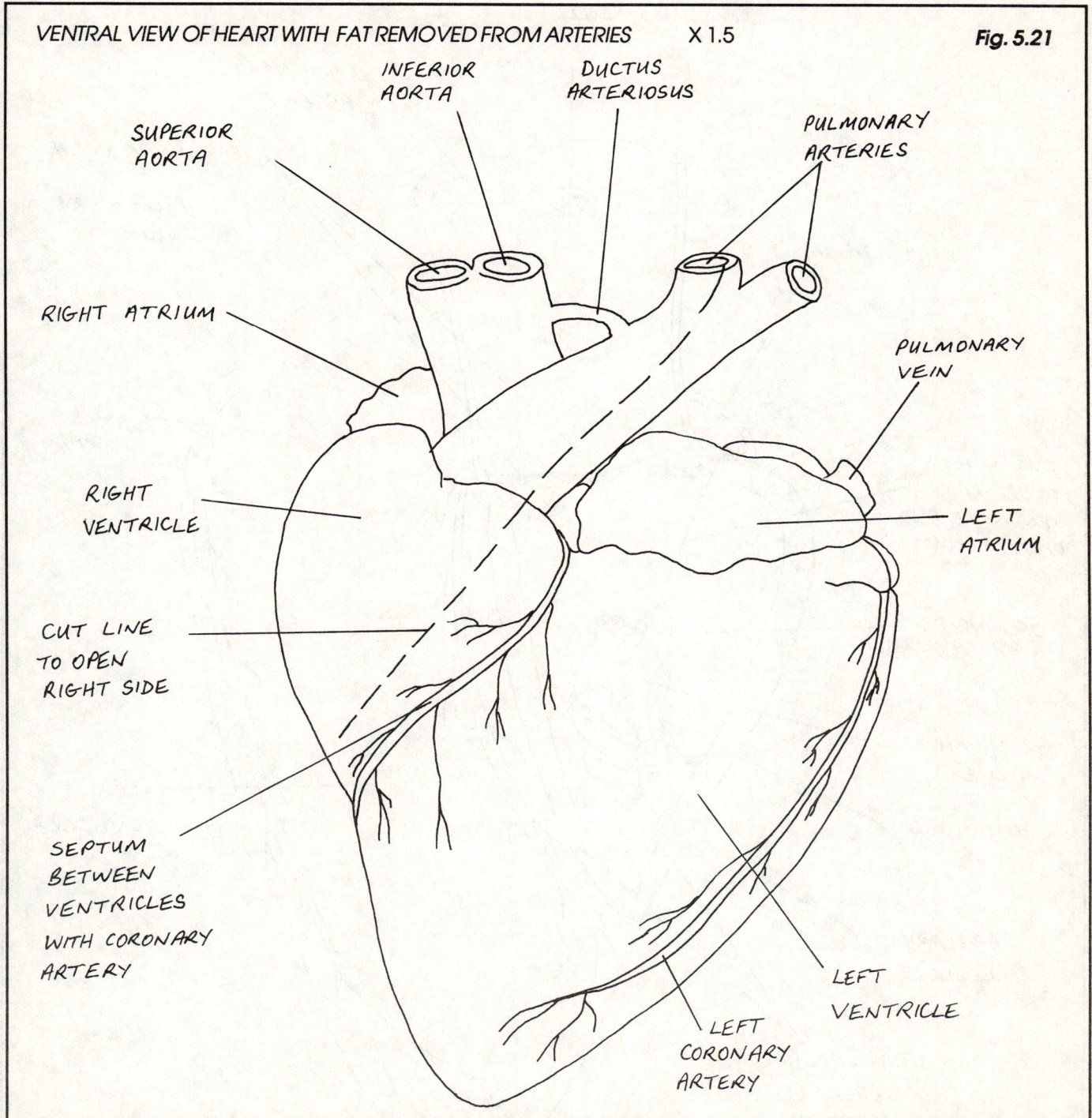

INFERIOR AORTA

DUCTUS ARTERIOSUS

SUPERIOR AORTA

PULMONARY ARTERIES

RIGHT ATRIUM

PULMONARY VEIN

RIGHT VENTRICLE

LEFT ATRIUM

CUT LINE TO OPEN RIGHT SIDE

SEPTUM BETWEEN VENTRICLES WITH CORONARY ARTERY

LEFT VENTRICLE

LEFT CORONARY ARTERY

5. Once the ventricle has been opened, you should be able to see the tricuspid valve and the opening from the right atrium above (*Fig. 5.22*)

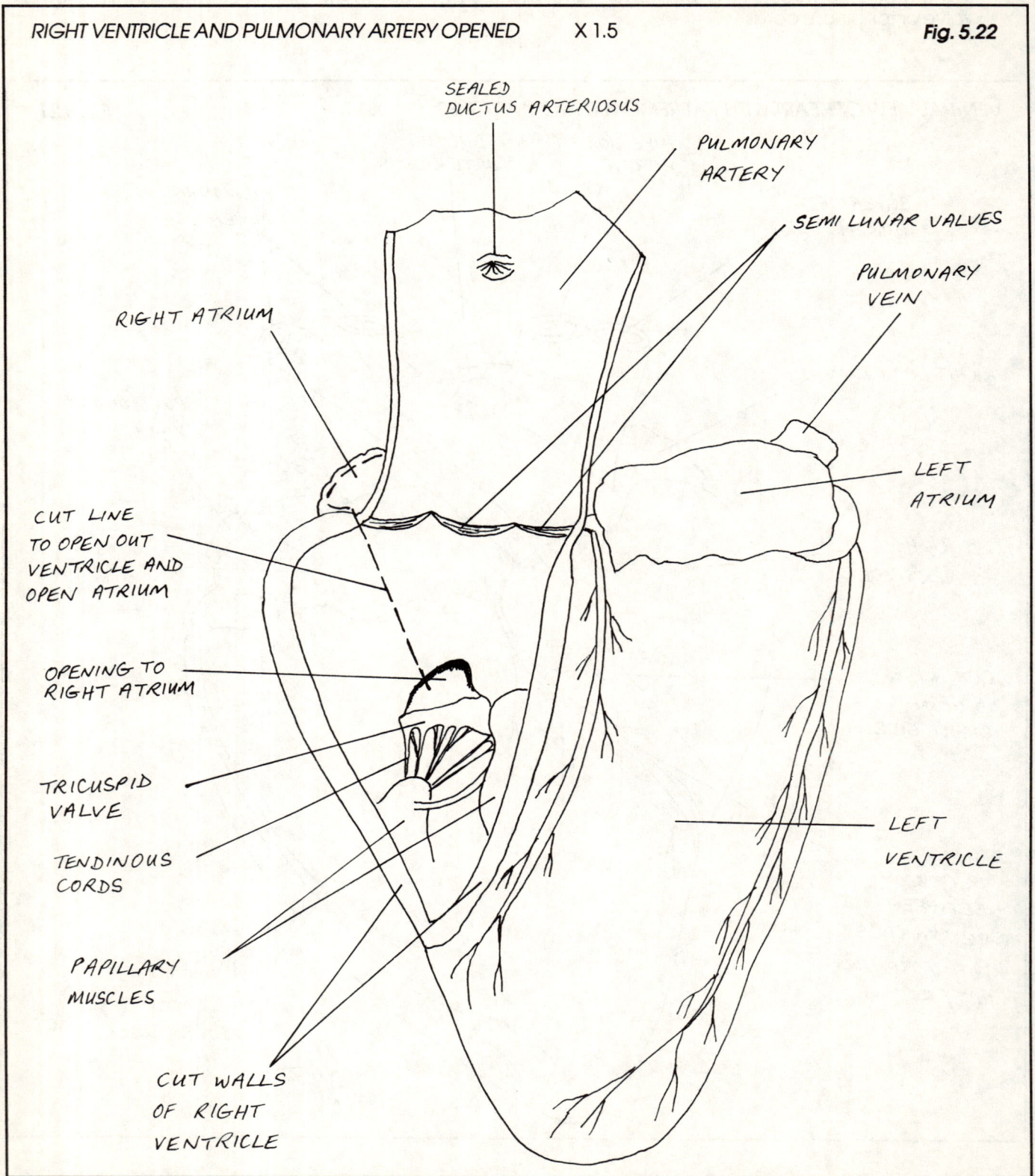

RIGHT VENTRICLE AND PULMONARY ARTERY OPENED   X 1.5   **Fig. 5.22**

SEALED DUCTUS ARTERIOSUS

PULMONARY ARTERY

SEMI LUNAR VALVES

PULMONARY VEIN

RIGHT ATRIUM

LEFT ATRIUM

CUT LINE TO OPEN OUT VENTRICLE AND OPEN ATRIUM

OPENING TO RIGHT ATRIUM

TRICUSPID VALVE

TENDINOUS CORDS

LEFT VENTRICLE

PAPILLARY MUSCLES

CUT WALLS OF RIGHT VENTRICLE

---

6. To expose the atrium, cut diagonally from above the tricuspid valve to the atrium and then cut round the edge of the atrium to open it flat. You can also cut open the vena cava if this is present.

7. You should now be able to see the complete route taken by the blood from the vena cava to the right atrium, through the tricuspid valve, into the right ventricle and up into the pulmonary artery, through the semi-lunar valves. Pin the structures flat and make a drawing of your dissection (*Fig. 5.23*)

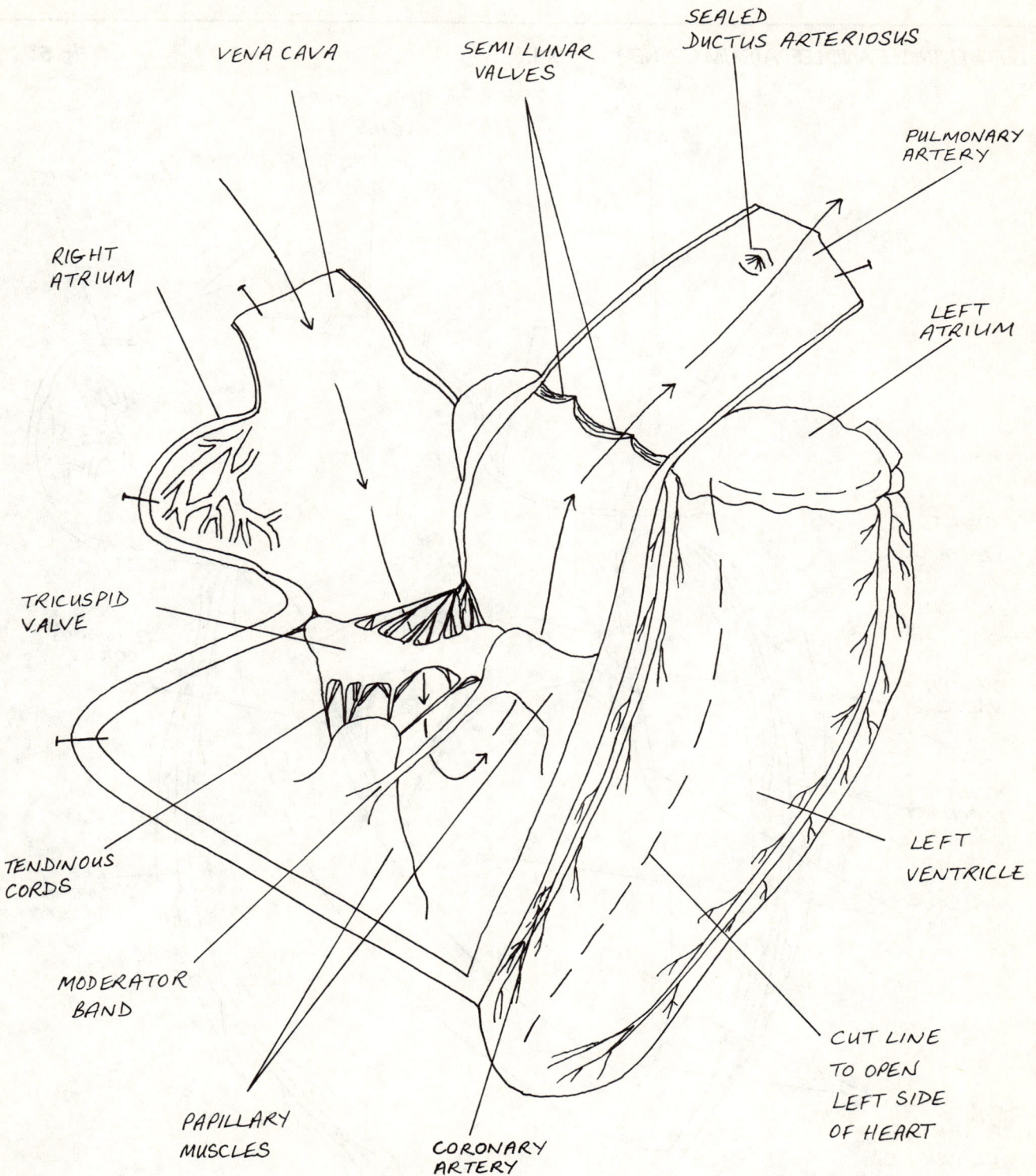

RIGHT SIDE OF HEART DISPLAYED   X 1.5   Fig. 5.23

VENA CAVA

SEMI LUNAR VALVES

SEALED DUCTUS ARTERIOSUS

PULMONARY ARTERY

RIGHT ATRIUM

LEFT ATRIUM

TRICUSPID VALVE

TENDINOUS CORDS

MODERATOR BAND

PAPILLARY MUSCLES

CORONARY ARTERY

LEFT VENTRICLE

CUT LINE TO OPEN LEFT SIDE OF HEART

■ IDENTIFYING & DISPLAYING LEFT SIDE STRUCTURES

8.   With the ventral surface of the heart uppermost, cut into the left ventricle about one centimetre to the left of the coronary vessels on the septum. The wall of the left ventricle is very thick, so the cuts have to be deep. Continue the cut parallel to the septum and into the left atrium. Cut round the edge of the atrium so that this can be laid flat (*Fig. 5.24*)

9.   Once the left ventricle is open, you should be able to see the bicuspid valve, tendinous cords and papillary muscles.

10. To open the aorta, use scissors and cut down through its wall to the edge of the bicuspid valve, leaving the valve attached to the papillary muscles via the tendinous cords (*Fig. 5.24*)

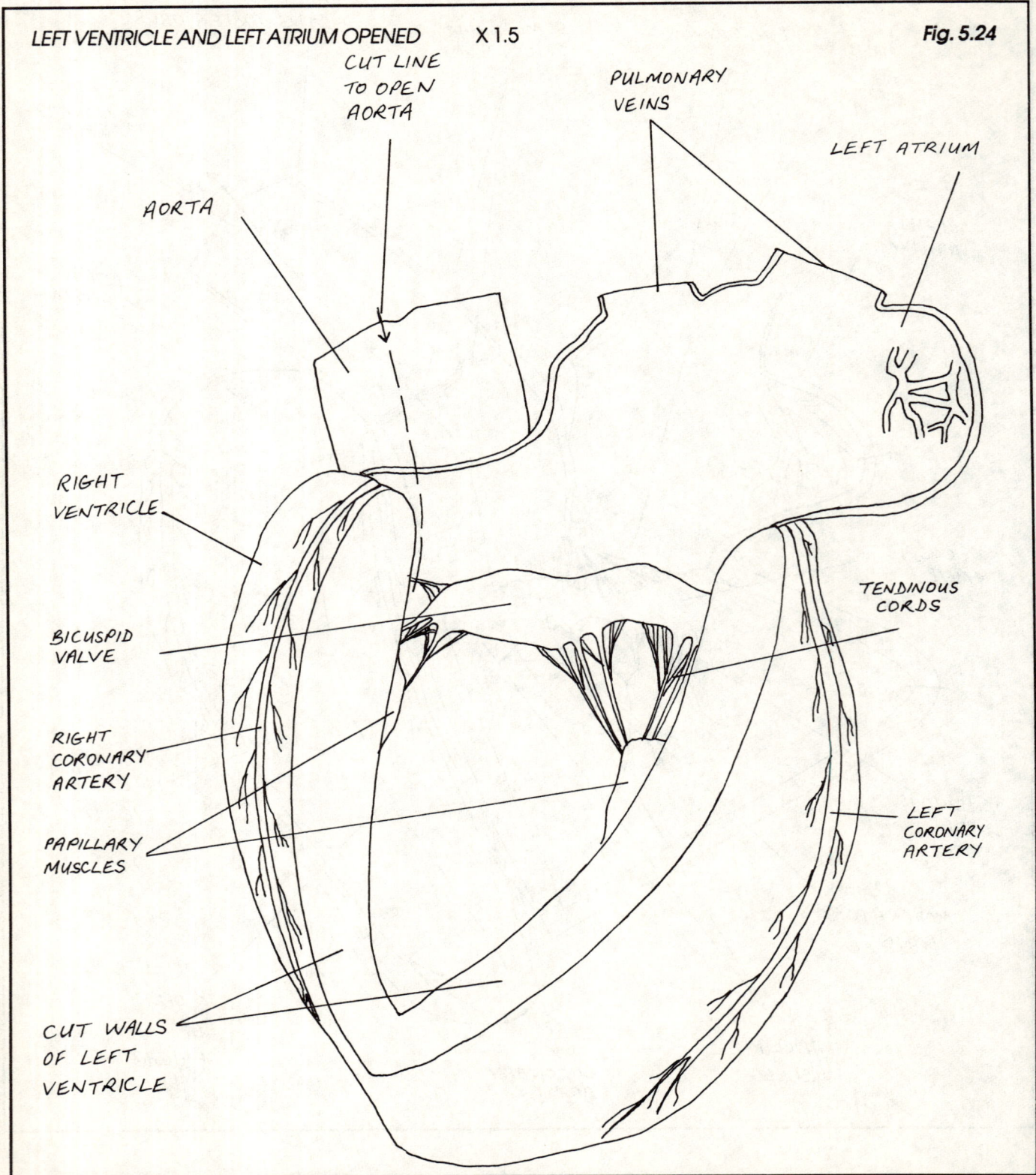

LEFT VENTRICLE AND LEFT ATRIUM OPENED   X 1.5   **Fig. 5.24**

CUT LINE TO OPEN AORTA

PULMONARY VEINS

LEFT ATRIUM

AORTA

RIGHT VENTRICLE

TENDINOUS CORDS

BICUSPID VALVE

RIGHT CORONARY ARTERY

LEFT CORONARY ARTERY

PAPILLARY MUSCLES

CUT WALLS OF LEFT VENTRICLE

11. You should now be able to see the semi-lunar valves at the base of the aorta, with openings to the coronary arteries just above these.

12. Pin out the left atrium, pulmonary veins and aorta.

13. You should be able to see the route taken by the blood from the pulmonary veins, into the left atrium, through the bicuspid valve into the left ventricle and up through the semi-lunar valves into the aorta. Make a drawing of your dissection (*Fig. 5.25*)

LEFT SIDE OF HEART DISPLAYED   X 1.5   Fig. 5.25

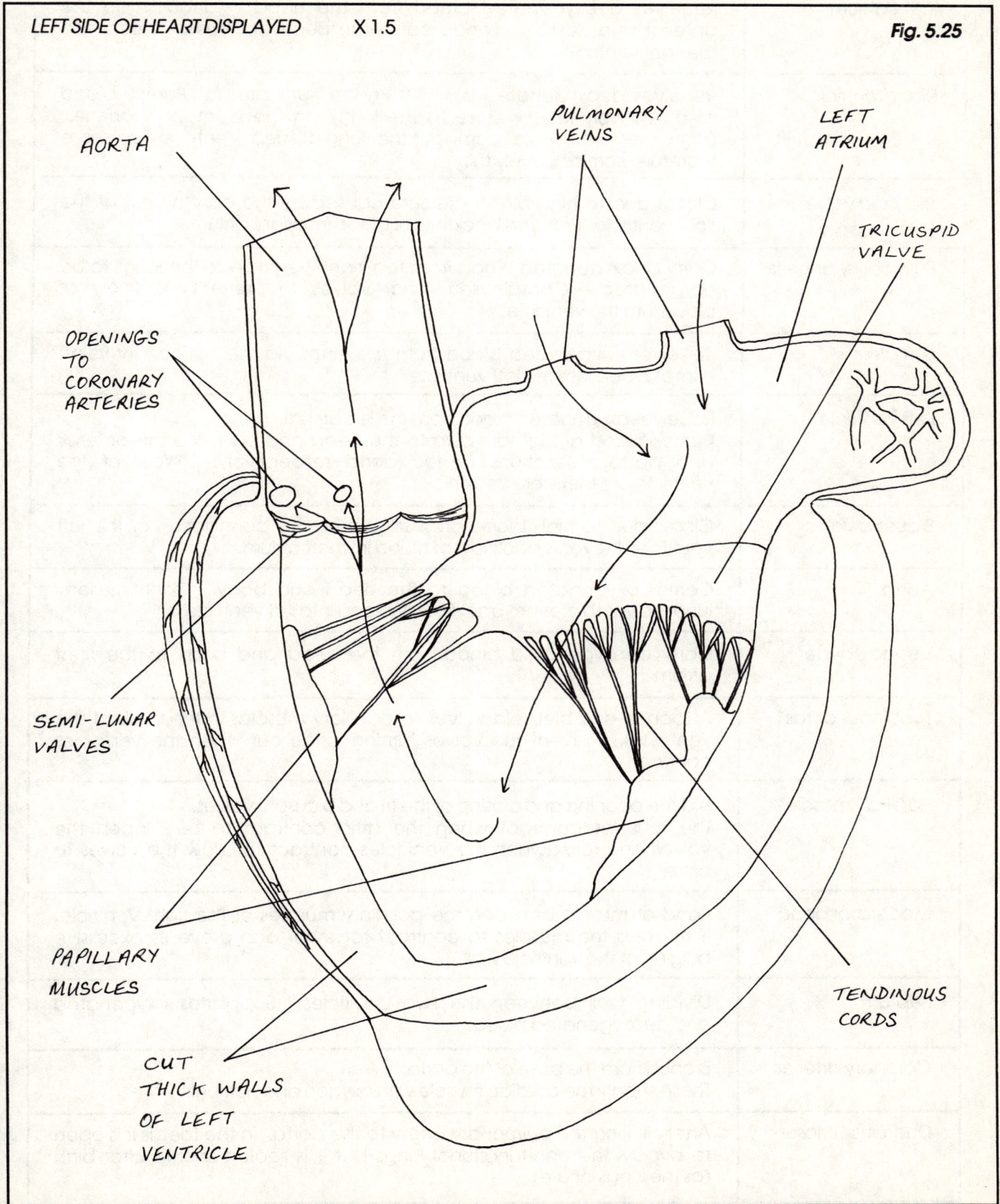

AORTA

PULMONARY VEINS

LEFT ATRIUM

TRICUSPID VALVE

OPENINGS TO CORONARY ARTERIES

SEMI-LUNAR VALVES

PAPILLARY MUSCLES

CUT THICK WALLS OF LEFT VENTRICLE

TENDINOUS CORDS

TABLE SHOWING FUNCTIONS OF THE HEART AND ASSOCIATED BLOOD VESSELS

STRUCTURE	FUNCTIONS
Right atrium	Receives deoxygenated blood from the head and body via the anterior and posterior venae cavae, respectively. Pumps blood into the right ventricle.
Right ventricle	Receives deoxygenated blood from the right atrium. Pumps blood at a relatively low pressure to the lungs via the pulmonary arteries. (High pressure would damage the lung tissue.) Ventricle walls are therefore comparatively thin.
Tricuspid valve	Closes due to high blood pressure caused by the contraction of the right ventricle. Prevents backflow of blood into right atrium.
Pulmonary arteries	Carry deoxygenated blood from the right ventricle to the lungs to be oxygenated. Contain semi-lunar valves to prevent backflow of blood into the ventricle.
Left atrium	Receives oxygenated blood from the lungs via the pulmonary veins. Pumps blood into the left ventricle.
Left ventricle	Receives oxygenated blood from the left atrium. Pumps blood at high pressure to the head and body via the anterior and posterior sections of the aorta respectively. Walls of the ventricle are therefore very thick.
Bicuspid valve	Closes due to high blood pressure caused by contraction of the left ventricle. Prevents backflow of blood into left atrium.
Aorta	Carries oxygenated blood to the head and body. Contains semi lunar valves to prevent backflow of blood into left ventricle.
Venae cavae	Carry deoxygenated blood from the head and body to the right atrium.
Tendinous cords	Attach tri-and bicuspid valves to papillary muscles in the walls of the ventricles. Prevent the valves turning inside out when the ventricles contract.
Papillary muscles	Aid the opening and closing of the tri and bicuspid valves. The muscles contract when the atria contract to help open the valves and relax when the ventricles contract to allow the valves to close.
Moderator band	Band of muscle between the papillary muscles of the right ventricle. It enables the muscles to contract together and prevents excessive bulging of the ventricle wall.
Septum	Dividing wall between the two ventricles. Separates oxygenated and deoxygenated blood.
Coronary arteries	Branch from the base of the aorta. These supply the cardiac muscle with oxygen and nutrients.
Ductus arteriosus	Artery linking the pulmonary artery to the aorta. In the foetus it is open to bypass the non-functional lungs but it is sealed shortly after birth (as the lungs inflate).

EXAM QUESTION 1

Dissect the mammalian heart in order to display the internal structures of the right atrium (*auricle*), right ventricle and the base of the pulmonary artery.

(The Examination Paper includes full instructions for the required procedure, including a diagram to help find the ventral surface, the coronary artery marking the septum between the ventricles and the pulmonary artery. The line of incision is also marked.)

a) Make a large, labelled drawing of your dissection to show the positions of the pulmonary artery, aorta, right ventricle, right atrium and the cut surface between the right ventricle and the rest of the heart. After careful examination, add the following to the drawing to show their structures and label them:
(i) the valves at the base of the pulmonary artery;
(ii) the valve separating the right atrium from the right ventricle, with details of its anchorage to the wall of the heart;
(iii) the two cut ends of the artery supplying the wall of the heart.

b) (i) Add arrows to your drawing to indicate the route and direction of the flow of blood through the dissected part of the heart.
(ii) Comment on the functional significance of the difference in thickness of the walls of the pulmonary artery and aorta.

(12 marks)
(University of Cambridge Local Examinations Syndicate)

ANSWER TECHNIQUE

a) and b) (i) Look at *Fig. 5.23* for the drawing and location of the structures and the direction of blood flow through the heart.

(ii) You would be expected to notice that the pulmonary artery has a thinner wall than the aorta. This is because the pulmonary artery carries blood at a lower pressure from the right ventricle to the lungs. The aorta has to withstand the much higher pressure created by the thick walled left ventricle. This is necessary to carry the blood to the rest of the body.

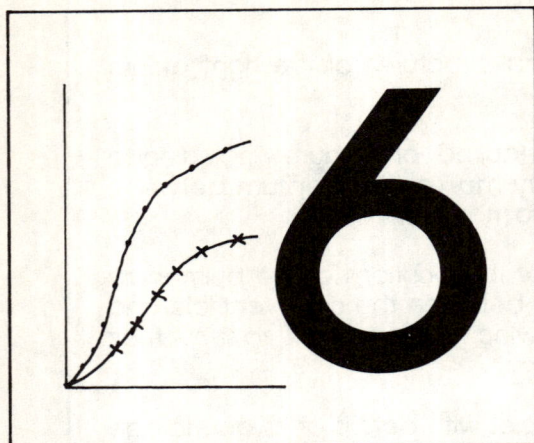

6

PRESENTING AND INTERPRETING DATA

This chapter describes the mathematical skills you will need for interpreting the data produced by your experiments. These skills can also be applied to the results of long-term or field investigations.

Although we shall be covering the maths most frequently used in the practical exams set by the majority of Examination Boards, you must check your own syllabus for the precise skills required.

The skills can be divided into three parts:

■ **Basic arithmetical techniques:** *eg.* addition and subtraction, use of decimals, percentages, volumes, areas and reciprocals. We shall assume that you have knowledge of these.

■ **Graphical techniques:** construction and interpretation of line graphs including choice of scale and axes, use of linear and logarithmic scales and calculation of rates of change; construction and interpretation of bar graphs, histograms and frequency polygons (kite diagrams).

■ **Simple statistical techniques:** calculation of means, modes and medians; use of standard deviation; calculation and use of the Chi-squared test; use of scatter diagrams to investigate correlation between two dependent variables.

GRAPHICAL TECHNIQUES

Linear & Logarithmic Scales
Rates of Change
Bar Graphs & Histograms
Frequency Polygons

STATISTICAL TECHNIQUES

Standard Deviation
Chi-Squared Test
Correlation between Variables

HINTS BOX ✔

CONSTRUCTION OF LINE GRAPHS

● The vertical (y) axis should bear values of the dependent (experimental) variables whilst the horizontal (x) axis should bear values of the independent (known) variables.

● The scale for each axis should be chosen carefully so that the finished graph makes full use of the paper available.

● The axes must be clearly labelled to indicate both the variable and its units.

● Each axis should begin at 0; if the interval between 0 and the first value on a particular axis is large then a break in the axis can be used (*eg. see Fig. 6.1*).

● All points should be plotted using a clear mark such as a X or ⊙ and not just a dot.

● The points should be joined with either a smooth curve or a straight line if all the points should lie on a straight line.

● If more than one set of data is plotted using the same axes then either the lines should be drawn in different colours or the points should be marked with different symbols. In either case a key to the lines should be used rather than writing on the lines.

● The graph should be given a clear title to indicate the relationship between the variables.

■ LINE GRAPHS

Fig. 6.1 shows the general format of a standard line graph, the most frequently required type of graph in the practical exam. In the exam you will be awarded marks for the way in which you present your line graph and you should therefore be careful to make sure that

● the axes are clearly labelled with variables *and* units
● there is a clear title
● the lines are smooth and well drawn
● a key is clearly shown if more than 1 set of data is plotted on the same axes
● plotting is accurate

GENERAL FORM OF LINE GRAPH   **Fig. 6.1**

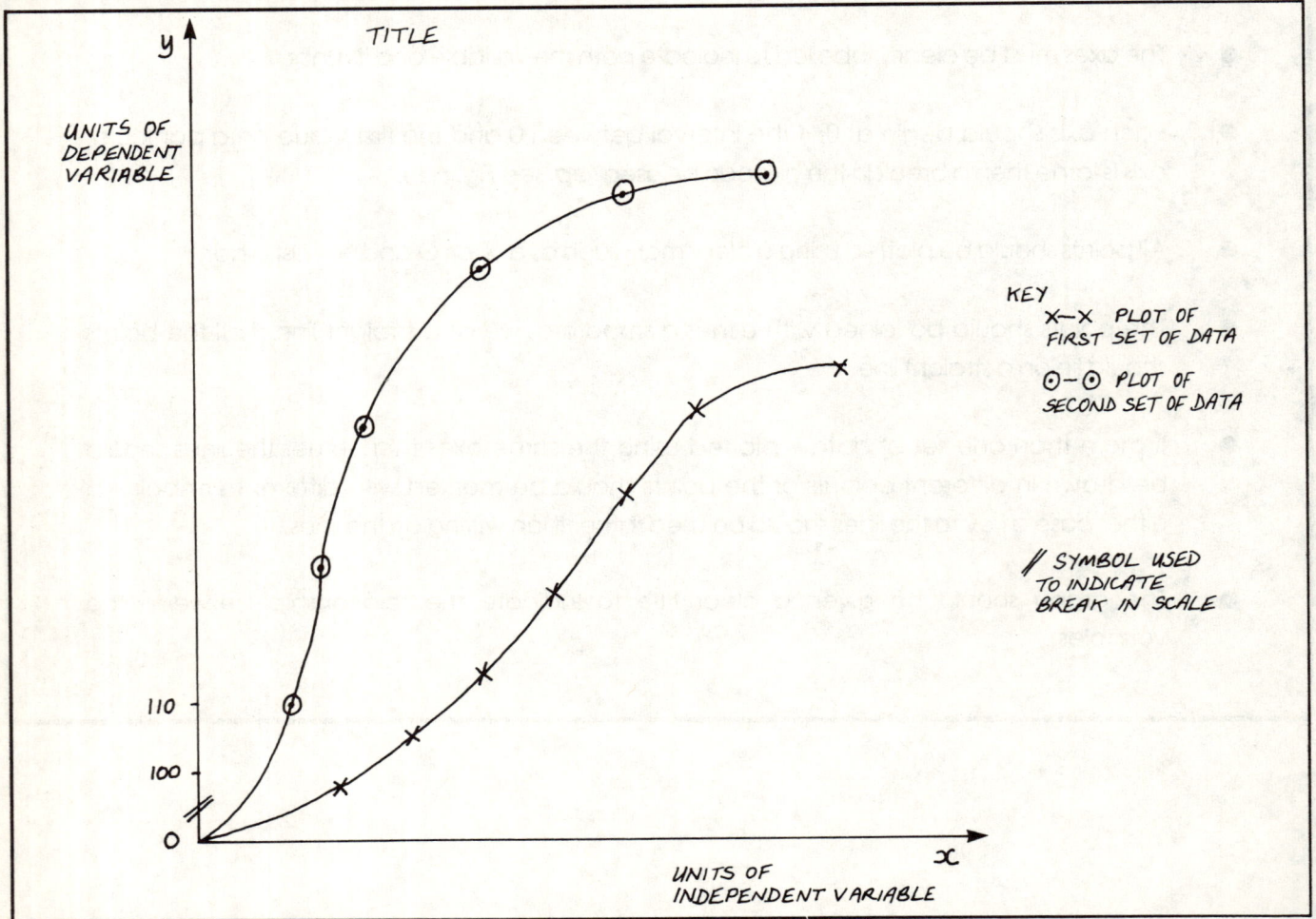

❑ Linear and Logarithmic Scales

In the exam you will generally be required to use only linear scales. In these the intervals between each point on an axis will represent the same numerical value. However, linear scales can be misleading. For example when representing data which expresses changes in a particular process, such as growth of a population, you may need to know the rate at which that process is changing. If the data is simply plotted on a linear scale, a change in population from 50 to 100 individuals is represented on the graph paper by the same distance on the y axis as a change in population from 1000 to 1050, even though the former represents a 100% increase whereas the latter is a 5% increase. Use of a logarithmic scale will show the rate of change of the population and, if this is constant, will produce a straight line.

The rate of growth of a population is more informative than simply knowing population numbers, because using the rate it would be possible to predict how long resources would continue to support a population in a particular area. This information would be useful both in small scale lab experiments and in making predictions for larger populations.

Normally it would be expected that a population would grow exponentially in the absence of limiting factors. Exponential growth can be illustrated by reference to certain bacterial cultures where the population doubles every 20 minutes *ie.* 1 cell divides to become 2, 2 divide to become 4 *etc.* Although this would produce large numbers in a comparitively short time, the rate of growth would remain constant. This can be checked by plotting the data as the logarithms ($\log_{10}$) of the numbers of individuals versus time. This should produce a straight line graph (*Fig. 6.2*).

TABLE OF POPULATION GROWTH DATA

Number of individuals	Log of number	Difference of logs
2	0.3	
4	0.6	0.3
8	0.9	0.3
16	1.2	0.3
32	1.5	0.3

From this table it can be seen that even though the magnitude of the difference in population varies each time it doubles, the log of numbers in the population increases by 0.3 thus producing a straight line.

The straight line is produced by converting the figures to logs because if the general equation of an exponential curve is **y = k^X** then converting to logs will produce **log y = x (log k)** which can be compared to the general equation for a straight line **y = mx + c**. You will remember from GCSE Maths that y and x are the numerical values on their respective axes and that m is the gradient of the line (which is constant) and c indicates the point at which the line crosses the y axis. In this case the line will go through the origin as **c = 0** and will have a gradient of **log k**.

The straight line graph in *Fig. 6.2* is a semi-logarithmic graph as only one axis has a log scale. It can be plotted either by calculating the logs of each individual value and then plotting them on normal graph paper or by plotting them directly onto special semi-logarithmic paper. This would not be given in an exam but you may have access to it when writing up projects or long term experiments and it is useful as you do not have to find the logs of your data.

GRAPH SHOWING EXPONENTIAL GROWTH IN A POPULATION OF ORGANISMS

Fig. 6.2

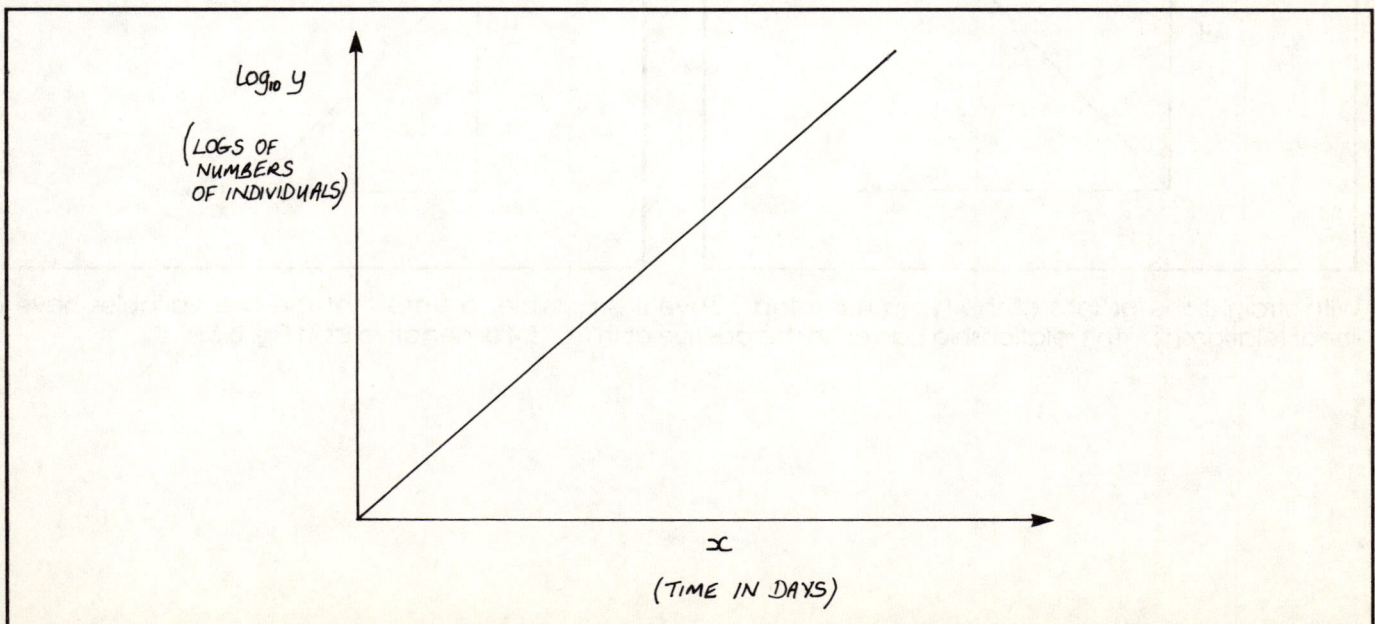

❑ Calculating rates of change

In questions involving the plotting of experimental data where the x axis represents units of time, you may be asked to calculate the rate of change of the process at a specific point. To do this you should draw a tangent to the curve at the specific point and then work out the gradient of the slope by constructing a triangle as shown in the diagram below (*Fig. 6.3*). You should try to make the tangent as long as possible.

Fig. 6.3

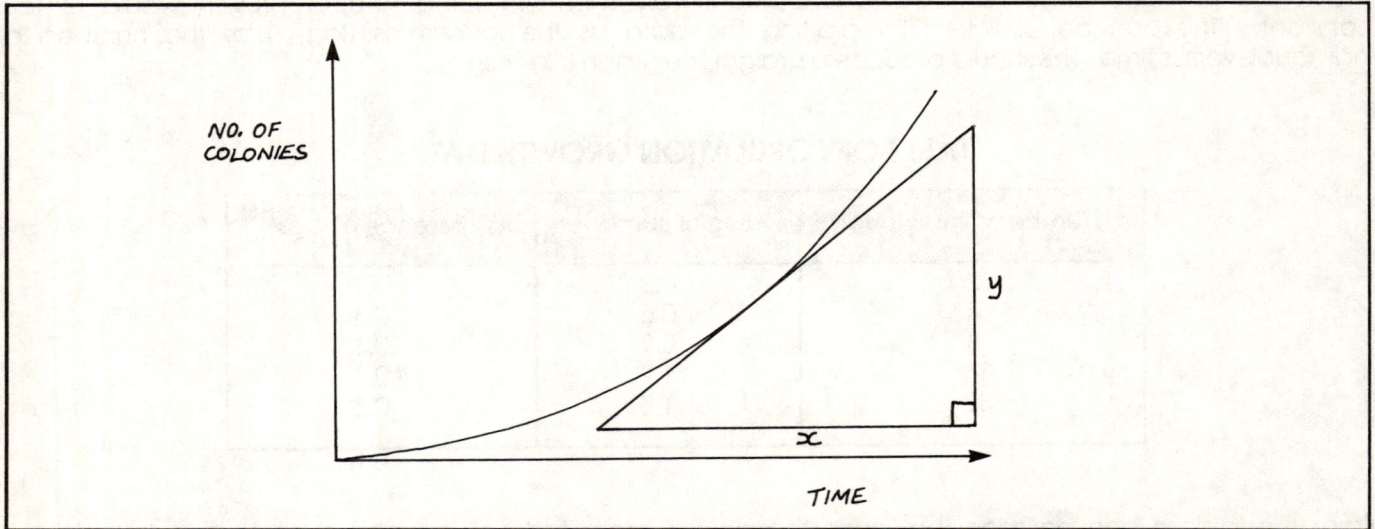

By dividing the value of y by the value of x, the gradient can be obtained. Your answer should be expressed in terms of the units used on the axes. In the example above this would be in colonies per day.

■ INTERPRETING LINE GRAPHS

The specific interpretations of a graph will depend upon the variables involved but a number of general points can be made:

Fig. 6.4   *Fig. 6.5*

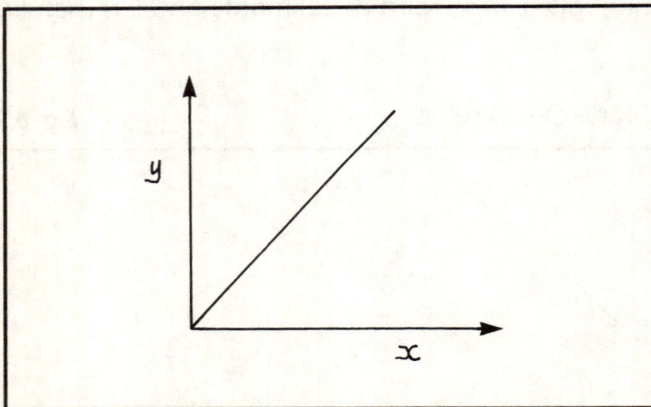

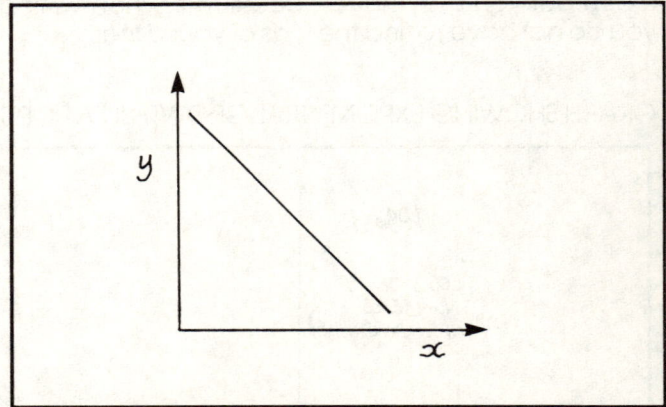

With straight line graphs of the types illustrated above it is possible to state that the two variables have a linear relationship. This relationship can either be positive as in *Fig. 6.4* or negative as in *Fig. 6.5*.

Fig. 6.6

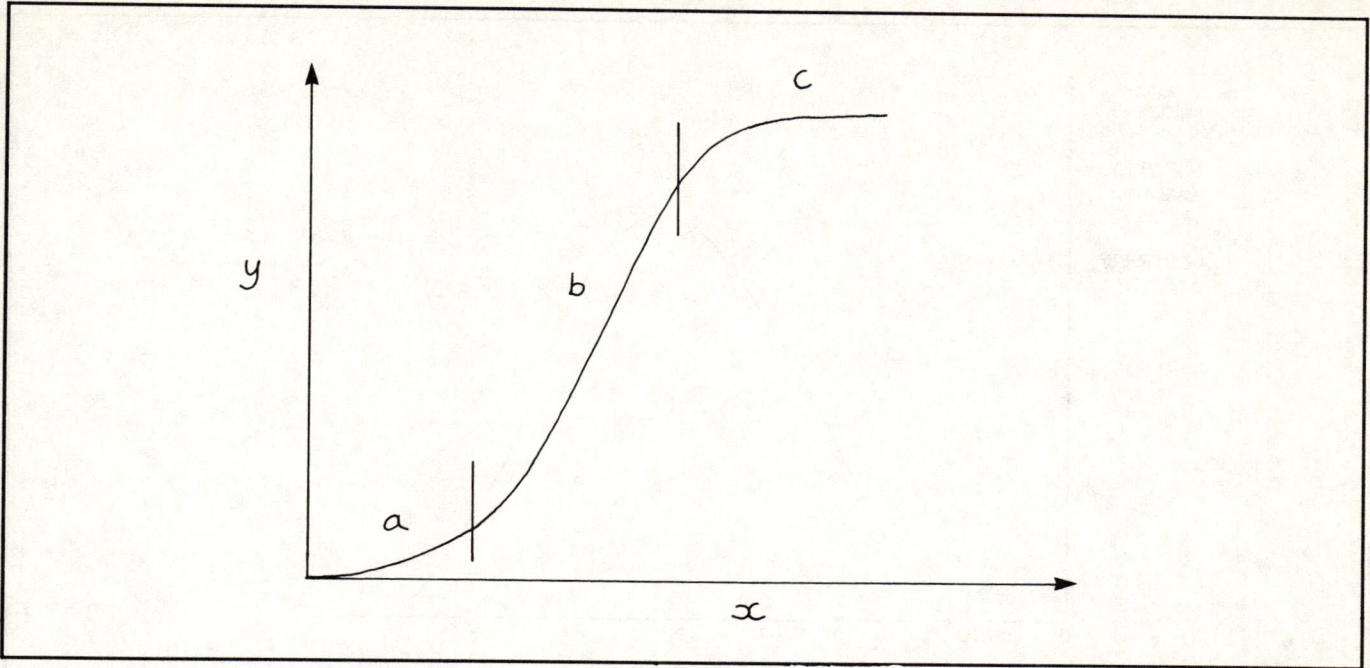

With a sigmoidal curve you would be expected to explain the significance of each of the three regions:
a)   Lag phase - here the process is slowly beginning to accelerate.
b)   Log phase - here the process is accelerating exponentially.
c)   Steady phase - here the process has reached its optimum rate or is being limited by another factor.

ACTION SPECTRUM FOR PHOTOSYNTHESIS

Fig. 6.7

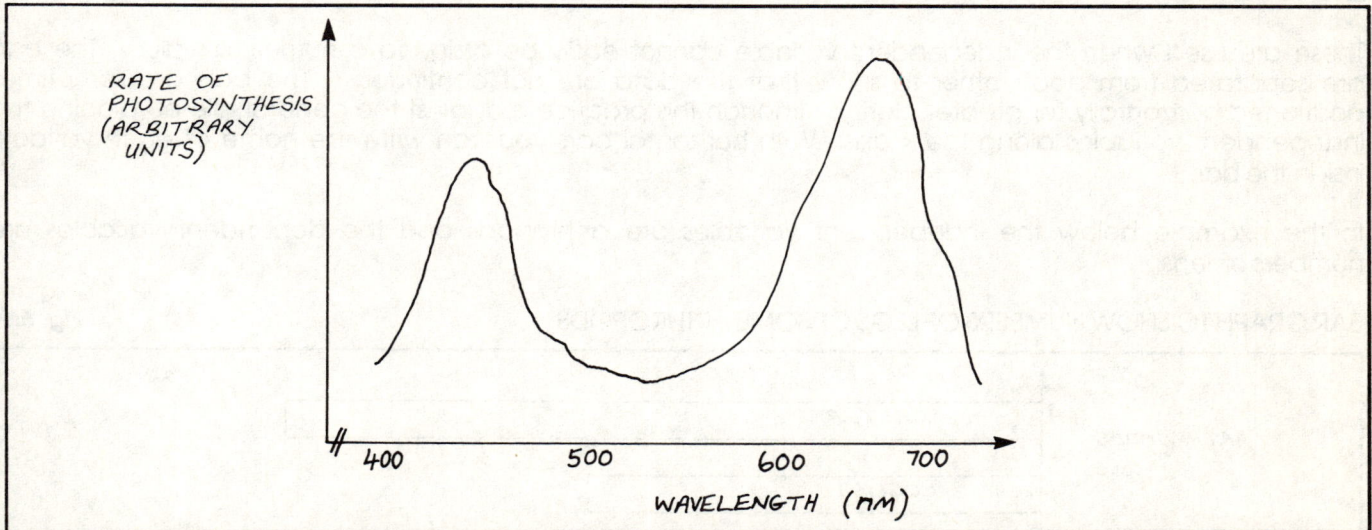

With a curve showing two clear peaks you should suggest that the x axis variable exerts its effects at two points. In the example above, the graph illustrates that photosynthetic activity is greatest in the blue and red areas of the visible spectrum.

GRAPH TO SHOW THE EFFECT OF TEMPERATURE ON ENZYME ACTIVITY   **Fig. 6.8**

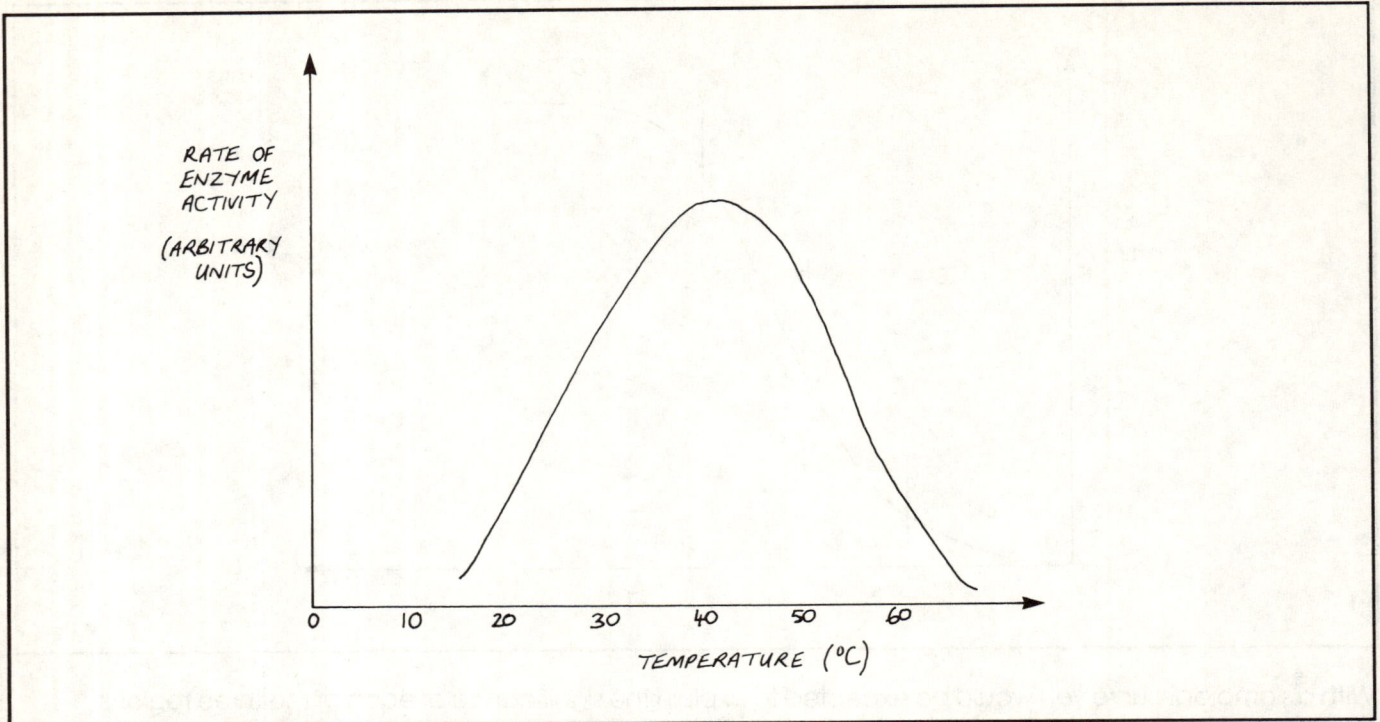

A bell shaped curve usually indicates that the process has clear minimum, optimum and maximum values.   The graph above illustrating enzyme activity versus temperature shows the optimum temperature at 40°C.   Bell shaped curves are also produced when plotting the frequency of certain characteristics of a population (normal distribution curve - see statistics section).

■ BAR GRAPHS

These are used when the independent variable cannot easily be assigned a numerical value.   The bars are separated from each other to show that the data are not continuous.   The bars are sometimes positioned horizontally for greater clarity, although this practice is against the general rule of placing the independent variables along the x axis.   With horizontal bars you can write the name of each variable inside the bar.

In the example below the independent variables are arthropods and the dependent variables are numbers of legs.

BAR GRAPH TO SHOW NUMBERS OF LEGS OF SOME ARTHROPODS   **Fig. 6.9**

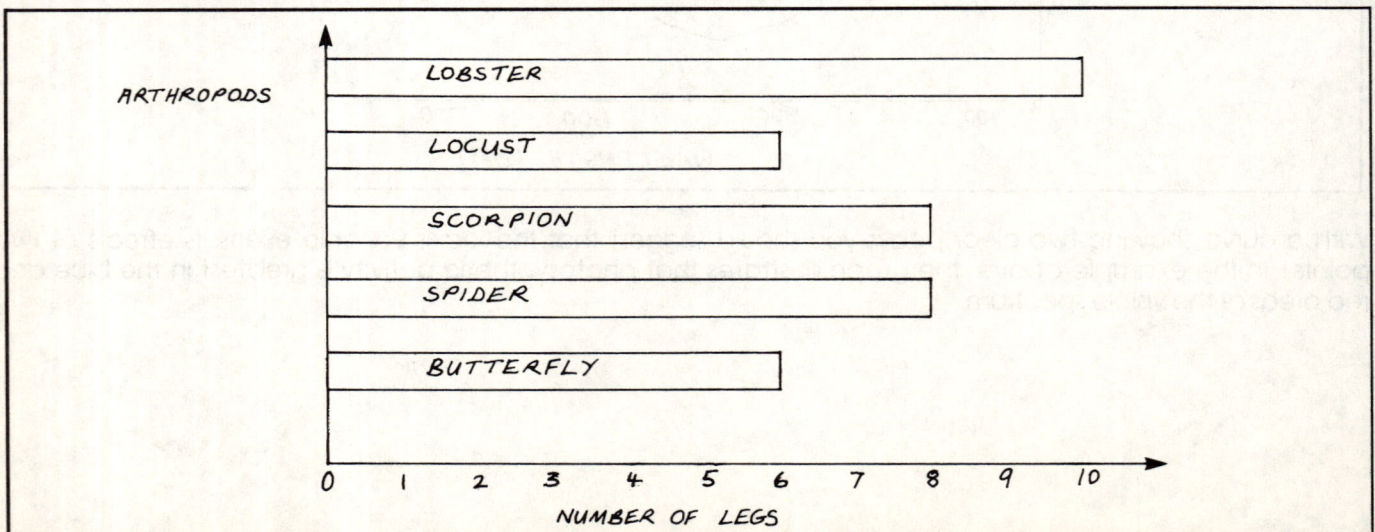

❑ Histograms

These are used when the data for the independent variable can be grouped into classes of equal size. The values for the independent variable must be on a continuous numerical scale. When plotting a histogram, each block should be of the same width and there should not be any gaps between the blocks.

In the example below, the independent variable (time) is grouped in three minute blocks as the oxygen production data was given as a volume produced per three minutes. It would not be appropriate to use a line graph as it is inaccurate to select one specific point during each three minute period as the value of the independent variable. This is because the plant would be giving out oxygen continuously during the time period.

HISTOGRAM TO SHOW VOLUME OF O_2 PRODUCED BY A PHOTOSYNTHESISING SHOOT OF ELODEA   **Fig. 6.10**

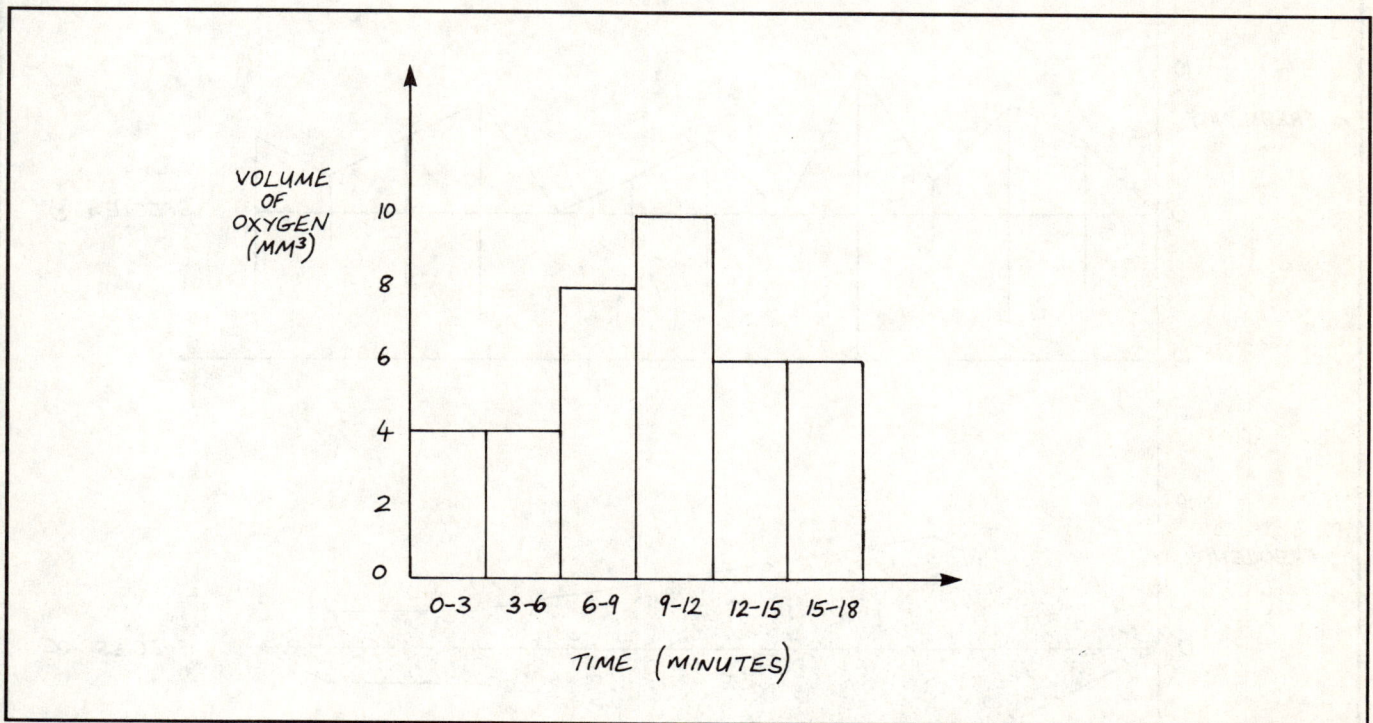

❏ Frequency polygons
(Kite Diagrams)

These are a modified form of bar chart and are usually used to represent the frequency and distribution of organisms along a specific line transect of a habitat.

The y axis is divided into sections for each organism. The frequency of each organism is plotted along its own x axis which dissects each section and indicates the distance along the transect. The frequency is plotted as a straight line drawn at right angles to the x axis and extending the same distance above and below the axis. The limits of these lines are then joined together, above and below the x axis. to form a figure which is symmetrical about the x axis. The figure is usually then shaded to form a solid polygon.

CONSTRUCTING A FREQUENCY POLYGON   *Fig. 6.11*

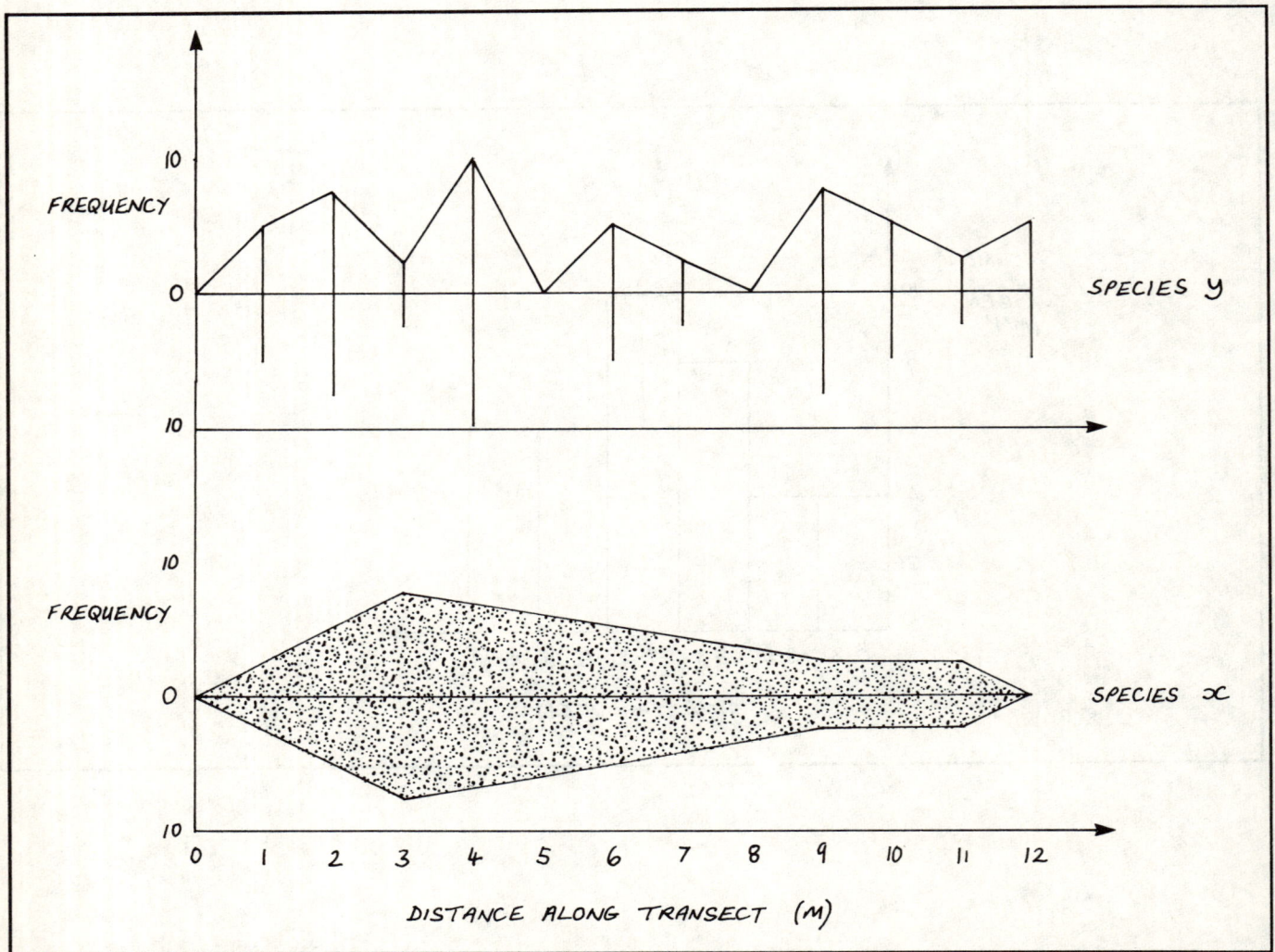

In *Fig. 6.11* the frequency polygon for species y shows the first stages of construction. The vertical lines representing frequency have been drawn and the upper limits have been joined. Once the polygon for species x was completed both sides were joined. The resulting polygon was then shaded to form a solid shape.

SIMPLE STATISTICAL TECHNIQUES

You may be expected to carry out simple statistical tests on your results, either in the exam or as part of your assessed practical work.

When recording data either in the laboratory or in the field it is often useful to know the average value. This average value can be the mean, the median or the mode.

○ **Mean** This is the arithmetic 'average' of a group of data obtained by adding their values together and then dividing the total by the number of individual data.

The formula for calculating the mean is:

$$\bar{x} = \frac{\Sigma x}{n}$$

where
$\bar{x}$ = mean
x = individual values
n = number of values
Σ = sum of values

○ **Median** This is the central value in a group of data written in ascending order. Example: In the series of numbers from 1 to 5 the median value is 3.

○ **Mode** This is the most frequently occurring value in a set of data. Example: In the following sequence: 1, 1, 2, 2, 2, 2, 2, 2, 3, 3, 4, 5, the mode is 2.

■ VARIATION WITHIN POPULATIONS

You would not be expected to calculate either the standard deviation or the variance of a set of data obtained from sampling a population but you are expected to have an understanding of standard deviation. Before explaining the use of standard deviation, the following two terms need to be defined:

○ **Continuous variation** This term refers to a characteristic within a population which shows a steady change between two extremes without jumps or gaps *eg.* shell size in limpets or height in humans.

○ **Discontinuous variation** This term refers to characteristics within a population which can be placed into discrete groups *eg.* Human ABO blood group system.

■ USE OF STANDARD DEVIATION

When the mean of a set of data is calculated, *eg.* height of trees, it does not give any indication of the spread or dispersion of the heights of the trees in the wood. The calculation of the standard deviation (σ) shows how far the data are spread out from the mean (*Fig. 6.12*).

COMPARISON OF TWO POPULATIONS WITH THE SAME MEAN

Fig. 6.12

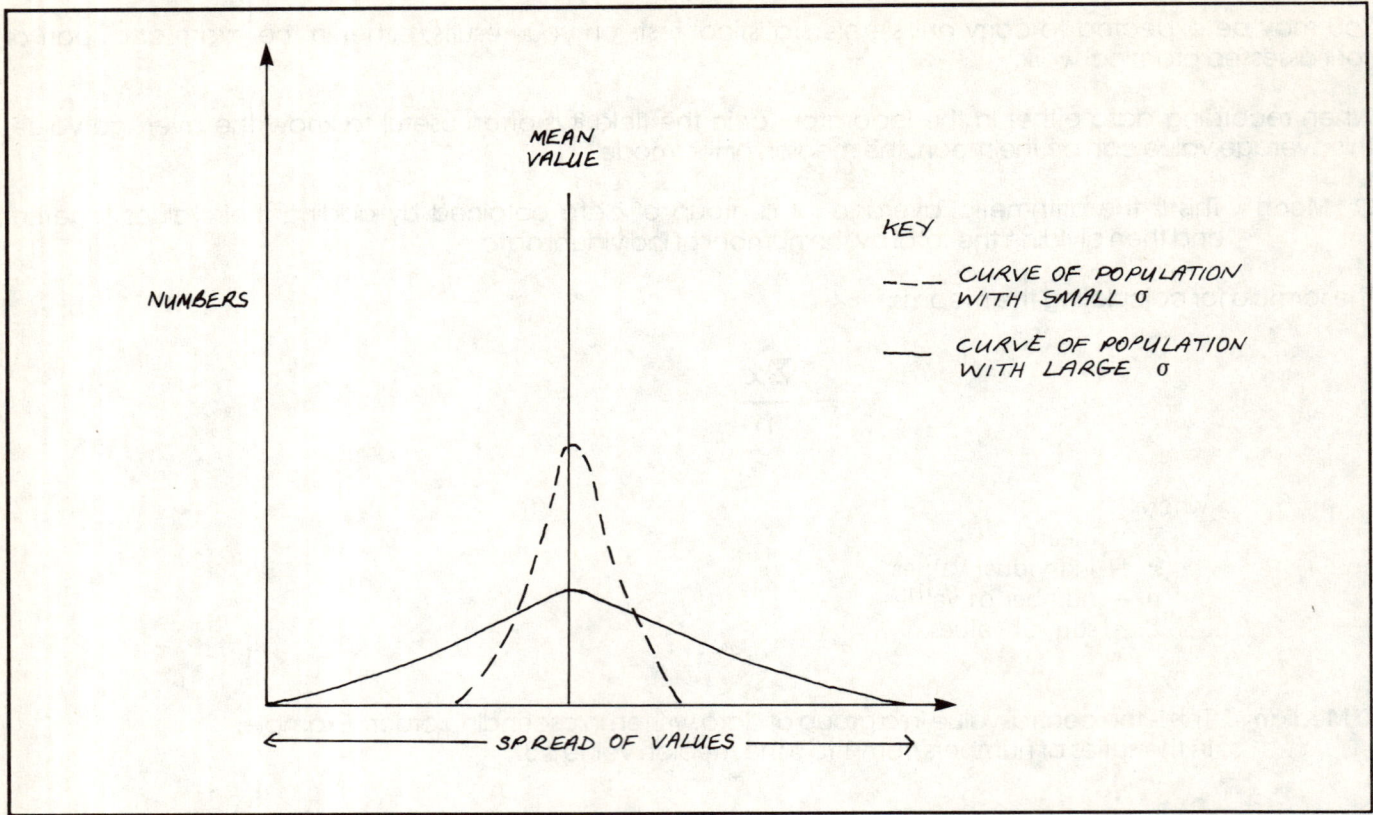

The standard deviation of a sample from a large population can be used to estimate the spread of values within the whole population. When the values are grouped around the mean the population shows little variation, whereas if they are spread out the population shows a large degree of variation.

When sampling a population of organisms which shows continuous variation in a particular characteristic eg. height, it would be expected that the values would be grouped around the mean. If the data was plotted on a graph, a bell-shaped curve would be produced. This is referred to as a curve of the normal distribution (Fig. 6.13).

STANDARD DEVIATION AND THE NORMAL DISTRIBUTION

Fig. 6.13

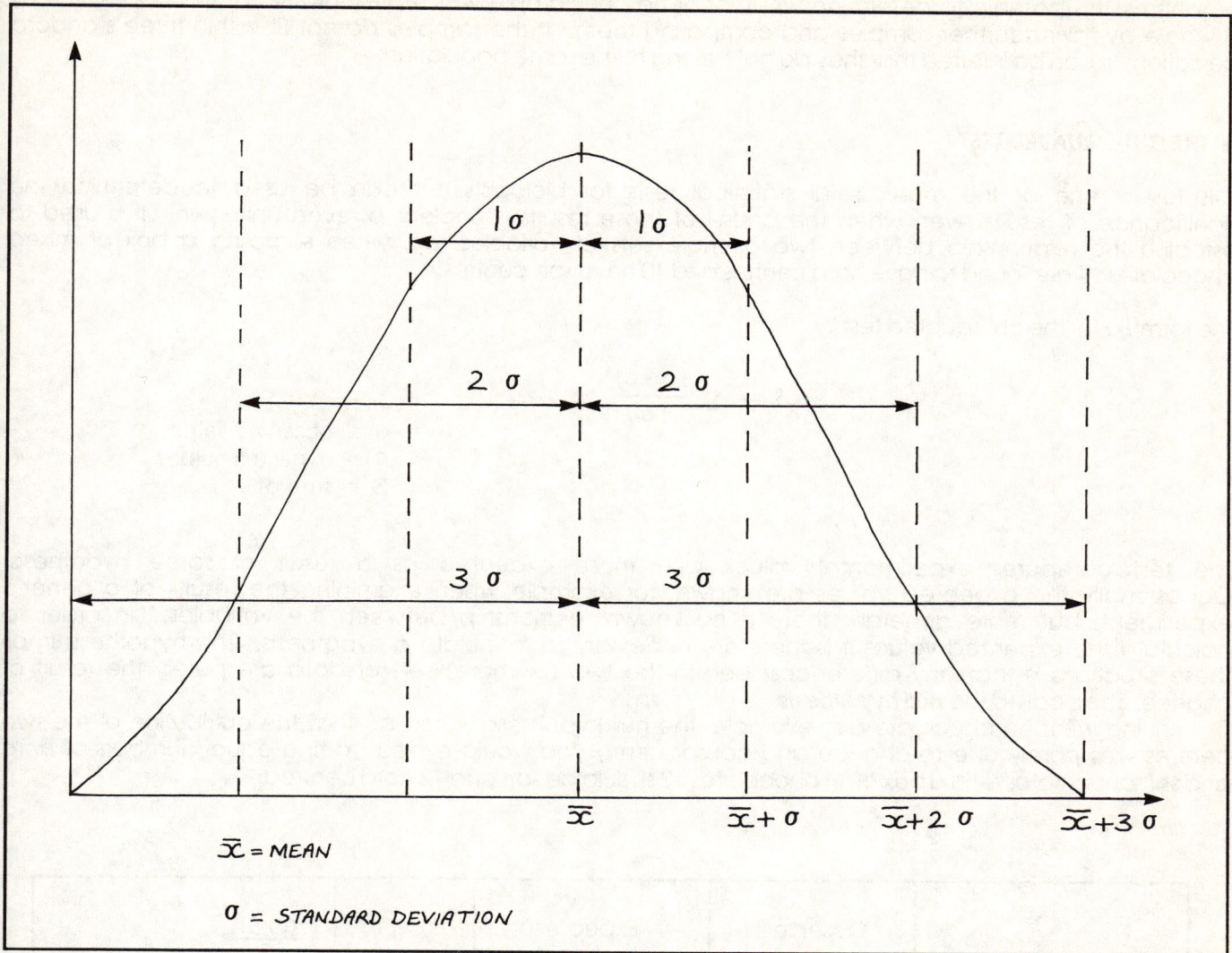

$\overline{x}$ = MEAN

σ = STANDARD DEVIATION

The area under the curve represents the whole population and from this it can be predicted that 68% of the population will be found within one standard deviation of the mean, 95% will be found within two standard deviations and 100% within three standard deviations.

The standard deviation of a set of data is calculated by first finding the mean value then subtracting this from all of the values in turn. This gives the deviation of each value from the mean. The results of this calculation are then each squared (making all values positive) and then added together. The resultant sum is divided by the total number of values. This gives the mean squared deviation from the mean, otherwise known as the **variance**. Finally, the square root of this last figure is taken to give the standard deviation.

The formula for standard deviation is:

$$\sigma = \sqrt{\frac{\sum (x - \overline{x})^2}{N}}$$

where
x = individual values
$\overline{x}$ = mean value
N = total number of values
Σ = sum of
$\sqrt{}$ = take the square root of

If the predictions made using the data from the sample are then applied to the general population of the organisms, it is possible to determine whether or not the sample was representative of the population as a whole by taking further samples and comparing them. If the samples do not fit within three standard deviations, it can be inferred that they do not belong to the same population.

■ THE CHI-SQUARED TEST

This test is one of the most useful statistical tests for biologists. It can be used to determine the significance of results even when the cause of those results is unclear or even unknown. It is used to establish the relationship between two or more sets of variables, *eg.* when sampling a box of mixed chocolates 14 are found to have hard centres and 10 have soft centres.

The formula for the chi-squared test is:

$$\chi^2 = \Sigma \frac{(o - e)^2}{e}$$

where
o = observed value
e = expected value
Σ = sum of

The test compares experimental values with those expected as a result of some hypothesis. Occasionally the expected values are known, for example when examining the results of a genetic experiment, but more generally there is no known relationship between the variables. In order to calculate the expected values it is therefore necessary to formulate a hypothesis. The hypothesis in all these situations is that any differences seen in the two (or more) sets of data are purely the result of chance. This is called the **null hypothesis**.

Continuing with the chocolate box example, the null hypothesis would be that the distribution of the two centres was purely due to chance and consequently you would expect to find equal numbers of hard and soft chocolates *ie.* in a box of 24 chocolates 12 should be soft and 12 hard centred:

	Observed	Expected	(O-E)	$\frac{(O-E)^2}{E}$
Hard centres	14	12	+2	0.33
Soft centres	10	12	-2	0.33
Totals	24	24		

Chi-squared   = 0.33 + 0.33
                 = 0.66

Having calculated a value for chi-squared the next step is to compare it with a standard table of values. Since in our example, we only need to know the value of one figure in order to know the other, there is said to be one degree of freedom. In general the degrees of freedom (*d.f.*) in any situation can be calculated using:

degrees of freedom = (numbers of sets of results - 1)

The standard tables give values for chi-squared for 1 to 30 degrees of freedom. In our example we only need to know the values for 1 degree of freedom:

PROBABILITY

d.f	0.99	0.95	0.90	0.70	0.50	0.20	0.05	0.001
1	0.000157	0.00393	0.0158	0.148	0.455	1.642	3.841	10.827

This table is used by looking along the second row for the last value which is lower than our calculated value (0.66). In this case the figure is 0.455. This means that our chi-squared value will occur by chance with a probability of 0.50 or 50%. Biologists generally accept that a probability of 0.05 or 5% is the level of biological significance. Any value of chi-squared which falls below this level (3.841 with 1 d.f.) fails to show a significant deviation from the expected result. Values above this level are regarded as highly significant and should cause the null hypothesis to be rejected and alternative explanations sought.

We can accept our null hypothesis that the distribution of chocolates in the box is due to chance alone.

■ CORRELATION BETWEEN TWO VARIABLES

In the exam you would not be expected to calculate the correlation coefficient but you would be expected to interpret a scatter diagram.

Generally in experimental situations the independent variable is controlled but in situations such as field investigations neither variable may be controlled. In this case the data is plotted on a graph (scatter diagram) and analysed by drawing a "line of best fit" through the points. The type of correlation (relationship) between the two variables can then be ascertained by examining the patterns formed by the plots (Fig. 6.14).

SCATTER DIAGRAMS

Fig. 6.14

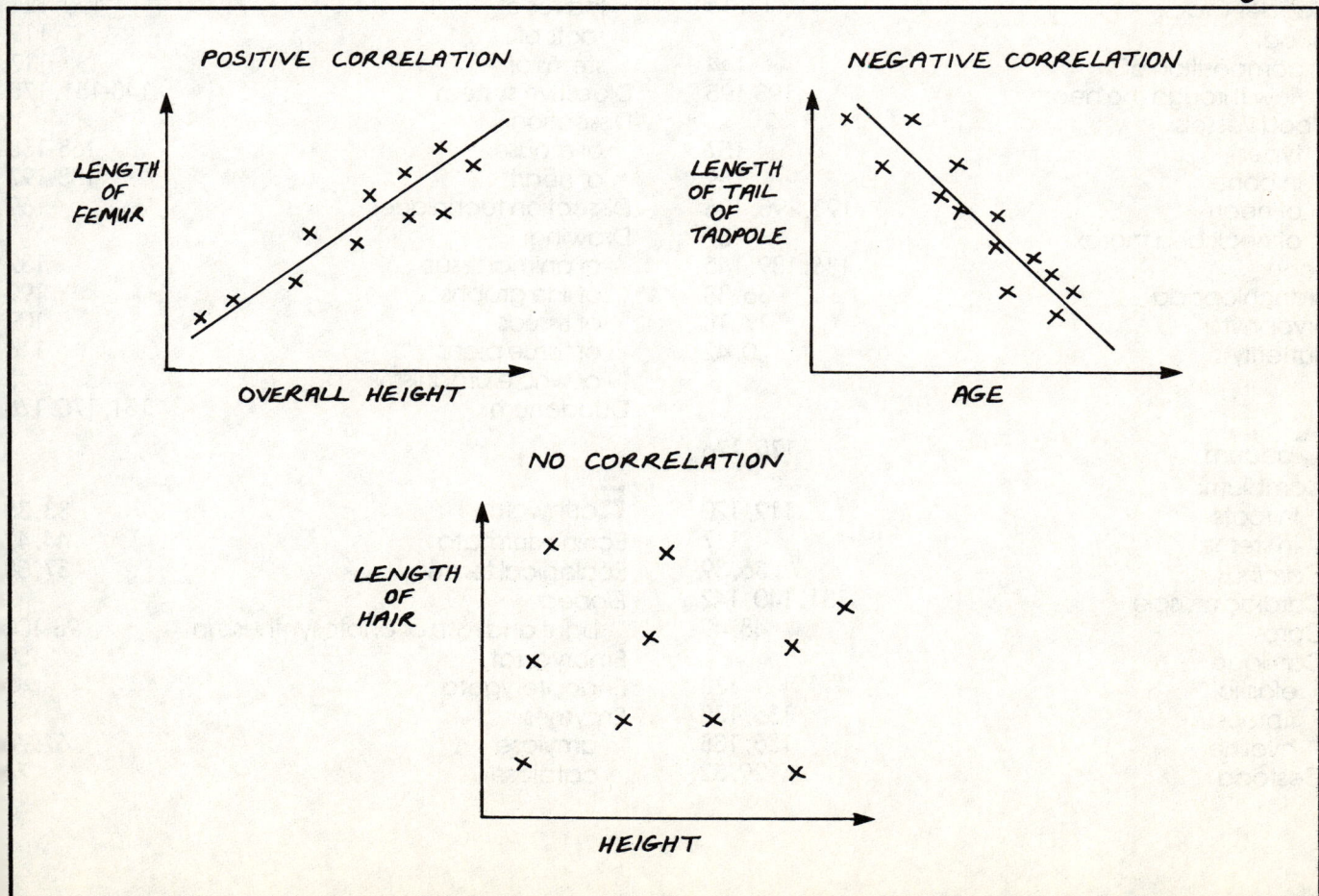